Augustine and the Catechumenate

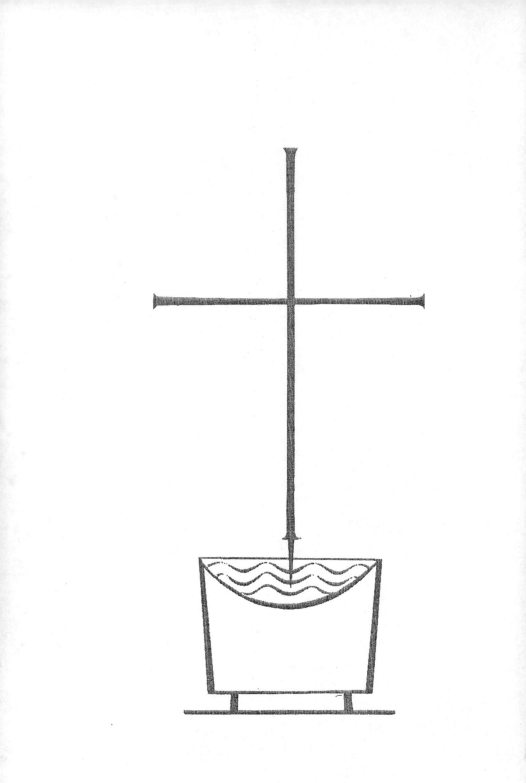

William Harmless, S.J.

Augustine
and the Catechumenate

A PUEBLO BOOK

The Liturgical Press   Collegeville, Minnesota

A Pueblo Book published by The Liturgical Press

Design by Frank Kacmarcik, Obl.S.B.

Library of Congress Cataloging-in-Publication Data

Harmless, William, 1953-
   Augustine and the Catechumenate / William Harmless.
      p.   cm.
   "A Pueblo book."
   Includes bibliographical references.
   ISBN 0-8146-6132-7
   1. Augustine, Saint, Bishop of Hippo—Contributions in work with catechumenate. 2. Catechumens—Algeria—Hippo (Extinct city)--History. 3. Hippo (Extinct city)—Church history. I. Title.
BR195.C38H37 1995
268'.092—dc20   95-7818
                                                              CIP

Contents

List of Charts

List of Abbreviations

ACW   Ancient Christian Writers (New York: Newman Press)

ANF   Ante-Nicene Fathers (reprint, Grand Rapids:
Wm. Eerdmans Publishing Co.)

BAug   Bibliothèque augustinienne (Paris: Desclée de Brouwer)

BAC   San Agustin, *Obras Completas*, Biblioteca de Autores
Cristianos (Madrid)

CCSL   Corpus Christianorum, Series Latina (Turnholt: Brepols)

CSEL   Corpus Scriptorum Ecclesiasticorum Latinorum (Vienna)

DACL   Dictionnaire d'archeologie chrétienne et de liturgie (Paris)

FC   Fathers of the Church (Washington: The Catholic University
of America Press)

LCC   Library of Christian Classics (Philadelphia: Westminster
Press)

LF   A Library of the Fathers of the Holy Catholic Church (Oxford)

MF   Message of the Fathers of the Church (Collegeville: The
Liturgical Press / Michael Glazier)

NPNF   Nicene and Post-Nicene Fathers (reprint, Grand Rapids:
Wm. Eerdmans Publishing Co.)

PG   Patrologia Graeca (Paris: J. P. Migne)

PL   Patrologia Latina (Paris: J. P. Migne)

PS   Patristic Studies (Washington: The Catholic University
of America Press)

RCIA   *Rite of Christian Initiation of Adults*, Revised edition
(Collegeville: The Liturgical Press, 1988)

SC   Sources chrétiennes (Paris: Éditions du Cerf)

Acknowledgements

I must thank a number of people for their guidance and encouragement on this project: first, Martin Elsner, S.J., and the people of St. Joseph's Parish in Houston who gave such support and brought such enthusiasm to the task of implementing the RCIA. I am particularly grateful to those who served on my dissertation committee: Thomas H. Groome, who directed my doctoral work and whose reflections on religious education have done so much to shape my own educational praxis; Rev. Robert P. Imbelli, whose insights on Christology alerted me to the melodic core of Augustine's catechesis; Michael S. Schiro, who guided my study of curriculum and educational philosophy; and especially Brian E. Daley, S.J., who first introduced me to patristic studies and whose insight, imagination, and sympathy did so much to bring Augustine and his era alive. I must also thank my Jesuit brothers and my parents, family, and friends who were so supportive through the years of research and writing, especially Paul Deutsch, S.J., Joseph Fortier, S.J., David Borbridge, S.J., Randall Rainey, S.J., Mel Halbert, Maureen O'Brien, Almeda Colby, and Ann Harmless. Finally, I must acknowledge my profound debt to Raymond Fitzgerald, S.J., who each week read through my scribblings, checked my translations, and acted as an astute discussion partner through it all.

I would also like to thank the following publishers for permission to quote from copyrighted texts and translations:

University of California Press for:

Peter Brown, *Augustine of Hippo: A Biography* (1968).

The Catholic University of America Press for:

St. Augustine, *Sermons on the Liturgical Seasons*, trans. Mary Muldowney, *Fathers of the Church* 38 (1959).

St. Augustine, *Tractates on the Gospel of John, 1–10*, trans. John W. Rettig, *Fathers of the Church* 78 (1988).

St. Augustine, *Tractates on the Gospel of John, 11–27,* trans. John W. Rettig, *Fathers of the Church* 79 (1988).

Paulist Press for:

St. Augustine, *The First Catechetical Instruction,* trans. Joseph P. Christopher, *Ancient Christian Writers* 2 (1946).

St. John Chrysostom, *Baptismal Instructions,* trans. Paul W. Harkins, *Ancient Christian Writers* 31 (1963).

Simon & Schuster for:

Saint Augustine, *On Christian Doctrine,* trans. D. W. Robertson, Jr., *Library of Liberal Arts* (New York: Macmillan, 1958).

Penguin Books Ltd. for:

Saint Augustine, *Confessions,* trans. R. S. Pine-Coffin (Penguin Classics, 1961).

Chapter 1

The RCIA: Its Catechetical Gaps and Silences

One hardly expects radicalism from Rome. Yet in 1972 the Vatican promulgated the Rite of Christian Initiation of Adults (RCIA) and, in so doing, reversed a thousand years of initiatory practice and attitude.[1] As Ralph Keifer has put it, "under the aegis of an ecumenical council, with the approval of the Roman see, and over the signature of the Roman pontiff, the primary rites of initiation . . . have been turned upside down and inside out, heralding a cry to begin a reform and renewal of the most radical sort."[2] The RCIA's contours are certainly revolutionary and its vision, breathtaking. Still, its official promulgation marked no more than a tentative first step. Its visionary hopes and high ideals can be easily tamed, watered down, or ignored.

1. *The Rite of Christian Initiation of Adults*, rev. ed., International Commission on English in the Liturgy (Collegeville, Minn.: The Liturgical Press, 1988)—listed hereafter as "RCIA." Note that the numbers of the 1974 provisional text differ significantly from those in the 1988 revised American edition; there have also been some modifications and rearrangement of different texts. In the notes that follow, I have used the numbers and text given in the 1988 edition. Also the 1988 version (approved by the American bishops in November 1986) contains several rites not found in the original text. The bishops designed these to deal with a problem specific to the American context: namely, baptized but uncatechized adults, including both Catholics preparing for confirmation and Eucharist and baptized Christians preparing to enter into full communion with the Church. For a discussion of this, see Ron Lewinski, "The Bishops and the RCIA in Washington: November 1986," *Catechumenate* 9 (January 1987) 15-19.

2. Ralph Keifer, "Christian Initiation: the State of the Question," in Aidan Kavanagh, et al., *Made, Not Born: New Perspectives on Christian Initiation and the Catechumenate*, Murphy Center for Liturgical Reflection (Notre Dame: University of Notre Dame Press, 1976) 138. The immediate impetus for the development of the RCIA was the official mandate of Vatican II: see *Sacrosanctum Concilium* 64-66; *Lumen gentium* 14; *Ad gentes* 13-14; *Christus Dominus* 14.

If the RCIA is to become more than another unrealized blueprint for reform, if it is in fact to work the renewal it heralds, then it will have to be faithfully implemented and become an integral part of ordinary parish life. That will not be easy. First, the RCIA is a lengthy, complex document that demands both careful study and prudent interpretation. Second, its vision of initiation is at odds with many of the Church's inherited liturgical, pastoral, and catechetical habits. And these habits may be so deeply ingrained as to resist any easy reversal. Finally, the RCIA, like any blueprint, sketches some matters in only the barest outline. This is particularly the case with its catechetical dimensions. If the rite is to be successfully implemented, then its catechetical principles will have to be concretized and its catechetical gaps filled in. It is precisely this sketchiness, this incompleteness, within the RCIA's blueprint that has prompted this study.

In this chapter I will begin by surveying two matters: first, what the RCIA legislates, and second, what it implies. These first two sections will introduce the RCIA's basic vocabulary and dynamics and will give some sense of the stakes involved in its implementation. In the third section I will address the problem: the RCIA's catechetical gaps and silences. Then in the fourth section, I will set out what I believe to be a fruitful way of dealing with these: examining the catechetical approaches used by the Church Fathers with their own candidates and drawing on their experience as a guide for our own work. I would like, in this study, to test the value and validity of this suggestion. So, in the fifth section, I will set out how this might be done more specifically: by conducting an in-depth inquiry into the forms and styles of catechesis found within a single ancient catechumenate—the catechumenate St. Augustine directed in Hippo.

WHAT THE RCIA SAYS

The RCIA describes the initiation of adults as "a spiritual journey," one that, throughout its length and breadth, "bears a markedly paschal character."[3] To plot out this journey, the concilium that drafted the RCIA turned to ancient "maps": to ancient sacramentaries and Church orders, to patristic sermons and apologetic works. This was sparked not by some romantic yearning for

3. RCIA 4 and 8.

the archaic. Rather the concilium found in these ancient maps a forgotten wisdom—a theological vision, a psychological sensitivity, a pastoral realism—a wisdom that, despite its antiquity, seemed surprisingly contemporary. Balthasar Fischer, the chairman of the concilium that drew up the new rite, put the board's reasoning this way:

"It was not our intention to keep ancient texts merely because they were old or for nostalgic reasons, but because these texts, while they linked us with the past, still answered contemporary needs: the ancient texts treated Christian initiation as what it really is, a *process*, and [they] related that process to human nature."[4]

Taking these ancient maps as guides, the concilium resurrected a complex ensemble of rites, stages, and practices which had guided the early Church in its formation of new members. The concilium thus divided the journey towards initiation into four distinct periods: (1) evangelization, (2) catechumenate, (3) enlightenment, (4) mystagogy. It then punctuated the transition between these with three rites of passage or steps: (a) acceptance into the order of catechumens, (b) election, (c) sacraments of initiation.[5] (For a schematic summary of these rites and stages, see chart 1.)

   The first period, evangelization, is to be a time for hearing the Gospel of "the living God" and "Jesus Christ whom he has sent for the salvation of all." During it, the inquirer should taste some initial conversion. This conversion should be powerful enough to "cause a person to feel called away from sin and drawn into the mystery of God's love." After this period, the Church officially welcomes candidates at the first of the public rites, the Acceptance into the Order of Catechumens. This rite serves not only as an occasion for welcome, but also for mutual commitment. In it, "candidates . . . declare their intention to the Church and the

---

4. Balthasar Fischer, "RCIA: Looking Back—an Interview with Fr. Balthasar Fischer," an interview by William Ciesiak, *Modern Liturgy* 11 (June–August 1984) 7.
   5. RCIA 6 refers to these rites of passage as "steps" or "gateways" through which candidates pass to "ascend to the next level." For detailed look at the evolution of the distinction between *tempus* and *gradus* in the work of the concilium, see Robert Duggan, "Conversion in the *Ordo Initiationis Christianae Adultorum*," *Ephemerides Liturgicae* 96 (1982) 77–83.

Church in turn . . . embraces the catechumens as its own with a mother's love and concern."[6] Candidates are then signed with the cross, first on the forehead, then on the ears, eyes, lips, heart, shoulders, hands, and feet. The community then invites them "to share with us at the table of God's word."[7] After the sermon but before the Liturgy of the Eucharist, the catechumens are prayed for, then dismissed with a formal blessing.[8] This initial rite "marks their reception and first consecration by the Church." Henceforth, the catechumens are to be regarded—as they were in the early Church—as "Christians," as "part of the household of Christ."[9]

This rite serves as the gateway into the second period, the catechumenate. This new phase is to be a time for more than mere schooling in Christian doctrine; rather it is to be, as Vatican II puts it, an "apprenticeship" in Christian living.[10] The catechumenate is thus an intricate venture accomplished not in a few hurried sessions, but more leisurely, over a span "long enough—several years if necessary—for the conversion and faith of the catechumens to become strong."[11] During this period, catechumens continue to attend the Sunday Liturgy of the Word—just as they did in the early Church. Week after week, the same pattern is kept: readings, sermon, prayer, blessing, dismissal.

Also during this period, catechumens receive "suitable catechesis, . . . gradual and complete in its coverage, accommodated to the liturgical year."[12] This catechesis should do more than instruct in dogmas and precepts. First, it should instill in the catechumens a "profound sense of the mystery of salvation."[13] Second, it

6. RCIA 36–37, 41, 47.

7. RCIA 60. Only the signing on the forehead is required; the others are optional (55–56). The signing on the forehead was the patristic practice. According to Michel Dujarier, the multiple signations was a Gallican addition: see *The Rites of Christian Initiation: Historical and Pastoral Reflections* (New York: Sadlier, 1979) 36.

8. The rite stresses that the "catechumens are normally dismissed" before the Eucharistic liturgy itself; however, it does make such a dismissal optional, but only for "serious reasons": RCIA 67, 75.3.

9. RCIA 41, 47. This phrase is from Augustine, *Tractatus in evangelium Ioannis* 11.4 and is quoted in Vatican II's *Ad gentes* 14.

10. Vatican II, *Ad gentes* 14.

11. RCIA 76.

12. RCIA 75.1.

13. RCIA 75.

should not only instruct them in the different ways of prayer, but also give them some experience of these. Third, it should focus on the practical and the moral—"implanting in their hearts . . . the morality of New Testament, the forgiveness of injuries and insults, a sense of sin and repentance, the duties Christians must carry out in the world."[14] Finally, this catechesis should take place, at least some of the time, not within the confines of a classroom, but rather within a liturgical setting.[15]

All this clearly moves against the grain of inherited practices. No longer can catechists content themselves with presenting tidy theological summaries lifted from official catechisms; no longer is it sufficient to win a nodding assent to propositions. The goal and measure of catechesis should be not only changed minds, but changed hearts and changed lives. That means that catechumens should give public witness to a "progressive change of outlook and conduct," and that that progress should be "manifest by its social consequences." Catechumens should begin to embody a vigorous love of neighbor, a virtue honed and won at the cost of self-renunciation. In all this, the RCIA is concerned that catechumens should come to mirror the Church's own life. And since the Church's life is apostolic, that of the catechumens should be so as well. To strengthen their resolve and progress, catechumens are to receive a whole complex of blessings, exorcisms, and anointings. Obviously, this process depends heavily both on the grace of God and on local circumstance (that is, on the needs of catechumens, the character of the local assembly, the availability of ministers). For this reason, "nothing . . . can be settled a priori."[16]

14. RCIA 82.

15. On this matter there are several differences between the 1974 provisional text and the recently revised American edition. Both suggest holding special celebrations of the word (i.e., besides the Sunday liturgy). The provisional text mentions that "celebrations of the word of God may be held after catechesis" (108 in the 1974 text); the revised American rite, on the other hand, suggests that "celebrations of the word may be held *in connection with* catechetical or instructional meetings of the catechumens, *so that these will occur in a context of prayer*" (81–89). In addition, the revised rite suggests a model for such celebrations: (1) an opening song, (2) readings and responsorial psalms, (3) a homily, (4) concluding rites (an exorcism, a blessing, or an anointing). Thus the revised American rite highlights more clearly than the provisional text what seems to have been the presumption of the ancient texts: that catechesis normally takes place within a liturgical context.

16. RCIA 76.

Throughout this period, sponsors play a key role. No longer are they to serve as mere ceremonial fixtures, rather they are once more to apprentice the catechumens into the everyday rhythms and demands of Christian living. Sponsors should show catechumens "how to practice the Gospel in personal and social life, to sustain [them] in moments of hesitancy and anxiety, to bear witness, and to guide [their] progress in the baptismal life." It is because of this close relationship that sponsors are so aptly suited to "stand as witnesses to candidates' moral character, faith, and intention."[17] In other words, sponsors play a dual role. They are, on the one hand, witnesses to the catechumens—testifying more by deed than word how one incarnates gospel imperatives. They are, on the other hand, witnesses for the catechumens—testifying on their behalf before the liturgical assembly.[18]

The third period, that of purification and enlightenment, coincides with Lent. It begins officially with the Rite of Election, held on the first Sunday of Lent. In this rite, the Church solicits the public testimony of sponsors and catechists—much as it did in the early Church. Then the catechumens are enrolled for baptism, and their names are formally inscribed in the Book of the Elect. During the weeks that follow, the candidates (now called the "elect") go through a "more intense spiritual preparation, consisting more in interior reflection than in catechetical instruction"; they are to purify mind and heart and to do penance.[19] On the third, fourth, and fifth Sundays of Lent, special readings are assigned which invite the candidates to grapple with three classic Johannine images: Christ the living water (John 4), Christ the light of the world (John 9), and Christ the resurrection and the life (John 11).[20] On these same weeks, after the homily, candidates undergo the great exorcisms known as the scrutinies.[21] These rites are meant to inspire

17. RCIA 9–11.

18. Michel Dujarier and Theophile Villaca, "The Various Ministries of Christian Initiation," in William Reedy, ed., *Becoming a Catholic Christian: a Symposium on Christian Initiation* (New York: Sadlier, 1978) 136–37.

19. RCIA 139.

20. RCIA 143. For an overview of this ancient tradition, see Thierry Maertens, "History and Function of the Three Great Pericopes: The Samaritan Woman, the Man Born Blind, the Raising of Lazarus" in Johannes Wagner, ed., *Adult Baptism and the Catechumenate*, Concilium 22 (New York: Paulist Press, 1967) 51–56.

21. For a survey of the history and meaning of the scrutinies, see A. Don-

self-searching and repentance and to "uncover, then heal all that is weak, defective, or sinful in the hearts of the elect; to bring out, then strengthen all that is upright, strong, and good."[22] Also during these weeks, the elect receive—as they did in the early Church—the Creed and the Lord's Prayer, those "ancient texts that have always been regarded as expressing the heart of the Church's faith and prayer."[23] Finally, on Holy Saturday, the elect withdraw to a quiet place, and there gather to pray, reflect, and fast. Two rites are held at this time: the Recitation of the Creed in which the elect formally give back the symbol of faith they have been handed; and the Ephphetha Rite, an exorcism of ear and mouth meant "to impress on the elect their need of grace in order that they may hear the word of God and profess it for their salvation."[24]

That night, at the Easter Vigil, the most intricate and sacred liturgy of the year, the Church celebrates the climax of this long journey: the candidates' initiation into the "awe-inspiring" rites of baptism, confirmation, and Eucharist.[25] The choice of the vigil is critical. As Aidan Kavanagh notes:

"The insistence on the Easter Vigil as the normal setting for Christian initiation is neither ecclesiastical nostalgia nor doctrinal wistfulness. There is simply no other time of the year, and certainly no other liturgical context, that serves as so rich a setting for sacramental initiation and its meaning. Not only are the initiates

deyne, "La discipline des scrutins dans l'église latine avant Charlemagne," *Revue d'histoire ecclésiastique* 26 (1932) 5–33 and 751–87; Roger Béraudy, "Scrutinies and Exorcisms," in Wagner, *Adult Baptism and the Catechumenate*, 57–61. The exorcisms in the RCIA are no longer "imprecatory" but "deprecatory"; that is, as Balthasar Fischer points out, "we no longer speak to the Devil (considered as being present); we speak with God about the Devil (still considered as personal)." Fischer, "Baptismal Exorcism in the Catholic Baptismal Rites after Vatican II," *Studia Liturgica* 10 (1974) 53.

22. RCIA 141, 143.

23. RCIA 147. The rite specifies that the presentation of the Creed takes place during the third week of Lent (i.e., following the first scrutiny); the presentation of the Lord's Prayer takes place during the fifth week of Lent (i.e., following the third scrutiny).

24. RCIA 193–99.

25. John Chrysostom was especially fond of the phrase "awe-inspiring" as a description of the rites of initiation. See, for instance, *Baptismal Instructions* 2.12, 14; 6.15.

dying and rising in Christ as the Church commemorates his passage from death to life long ago. More importantly the initiates are entering into his corporate real presence which is the Church. . . . Only the Easter Vigil yields up an ecclesiology worthy of baptism."[26]

Also striking is the RCIA's insistence that the sacraments be celebrated not as though these were separate entities, but as they were originally: a unified integral succession of rites. No longer is confirmation to be separated from baptism—whether by days or by years—but is to take place immediately afterward.[27] For this to occur, the RCIA had to make a significant provision: namely, that the priest who confers baptism is, in most cases, the one who also confers confirmation.[28] This obviously moves against the long-standing Latin tradition of reserving the conferring of confirmation to bishops. In addition, the RCIA sets out full immersion as the preferred form of baptism.[29] No longer should baptism be a few dribbles of water on the forehead. It is again to resemble what it in fact is: a bath, a plunge into enough water that one can taste and feel water's death-dealing and life-giving power.

26. Aidan Kavanagh, *The Shape of Baptism: The Rite of Christian Initiation* (New York: Pueblo Publishing Co., 1978) 134–35.

27. RCIA 215. The text gives weighty theological reasons for this: "In accord with the ancient practice followed in the Roman liturgy, adults are *not to be baptized without receiving confirmation immediately afterward*, unless some serious reason stands in the way. The conjunction of the two celebrations signifies the unity of the paschal mystery, the close link between the mission of the Son and the outpouring of the Holy Spirit, and the connection between the two sacraments through which the Son and the Holy Spirit come with the Father to those who are baptized. . . . Finally in the celebration of the eucharist, as they take part for the first time and with full right, the newly baptized reach the culminating point in their Christian initiation." For a discussion of this key passage, see Kavanagh, *Confirmation: Origins and Reform* (New York: Pueblo, 1988) 85–86.

28. RCIA 14. Balthasar Fischer has remarked that "if I am proud of anything, I am proud of having convinced the bishops that they should give permission to the priest to confirm." "Interview with Balthasar Fischer," *Chicago Catechumenate* 6, no. 2 (December 1983) 11.

29. RCIA 26. Note that while the RCIA does allow for pouring water over the head as a possible option, it lists immersion first. What is true of any liturgical document is true here: the preferred is listed first. See Kavanagh, *The Shape of Baptism*, 138.

The fourth and final period, that of mystagogy, begins after initiation and extends from Easter to Pentecost. During it, the newly baptized (now known as "neophytes") receive a form of catechesis widely used in the ancient Church, but almost unknown in the present: mystagogy, that is, a "teaching of the mysteries," a series of explorations which probe the rites of initiation—the gestures, the symbols, the words—in terms of their biblical resonances and their import for Christian life. During the liturgies of this period, the neophytes sit in a special section of the church.[30] This silently but powerfully highlights their new status and marks them as people deserving the assembly's special care and attention.

This fourth phase of the initiates' journey ends on Pentecost. The RCIA thus suggests that the community make Pentecost an occasion to celebrate the neophytes' completion of their long pilgrimage. The rite also adds one final suggestion: that "on the anniversary of their baptism the neophytes should be brought together in order to give thanks to God, to share with one another their spiritual experiences, and to renew their commitment."[31]

WHAT THE RCIA IMPLIES

The RCIA is much more than a collection of rites and rubrics; it is ultimately a pastoral statement that re-envisions both the mission and character of Christian community. Not only does it resurrect ancient rituals, practices, and stages. It also attempts to retrieve an ancient and quite radical vision of the Church—one which places conversion at the heart of things, which reshapes community roles, which radically redefines the meaning of catechesis, and which sees baptism as the taproot and catalyst for life-long transformation. Let us now probe some of these implications in more detail.

First, RCIA reverses a centuries-old habit: privatizing Christian initiation. No longer is the formation of converts a few hasty months of private instruction in doctrine. No longer is their conversion a private matter—worked out in hushed anonymity be-

30. RCIA 248.
31. RCIA 250. The RCIA differs from the custom of the early Church in extending this period through the fifty days between Easter and Pentecost. Quite often the period of mystagogy lasted only one week; see chapter 8.

tween convert and parish priest. No longer is their baptism to be a quiet little affair, a small gathering of family and friends held any Saturday afternoon. Rather their initiation is to assume once more the honor, the centrality, and the symbolic richness it enjoyed in the patristic era.

Because of the new rite, converting individuals assume center stage in the assembly's worship. Before the whole assembly, their motives and commitments are examined. Before it, they are lavished with blessings, healed with exorcisms, strengthened with anointings. Week after week, they are solemnly dismissed in a vivid, even threatening, gesture meant to catechize faithful and catechumen alike on the high dignity of baptism. Through it all, "their faith, progress, and prognosis in communal faith-living are the concerns of the entire local church met for solemn public worship."[32] Candidates are to be public persons, and the witness of their conversion, a matter of public record. This public witness assumes its richest expression at the vigil. According to Keifer, this means that:

"the celebration of the paschal mystery finds its axis and concrete manifestation in the baptism, confirmation, and eucharist of newly baptized adults. . . . The revelation of Christ's saving, healing, and redeeming power in our midst is the making of Christians. [This marks] a breathtaking departure from the recent past."[33]

Second, the RCIA insists that lay ministry—of sponsors, of catechists, of the assembly—must be vital, indeed, must be constitutive of the life of the whole Church. In particular, it presumes that within every assembly there are enough master Christians to apprentice catechumens in the intricate art of gospel-living. As Kavanagh has cogently put it: "One learns how to fast, pray, repent, celebrate, and serve the good of one's neighbors less by being lectured on these matters than by close association with people who do these things with regular ease and flair."[34] Restoring the catechumenate may not only renew traditional ministries (of deacons, catechists, and sponsors); it may also catalyze the growth of other less ordered, more informal ministries: that of

32. Kavanagh, *The Shape of Baptism*, 128.
33. Keifer, "Christian Initiation," 139.
34. Kavanagh, *The Shape of Baptism*, 131.

10

evangelists and healers, song leaders and storytellers, specialists in hospitality and in spiritual direction.[35] Such diversification may help de-clericalize the Church's ministry. It may also give fresh substance to the phrase "priesthood of all believers" and may help us again see that "*laos* is a priestly name for a priestly person."[36] After all, the RCIA insists that this ministry of initiation is not the preserve of some elite—ordained or otherwise—but is the responsibility of all the baptized, that in the last analysis it is the whole local assembly who is evangelist, catechist, sponsor, and priest. Put another way, the RCIA calls the Church to see and to be what it is: the people of God sent on a world-shaking and world-transforming mission—evangelizing, witnessing, teaching, serving, healing, dying to self and rising to new life.

Third, the RCIA resurrects the order of catechumens. That means that we will need to adjust our conceptions about what constitutes membership and begin to take seriously the rite's (and Vatican II's) words about catechumens as "already part of the household of Christ." It also implies something about the catechumens' role in the ecology of the Church's apostolic life. As Kavanagh notes, "catechumens together form a corporate presence that discharges a true ministry in the Church by witnessing constantly to the Church her need for continuing conversion in Christ."[37] For instance, when the community witnesses catechumens feasting at the table of God's Word, it should find itself called to examine how that Word nourishes its own heart and mind; when it witnesses catechumens who spend years hungering

35. For this reason, some commentators see the RCIA as a source for parish renewal. Raymond Kemp, in his book *A Journey in Faith* (New York: Sadlier, 1979), offers a vivid personal account of the way the RCIA has renewed his inner-city parish. However, as Kavanagh warns, parish renewal is not the RCIA's purpose: "Parish renewal, which is a good thing on the whole, may well be (and should be) a *by-product* of the church's rites of initiation. But these rites are not in themselves a plan for parish renewal." Rather their purpose "is to initiate by catechesis, exorcism, prayer, example, and sacrament those who are coming to faith lived in the church." Kavanagh, "Critical Issues in the Growth of the RCIA in North America," *Catechumenate: a Journal of Christian Initiation* 10 (March 1988) 11.

36. Kavanagh, "Unfinished and Unbegun Revisited: the Rite of Christian Initiation of Adults," *Worship* 53 (July 1979) 336.

37. Kavanagh, *The Shape of Baptism*, 112.

for the Eucharist, it should find itself called to examine how that Eucharist sustains its own graced life; when it witnesses catechumens feeding the hungry, clothing the naked, visiting the dying, it should find itself called to ponder the meaning and cost of its own apostolic vocation. In this sense then, catechumens are not simply recipients of the Church's ministry, but also ministers to the Church itself, agents of its transformation.

Fourth, the RCIA restores the sacraments of initiation to their original order and their original ritual proximity. No longer is baptism to be separated from confirmation by weeks or even years, as had happened in the medieval Church.[38] No longer is first Eucharist (and consequently first penance) to be inserted between baptism and confirmation, as has been the case ever since Pius X's 1910 decree.[39] Rather, the RCIA insists that the sacraments be celebrated in the same order and the same ritual proximity that they were in the Latin Church of the early centuries. In essence, it attempts to reverse what Nathan Mitchell has called the "dissolution of Christian initiation," a "ritual breakdown" that "resonate[ed] throughout Christian faith, catechesis, theology, and praxis."[40] In other words, this reform is more than simply ritual fine-tuning or archaeological restoration. It is an attempt, according to Mark Searle, to present "a powerful symbolic redescription of what it means to be Christian:" "that a Christian is one who is identified with the dead and exalted Christ by the power of the

38. For a study of the breakdown of Latin initiatory polity during the Middle Ages, see Nathan Mitchell, "Dissolution of the Rite of Christian Initiation," in *Made, Not Born*, 50–82.

39. Pius X's "Decree on Frequent and Daily Reception of Holy Communion" (1905) helped reverse a millennium-old practice of infrequent communion. Then the "Decree of the Sacred Congregation of the Discipline of the Sacraments on First Communion" (1910) lowered the age of communion from early adolescence to early childhood. For the texts, see *Official Catholic Teachings: Worship & Liturgy*, ed. James J. Megivern (Wilmington, N.C.: McGrath Publishing Co., 1978) 27–40. While these decrees helped increase the frequency of Eucharistic reception, they had a side effect: namely, first Communion (and with it, first penance) became inserted between infant baptism and confirmation, thereby disrupting the ancient sequence. Kavanagh, *The Shape of Baptism*, 81, notes: "The state of initiatory practice in the Roman Rite during the four decades preceding the Second Vatican Council was in a degree of confusion intensified if not wholly induced by unilateral papal action."

40. Mitchell, "Dissolution of the Rite of Christian Initiation," 50.

Spirit" and who is united with his Body by that common fellowship, meal, and sacrifice we call Eucharist.[41]

This shift towards an integral celebration may affect our corporate consciousness in subtle ways. For Catholic Christians, sacraments are essential elements for the grammar of faith. And this grammar, like that of any language, generally works beneath the surface: mediating meanings, establishing canons of intelligibility, structuring what is expressible and what is not. Because of this grammatical shift, we may more readily recognize confirmation's baptismal moorings and begin to savor and probe its messianic and pneumatic themes. Because of this, we might once again appreciate the way confirmation serves as a Spirit-filled rite of passage that leads one *from* the Spirit-imbued waters of baptism and *to* the Spirit-endowed table of Eucharist. And because of this, we might once more come to think of Eucharist—rather than confirmation—as the apex of Christian initiation, as *the* sacrament of Christian maturity.[42] In other words, in altering our symbols—particularly ones as important as how one becomes and remains Christian—we may subtly alter our corporate self-understanding.

Fifth, the RCIA implies that adult baptism should once more serve as the *norm* for Christian initiation.[43] This does not mean that we will abandon infant baptism. Nor does it mean that infant baptism will cease being the most common way people enter the ranks of the faithful. To raise such concerns would be to misunderstand what a norm is and how it functions. As Kavanagh has noted, "a norm has nothing to do with the number of times a thing is done, but it has everything to do with the standard to which a thing is done."[44] Thus, norms—whether those of the Church or of civil society—set standards of judgment: they help us decipher what is normal, what is abnormal but permissible, and

41. Mark Searle, "Issues in Christian Initiation: Uses and Abuses of the RCIA," *Living Light* 22 (March 1986) 200.

42. Kavanagh, *The Shape of Baptism*, 177. These suggestions touch on a complex and much disputed area of liturgical theology; for a fuller discussion, see Kavanagh, *Confirmation*; also Gerard Austin, *The Rite of Confirmation: Anointing with the Spirit* (New York: Pueblo, 1985).

43. For an extended discussion of this question, see Kavanagh, *The Shape of Baptism*, 102–25, a revision of his initial article on the question: "The Norm of Baptism: the New Rite of Christian Initiation of Adults," *Worship* 48 (1974) 143–52.

44. Kavanagh, *The Shape of Baptism*, 109.

what is abnormal and impermissable. What does this mean for baptism? It means that once we come to experience the RCIA as our operative norm, we may again come to recognize the weighty demands and spacious contours of Christian initiation: that is, initiation, in the richest sense, should happen in stages and with a panoply of rites; it demands faith and conversion; it involves community and apostolic commitment; it is accomplished slowly—over a period of years; it is best celebrated at the vigil; and its sacramental expression includes not just bathing, but also anointing and feasting. Set against such a norm, infant baptism will seem a mere "piano reduction" compared to the RCIA's "symphonic orchestration": the key melodies may all be there, but scarcely with their proper richness and full-voiced tonality. In other words, the RCIA should, over time, quietly but profoundly challenge the standards and presuppositions that undergird our long-standing habit of infant baptism.[45]

Sixth, the RCIA puts forward the Church's *canonical* vision of conversion. This may seem, at first sight, a rather grandiose claim. But, as Robert Duggan has insisted, this is simply to take seriously the classic patristic dictum: *lex orandi, lex credendi* (what the Church prays is what the Church believes).[46] Duggan has thus

45. Some commentators use the RCIA as a way of raising challenging questions about our current practice of infant baptism. For example, see Kemp, "The Rite of Christian Initiation of Adults at Ten Years," *Worship* 56 (July 1982) 320–21 and Kavanagh, *The Shape of Baptism*, 109–14. Kemp questions why we do not complete sacramental initiation (as the Orthodox do) and why we exclude newly baptized infants or children from the Eucharistic table—in effect, "excommunicating" them. Kavanagh is especially critical of *quamprimum* infant baptism and regards certain cases of infant baptism as a "benign abnormality" (in case of emergencies or of especially faithful parents); however, he considers much of our current practice as "pastoral malfeasance" and "theological obsession." Mark Searle has strongly criticized some of this discussion and has tried to offer a fresh approach to infant baptism in ways that respect the richness of the RCIA and the ancient traditions. For instance, he suggests that baptism possesses a meaning beyond simply the Pauline "death-resurrection" motif; for instance, "adoption" "divinization," "indwelling." And he believes that some of these are better highlighted by infant baptism. He also warns of our need to learn from the experience of churches that practice "believers' baptism" and have learned how "an adult decision for Christ can be subverted." See Searle, "The RCIA and Infant Baptism," *Worship* 56 (July 1982) 327–32.

46. The classic formulation is that of Prosper of Aquitaine. See Jaroslav Pelikan, *The Christian Tradition*, vol. 1, *The Emergence of the Catholic Tradition*

argued that a "careful listening" to the RCIA text gives us "what the praying Church says genuine conversion is and should be," and such listening "springs from the deep conviction that in the *ecclesia orans* we are in vital contact with the voice of the Spirit."[47] Clearly the RCIA proposes an intricate vision of conversion. Duggan has isolated eight distinct, though often interrelated, facets of that vision:

(1) *Radical transformation:* Authentic conversion involves more than some sudden moment of illumination, more than some shift of institutional allegiance: it means nothing less than a radical transformation of the whole person. And this metamorphosis springs from an encounter with the mystery of Christ dying and rising in his people—in their life of shared teaching, fellowship, service, and worship.

(2) *Journey:* The RCIA envisions human life as a journey of ongoing conversion and sees the path towards initiation simply as one segment of that larger journey. It acknowledges that the journey begins long before the person approaches the local church and will continue long after the person has entered its ranks. The rite also presumes that this ongoing journey touches not only the candidate, but the local church as well. As James Lopresti has noted, "if initiation is a journey begun, then the community that receives the new Christian must be seen to be a journeying people, a people going somewhere."[48]

(3) *"Times and seasons":* The RCIA acknowledges that conversion has its "times and seasons" and so maps out four different periods, each with its unique character and emphases. And it recognizes that at certain pivotal moments the conversion experience crystallizes in ways that demand ritual expression.

(4) *Covenantal:* The RCIA, drawing on biblical imagery, envisages conversion as covenant-making.[49] However inchoate it may seem,

(100–600) (Chicago: University of Chicago Press, 1971) 339. It had been an operative principle in patristic debates long before Prosper set it out as an axiom.

47. Robert Duggan, "Conversion in the *OICA*," *Ephemerides Liturgicae* 97 (1983) 208.

48. James Lopresti, "New Christians, New Faith," *New Catholic World* 222, no. 1330 (July–August 1979) 167.

49. Louis Ligier, one of the rite's architects, draws this theme out in his essay "The Biblical Symbolism of Baptism in the Fathers of the Church and the Liturgy," in Wagner, *Adult Baptism*, 17–23.

however dimly the candidate may grasp it, the heart of this journey is the forging of a sacred pact between God and candidate. But as Duggan notes, "no parity of roles is implied; the initiative is always God's."[50] The human response is thus always hearing, answering, following. Because of this covenant, the candidate can lay claim to certain blessings but must also embrace certain responsibilities.

(5) *Christocentric:* The RCIA text speaks of conversion as Christ-centered: the catechumen is signed with the cross of Christ and presented with the Gospel book, which is the "good news of Christ"; in the years of the catechumenate, candidates "come to reflect the image of Christ"; baptism is a "sharing in the death and resurrection of Christ"; confirmation makes them "more like Christ"; and Eucharist marks the culminating point of their incorporation into Christ.[51]

(6) *Ecclesial:* The RCIA conceives of conversion as an ecclesial event. Conversion "takes place step by step in the midst of the community of the faithful." Over the years, candidates slowly form a network of relationships: with sponsors, catechists, priests, the bishop, the whole local assembly. Fellowship with this local community is seen as one of the fruits of conversion. Ultimately, such conversion is the genesis of the Church—transforming both candidate and community.[52]

(7) *Sacramental:* Conversion demands sacramental expression. Certainly the RCIA sees the vigil as the culminating moment, but it regards the other rites—signing with the cross, blessings, exorcisms, election, etc.—as sacramentlike junctures within the larger pilgrimage.

(8) *Comprehensive:* Conversion touches the whole person: one's body which is signed, immersed, anointed, fed; one's mind which delves intuitively into the great mysteries and grapples with specific theological insights and tenets; one's heart which savors the love of God and of God's people and which is touched by the rite's play of images, metaphors, and symbols; one's behavior— both the break with sin and the forging of virtue, especially charity.

50. Duggan, "Conversion in the *OICA*," 97:209.
51. RCIA 55, 64; 66; 8; 233; 217.
52. Duggan, "Conversion in the *OICA*," 96:211.

16

Finally, the RCIA proposes a formidable agenda for religious educators. Balthasar Fischer has stated that he and the other members of the concilium explicitly intended "to do away with [the] school mentality, that cerebral way of entering the Church."[53] They were concerned that catechists recognize that "the catechumenate is not a school, but an initiation: the school has some students who learn a lesson; initiation has some disciples who discover a life."[54] Thus the rite presumes that catechists are multilingual, that they can speak with equal fluency the plural languages of catechesis: certainly that of instruction, but also of evangelization and apprenticeship, of spiritual direction and mystagogy. It demands not only that catechists be capable of handing on the Church's rich, pluriform traditions; it also insists that they propose a practicable ethics, that they catalyze interior explorations, guide prayer, and discern spirits, that they nurture apostolic action and embody a virtue worth imitating. It asks that catechists not only be fluent in a host of catechetical languages and disciplines, but also be attuned to a process more circular than linear: not so much "a graduated program" as a "series of explorations that radiate outward from the gospels into every area of personal, ecclesial, and social living, flowing back again into the meditative reading of the scriptures; the practice of prayer, and the elicitation of commitments."[55]

In other words, it presumes that catechists be experts in the fine art of "conversion therapy"—to use Kavanagh's popular and often misunderstood coinage. By this phrase, Kavanagh does not mean a therapy that is merely psychological or individualistic—as the term tends to connote in our culture.[56] Rather he gives this

53. Fischer, "An Interview with Balthasar Fischer," 7.
54. André Aubry, quoted in Thomas Ivory, "The Restoration of the Catechumenate as a Norm for Catechesis," *The Living Light* 20 (Summer 1976) 230.
55. Searle, "Issues in Christian Initiation," 202.
56. Robert Duggan seems to lapse into such an individualist model in his article "Implementing the *Rite of Christian Initiation of Adults*," 329: "Proper implementation of the RCIA requires 'conversion therapy' that can *only* be administered according to personal needs. . . . We need to reach a point where the first association with 'catechumenate' is 'catechumen.' The term 'catechumenate' should make us think of a group of *individuals* who have this in common—that they are preparing for baptism—but whose conversion journeys are *so individual* that each must be dealt with according to its own needs" [my emphasis]. Anthony Garascia makes a similar error in his article, "Forum:

suggestive term a somewhat idiosyncratic meaning. He means a catechesis capable (1) of nurturing people through the trauma of God's iconoclastic grace, (2) of protecting them "from the Church's insensitivity to the crisis," and (3) of bringing both the Church and the converting individual into a sustained relationship, that is, into communion.[57] Clearly this presumes both high standards and considerable expertise. And as we shall see, the RCIA offers few resources for fulfilling such an agenda. This mix of high expectations and poor resources leads thus to the problem and impetus for this study.

WHAT THE RCIA DOES NOT SAY

In 1982, I helped a small Hispanic parish in Houston begin implementing the RCIA. Careful study had alerted me to its potential. But as we began to implement the new rite, we soon discovered a disparity within it: between what it says and what it does not say. On the one hand, we found that it provides fairly detailed directions for executing its complex of rites. These made implementation of the rituals fairly straightforward. On the other hand, its directions and goals for catechesis, while provocative and innovative, seemed rather sketchy. In particular, we found that the RCIA fails to address four catechetical issues critical to its implementation:

1. *Curriculum:* The rite is, for most part, silent about curriculum. Admittedly, it specifies that each period has its own unique curricular goals: e.g., evangelization, apprenticeship, repentance, immersion into mystery. But it offers few specifics. Yet educators who implement it must ask: What are we to teach? What specific experiences should catechumens have of God and of community? What do they need to know, feel, taste, and do? What stories, beliefs, or practices? What order should these things be given in? And in what depth?

The RCIA as Conversion Therapy." *Worship* 62 (July 1988) 360–65. He takes up Kavanagh's coinage and claims that "we are justified in calling the RCIA 'conversion therapy' for there is a resemblance to what happens in a therapy group combined with a focus on conversion." Garascia goes on to apply principles of group therapy to the way one forms catechumens.

57. Kavanagh, "Christian Initiation: Tactics and Strategy," in *Made, Not Born,* 4.

2. *Models of Teaching:* In the same way, the RCIA is largely silent about appropriate teaching styles. Yet educators must ask: How might specific beliefs, moral precepts, and habits be best taught or nurtured? What methods best respect the dignity, call, and needs of catechumens? How specifically should catechists—in conjunction with sponsors, pastors, and assembly—apprentice catechumens in the Christian life? The revised American rite suggests using the Liturgy of the Word as a model for structuring sessions during the catechumenate phase. But does this framework allow catechumens to share their own experience of conversion or to participate actively in the reflection on the Word? How should sermons or instructions in these services mix biblical, doctrinal, and moral themes? And if this is a possible framework for the catechumenate phase, what should one do during the other periods? Does each period, in accord with its specific character, demand using different methods, processes, and settings?

3. *Conversion:* Clearly, the RCIA offers a rich, multifaceted vision of conversion. Yet educators must worry about how this is to be fostered and discerned in the concrete. In other words: How will such conversion manifest itself in the life of the candidate? What evidence should we look for? In particular, how should curriculum and teaching converge so as to aid and nurture the intricate conversion the rite calls for? Yet educators must be attuned not only to the conversion of candidates, for the RCIA speaks of the community of the faithful "joining the catechumens . . . [in] renewing *their own* conversion."[58] Implied in this is a recognition that the Church is a pilgrim people, that it too is in need of conversion. The problem is this: catechumens confront a Church, both locally and world-wide, that needs reform. As a catechist, I have had to ask: How does one bring the energy, insights, and charisms of the catechumens to challenge both the local community and the larger Church? How does one avoid using the RCIA simply as an instrument for socialization, as a subtle tool for maintaining the status quo?[59] How does one give catechumens a

58. RCIA 4.

59. It is somewhat alarming to see some commentators interpret the RCIA simply as dependent on a socialization model of catechesis: for instance, Duggan, "Implementing the RCIA," 330; Searle, "Issues in Christian Initiation," 211–14. Admittedly the RCIA rejects a purely instructional model. But

realistic sense of both the wisdom and weaknesses of the Church and at the same time honor their idealism and encourage them to help reform our communities?

4. *Faith and culture:* The RCIA is a document for the universal Church, but new members are initiated not only into the universal Church but into quite specific local communities. For example, the Houston church I worked in was shaped both by its Hispanic cultural traditions and by its American setting. This bicultural character in turn shaped its social life, its liturgical habits, its popular piety. Thus I had to discern: What is the interplay of the faith of the larger Church and its local embodiment? Which of the culturally embedded traditions of the local community does one pass on: for instance, devotion to Our Lady of Guadalupe or participation in *las posadas*? Which of these are helpful or nurturing and which are simply peripheral or even superstitious? In addition, the people in this parish were quite poor. They daily faced prejudice and suffered terribly from our country's prevailing economic and political structures. Thus it became critical to ask: How does one help catechumens make an option for the poor? How does one help them develop a faith-tempered critical stance to the dominant American culture?

The RCIA's silence on such catechetical issues seems to be a weakness of the document. Admittedly, it is what it calls itself: a rite.[60] But it is a rite in which the catechetical dimension is woven

---

such commentators seem unaware of the hazards of such a "socialization" interpretation. For a critical discussion of the strengths and weaknesses of the socialization model, see Thomas Groome, *Christian Religious Education: Sharing Our Story and Vision* (San Francisco: Harper & Row, 1980) 115–27.

60. On this point, I both agree and disagree with Kavanagh's position in his article "Critical Issues in the Growth of the RCIA in North America," 10–11. In it he claims: "The RCIA must not be perceived to be a program or, as one often hears, a process. It is what it says it is: a rite. . . . [It]must be perceived and dealt with as such. And good liturgy does not proceed from our confusing it with educational programs or therapeutic processes, any more than automotive efficiency proceeds from confusing an engine with a hubcap." True, but Kavanagh consistently tends to overestimate the liturgical at the expense of the catechetical. He fails to see that the conundrums surrounding the implementation of the RCIA's catechetical dimensions are in large measure due to the rite's sketchiness. For instance, he claims: "The directions given for each stage of the rite are *clear* on the whole; often they are well detailed and filled with helpful options at every point." That may be true for

into its very fabric. And if pastors and catechists rely on an ill-conceived or inappropriate catechesis, then they will undermine its power and subvert its pastoral vision. In any case, the RCIA's silence does at least open the way for creative local adaptation.

For over a decade now, religious educators have been at work concretizing the RCIA's sketchy ideals and filling in its gaps. In particular, they have wrestled with the problems of creating appropriate curricula and teaching styles. The first impulse in many parishes has been to rely on contemporary catechisms to help shape their curriculum. Quite often they couple this catechism-framework with a lecture approach—effectively reducing inquirers and catechumens to passive recipients. The theological content they offer may be erudite and up-to-date, but the dynamic remains that of the old convert class: doctrinal in focus, abstract in content, cognitivist in conception of faith. Other parishes have used catechisms for their curricular outline, but couple them with more experience-based methods. Admittedly both of these approaches honor the RCIA's call for a catechesis that is "complete in its coverage." But they ignore its very next phrase: that catechesis be "accommodated to the liturgical year."[61] Even more importantly, they can lose sight of the RCIA's central focus: conversion. As Duggan warns:

"Because the American parish has such a strong record of successful educational programs, the danger of identifying the catechumenate as 'yet another program' is immense. In fact, the didactic bias of many currently operating 'catechumenate programs' reveals that what is really at issue is basically a re-tooled version of the old 'convert class instructions.' . . . . It is relatively easy for someone to 'learn about' the Catholic faith in this fashion, even in programs that are experientially based and quite sophisticated pedagogically. But the RCIA calls for more than 'learning about' our faith. What is actually at stake is conversion—change of heart and change of life. The mysterious interaction of divine grace and human freedom which results in conversion cannot be managed. . . ."[62]

parish liturgists, but their colleagues working in catechesis enjoy no such clarity or specificity.

61. RCIA 75.1.
62. Duggan, "Implementing the RCIA," 328.

Other religious educators have suggested approaches more attuned to the RCIA's conversion dynamic. For instance, James Dunning, founder of the North American Forum on the Catechumenate, has argued strongly against our inherited didactic and cognitivist biases. He insists that the RCIA is "a process not a program";[63] that its central focus is "journeying"—a graced venture into mystery that defies any single model or method. Over the years, he has suggested several catechetical approaches. For instance, in his book *New Wine: New Wineskins*, he argues that the RCIA's four periods contain a built-in catechetical method: (1) the precatechumenate should be a time for listening to and for telling stories—certainly those from Scripture but also personal stories, especially those of the inquirers themselves—stories that raise ultimate questions about the meaning of our lives; (2) during the catechumenate, one should probe these stories and their meaning more deeply and put them into dialogue with the Tradition; the basic text should be the Scriptures and the basic lens should be either a salvation-history or Christological one; (3) Lent should be a time of recollection, a time for discerning the call to conversion; it should feel more like a retreat than a series of catechetical sessions, and its basic dynamic should be akin to spiritual direction; and (4) mystagogy should be a time to drink in and savor the power of the sacramental symbols; it should occasion both celebrating one's call and putting its imperatives into practice. In his widely anthologized article, "Method is the Medium is the Message," Dunning has suggested a "potpourri of methods": adapting the dynamics of Alcoholics Anonymous' twelve steps or of Ignatian directed retreats, tapping on the movements suggested by Lonergan's epistemology (attend, reflect, judge, decide) or John Shea's theology of religious experience (meeting with Mystery, enlightened by Mystery, acting in Mystery).[64] He also encourages educators to begin systematically applying Thomas Groome's model of shared praxis to the design of catechumenal curricula and sessions.

---

63. James B. Dunning, *New Wine: New Wineskins: Pastoral Implications of the Rite of Christian Initiation of Adults* (New York: Sadlier, 1981) 20.

64. See Dunning, "The Method Is the Medium Is the Message: Catechetical Method in the RCIA," *Christian Initiation Resources Reader*, vol. 1: *Precatechumenate* (New York: Sadlier, 1984) 86–94.

For some years now, Karen Hinman Powell has advocated using the lectionary as the basis for the RCIA's curriculum. Hinman Powell takes as her starting point the RCIA's call that "catechesis [be] accommodated to the liturgical year" and thus claims "the lectionary as *the way* for catechumenate":

"Human experience in dialogue with the word and our living tradition . . . leads catechumens to a rich understanding of dogmas and Church teachings. . . . The lectionary is the best tool for catechesis because it provides for the fact that catechesis can then be given in stages and the 'unique spiritual journey of candidates' be reverenced."[65]

To make this suggestion more a practical possibility, she has edited a three-volume work, *Breaking Open the Word of God.* In it, she and other contributors offer catechists a set of lesson plans designed to follow the lectionary's three-year cycle of readings. Hinman Powell's approach has gained increasing support. For instance, Dunning has recently joined her in arguing for such a lectionary-based curriculum. He stresses that "the goal is not to exegete texts but exegete lives—to look deeply into our personal and communal lives and to see them in the light of the persons and communities who have journeyed with the Lord before us."[66] Similarly, Catherine Dooley argues that the lectionary should serve as "*the* source book" for RCIA catechesis. She stresses that such liturgically based formation will give rise to a catechesis that is less "didactic" and more "intuitive." Moreover, such an approach will help "build up a lexicon of image and sign that enables catechumens to name more fully their own experience of God and to enter more deeply into God's presence."[67]

---

65. Karen M. Hinman Powell and Joseph P. Sinwell, eds., *Breaking Open the Word of God: Resources for Using the Lectionary for Catechesis in the RCIA* (New York: Paulist Press, 1986–1988) 1:10. Perhaps she (and others) state this view in such black-and-white terms for rhetorical effect. However, the RCIA's silence on curriculum seems to make allowance for freedom and for flexibility. At this moment at least, it seems imprudent to declare any approach as *the* way.

66. Dunning, "Foreword," in Hinman Powell and Sinwell, *Breaking Open the Word of God,* 1:vii.

67. Catherine Dooley, "The Lectionary as the Source Book of Catechesis in the RCIA," *Catechumenate: a Journal of Christian Initiation* 10 (May 1988) 10, 20. See also Gerard Sloyan, "Forming Catechumens through the Lectionary," in

This survey of current trends in RCIA catechesis is not meant to be exhaustive. Rather it should alert us to two points. First, catechesis for the RCIA remains an open question. Certainly some curricula and some methods are more faithful to the RCIA's spirit and vision than others. But these catechetical issues remain a matter of debate precisely because the RCIA is, for the most part, silent on such matters.

Second, the current debate divides catechists between those who opt for attitudes and practices of the recent past (i.e., a catechism-based curriculum, a lecture format, a cognitivist understanding of conversion) and those who opt for more contemporary attitudes and practices (i.e., a lectionary curriculum, a more experientially focused or shared praxis format, a more affective or praxis view of conversion). In other words, the debate focuses on essentially *modern* approaches.

THE HYPOTHESIS

Certainly religious educators are trying to deal with the RCIA's gaps and silences. Equally noteworthy is what they are not doing: turning to patristic authors for guidance. This may seem, at first sight, a rather strange suggestion. Yet this is precisely what the liturgists who created the rite did, and it is precisely what contemporary commentators on the rite do. These liturgists and these commentators have argued that *if we want to interpret the RCIA adequately, then we need to understand the patristic sources that gave rise to it.* Their hypothesis appears to be sound for several reasons. First, the concilium used patristic documents as its map for plotting out the initiatory journey. Second, the Church has not had a vital adult catechumenate for over thirteen hundred years. This means commentators lack contemporary models to point to or draw upon. Third, the RCIA seems to open a virtual chasm between its vision of initiation and our inherited liturgical, pastoral, and catechetical habits.

In this study, I will take the hypothesis of these liturgists and these commentators one step further and apply it to the RCIA's catechetical dimension: that is, *if the Church has found itself increasingly renewed by the wisdom and richness of these ancient rituals and*

Before and After Baptism: the Work of Teachers and Catechists, ed. James A. Wilde (Chicago: Liturgy Training Publications, 1988) 27-38.

their underlying pastoral vision, then the Church might find itself similarly renewed by our gleaning the best from ancient styles of catechesis.

A few comments about my hypothesis are in order: First, the catechumenate—both its liturgy and its catechesis—was a patristic creation, and the Fathers who shaped it were splendid teachers and, on occasion, splendid theorists of teaching. Perhaps their example and their counsels can help us not only restore the rites of the catechumenate but also enrich our pedagogy. Over the years, I have found that these patristic sources—Hippolytus, Tertullian, Cyril of Jerusalem, Ambrose—have helped me contextualize the rite: its vocabulary, its dynamics, its spirituality. But more importantly, I have found in them an unexpected wisdom and richness, one which both exposes and challenges often unreflected habits and attitudes about the "what" and the "how" of catechesis. For example, the Fathers worked in a period prior to what Aidan Kavanagh has called the "deritualization of catechesis." For the Fathers, religious education and liturgy were not such separate endeavors, each with its own expertise, ideologies, and methods. Rather the two intertwined, each one subtly influencing the other: catechesis usually took place in a liturgical setting; its learnings prompted ritual expression; and each new rite of passage led in turn to new and deeper catechetical exploration. According to Kavanagh, this intimate proximity of liturgy and catechesis occasioned a quite specific dynamic:

"The Fathers understood catechesis to be a process the nature and form of which were determined entirely by its 'final cause,' namely sacramental initiation. Catechesis was thus permeated from beginning to end with a rich and carefully calibrated sacramental ethos. It was a process of 'enlightenment' consummated in the illumination (*photismos*) of baptism-in-its-fullness, that is baptism, chrismation or consignment, and eucharist. . . . Catechesis was thus intrinsically sacramental from beginning to end, and the catechumenate was a sacramental structure in the Church."[68]

In addition, the Fathers offer us a sober realism. For us, the catechumenate is a novelty and—at least in some circles—a panacea for the ills of the Church. It was not that for the ancients. It

68. Kavanagh, "Unfinished and Unbegun Revisited," 328.

25

was simply a part of the Church's ordinary life. The Fathers knew well its power and its limits. They devoted great energy to its maintenance, but they had no illusions about its weaknesses for shaping the sort of Christians they hoped would people their assemblies.

Second, I use the word "gleaning" quite deliberately. I am not suggesting that one uncritically resurrect patristic catechetical practices any more than the RCIA suggests uncritically resurrecting patristic liturgical habits. Rather, just as the RCIA gleaned the best of ancient liturgical practice, so religious educators might well glean the best of ancient catechetical practice. In other words, my suggestion is that we put current debates (such as catechism vs. lectionary) aside for the moment, that we try stepping behind them, and that we let the Fathers—people more experienced with the catechumenate than ourselves—teach us how to teach. This is not to denigrate contemporary efforts. Far from it. We plainly enjoy certain insights they did not have, and we have integrated these into the fiber of our thought and our work. To name but a few: we possess a highly developed historical consciousness; we recognize the intricacy and sweep of the physical universe in ways they could not; we are sensitive to the subtleties of the unconscious and to the dynamics of class, race, and ethnicity; we recognize the power and intractability of sinful social structures and have new insights into the weighty demands of human dignity and of social justice. Still, the Fathers have much to teach. Their example might help us search out new and more appropriate models, and their experience might warn us of unforeseen hazards. In particular, they might offer us fresh approaches to the open questions surrounding the RCIA's catechetical gaps and silences.

Third, if educators hope to act upon this suggestion, then they will need a wealth of scholarly literature that spells out in detail what catechetical approaches the Fathers used with their candidates. The problem is that the existing scholarly literature on the ancient catechumenate gives little attention to the specific concerns and questions of educators. Most of this literature has been done by and for liturgists. Certainly their contributions have been extraordinary, and the RCIA is but one of the fruits of their research. But their analyses tend, naturally enough, to focus on passages and perspectives relevant to liturgy. Few have approached the texts with an educator's eye, at least in a sustained, systematic way.[69] As Charles Paliard has poignantly remarked, "in the literature on the catechumenate, [catechesis] takes on the image of a 'poor relation.' "[70] This state of affairs is quite ironic. After all, the primary fourth- and fifth-century documents that these liturgists study are generally not liturgical documents per se (church orders, ordines, sacramentaries), but are transcripts of actual catecheses. And liturgical scholars use these documents not to study catechesis, but to reconstruct from them the course and structure of the ancient rites. This is certainly legitimate, but these ancient documents also need to be studied in terms of what they are: records of catechesis.

In addition, there is as yet nothing like a general critical history of the ancient catechumenate—certainly not one comparable to the histories we have on the ancient Trinitarian or Christological debates. Those that exist are far too brief, and the most accessible of these, Michel Dujarier's, is rather uneven.[71] In addition, these surveys too often present what "the Fathers said" or what "the Fathers did."[72] This approach can lull the unwary reader into

69. A notable exception to this is Hugh M. Riley, *Christian Initiation: A Comparative Study of the Interpretation of the Baptismal Liturgy in the Mystagogical Writings of Cyril of Jerusalem, John Chrysostom, Theodore of Mopsuestia, and Ambrose of Milan* (Washington: Consortium Press, 1974).

70. Charles Paliard, "The Place of Catechesis in the Catechumenate," in Wagner, *Adult Baptism,* 88.

71. Michel Dujarier, *A History of the Catechumenate: the First Six Centuries,* trans. Edward J. Hassl (New York: Sadlier, 1979). Dujarier relies heavily on arguments from silence, using them to justify his claim that the third century (and not the fourth) was the "golden age" of the catechumenate. Other surveys of the history of the ancient catechumenate include: P. de Puniet, "Catechuménat," *Dictionnaire d'archéologie chrétienne et de liturgie* 2:2579-2621; Josef Jungmann, *The Early Liturgy to the Time of Gregory the Great,* trans. Francis A. Brunner (Notre Dame: University of Notre Dame Press, 1959); Jungmann, "Catechumenate," *New Catholic Encyclopedia* 3:238-40; Robert M. Grant, "Development of the Christian Catechumenate," in *Made Not Born,* 32-50; Alois Stenzel, "The Temporal and Supra-Temporal in the History of the Catechumenate and Baptism," in Wagner, *Adult Baptism,* 31-44. See also the next note.

72. For instance, A. Turck, "Catéchein et Catéchèsis chez les premiers Pères," *Revue de sciences philosophiques et théologiques* 47 (1963) 361-72; Maurice Jourion, "Catéchèse et liturgie chez les Pères," *La Maison-Dieu* 140 (1979) 41-54; Ligier, "The Biblical Symbolism of Baptism in the Fathers of the Church and the Liturgy," 16-30; Jean Danielou, *The Bible and Liturgy* (Notre Dame: Univer-

thinking that the structure and style of the different ancient catechumenates was largely the same. As these authors too infrequently point out, we cannot presume any uniformity of practice given what we know of the diversity and localism in other areas of Church life (doctrine, ministry, Eucharistic practice). Put simply, what may have been practiced in one area may have been absent in another. This survey approach also tends to gloss over the fact that our knowledge of the ancient catechumenate is fragmentary; that, all too often, mention is made in passing so that we usually get more of a glimpse than a sustained portrait. Moreover, only a few studies have focused on a single locale and sought to reconstruct, with all deliberate caution, what its specific catechumenate looked like.[73] Only from a series of such studies can we hope eventually to have a general critical history of the ancient catechumenate.

To sum up: I propose that if we want to develop a catechesis appropriate to the RCIA, we might do well to learn what we can from those for whom the catechumenate was an ordinary reality, that is, the Fathers who directed the ancient catechumenate. It is a hypothesis in accord with those liturgists who created the rite and with those liturgists who have provided us with such fine commentaries on it. Yet it is one that educators cannot easily act upon—for while there exists a body of literature on the ancient catechumenate, it is one more attuned to the needs of parish liturgists than parish catechists. Thus in this investigation, I would like to examine the ancient catechumenate from an educator's point of view. The next section spells out more specifically how this will be done.

---

sity of Notre Dame Press, 1956); Edward J. Yarnold's introductory essay in *The Awe-Inspiring Rites of Initiation*; and Joseph Lecuyer, "Théologie de l'initiation chrétienne chez les Pères," *La Maison-Dieu* 58 (1959) 5–26. For instance, Lecuyer (5) does admit that he is "négligeant délibérément les différences accidentelles dues à la diversité des situations historiques et des cultures"; yet he fails to note the inherent methodological problem in such a synthetic history-of-ideas approach: that it divorces ideas from the fabric of their social context, that it creates an artificial unanimity, that it presumes such differences are mere accident and not perhaps critical to their theology of initiation.

73. The best known extended study is that of Thomas Finn, *The Liturgy of Baptism in the Baptismal Instructions of St. John Chrysostom* (Washington, D.C.: Catholic University of America Press, 1967).

THE INVESTIGATION

This study will focus on a single instance of the ancient catechumenate: Augustine's catechumenate in Hippo. In other words, this
will be a case study. It will explore in detail what Augustine did
with his baptismal candidates, what he said to them, and what his
reflections on the experience were. And the approach will be to
read the texts with an educator's eye: to chart the course and
rhythms of his catechesis; to note what issues he thought important, what language he used, what feelings he roused, what actions he called for; in other words, to discern how he envisioned
conversion and how he nurtured it.

A. Why Study Augustine

Before I set out the questions of scope and method, I would like
to explain why this focus on Augustine. After all, there are other
patristic figures whose works deserve study from a catechetical
perspective: e.g., Cyril of Jerusalem or Ambrose or John Chrysostom. However, focusing on Augustine offers several advantages:

First, Augustine wrote several treatises that give one or another
aspect of his understanding of catechesis and the catechumenate:
*On Catechizing Beginners; On Faith and Works; On Christian Doctrine;
Answers to the Inquiries of Januarius* (i.e., *Letters* 54 and 55). And
these can be compared with his actual practice; even by a conservative count, there are at least twenty-two sermons directed, at
least in part, to catechumens; at least nineteen sermons directed to
the elect; and at least thirty-five sermons directed to neophytes. In
addition, Augustine's numerous theological works can help to
interpret themes alluded to in his catechetical instructions.

Second, Augustine seems to be the only patristic author from
whom there is a sampling of material for each of the four periods
of initiation: (a) evangelization: *On Catechizing Beginners;* (b) catechumenate: e.g., *Sermon* 132, *Enarratio* on Psalm 80, *Tractates on the
Gospel of John* 4, 10, and 11; (c) Lent: e.g., *Sermons* 56–59, 212–216;
(d) mystagogy: e.g., *Sermons* 225, 227, 228, 260, 272. (For a complete
list of these, see charts 7, 12, and 16). The sermons Augustine
directed to ordinary catechumens are especially valuable since information on this often lengthy phase of formation is scarce.

Third, scholars have produced fine critical editions of most of
Augustine's works. Moreover, a complete edition of Augustine's
sermons has recently been published by the Biblioteca de Autores

Cristianos (Madrid). While not a critical edition, it does at least bring together the best texts currently available. It also incorporates the findings of the most recent text-critical study of Augustine's sermons.[74]

Fourth, over the last forty years, scholars have uncovered extraordinarily detailed information about Augustine and his Church in Hippo. Thus one can peer into the life of his Church with a precision that is simply not possible with other ancient sees. For example, Frederic Van der Meer's *Augustine the Bishop* offers a richly detailed portrait of daily life in Hippo; Peter Brown's acclaimed biography sets Augustine's thought and practice within the context of social and intellectual movements of the fourth and fifth centuries; and W. H. C. Frend's *The Donatist Church* offers valuable perspectives on the economic, ethnic, and social structures that lay behind pastoral conflicts within the North African Church.[75]

Despite this, both Augustinian scholars and liturgical historians have, for the most part, neglected his catechumenal treatises and sermons. Admittedly, most surveys of the ancient catechumenate mention *On Catechizing Beginners*, but generally touch on little else.

74. *Sermones*, in *Obras Completas de San Agustín* 7, 10, 23, 24, 25, and 26, ed. Miguel Fuertes Lanero, text with Spanish trans. Pio de Luis and others (Madrid: Biblioteca de Autores Cristianos, 1981–1985). The editors made use of the work of Pierre-Patrick Verbraken, *Études critiques sur les sermons authentiques de saint Augustin*, Instrumenta Patristica 12 (Steenbrugis, 1976). In particular, they followed Verbraken's suggestion for numbering the sermons. Verbraken suggests using the standard Maurist—and Migne—numbering as the base (that is, PL 1–396) and then inserting the remaining 196 sermons found by Morin and others according to their subject matter or occasion. In my own notes, I list first the number given in Verbraken's scheme and then the older numbering found in the Maurist edition and in the edition by G. Morin, *Sermones post Maurinos reperti* (e.g., Guelferbytanus, Lambot, Mai, Frangipane). A complete English translation of Augustine's sermons has—at long last—begun to be published: see Sermons, vol. 1, trans. Edmund Hill, in *The Works of Saint Augustine: A Translation for the 21st Century*, ed. John E. Rotelle (Brooklyn: New City Press, 1990). Because this new translation was not available to me, many of the passages cited from Augustine's *Sermones ad populum* are my own translation.

75. Frederic Van Der Meer, *Augustine the Bishop*, trans. Brian Battershaw and G. R. Lamb (London: Sheed & Ward, 1961); Peter Brown, *Augustine of Hippo: a Biography* (Berkeley: University of California Press, 1967); W. H. C. Frend, *The Donatist Church*, rev. ed. (Oxford: Clarendon Press, 1985).

There have been only a handful of studies on Augustine's catechumenate, and only one of these is available in English. The
most significant of these are: two lengthy articles by Benedict
Busch (1938, in Latin!); a forty-page chapter in Van der Meer (1947;
translation: 1961); a lengthy introduction by Suzanne Poque in the
Sources Chrétiennes edition of Augustine's Easter Sermons (1966);
and a survey article on initiation in Augustine's Church by R.
DeLatte (1975).[76] Busch's and DeLatte's studies focus mainly on
liturgical matters; Poque limits her work to Augustine's Lenten
and Easter sermons, and devotes only a portion of her valuable
analysis to catechesis. Van der Meer's study offers the most
expansive treatment, but his work is more descriptive than analytical.

B. Design

Chapter 2 serves as a backdrop and offers an overview of the
fourth-century catechumenate. In chapter 3, I examine Augustine's
Confessions and Ambrose's sermons to uncover some aspects of
Augustine's experience as a catechumen in Milan. These give
some important clues about Augustine's own habits as a director
of a catechumenate. After all, Augustine, like most of us, drew
guidance from his own experience and, to some extent, taught
others as he had been taught. The remainder of the investigation
parallels the four periods of the RCIA. Chapter 4 examines Augustine's understanding and practice of evangelization, particularly as
he sets it out in *On Catechizing Beginners*. Chapters 5 and 6 will
deal with the catechumenate phase. During the fourth century,
catechumens did not—it seems—receive special instruction. Instead, they simply attended Liturgies of the Word together with
the faithful; in other words, their catechetical instruction came

76. Dom Benedict Busch, "De initiatione christiana secundum sanctum
Augustinum," *Ephemerides Liturgicae* 52 (1938) 159–78; "De modo quo sanctus
Augustinus descripserit initiationem christianam," *Ephemerides Liturgicae* 52
(1938) 385–83; Van der Meer, *Augustine the Bishop*, 347–87 and 453–67; Suzanne
Poque, "Introduction," *Sermons pour la Pâque*, SC 116 (Paris: Les Éditions du
Cerf, 1966); and R. DeLatte "St. Augustin et le baptême. Étude liturgico-
historique du rituel baptismal des adultes chez saint Augustin," *Questions
liturgiques* 56 (1975) 177–223. Philip T. Weller, in his introduction to the *Selected
Easter Sermons of Saint Augustine* (St. Louis: B. Herder Book Co, 1959), touches
on some relevant issues.

from whatever they could glean from ordinary sermons. Thus chapter 5 surveys Augustine's habits as a preacher, while Chapter 6 examines a sequence of sermons which Augustine delivered over a four-month period and in the course of which he repeatedly turned his attention to catechumens present among the larger assembly. Chapter 7 focuses on his Lenten sermons; these include sermons given on the occasion of the Scrutiny, the Presentation of the Creed, and the Presentation of the Lord's Prayer. Chapter 8 examines his mystagogical sermons, especially those given on Easter Sunday morning during which he instructed the neophytes on the Eucharist, and those given eight days later when the neophytes would take off their baptismal robes and once more mix in with the larger assembly. Finally, in chapter 9, I explore some ways that Augustine's catechetical practices and reflections may be of value for contemporary RCIA catechesis.

C. Method

In this investigation I hope to construct a portrait of Augustine's catechumenate: to see what he did, what he said, and what his reflections were. And I try to do this with an educator's eye. Let me specify what I mean by this phrase—for education can mean many things, depending on one's context, individual discipline, and overall philosophy. Moreover, contemporary educational theory and its categories have been, to some degree, shaped by the realities of schools; and as we have seen, the catechumenate involves much more than schooling, instruction, or intellectual development. Thus a certain balance needs to be maintained: to ask the sort of questions that concern educators, yet to try to do so in a way that respects the dynamics of the catechumenate. I have listed below what I believe to be appropriate questions and have loosely grouped these under the four headings cited earlier:

1. *Curriculum*—that is, the "what" of catechesis: What *past* traditions (stories, beliefs, practices, prayers) of the Christian community did Augustine hand on? What *present* experiences of God and of community did he see as constitutive?[77] Specifically: What

77. See Groome, *Christian Religious Education*, 5–29, and Mary Boys, *Biblical Interpretation in Religious Education* (Birmingham: Religious Education Press, 1980) 278–93; Michael Schiro, *Curriculum for Better Schools: The Great Ideological Debate* (Englewood Cliffs, N.J.: Educational Technology Publications, 1978) esp.

topics did Augustine touch upon? What order did he follow? In what depth did he treat them? Through what other formative experiences (liturgies, prayers, ascetical practices) did he guide his candidates? What social habits and attitudes did he expect candidates to manifest in their day-to-day lives? What dynamic did he envision between different aspects of his curriculum: i.e., between instruction, liturgy, and the day-to-day apprenticeship in Christian living? Obviously, Augustine has not left us anything like a textbook or a scope-and-sequence chart. Thus one has to view his work as a curriculum-in-action, or as William Pinar has put it, a *currere*, "living experiences encountering the curriculum."[78]

2. *Models of Teaching*—that is, the "how" of catechesis: In a way similar to curriculum, it is clear that Augustine has not left us anything like a set of lesson plans. Thus his models of teaching will have to be discerned from the records we have of his actual practice. Specifically: How did he instruct? What language did he use? How did he gear his message to the mind and to the heart? How did he try to educate the body (as a teacher of athletes would)?[79] How did he shape the symbolic imagination of his candidates (as a teacher of artists would)? Did he see the rites as educative? How did he interrelate them with his sermons? In what setting(s) did formal instruction take place? Were they set within a liturgical context? Did he use or suggest other formative environments, such as the home or the marketplace?

3. *Conversion*—that is, the "why" of catechesis: Education is—or should be—a teleological activity. And thus its curriculum and

24–29. Boys, for example, suggests that "religious education is the making accessible of the traditions of religious communities and the making manifest of the intrinsic connection between tradition and transformation" (282). My accent concerning curriculum is on "past" and "present." I take up teleology (i.e. "future" and "transformation") in the questions on conversion.

78. William Pinar, "Currere: Toward Reconceptualization," in *Curriculum Theorizing: The Reconceptualists* (Berkeley: McCutchan, 1974) 402.

79. Seeing the body as a focus of education seems to be largely neglected in much contemporary educational discussion. Ancients, however, were quite conscious of it in their own educational reflections. See Henri Iréné Marrou, *A History of Education in Antiquity*, trans. George Lamb (Madison: University of Wisconsin Press, 1982) esp. 116–32. Relevant perspectives are also found in Peter Brown, *The Body and Society: Men, Women, and Sexual Renunciation in Early Christianity* (New York: Columbia University Press, 1988).

teaching styles should converge so as to foster specific goals, aims, and intents or to promote a particular vision of the future.[80] And as we have seen, the overarching goal of the RCIA is conversion. Thus: How did Augustine see his curriculum and teaching styles contributing to his candidates' conversion? Did he envision this conversion (to use Duggan's categories) as radically transformative? as a journey? as having times and seasons? as Christocentric? as covenantal? as ecclesial? as sacramental? as comprehensive? By what standards did he evaluate their conversion? Was the conversion of his candidates his primary aim or were there others? In addition, did he simply try to socialize his candidates into the ecclesial status quo? Or did he alert them to the community's weaknesses and sinfulness? If so, how?

4. *Faith and Culture*—that is, the "where" of catechesis: Educators necessarily deal with specific people living in a specific cultural, economic, social, ethnic, and intellectual milieu. This fact implies the need to use the methods of social history so as to respect the social roots and moorings of Augustine's thought and practice. Thus it will be important to ask: How was his message shaped by his fourth- and fifth-century North African context? What economic, social, and ethnic realities did he address? How did contemporary religious movements and intellectual frameworks shape his formulation? Did he envision any clash between the faith of his community and the larger (pagan or nominally Christian) culture? If so, how did he address it? How did he deal with differences between the faith expression of his local community and that of other churches?

These questions, while not exhaustive, seem to be significant ones for charting how Christians educate. Admittedly, they are preliminary. Some of these may not be fully answerable; others may better define current concerns than those of Augustine. Still, it seems important that one's categories and questions not be left implicit. Historical research is not a matter simply of observing texts and then reconstructing from them a purely objective history.

80. John Dewey gave the question of teleology special emphasis. In part because of his influence, it occupies a central place in modern educational theory. See especially his discussion of the "criteria of experience" in *Experience and Education* (New York: Collier Books, 1938) 33–50. For a discussion of its place in religious education, see Groome, *Christian Religious Education*, 9–10 and 35–55.

As philosophers of history and of interpretation are quick to point out, objectivist and historicist claims are neither accurate nor adequate since they ignore the historical situation of the interpreter.[81] And as these philosophers go on to note, one necessarily comes to historical documents with specific questions, concerns, and assumptions. These open and in some measure guide the dialogue (to use Gadamer's language) of interpreter and text. This dialogue is always a risky endeavor, for one's questions can be so foreign, so alien, that they miss the horizon of the texts and so distort the subsequent dialogue. The dialogical task, if it is to be authentic, means not simply asking and probing, but listening and adjusting. It means being willing to shift perspectives, to let the world view of the text touch one's own, and thus call into question unrecognized assumptions and attitudes. Thus these four sets of questions provide not a fixed hermeneutic, but rather background perspectives or initial angles of vision.

In addition, I should note several limits. First, I will concentrate more on Augustine's sermons than on his treatises. Admittedly his sermons touch on many of his favorite themes: for instance, the two cities, the inner teacher, the disputes with the Donatists on rebaptism. And within his treatises he gives a highly nuanced treatment of these themes. However, few of his candidates likely ever read his theological treatises. Thus the concern will be with what his candidates actually heard. In other words, I will focus less on Augustine the theologian and more on Augustine the practicing catechist.

There will be, however, a few important exceptions to this principle. In particular, I will focus on two important treatises: *On Catechizing Beginners* (when examining evangelization) and *On Faith and Works* (in which he makes some important comments about the Lenten period). Also, since Augustine's catechumenal instructions were for the most part sermons, I will examine his *On Chris-*

81. For a survey of hermeneutical theory, see Richard Palmer, *Hermeneutics: Interpretation Theory in Schleiermacher, Dilthey, Heidegger, and Gadamer* (Evanston, Ill.: Northwestern University Press, 1969); an excellent and more popular treatment is given by David Tracy in *A Short History of the Interpretation of the Bible*, 2d ed. (Philadelphia: Fortress, 1984) 153–66. In this discussion I have used Gadamer's terminology. It is not without its weaknesses. See Paul Ricoeur, *Interpretation Theory: Discourse and the Surplus of Meaning* (Fort Worth: Texas Christian University Press, 1976).

tian Doctrine (especially book 4 on the task of the preacher) as a backdrop for chapters 5–8.

Second, this is, as I have stated, only a case study. Thus, while I will cite parallel accounts from other ancient authors, the primary concern is with Augustine and his North African congregation. Moreover, one cannot presume that the traditions of North Africa were identical with those found elsewhere. In other words, I begin from the presupposition of local pluralism.

Third, the evidence, while abundant, is still fragmentary. Thus there will always be a certain tentativeness to generalizations and reconstructions. Moreover, much of it is scattered in a variety of literary (and oral) genres: sermons, polemical works, letters, etc. Thus I will try to take account of the way both Augustine's immediate concern and the genre he used may have colored the description. Finally, the works that have come down to us do not, as a rule, represent what Augustine actually did in a given year. There are a few exceptions to this: e.g., his four-month catechumenal sequence; several of his special Easter Week series. However, in most cases, we possess only fragments from different periods of his life. Some of these can be dated precisely; many cannot be. However, the material is sufficiently rich to recreate a set of tableaux from Augustine's catechumenate. For the purposes of this investigation, that should suffice.

Chart 1
The Rites and Structure of the RCIA

PERIOD/RITE	LENGTH/DATE	GOAL	CATECHESIS/SYMBOLS
First Period: Evangelization	Not specified	*Initial conversion	*Hearing the Gospel
Name for Candidates: Inquirers			
First Step: Acceptance into Order of Catechumens	Not specified	*Welcome *Mutual commitment	*Signed with cross *Liturgy of Word *Receive bible [*Renunciation of false worship *New name]
Second Period: Catechumenate	1-3 years	*Strengthen faith *Sense mystery of salvation *Change of outlook and conduct	*Setting: Liturgies of Word *NT morality *Prayer experience *Dogmas, precepts *Apprenticeship in Christian life by sponsors, etc.
Name for Candidates: Catechumens			
Other rites during catechumenate:			
a. Blessings	Anytime during this time	*Sign of God's love/Church's care	
b. Exorcisms		*Need for God's help in struggle	
c. Anointings		*Strengthening faith, hold to it	
Second Step: Election, enrollment of names	First Sunday of Lent	*Approval of candidates for baptism	*Inquiry by bishop on worthiness of candidates *Affirmation by godparents *Enroll names
Third Period: Purification/ Illumination	Lent	*Intense spiritual preparation *Purify mind and heart	*Do penance *Guide interior reflection more than instruct
Name for Candidates: the Elect			
Rites during third period:			
a. Scrutinies	Third, Fourth, and Fifth Sundays of Lent	*Inspire self-search *Uncover, heal the defective and sinful *Strengthen the good	*Christ, the living water *Christ, the light of the world *Christ, the resurrection and the life
b. Present Creed	Third Week of Lent	*Recall salvation history	*Hand over, instruct on heart of Church's faith
c. Present Lord's Prayer	Fifth Week of Lent	*Fill with spirit of adoption	*Hand over, instruct on heart of Church's prayer

Chart 1 *(cont.)*
The Rites and Structure of the RCIA

PERIOD/RITE	LENGTH/DATE	GOAL	CATECHESIS/SYMBOLS
d. Recite Creed	Holy Saturday	*Elect recite Creed	*Instruct on duty to proclaim gospel
e. *Ephphetha*	Holy Saturday	*Need to hear, speak Word of God	*Touch ears and lips
Third Step: Sacraments of initiation *Baptism *Confirmation *Eucharist	Easter Vigil	*Rebirth, Inaugurating life of baptized	*Vigil readings *Renunciation of sin/devil *Profession of faith *Baptism-immersion *Clothe with robe *Lighted candle *Anoint—chrism *First Eucharist
Fourth Period: Mystagogy	Easter to Pentecost	*Deepen grasp of paschal mystery *Experience welcome of faithful	*Celebrate Eucharist *Mystagogical catechesis *Do works of charity

Name for Candidates: Neophytes

The Fourth-Century Catechumenate

In Augustine's day one of the most popular art forms was the mosaic. Late Romans used mosaics to adorn their villas, the floors of their basilicas, and, of course, their baptisteries.[1] In this chapter, I would like to create a mosaic of a different sort: a "mosaic" of the fourth-century catechumenate. First I will draw on fragments from the third-century catechumenate to illustrate inherited patterns; then I will sort through some pieces from the fourth-century to map out general trends. Some will illustrate continuities; others, discontinuities; still others, subtle shifts in tone and theme. With this mosaic as backdrop, we will then be in a better position to set Augustine's catechetical artistry in its proper frame.

INHERITED PATTERNS FROM THE THIRD CENTURY

In the 180s, the pagan philosopher Celsus, a shrewd and caustic critic of the Christian movement, quipped: "If all people wanted to be Christians, the Christians would no longer want them."[2] Celsus's remark, for all its irony, may have had more than a grain of truth in it. One detects a rigorist, sectarian strain running through much third-century catechumenal literature.[3] To get a sense

1. Erwan Marec, *Monuments chrétiens d'Hippone: Ville épiscopale de saint Augustin* (Paris: Arts et Métiers Graphiques, 1958) 31–95; and Katherine M. D. Dunbabin, "A Mosaic Workshop in Carthage around 400 A.D.," in *New Light on Ancient Carthage,* ed. John Griffiths Pedley (Ann Arbor: University of Michigan Press, 1980) 73–84.

2. Celsus, quoted by Origen, *Contra Celsum* 3.9 (trans. Henry Chadwick [Cambridge: Cambridge University Press, 1980], 133). For a reconstruction of the original treatise, see Celsus, *On the True Doctrine,* ed. and trans. R. Joseph Hoffman (New York: Oxford University Press, 1987).

3. Joseph Trigg, *Origen: The Bible and Philosophy in the Third-Century Church* (Atlanta: John Knox Press, 1983) 30. For a detailed social analysis of third-century Christianity, see Robin Lane Fox, *Pagans and Christians* (New York: Alfred A. Knopf, 1987).

of this, let us look at two authors from the period: Hippolytus and Tertullian. The two illustrate, each from a different angle, the shape and tenor of the third-century catechumenate: Hippolytus gives an overview of stages and rites, while Tertullian reveals the way rigorist attitudes permeated the catechumenate in Augustine's native milieu, North Africa.

Perhaps the clearest blueprint we have of a third-century catechumenate—at least, of its rites and stages—is that found in *The Apostolic Tradition*. This document, first discovered in Coptic in the middle of the last century, is now generally recognized as the work of Hippolytus of Rome (d. 235).[4] The document itself is a Church order, that is, a hodge-podge of rules and rubrics for Christian life, Church discipline, and liturgy; and like so many of these, it claims apostolic authority. The descriptions and prescriptions it gives may, at first sight, seem neutral enough, but as the prologue makes clear, it also has a strong polemical thrust: "We have set down these things . . . in order that those who have been well taught by our exposition may guard that tradition . . . and remain firm [against] that backsliding or error which was recently invented through ignorance. . . ."[5] Such sentiments square with what we know of Hippolytus: he was a presbyter of the Church of Rome and an outspoken defender of certain traditionalist standards on the purity of the Church. At some point, it seems, he broke communion with the bishop Callistus over innovations in doctrine and discipline and may have been elected as a rival bishop for a dissident party within the community at Rome.[6]

4. Throughout this section, I have followed the most recent reconstruction and translation of the *Apostolic Tradition*: Geoffrey J. Cuming, *Hippolytus: A Text for Students* (Bramcote: Grove Books Limited, 1987); see also *La tradition apostolique*, ed. Bernard Botte, SC 11 bis (Paris: Édition du Cerf, 1968). Cuming (3–7) and Botte (11–24) trace the complex process of the document's discovery and its attribution to Hippolytus.

5. Hippolytus, *Apostolic Tradition* 1 (Cuming, 8).

6. On Hippolytus and the Church in Rome, see Robert M. Grant, *Augustus to Constantine: the Rise and Triumph of Christianity in the Roman World* (San Francisco: Harper & Row, 1970); and W. H. C. Frend, *The Rise of Christianity* (Philadelphia: Fortress Press, 1984), especially 344–46. Hippolytus did not have a rigid sense of apostolic tradition in one sense: he allowed for considerable freedom in improvising certain liturgical prayers. For a fine study of Hippolytus's notion of tradition, see A. F. Walls, "A Note on the Apostolic Claim in the Church Order Literature," *Studia Patristica* 2, ed. Kurt Aland and F. L. Cross (Berlin: Akademie-Verlag, 1957) 83–92.

In chapters 15–21 of *The Apostolic Tradition*, Hippolytus set out guidelines for the catechumenate and baptism. First, he insisted that when newcomers were brought to church, teachers were to conduct an interview, questioning not only the newcomers, but also "those who brought them." The latter—we would call them sponsors—were to "bear witness about them, whether they are capable of hearing the word."[7] This probe, at least as Hippolytus details it, focused less on motive and more on lifestyle: Did these new inquirers have a mistress? Were they slaves trying to please a master? Were they charioteers, gladiators, sculptors of idols, actors, brothel-keepers, theatre producers, city magistrates—in other words, anyone connected with the pervasive apparatus of paganism, its idolatry, its violence, its impurity?[8] If so, then—in what seems to be a ringing refrain—"let them cease or be rejected."[9] Some people (prostitutes, eunuchs, magicians, astrologers) were rejected outright; others (teachers and soldiers) were accepted under certain strict conditions.[10] The tone set by Hippolytus was stern, uncompromising. In his view the new convert had to be willing to make a sharp and probably costly break from the larger culture, and this turnabout was to take place not after some months, but from the very outset. Clearly, Hippolytus worried less about the size of his congregation and more about the standards it lived by.[11]

Once accepted, catechumens were "to hear the word for three years."[12] What this involved is not clear. Perhaps it meant catechumens attended the first part of the Eucharistic liturgy; it may also refer to their joining the faithful at the daily early-morning service of readings, instruction, and prayer.[13] In any case, there

7. Hippolytus, *Apostolic Tradition* 15 (Cuming, 15).

8. Ibid., 15–16 (Cuming 15–16). He does not give any explicit rationale for this list, but Tertullian does: see the discussion of his *De idololatria* below.

9. Ibid.

10. Ibid., 16.

11. Jungmann, *The Early Liturgy*, 76, makes this point, but somewhat questionably describes it as the attitude of "the Church." His language is problematic on two counts: (1) in this period, it is better to speak of "churches" rather than "the Church"; and (2) Hippolytus may not be reflecting normative practice, but rather the views of a more extremist wing.

12. Hippolytus, *Apostolic Tradition* 17 (Cuming, 16).

13. Ibid., 39 (Cuming, 28): "The deacons and priests shall assemble *daily* at the place which the bishop appoints for them. . . . When all have assembled,

seems no reason to postulate, as Kavanagh does, that catechumens received instruction at special catechetical sessions modeled on the Liturgy of the Word.[14] Hippolytus was, however, specific on one matter: after "the teacher has finished giving instruction," catechumens are to "pray by themselves, separated from the faithful"; moreover, "they shall not give the Peace, for their kiss is not yet holy."[15] Then the teacher, whether "a cleric or layman," would lay hands on them in blessing and dismiss them—implying

---

let them teach those who are in the church, and in this way, when they have prayed, let each one go to the work which falls to him." (Note: "presbyters" rather "priests" would be the more accurate term in this period.)

14. Kavanagh, *The Shape of Baptism*, 56, claims that Hippolytus in *AT* 18–19 is alluding to special catechetical sessions: "This is rare information on the form taken by catechetical sessions in the early church. It suggests that instruction did not take place in a classroom setting. . . . Rather, it seems to have taken place at least within a prayer context. . . . [The *Apostolic Tradition*] strongly implies that so similar is the form in which catechumens are instructed each Sunday before the eucharist that catechumens, being familiar with it, must be cautioned by their teachers that their prayer is not that of the Faithful and must therefore not conclude with the kiss of peace." There seems no reason, however, to postulate such special catechetical sessions modeled on the service of the Word. Note that Kavanagh focuses his remarks only on *AT* 18–19 and ignores the daily gatherings mentioned in *AT* 39. Pierre Nautin sees in *AT* 39 a confirmation of something he finds in Origen: daily non-Eucharistic Liturgies of the Word. In Origen's church in Caesarea, catechumens joined the faithful at the daily service of the Word. Thus their primary—and perhaps, their only—catechesis came from whatever they would glean from sermons given at these gatherings. Nautin remarks that "liturgical historians have paid hardly any attention to these daily assemblies in which Origen gave his homilies." According to Nautin, these liturgies had (1) an opening prayer, (2) a lengthy reading from the Old Testament, (3) a lengthy sermon, and (4) formal blessings, prayers, and dismissal. Apparently, the church in Caesarea did not follow a fixed lectionary, but simply used the Jewish *lectio continua* method for reading through the Scriptures. Nautin estimates that, given the length of the readings and sermons, the whole service probably lasted an hour. In addition, on Sundays and Christian fast days (Wednesdays and Fridays), a Eucharistic liturgy was added to an abbreviated service of the Word. On these days, there were brief readings from the Old Testament, the Epistles, and the Gospels; and there may well have been a short sermon *after each*. Nautin believes that this procedure would have made it possible for catechumens, over the course of three years, to hear the whole Bible read and commented on. If true, this would explain why Hippolytus had legislated a three-year catechumenate. See Pierre Nautin, "Introduction," in Origen, *Homélies sur Jérémie*, SC 232:102–5.

15. Hippolytus, *Apostolic Tradition* 18 (Cuming, 16–17).

that catechumens were barred from attending the Eucharist.[16] The mention of laymen here is intriguing. It implies that lay teachers played an official role in the liturgical life of the Roman Church.[17]

Hippolytus legislated a second examination once catechumens had completed their three-year probation and were deemed ready for baptism. Again it was "those who brought them" who offered testimony, and again the interrogation focused on lifestyle: "Have they honored the widows? Have they visited the sick? Have they done every good work?"[18] In other words, the concern was not theological expertise or orthodoxy, but lived faith and the practice of charity and justice. If accepted, candidates were allowed "to hear the gospel."[19] Scholars have speculated about what Hippolytus meant by this, but it remains one of the text's tantalizing obscurities.[20] From this time until their baptism (Hippolytus never

16. Hippolytus does not make any explicit mention of this, though he does forbid catechumens sitting "at the Lord's Supper" (*Apostolic Tradition* 27)—presumably referring to an *agape* (a common community meal). Both the *Didache* 9.5, and Justin, *Apologia prima* 65–66, explicitly forbid allowing any of the uninitiated to attend the Eucharist.

17. See G. Bardy, "Les écoles Romaines au second siècle," *Revue d'histoire ecclésiastique* 28 (1932) 501–32. Bardy traces the role of lay teachers in the second century. Their "schools" seem to have been small, free-lance operations where they, like their pagan counterparts, offered private instruction. These teachers apparently enjoyed no official mandate from the Church. Some were quite orthodox, like Justin Martyr, but others, such as Theodotus and Tatian, seem to have promoted heretical positions. Apparently the problems such teachers posed became severe enough that under Victor (189–98) condemnations were issued. Around the turn of the second century, greater centralization and control over catechesis seems to have occurred. In view of this, Hippolytus here may be witnessing to the possibility that lay teachers (officially recognized ones?) were still permitted to preach at some official community gatherings (or at least within his circle). In other words, this seems to testify to the preservation of a somewhat archaic ordering of ministries—one that was being eliminated elsewhere.

18. Hippolytus, *Apostolic Tradition* 20 (Cuming, 17).

19. Ibid.

20. Jungmann, *The Early Liturgy*, 78, thinks this means a "more systematic instruction" whose "main content was no longer the moral law, but dogmatic theology, the glad tidings of salvation, presented in a coherent form." In other words, he reads this in light of fourth-century practice. Nautin takes Hippolytus more literally and suggests that this meant candidates were finally allowed to stay for the reading of and exposition on the Gospels given at Eucharistic liturgies and that ordinary catechumens were dismissed prior to the reading of the Gospels. See Nautin, *Origène: Sa vie et son oeuvre*, Christianisme

specifies how long), candidates were "set apart" and exorcised daily. On Thursday (presumably before Easter, but Hippolytus never says), they bathed (presumably because they had not bathed during this time). On Friday they fasted and on Saturday were exorcised. Candidates then spent the whole night in vigil and were "read to and instructed."[21]

Baptism took place early the next morning (presumably on Easter). Several features of this liturgy differ markedly from our own. First, candidates were baptized in the nude; thus the washing took place not in full view of the assembly, but in relative privacy.[22] Second, the three interrogations—their belief in Father, Son, and Spirit—were interspersed between three immersions, leaving the impression that these interrogations substituted for the baptismal formula we use.[23] Third, there were three anointings: one with "the oil of exorcism" before immersion; the second with "the oil of thanksgiving" after immersion; and a third by the bishop once the baptismal party had rejoined the larger assembly.[24] Fourth, the newly baptized enjoyed what had not been permitted them as catechumens: the prayer of the faithful, the kiss of peace,

---

Antique 1 (Paris: Beauchesne, 1977) 394–96. Both explanations of these are plausible, but venturesome.

21. Hippolytus, *Apostolic Tradition* 20.

22. Ibid., 21 (Cuming, 18).

23. Ibid. (Cuming, 19). In the Ethiopic and Sahidic versions, a declaratory form of the Creed is given. But Cuming and other experts on the text regard this as a later interpolation. On the use of the interrogations as a baptismal formula, see P. De Puniet, "Baptême," DACL 2:342; E. C. Whitaker, "The History of the Baptismal Formula," *Journal of Ecclesiastical History* 16 (1965) 1–12; J. N. D. Kelly, *Early Christian Creeds*, 3d ed. (London: Longmans, Green, and Co. Ltd, 1971) 40–49.

24. Hippolytus, *Apostolic Tradition* 22 (Cuming, 20). This whole sequence has received considerable attention because of its resemblance to what will later become the sacrament of confirmation. Particularly striking is the fact that there is a double postbaptismal anointing. Cuming (20) notes that "a second postbaptismal anointing is unparalleled until the Gelasian Sacramentary." See also Kavanagh, *Confirmation*, 41–52. His argument is too complex to cite in detail here. Basically, he suggests that in the *Apostolic Tradition*, the ritual complex of blessing, hand-laying, signing, and kiss functions as a "baptismal *missa*" (or dismissal); that is, it structurally serves to draw the baptismal rite publicly to a close (it also "seals" the waiting community's prayer vigil). He goes on to note that the prayer of the bishop over the candidates is not an epiclesis of the Holy Spirit as it will become in the Gelasian sacramentary, but a Trinitarian prayer paralleling that of the baptismal rite.

and of course, the Eucharist. Finally, they received not only the "bread of heaven in Christ Jesus" but also three cups: one with water to wash "the inner man"; one with a mixture of milk and honey; and one with wine.[25] Then, according to Hippolytus, the newly baptized were to "hasten to do good works and to please God."[26] He also suggested that the neophytes would need further catechesis, but that the "bishop should say [these things] privately to those who have received baptism"; "unbelievers must not get to know it."[27] This secrecy—what scholars refer to as the *disciplina arcani*—would become a standard feature of later postbaptismal catechesis. As for the sort of catechesis Hippolytus had in mind here, we can do no more than speculate.

The rigorist strain one finds in Hippolytus is even more prominent in his North African contemporary, Tertullian (d. after 220). It is not clear precisely what role Tertullian played in the Church of Carthage, whether he served as a presbyter, as Jerome claims, or whether he was a layman.[28] Whatever the case, his writings display an abiding and passionate concern for the formation of catechumens, those "recruits who have just recently begun to give ear to the flow of divine discourse and who, like puppies newly born, creep about uncertainly, with eyes as yet unopened."[29] Tertullian's works also set in high relief what Timothy Barnes has called "the dominant motif of African Christianity: uncompromising rejection of an alien world."[30] For example, Tertullian addressed one of his early works, *The Spectacles*, explicitly to catechumens and neophytes and warned that they inhabit a demon-possessed world: "There is no place—whether streets or

25. Hippolytus, *Apostolic Tradition* 21 (Cuming, 21).

26. Ibid. (Cuming, 22).

27. Ibid. For a survey of the tradition of the *disciplina arcani*, see Edward Yarnold, *The Awe-Inspiring Rites of Initiation: Baptismal Homilies of the Fourth Century* (Middlegreen: St. Paul Publications, 1972) 50–54.

28. Jerome claims in *De viris illustribus* that "Tertullian was a priest of the church until middle age, but then, because of the envy and insults of the clergy of the church of Rome, he lapsed into Montanism. . . ." Many commentators have taken this and other remarks by Jerome at face value. Timothy Barnes, *Tertullian: A Historical and Literary Study* (New York: Oxford University Press, 1971) 3–59, has raised significant doubts on Jerome's accuracy on this point and argues that Tertullian was a layman.

29. Tertullian, *De paenitentia* 6.1 (trans. William LeSaint, ACW 28:24).

30. Barnes, *Tertullian*, 62.

marketplace or baths or taverns or even our own homes—that is completely free of idols: Satan and his angels have filled the whole world."[31] In this work Tertullian tried to convince his hearers to avoid four popular locales and the entertainment they offered: horse races in the circus; gladiatorial combats and wild-animal hunts in the amphitheater; athletic competitions in the stadium; and bawdy plays in the theatre. The linchpin of his argument was that these amusements were at base "pomps of the devil" and thus were contrary to the baptismal vows:

"I shall now appeal to the prime and principal authority of our seal itself. When we step into the water and profess the Christian faith in the terms prescribed by its law, we bear public witness that we have renounced the Devil and his pomp and his angels. . . . So, if it shall be proved true that the entire apparatus of the spectacles originates from idolatry, we will have reached a decision in advance that our profession of faith in baptism refers also to the spectacles, since they belong to the Devil and his pomp and his angels because of the idolatry involved."[32]

This same argument appears again and again in Tertullian. In fact, one could rightly regard his disciplinary works as an extended commentary on the baptismal renunciation and its implications for Christian living. In *The Crowns* he used this argument to condemn Christian soldiers who joined their pagan confreres in wearing victory crowns and swearing oaths of allegiance.[33] In *The Apparel of Women* he appealed to it to denounce women who used rouge or hair-dyes or wore gold jewelry or fashionable seashells.[34] But his most far-reaching use of it appears in his work *On Idolatry*.[35] In this treatise, he explained why certain professions were

31. Tertullian, *De spectaculis* 8.9 (trans. Rudolph Arbesmann, FC 40:69). The mention of catechumens and neophytes is in 1.1.
32. Ibid., 4.1 (Arbesmann, 56). For a treatment of this theme, see J. Waszink, "Pompa diaboli," *Vigiliae christianae* 1 (1947) 13–41.
33. Tertullian, *De corona* 13.7.
34. Tertullian, *De cultu feminarum* 1.2.4; also 2.5.1–3.
35. Barnes, *Tertullian*, 100, notes that "Tertullian is writing for recent converts," though the text has no explicit reference to either catechumens or neophytes. Earlier commentators presumed that this treatise dated from Tertullian's later Montanist phase. Contemporary critics now date it between 198 and 208. See the discussion by J. H. Waszink and J. C. M. Van Winden, "Introduction," in Tertullian, *De idololatria: Critical Text, Translation, and Commentary* (Leiden: E. J. Brill, 1987) 10–13.

forbidden—repeating, even extending the list found in Hippolytus. He argued that because of baptismal vows, craftsmen could not sculpt or paint pagan figures; weavers, bronze workers, silversmiths, stone masons, building contractors, and engravers could not work on temples, altars, or shrines—thus barring them from the most lucrative construction projects of the day. Similarly, Christians could not be teachers: the school curriculum required teaching books that glorified pagan gods, and the school calendar revolved around pagan feasts. Nor could Christians feasibly serve as magistrates since they would be required, either in person or by delegation, to help with sacrifices, raise taxes for maintenance of pagan temples, sponsor gladiatorial games, and order the torture and execution of criminals.[36] Christian businessmen were to scrupulously avoid oaths—a near impossibility since business contracts in those days contained an oath to the gods.[37] This advice, if followed, meant Christians had to make a radical break from their everyday world. Not surprisingly, many complained: "I have nothing else to live by."[38] Tertullian was unsympathetic. As he saw it, the baptismal renunciation formed the bedrock of Christian morals—or at least, his interpretation of them—and its exigencies had to be followed no matter what the cost.

Two of Tertullian's catechumenal works, On Penitence and On Baptism, are in the form of sermons and may have actually been delivered as such—perhaps at a community meal or some other community gathering.[39] In the first he complained about two pastoral problems that, in Augustine's time, would become commonplace: (1) catechumens who delayed baptism because they feared

36. Tertullian, De idololatria 3–17.

37. Ibid., 23. Waszink and van Winden (285) note that "in business contracts of the day, there were oaths to pagan gods. While a Christian only had to sign the document, they—in Tertullian's view—made the words of the document their own."

38. Tertullian quotes the complaint in De idololatria 5 (Waszink, 29).

39. Barnes, Tertullian, 117, notes that Tertullian, in Apologeticum 39, mentions that at their common meal Christians were afterwards invited to read from Scripture or to speak. Barnes concludes that "the hypothesis of actual delivery can be plausibly entertained" for these and several other works (e.g., De oratione, De patientia). Given Hippolytus's mention of lay teachers, it might plausibly be argued that Tertullian actually gave these in a liturgical setting (though the versions we have may have been reworked by Tertullian somewhat later).

the rigorous penitential discipline; (2) catechumens who felt justified in maintaining a lower moral standard, that they might "steal the intervening time and make of it an interlude for sinning rather than for learning not to sin."[40] He castigated both and encouraged catechumens to strive for rigor of life: "We are not baptized so that we may cease committing sin but because we have ceased, we are already clean of heart. This, surely, is the first baptism of the catechumen."[41] Clearly Tertullian, for all his awe of baptism, did not regard its power as magical. Rather, the water bath ratified what the discipline of the catechumenate had wrought.

The second, *On Baptism*, is a rare example of third-century baptismal catechesis. Given both its tone and themes, it has the earmark of a final address to those awaiting baptism.[42] Tertullian opened his last-minute instructions with an intriguing claim—that baptism made Christians "fish": "We, being little fishes, as Jesus Christ is our great Fish, begin our life in the water, and only when we abide in the water are we safe and sound."[43] Tertullian then took up a problem that Augustine's teacher, Ambrose, would also address: that candidates were disappointed by the simplicity of the Christian mysteries. At that time, pagan shrines sometimes used elaborate apparatus to create the impression of miraculous events: reflecting pools which caused strange light-effects; fireworks to suggest a god's departure; mirrors that allowed initiates to see the god through a glass darkly; underground channels and piping which made it possible to convert a stream of water into one of wine; doors equipped with spring mechanisms so that they appeared to open miraculously; statues that seemed to speak in an eerie, distant voice.[44] Given such "miracles," it is little wonder that Christian neophytes would be downcast. Tertullian tried to head off any such disappointment:

40. Tertullian, *De paenitentia* 6.9 (LeSaint, 24).

41. Ibid., 6.17 (LeSaint, 26).

42. Johannes Quasten, *Patrology* (Westminster, Md.: Newman Press, 1953) 2:278, notes that in this work Tertullian "speaks like a teacher to his catechumens." In *De baptismo* 20, Tertullian closes with an appeal for prayer. Such an appeal appears also in Chrysostom's final instructions to candidates before their baptism; see *Baptismal Instruction* 11.30–31.

43. Tertullian, *De baptismo* 1 (trans. Ernest Evans, *Tertullian's Homily on Baptism* [London: SPCK, 1964] 5).

44. For a description of such apparatus, see Fox, *Pagans and Christians*, 135–36.

"There is nothing which so hardens people's minds as the simplicity of God's works as they are observed in action, compared with the magnificence promised in their effects. So in this case too, because with such complete simplicity, without display, without any unusual equipment, and (not least) without anything to pay, a person is sent down into the water, is washed to the accompaniment of very few words, and comes up little or no cleaner than he was, his attainment to eternity is regarded as beyond belief."[45]

Tertullian then gave a panegyric on the high dignity of water.[46] First he traced its role in classic biblical texts: the waters at creation which became "the resting place of the Spirit"; the waters of the flood and the dove of Noah which heralded "to the earth peace from the wrath of heaven"; the Red Sea signifying "that the gentiles are set free from the present world by means of water, and leave behind, drowned in the water, their ancient tyrant, the devil"; Moses sweetening a desert spring by throwing in a piece of wood ("that tree was Christ"); the consecration of Aaron as priest by washing and anointing; the healing waters of Bethsaida which "used to administer temporal health, but now restore the health which is eternal."[47] He then, in lapidary fashion, asserted, "where Christ is, there is water," and gave a terse compendium of gospel episodes that mentioned water:

"[Christ] himself is baptized in water; when called to a marriage he inaugurates with water the first rudiments of his power; when engaged in conversation he invites those who are athirst to come to his everlasting water; when teaching of charity he approves of a cup of water offered to a little one as one of the works of affection; at a well-side he recruits his strength; he walks upon the water, by his own choice he crosses over the water, with water he makes himself a servant to his disciples. He continues his witness to baptism right on to his passion: . . . when he receives a wound, water bursts forth from his side, as the soldier's spear can tell."[48]

45. Tertullian, *De baptismo* 2 (Evans, 5).
46. Ibid., 3 (Evans, 9).
47. Ibid., 3–9 (Evans, 6–21).
48. Ibid., 9 (Evans, 21).

Tertullian clearly presumed that catechumens possessed a high level of biblical literacy. Otherwise, how would he have dared use such rapid-fire and often oblique allusions?

Towards the end of the sermon, he argued that "baptism ought not to be rashly granted."[49] He thus encouraged the unprepared to defer and counseled against the baptism of children. Finally he exhorted the catechumens to "invoke God by fervent prayers, fastings, kneelings, and all-night vigils, along with the confession of all their former sins."[50] In closing, he asked for their prayers, implying that they would possess unusual intercessory powers when they emerged from the font:

"Therefore, you blessed ones, for whom the grace of God is waiting, when you come up from that most sacred washing of the new birth, and when for the first time you spread out your hands with your brethren in your mother's house, ask of your Father, ask of the Lord, that special grants of grace and apportionments of spiritual gifts be yours. Ask, he says, and you shall receive. So now, you have sought, and have found: you have knocked, and it has been opened to you. This only I pray, that as you ask, you also have in mind Tertullian, a sinner."[51]

The third-century catechumenate should neither be romanticized nor underestimated.[52] On the one hand, its selectivity and rigor would produce a spate of martyrs. The heroics of North African

49. Ibid., 18 (Evans, 37).
50. Ibid., 20 (Evans, 41).
51. Ibid. (Evans, 43).
52. Some modern commentators on the catechumenate have romanticized this era. Dujarier, *History of the Catechumenate*, 30, claims this period represents the catechumenate "in its most authentic form" (see also 107–11). Jungmann, *The Early Liturgy*, 74–75, also idealizes things: he makes the unsubstantiated claim that *The Apostolic Tradition* "is proof of the extraordinarily fine standing and reputation of the Christian communities of those days" and that its "strictness and high standards only served to increase all the more the magnetic power of the Church." Such claims are problematic on several counts: (1) they ignore the rigorist temperaments of these authors and the polemical intent of their works; (2) they ignore the link between initiatory polity and ecclesiology (and few—I believe—would find the sectarian attitudes of the third-century Church an ideal); (3) they do not examine the extent to which these documents actually reflect normative pastoral practice (i.e., how much of the rigorism of *The Apostolic Tradition* reflects routine third-century practice, and how much the more sectarian standards held by Hippolytus and the party he

martyrs such as Perpetua (d. 203), a catechumen who enjoyed extraordinary dream-visions before her death in the arena, and Cyprian (d. 258), the shrewd and dynamic bishop of Carthage, would be celebrated by Augustine's congregation.[53] On the other hand, the third-century catechumenate, for all its sectarian rigor, did not guarantee high standards or stalwart congregations. During the persecution of Decius (250–251), thousands of Christians lapsed, fomenting a massive pastoral crisis not only in North Africa, but across the empire.[54] On a more mundane level, there were always those less-than-zealous Christians who, according to Origen, came to church erratically, disturbed liturgies with noisy chit-chat, and spent their best energies not on faith but on money-making.[55]

SHIFTS IN THE FOURTH CENTURY

The official toleration of Christianity under Constantine profoundly altered the catechumenate. This should not be surprising. As Kavanagh has noted, the catechumenate, by its very nature,

---

apparently spoke for); and (4) they tend to gloss over pastoral problems explicitly mentioned in third-century texts (hesitancy of candidates, apostasy, indifference within congregations).

53. See W. H. C. Frend, *Martyrdom and Persecution in the Early Church* (Garden City, N.Y.: Doubleday, 1967), especially 1–21 and 254–323; also Augustine's sermons on Perpetua (*Sermones* 280–82) and on Cyprian (*Sermones* 309–13 and 313A–313F).

54. Cyprian, *De lapsis* 8, complained that so many Christians rushed out to sacrifice that imperial officials found themselves overwhelmed by the crowds and had to beg people to come the next day. For a fine treatment of the Decian persecution and the crisis it caused, see Frend, *Rise of Christianity*, 318–24.

55. Origen, *In Genesim* 10.1–2 (trans. Ronald E. Heine, FC 71:157–60): "You spend most of this time, no, rather almost all of it in mundane occupations. . . . Even when you are present and placed in the Church, you are not attentive, but waste your time on common everyday stories. . . . What, then, shall I do, to whom the ministry of the word has been entrusted? The words which have been read are mystical. They must be explained in allegorical secrets. Can I throw 'the pearls' of the word of God to your deaf and averted ears?" Also in *In Exodum* 13.3 (trans. Heine, FC 71:378), Origen complains about those "who are preoccupied and can scarcely stand in the presence of the word of God a fraction of an hour," and have "their mind and heart on business dealings" and "profit" and "chatter so much, who disturb with their stories so much that they do not allow any silence." See Joseph Trigg, "Origen's Understanding of Baptism," *Studia Patristica* 17.2, ed. E. A. Livingston (Oxford: Pergamon Press, 1982) 959–65.

"lies on the turbulent leading edge of the Church's ministry to the world."[56] Thus shifts either within the larger culture or within the Church itself touch the catechumenate and often alter, if not its structure, at least its quality and tenor. The fourth century saw several such shifts, and these in turn left their impress on the catechumenate.

First, Christians ceased to be a minority vulnerable to intermittent and sometimes fierce persecutions; rather, they began to enjoy, because of imperial favors, a new privileged status. What Constantine did for Christianity was not without venerable precedent. Emperors before him had lavished benefactions on their favorite cults, and such patronage was considered good piety; that is, if a god rewards one with health, good fortune, or military success, then it is only fitting to express one's gratitude, conversion, and obeisance by acting as a patron for the god's cult.[57] Constantine shared this traditional view. He attributed his victories to the God of the Christians and in recompense offered the churches his patronage. He built spacious basilicas and richly adorned shrines in Rome, Jerusalem, Antioch, and Constantinople; he bequeathed large endowments of land; he offered grain allowances and shelter to widows and orphans; he even provided dowries for poor women seeking second husbands. Most importantly, he accorded bishops a host of special privileges: they were granted immunity from burdensome and often financially disastrous civic obligations; they received judicial powers comparable to high magistrates, allowing them to hear court cases and to preside over the manumission of slaves; they were allowed to use the imperial post for transportation (something previously reserved only for imperial messengers and high state officials).[58] With these new powers came new expectations. Bishops found themselves, almost overnight, called upon to serve as patrons for their subjects and thus to enmesh themselves in the intricate and often corrupt system of patronage that held together late Roman society. This meant wielding their new powers and influence in matters both spiritual

56. Kavanagh, *The Shape of Baptism*, 154.

57. Ramsay Macmullen, *Christianizing the Roman Empire*, A.D. *100–400* (New Haven: Yale University Press, 1984) 48–49.

58. Timothy D. Barnes, *Constantine and Eusebius* (Cambridge, Mass.: Harvard University Press, 1981) 44–53; Macmullen, *Christianizing the Roman Empire*, 49; Fox, *Pagans and Christians*, 622–23 and 667–69.

and secular: settling local feuds, forwarding lawsuits, getting debts canceled, even lobbying for favors in the imperial court.[59]

Second, the churches faced a flood of new converts. To account for such a mass movement is no easy matter. As Ramsay Macmullen notes, it is not enough to study conversion accounts from intellectuals like Augustine; scholars have given these "disproportionate attention" so that "we see only a church all head and no body, a phenomenon that affected only a few lives, a change without mass and therefore without historical significance."[60] To account for a movement touching disparate ethnic groups, social classes, and geographic locales is much more complex and difficult—particularly since the historical record gives scant attention to the lives and feelings of this mass of ordinary people.

Macmullen and A. H. M. Jones have suggested several factors that at least would have made people more receptive to Christianity: (1) the new tolerance allowed Christian evangelical campaigns to take place unchecked by government authorities; (2) the conversion of Constantine gave Christianity considerable publicity, and probably did much to make it at least socially acceptable; (3) the benefits that Constantine lavished on the churches drew public attention to them and helped make them major public centers (i.e., for settling lawsuits, for distributing bread for the needy); (4) the favors Constantine and his sons gave to their co-religionists made it politic in some circles (e.g., government, the military) to become a Christian; (5) pagan cults faced a slowly mounting body of legislation that curtailed their activities and depleted their state-supported revenues.[61] None of these, of course, guaranteed conversion. Moreover, fourth-century emperors did not go about forcing conversions as some Moslem or medieval Christian rulers would

59. On the patronage system, see Paul Veyne, "The Roman Empire," *A History of Private Life*, vol. 1: *From Pagan Rome to Byzantium*, trans. Arthur Goldhammer (Cambridge, Mass.: Harvard University Press, 1987) 95–115. Concerning the effect of this on the Church, see Brown, *Augustine of Hippo*, 194–95; he develops this in more detail in his influential article, "The Rise and the Function of the Holy Man in Late Antiquity," reprinted in *Society and the Holy in Late Antiquity* (Berkeley: University of California Press, 1982) esp. 116–20.

60. Macmullen, *Christianizing the Roman Empire*, 1; see also his discussion of the difficulties of such studies, 1–9.

61. A. H. M. Jones, *The Later Roman Empire, 284–602: A Social, Economic, and Administrative Survey* (Baltimore: Johns Hopkins Press, 1986) 1:90–96; Macmullen, *Christianizing the Roman Empire*, 49–67, 86–99.

do.[62] Also, as Jones notes, paganism continued to maintain strongholds both in the countryside (except in North Africa and Egypt) and among the aristocracy. Thus Christianity remained a largely urban movement dominated by the lower and middle classes. Its progress was fitful and subject to enormous local variation.[63]

Third, the fourth century witnessed a series of bitter controversies over doctrine. Such disputes had long plagued local communities in the third century, but in the fourth these assumed a more public stature. There was, of course, the succession of councils and synods that punctuated the century, not only those accepted today like Nicaea and Constantinople but also those later repudiated like Sirmium and Seleucia. However, such theological controversy was not confined to bishops or councils; it also became part of the routine banter one heard in bazaars or bathhouses. As Gregory of Nyssa once complained:

"If you ask anyone for change, he will discuss with you whether the Son is begotten or unbegotten. If you ask about the quality of bread, you will receive the answer that 'the Father is greater, the Son is less.' If you suggest that you require a bath, you will be told that 'there was nothing before the Son was created.'"[64]

Given this milieu, it is little wonder fourth-century catechists devoted great care to doctrinal issues. Catechists particularly focused on the intricate Trinitarian debate—partly because this was the faith into which catechumens would be baptized and partly because this was the faith that catechumens would have to defend in public fora.

---

62. Coercive legislation was used later in the century against heretical groups. People, however, were not forced to convert from paganism to Christianity; rather paganism was disestablished. Also the withdrawal of government support of pagan cults left them vulnerable to Christian mobs bent on tearing down pagan shrines and temples. See the discussion in Macmullen, *Christianizing the Roman Empire*, 86–101. Macmullen, 145 note 31, mentions that "Islamization" took place by similar mechanisms: less through force and more through withdrawal of government support and government protection from mobs.

63. A. H. M. Jones, "The social background of the struggle between paganism and Christianity," *The Conflict between Paganism and Christianity in the Fourth Century*, ed. A. Momigliano (Oxford: Clarendon Press, 1963) 17–37.

64. Gregory of Nyssa, *De deitate Filii et Spiritus sancti* (trans. Frend, *Rise of Christianity*, 636).

Fourth, this century witnessed the rise of several generations of extraordinary Christian thinkers, all highly educated, many trained as rhetoricians.[65] Most served as bishops of local Churches and made the teaching of catechumens and neophytes one of their routine pastoral duties. In fact, the major catechumenal documents from this period are verbatim transcriptions of their talks. The quality of their catechesis was extraordinary—a rich blend of biblical spirituality, doctrinal precision, and rhetorical flare. Not surprisingly, some modern commentators have characterized this as the "golden age of catechesis."[66]

Fifth, there was an uneasy shift in ecclesiology: away from a Church of the pure and the few and towards a Church of the many—a *corpus permixtum*, as Augustine would describe it. Some of the old rigor still persisted: the cult of the martyrs remained a potent and sometimes disruptive force; the rising monastic movement, with its athletic asceticism, retained and even accentuated old rigorist strains; and the vitality of protest movements such as the Donatists and Pelagians suggests the continuing strength of purist sentiments.[67] On the other hand, the orthodox Churches, while counter-cultural in many respects, seemed more prepared to

65. For example, within the lifetime of Augustine, the following were active: Athanasius, Cyril of Jerusalem, Basil of Caesarea, Gregory of Nyssa, Gregory of Nazianzus, Ambrose, Jerome, John Chrysostom, Theodore of Mopsuestia, Paulinus of Nola, and Cyril of Alexandria. See Peter Brown, *The World of Late Antiquity* (New York: Norton, 1971) 108 and the chronological charts on 204–5.

66. De Puniet, "Catechuménat," DACL 2:2589; Searle, *Christening: the Making of Christians* (Collegeville, Minn.: The Liturgical Press, 1980) 11.

67. "Purist" might seem an unusual description of Pelagianism. However, scholars in recent years have shown how elitist and ascetical strains figured prominently in Pelagian movement; it was, in large measure, a movement influential among aristocrats in the Latin West. Moreover, the actual content of its message varied considerably: the message of Pelagius was not the same as those of Rufinus the Syrian, Caelestius, Julian of Eclanum, etc. For an excellent summary of this, see Gerald Bonner, *Augustine and Modern Research on Pelagianism*, St. Augustine Lecture Series (Villanova: Villanova University Press, 1972). See also Peter Brown, "Pelagius and His Supporters: Aims and Environment," *Journal of Theological Studies* n.s. 19 (1968) 93–114; reprint, in *Religion and Society in the Age of Saint Augustine* (New York: Harper & Row, 1972) 183–207; and "Patrons of Pelagius: The Roman Aristocracy Between East and West," *Journal of Theological Studies* n.s. 21 (1970) 56–72; reprint, *Religion and Society in the Age of Saint Augustine*, 208–26.

absorb the larger culture. However, as Kavanagh notes, this "did not mean that the churches would do so indiscriminately. The fathers' catechumenal homilies suggest that they still needed more Christians less than they needed better ones, even as they wished and worked for the conversion of all."[68]

These shifts within both the Church and its cultural milieu combined to tax and redefine structures inherited from the third century. Let us now survey the effect of these shifts on each phase of initiation. I will document trends using examples from the East since we will examine the catechumenate in Milan in the next chapter and the catechumenate in Hippo in the remaining chapters.

CATECHUMENATE: TRENDS IN THE GREEK EAST

We do not have a great deal of information about the catechumenate phase—at least relative to what we know about formation immediately prior to and following baptism. It seems that basic catechetical structures continued unchanged.[69] Catechumens still attended Liturgies of the Word.[70] It was during these liturgies that ordinary catechumens received their primary—and in all probability, their only—formal instruction.[71] Fourth-century preachers

68. Kavanagh, *The Shape of Baptism*, 119.

69. On this point, I disagree with Dujarier who makes the far-fetched claim that in the fourth century "the catechumenate, properly speaking, no longer existed" (*History of the Catechumenate*, 94). Apparently, by "catechumenate" he means the sort envisioned in Hippolytus. First, it is not at all clear how much of Hippolytus's "catechumenate" was more than an ideal-type. Dujarier also seems to ignore the fact that the fourth-century Fathers certainly felt the catechumenate was very much in existence, and that they took great pains to deal with the new flood of catechumens that swelled the ranks of their assemblies. Admittedly, the intimacy of the third century was gone, and the inherited structures were less than adequate for coping with the new milieu. However, such idealizing claims seriously distort the historical record and ignore the historical context. In chapter 5, I will take up these issues in detail.

70. Catechumens also seem to have attended the services of psalms (what we call the "Liturgy of the Hours" or, in older parlance, the "Divine Office"). Egeria, a fourth-century Spanish pilgrim, constantly mentions the presence of catechumens at the different prayer services of the Jerusalem church; *lucernarium* (Vespers) seems to have been particularly popular. See her description of the dismissal of catechumens at Vespers: Egeria, *Peregrinatio* 24.

71. However, in the *Constitutiones apostolorum* 7.39.1-4 (trans. James Donaldson, ANF 7:4375-476), there is an interesting passage: "Let him, therefore, who is to be taught the truth in regard to piety be instructed before his bap-

sometimes addressed the catechumens directly, particularly when they came across texts with baptismal overtones. For instance, when John Chrysostom preached on the story of Nicodemus, he first pleaded with the baptized to lead "a life worthy of . . . the mysteries"; he then turned to the catechumens: "You who have not yet been deemed worthy of them, do everything so as to become worthy, that we may be one body, that we may be brethren."[72] After the sermon, prayers were offered for the catechumens in a pattern reminiscent of Hippolytus. In Antioch, for example, catechumens did not mingle with the baptized, but stood apart—"far from the sacred precincts," as Chrysostom put it.[73] At the deacon's call for prayer, they would kneel or prostrate themselves full-length on the floor. Then the deacon would intone a long and quite beautiful prayer asking:

". . . that [God] would open the ears of their hearts and instill into them the word of truth, . . . that He would unveil to them the gospel of righteousness, that He would grant to them a godly mind, sound judgment, and virtuous manner of life, . . . that He would count them worthy in due season of the regeneration of the Laver, of the remission of sins, of the clothing of incorruption, that He would bless their comings in and goings out, the whole course of their life."[74]

---

tism in the knowledge of the unbegotten God, in the understanding of His only-begotten Son, in the assured acknowledgement of the Holy Spirit. Let him learn the order of the several parts of the creation, the series of providence, the different dispensations of your laws. Let him be instructed why the world was made, and why man was appointed to be a citizen there; let him also know his own nature, of what sort it is; let him be taught how God punished the wicked with water and fire, and glorified the saints in every generation . . . and how God still took care of, and did not reject, mankind, but called them from their error and vanity to acknowledge the truth at various seasons, leading them from bondage and impiety to liberty and piety, from injustice to justice, from death eternal to everlasting life." Finn, *The Liturgy of Baptism*, 35, thinks this may possibly be a curriculum for the ordinary catechumen. That seems questionable; more likely, it is an outline for the Lenten instruction.

72. Chrysostom, *In s. Johannis evangelium*, Homily 25.3 (trans. T. A. Goggin, FC 41:248). See also Homily 18.1.

73. Chrysostom, *In epistolam 2 ad Corinthios*, Homily 2.6 (trans. Talbot Chambers, NPNF 12:282). See Finn, *The Liturgy of Baptism*, 35.

74. The reconstruction of this prayer was done by Talbot Chambers (NPNF 12:281–82, note 11). Chrysostom, *In epistolam 2 ad Corinthios*, Homily 2.6–8, gives

After the deacon's prayer and the faithful's amen, the catechumens would rise, receive a blessing, and be dismissed.[75] As in the third century, catechumens were not allowed to witness the Eucharist itself.

While this basic structure remained, its viability seems to have been severely taxed. In the third century, there had been few catechumens. Thus their presence or absence at liturgies could be dutifully noted; their progress and lifestyle, carefully scrutinized. But in the fourth century, this was no longer feasible. The flood of new converts made such intense pastoral care much more difficult. Also, catechumens no longer enjoyed the security of an intimate, if sometime embattled, community; they could now drift in and out more anonymously; they could be simply one more face among the crowds that filled the basilicas.

Not only was the catechumenate weighed down by increased numbers; it was also populated by candidates whose lifestyle and motives—when compared to inherited standards—seemed sullied. There were, of course, opportunists. Eusebius of Caesarea, a bishop who moved among the elite circles in the empire, complained of "the unspeakable hypocrisy of men who crept into the Church and who took on the name and the character of Christians" to win political favors.[76] Similarly, Cyril of Jerusalem suspected that even some in immediate preparation for baptism were there for less-than-exemplary motives: that a man may have come because he is courting a woman or that "a slave has wished to please his master, or a friend, his friend."[77] While there seem to have been enough conversions of this type to merit such remarks, most probably converted for sincerely religious motives.[78] The

---

a line-by-line commentary on this prayer for the catechumens. A similar prayer is found in the fourth-century Syrian *Constitutiones apostolorum* 8.6.

75. Egeria reports that a similar pattern took place in Jerusalem at the end of Liturgies of the Hours; these dismissals must have been quite lengthy affairs because she notes them no less than seventy-two times. See Kavanagh, *Confirmation*, 12–14.

76. Eusebius, *Vita Constantini* 4.54 (trans. Colm Luibheid, *The Essential Eusebius* [New York: New American Library, 1966] 208). See Jones, *The Later Roman Empire*, 1:91.

77. Cyril, *Procatechesis* 5 (trans. Anthony A. Stephenson, FC 61:74).

78. See Jones, *The Later Roman Empire*, 2:979–80. Some surveys of the ancient catechumenate take the complaints about politic conversions and suspect motives too much at face value and ignore the historical context: e.g., Dujarier,

greater problem seems to have been weaning people from deeply ingrained cultural habits which, to Christian eyes, seemed pagan: theatre-going, attending the public games, consulting astrologers, wearing charms. Thus, some preachers were apt to portray catechumens in less-than-favorable terms. For instance, John Chrysostom once remarked that "the catechumen is a sheep without a seal; he is a deserted inn and a hostel without a door, which lies open to all without distinction; he is a lair for robbers, a refuge for wild beasts, a dwelling place for demons."[79]

An even more severe pastoral problem soon developed: many who became catechumens never advanced further. Earlier, Tertullian had complained of hesitant catechumens and had even advised delay in some cases. During the fourth century, this deferring of baptism reached epidemic proportions. According to Frederic Van der Meer, this was, in part, because "the catechumenate was the customary status of the nominal Christian, the one who lacked the courage for baptism but was ashamed to be called a heathen."[80] However, it was not simply new converts who delayed. Even those raised in pious Christian families did so: for instance, Chrysostom had deferred his baptism until age twenty-five; Basil of Caesarea, until age twenty-six; Gregory of Nazianzus, until twenty-eight.[81] Some even delayed until they were on their deathbed. The most prominent convert of the period, Constantine, had done as much.

These delays may have been prompted less by people's ill will and more by their response to Christianity's ethical rigor. As we saw earlier, Hippolytus and Tertullian had banned some people from the catechumenate; for instance, magistrates or men with concubines. Fourth-century churches both altered and maintained such standards: they admitted such people into the catechumenate, but barred them from baptism. Gregory of Nazianzus, for example, reports that those in politics feared that they were

---

History of the Catechumenate, 94ff.; Alois Stenzel, "Temporal and Supra-Temporal in the History of the Catechumenate and Baptism," 34.

79. Chrysostom, *Baptismal Instruction* 10.16 (trans. Paul W. Harkins, ACW 31:155). The numbering of Chrysostom's baptismal instructions varies from edition to edition; I have followed that used by Harkins.

80. Van der Meer, *Augustine the Bishop*, 357.

81. For a narrative summary of delays among those from Christian families, see H. Thurston, "When Baptism was Delayed," *Month* 152 (1928) 529–41.

"stained" by such business; he thus advised that they "flee . . .
from the forum . . . for what have you to do with Caesar or the
things of Caesar."[82] According to A. H. M. Jones, the source of
the problem was the Church itself: it "had built up its code when
it was a small exclusive society of the elect" and thus "set its
standards too high, and insisted too strongly that any major lapse
entailed eternal damnation."[83] Also, as Jungmann notes, delaying
meant "baptism was still ahead, and with it the possibility of
obtaining the remission of sins without undergoing the terrible
conditions associated with ecclesiastical penance."[84]

Denunciations against these delays were strong and frequent.
For instance, Chrysostom, when commenting on John 1, noted
that the apostles Andrew and Peter "merely heard of Him who
takes away the sin of the world and at once they ran to Him"; he
then remarked: "Is it not, then, utter senselessness to defer ac-
cepting the gift? Let the catechumens listen to this—those who are
putting off to their last breath their own salvation."[85] Chrysostom
found such delays a woeful abuse and would sometimes use
biting satire to denounce it. In one sermon, he entertained his
candidates with a portrait of a typical deathbed baptism:

"Even if the grace is the same for you and for those who are initiated on their deathbeds, neither the choice nor the preparations
are the same. They receive baptism in their beds, but you receive
it in the bosom of the common mother of us all, the Church; they
receive baptism amidst laments and tears, but you are baptized
with rejoicing and gladness; they are groaning, while you are giving thanks; their high fever leaves them in a stupor, while you are
filled with an abundance of spiritual pleasure. . . . The dying
man weeps and laments as he is baptized, his children stand
about in tears, his wife mars her cheeks with her nails, his friends
are downcast, his servants' eyes well with tears, and the whole
house gives the appearance of a gloomy winter's day. . . . Then,
in the midst of such tumult and confusion, the priest comes in,
and his arrival is a greater source of fear than the fever itself and

82. Gregory of Nazianzus, *Oratio 40: In sanctum baptisma* 19 (trans. Charles
G. Browne and James F. Swallow, NPNF, second series, 7:366).

83. Jones, *Later Roman Empire* 2:979; see his excellent discussion of the problems posed by this inherited code: 2:979–85.

84. Jungmann, *The Early Liturgy*, 248.

85. Chrysostom, *In s. Johannis evangelium*, Homily 18.1 (Goggin, 175).

harder than death for the sick man's relatives. When he enters, their despair is deeper than when the physician said he had given up all hope for the patient's life. Thus, he who is an argument for eternal life is seen as a symbol of death."[86]

Like Chrysostom, the Cappadocians found such delays an abuse. On Epiphany—a feast commemorating not only Jesus' birth, but his baptism as well—they would try to rally their catechumens, calling them to set aside their anxieties and to put in their names for baptism.[87] In one of these Epiphany sermons, Gregory of Nazianzus exploited a number of rhetorical tactics. For example, he would appeal to his catechumens' common sense: "How absurd it would be to grasp at money and throw away health, to be lavish in cleansing the body, but economical over cleansing the soul; to seek freedom from earthly slavery, but not to care about heavenly freedom."[88] He would tantalize the catechumens by claiming that baptism would give them access to ineffable mysteries: "As long as you are a catechumen you are but in the vestibule of religion; you must come inside, and cross the court, and observe the holy things, and look into the Holy of Holies, and be in company of the Trinity."[89] He even played upon their fears of hell and warned that death might come unexpectedly—through war, earthquakes, sudden illness, a political purge, choking on food, falling from a horse.[90] These sermons by the Cappadocians contain sparkling theology and rhetorical acumen, but the intent behind them was the same as an evangelical preacher's altar call: to bring people to the water.

LENT: TRENDS IN THE GREEK EAST

By 325, Lent (or "the forty days," as it was called) was already part of the liturgical calendar—though its exact length and order-

86. Chrysostom, *Baptismal Instruction* 9.5-6 and 8 (Harkins, 133-34). For a survey on the practice of "clinical (i.e., deathbed) baptisms," see Finn, *The Liturgy of Baptism*, 27-30 and Jones, *The Later Roman Empire*, 2:981.

87. De Puniet, "Catechuménat," DACL 2:2591. Other examples not examined here include: Basil of Caesarea, *Homilia XIII: Exhortatio ad sanctum baptisma* (PG 31:424-44); Gregory of Nyssa, *Ad eos qui differunt baptismum oratio* (PG 46:415-32).

88. Gregory of Nazianzus, *Oratio* 40.13 (Browne-Swallow, 364).

89. Ibid., 40.16 (Browne-Swallow, 365).

90. Ibid., 40.14. Chrysostom, likewise, was quite willing to play on such fears: *In s. Johannis evangelium*, Homily 25.3.

ing apparently differed from place to place.[91] It was customarily used as a time for more intensive formation of those ready for baptism. The contours and tenor of this formation can be gleaned from the collections of Lenten catecheses that have come down to us: nineteen by Cyril of Jerusalem (delivered c. 350); the fourteen by Theodore of Mopsuestia (delivered sometime between 392 and 428); and six by John Chrysostom (delivered in Antioch, c. 388–90).[92] (See charts 2, 3, and 4). In addition, we have a journal from a Spanish pilgrim named Egeria who visited the Holy Land near the end of the fourth century; it contains vivid descriptions of liturgies and catecheses she witnessed in Jerusalem.

Special prebaptismal formation was nothing new; we saw mention of it in Hippolytus. However, these fourth-century documents have several important features. First, they testify to a sharpening of the old distinction between beginning and advanced catechumens. Cyril of Jerusalem highlighted this distinction in his opening address, the *Procatechesis*:

"What honor Jesus bestows! You used to be called a catechumen, when the truth was being dinned into you from the outside: hearing about the Christian hope without understanding; hearing about the Mysteries without having a spiritual perception of them; hearing the Scriptures but not sounding their depths."[93]

A special vocabulary developed at this time to distinguish those preparing for baptism from ordinary catechumens: Eastern sources typically referred to the former as *photizomenoi* ("those being illu-

91. Canon 5 of Nicea mentions Lent in passing; the text is given in J. Stevenson, *A New Eusebius: Documents Illustrating the History of the Church to A.D. 337*, rev. ed. by W. H. C. Frend (London: SPCK, 1987) 339–40. According to festal letters of Athanasius (after 330), Lent in Alexandria lasted six weeks; according to Cyril and Egeria, it lasted eight weeks (i.e., not counting Saturday and Sunday). For the practice in Alexandria, see L. W. Barnard, "Some liturgical elements in Athanasius' Festal Epistles," *Studia Patristica* 13.2, ed. E. A. Livingston (Berlin: Akademie-Verlag, 1975) 337–42. For the practice of Jerusalem and Antioch, see Finn, *The Liturgy of Baptism*, 45–47.

92. For a discussion on the dating, authorship, and locale of these sermons, see Riley, *Christian Initiation*, 10–17.

93. Cyril of Jerusalem, *Procatechesis* 6 (Stephenson, 75—altered). Note the way Cyril plays on the root meaning of the word *catechesis:* "echoing." No longer does God's Word "echo" from the outside, but reaches down so that it touches the depths of the person. Cyril makes the same point several times in the course of his talks: *Catechesis* 1.4; *Catechesis* 5.1.

minated"), while Western sources called them *competentes* ("petitioners"); Rome had the unique custom of calling them *electi* ("chosen ones").[94]

Second, these sources testify to a quite sophisticated and structured process of formation. Commentators are divided on how to interpret its sudden appearance. At one extreme is Dujarier who claims that this Lenten formation was new, that it was a way of squeezing the old three-year catechumenate into a few weeks.[95] At the other extreme is Jungmann who claims that "the catechesis in Lent was what it had always been: a systematic introduction into the entire Christian doctrine, summed up in the *symbolum* [the Creed]."[96] Frankly, it is impossible to say given the paucity of third-century evidence. Some practices may represent a continuation of earlier ways; others, a refinement and expansion; and still others, new developments.

This Lenten phase typically began with a formal enrollment of names. The Jerusalem rite described by Egeria had an air of high solemnity. On the first day of Lent, those who had turned in their names came with their sponsors to the main church, the Martyrium. There the bishop would personally preside over the proceedings. Seated on the traditional *cathedra*, surrounded by a retinue of presbyters and deacons, he would question the godparent and neighbors of each candidate: "Does he lead a good life? Does he obey his parents? Is he a drunkard or a liar?" If accepted, the bishop would note down the person's name; if denied, the bishop would say: "Let him amend his life, and when he has done so, let him then approach the baptismal font."[97] This inquiry, while perhaps more courtly than Hippolytus's, retained the older concern: the public witness of one's lifestyle.

Once enrolled, candidates embarked on a complex regimen that wove together three elements: (1) asceticism, (2) instruction, and (3) exorcism. The Fathers envisioned this as a sort of spiritual fitness program meant to touch mind, heart, body, and behavior.

94. De Puniet, "Catéchuménat," DACL 2:2580, 2602. Finn, *The Liturgy of Baptism,* 32–33, notes that Chrysostom did not usually employ the traditional Eastern term, but referred to this group of candidates as "those about to be initiated."

95. Dujarier, *History of the Catechumenate,* 109.

96. Jungmann, *The Early Liturgy,* 249.

97. Egeria, *Peregrinatio* 45 (trans. George E. Gingras, ACW 38:122).

Chrysostom, for instance, compared it to a training camp for wrestlers:

"Let us learn during these days how we may gain the advantage over that wicked demon. . . . Let us learn, during this time of training, the grips he uses, the source of his wickedness, and how he can easily hurt us. Then, when the contest comes, we will not be caught unaware nor be frightened . . . because we have practiced among ourselves and have learned all his artifices."[98]

(1) *Asceticism.* During Lent, candidates took up a rigorous ascetical discipline. Typically it included all-night vigils, fasting, abstaining from alcohol, sleeping on the ground, weeping for one's sins, giving alms to the poor, even refraining from bathing.[99] Of these, almsgiving received the most catechetical attention. Gregory of Nazianzus, for example, insisted that a "Lazarus is at your gate" needing food and drink; that the sufferings of Christ are found in the masses of homeless; that candidates should "be a Zacchaeus, who yesterday was a publican, and is today a generous soul"; that if they find a debtor falling at their feet, they should, unlike the hard-hearted servant of the parables, "tear up every document, whether just or unjust."[100] Chrysostom—always the prophet—fought against the rigid class strictures of his day and insisted that the newly enrolled give witness to the justice of the kingdom: "That you may wear a single ruby, countless poor are starved and crushed. What defense will you find against this charge? . . . You received gold, not to bind your body with, but to help and feed the poor."[101]

(2) *Instruction.* The pedagogy found in these Lenten instructions is so complex and varied that I can do no more than highlight a few more salient features. Egeria provides the most vivid account of their setting, length, and audience. In Jerusalem, the talks were held, appropriately enough, in the Martyrium, the supposed site of the crucifixion. They lasted several hours and were given daily

---

98. Chrysostom, *Baptismal Instruction* 9.29 (Harkins, 140–41).

99. Ibid., 1.38; 12.7; 5.1–3.

100. Gregory of Nazianzus, *Oratio* 40.31 (Browne-Swallow, 371).

101. Chrysostom, *Baptismal Instruction* 12.41 (Harkins, 185). On Chrysostom's social thought, see Frances M. Young, *From Nicaea to Chalcedon: A Guide to the Literature and Its Background* (Philadelphia: Fortress Press, 1983) 145–48; and Peter Phan, *Social Thought*, MF 20 (Wilmington, Del.: Michael Glazier, 1984).

after the early morning service of psalms.[102] Typically, the bishop spoke from his *cathedra*. The *photizomenoi* would sit closely around him, while their sponsors stood nearby; some of the faithful also attended, but ordinary catechumens were barred.[103] Apparently the talks Egeria heard were stirring addresses, for she reports that they roused loud shouts and applause.[104]

The syllabus of these instructions varied considerably. Egeria reports that in Jerusalem the bishop spent the first five weeks surveying the entirety of Scripture, "expounding first its literal meaning and then explaining the spiritual meaning." After this, the candidates formally received the Creed, one of those secrets which, like the rites of baptism and Eucharist, was hidden from ordinary catechumens. The bishop then spent the remaining two weeks explaining the Creed as he did the Scriptures, "expounding first the literal and then the spiritual sense." Formal instruction ended just before Holy Week. At this time each one recited the Creed back to the bishop; then the bishop offered a final sermon noting that he could not instruct them about "things which belong to a still higher mystery, that of baptism" but would do so after initiation.[105]

Cyril's instructions followed a somewhat different arrangement. He used the tenets of the Jerusalem Creed as the overarching framework: Catecheses 1–3 treat the phrase "one baptism for the forgiveness of sins"; 4 gives an overview of essential Christian beliefs; 5–18 then take the remaining phrases of the Creed phrase by phrase. In the middle of catechesis 5, he formally handed over the Creed and at the end of 18, he formally received it back.[106]

---

102. Egeria, *Peregrinatio* 46. Some of these details are confirmed in Cyril. In *Catechesis* 18.32, Cyril mentions that "we have . . . delivered as many lectures as possible in these past days of Lent." Cyril's own talks were given sometimes on successive days, sometimes after breaks of some days—though he mentions other teachers who may have spoken on days when he did not (18.32). See Gingras, "Introduction," ACW 38:23–43, for comments on the various Jerusalem churches and the liturgies held in each.

103. Egeria, *Peregrinatio* 46. Cyril, *Procatechesis* 12, also stresses the need for such secrecy.

104. Egeria, *Peregrinatio* 46.

105. Ibid. (Gingras, 123–25).

106. *Catecheses* 1–3 do not explicitly refer to the credal phrase because the *photizomenoi* had not yet formally been handed over the Creed until *Catechesis* 5. However, in *Catechesis* 18.32, Cyril mentions that he skips an exposition on

Cyril likened this systematic approach to good construction techniques: "Let me compare the catechizing to a building. Unless we methodically bind and joint the whole structure together, we shall have leaks and dry rot, and all our previous exertions will be wasted."[107] While credal phrases charted the main lines of this catechetical edifice, biblical stories shaped its interior. In actual practice Cyril linked Creed and Scriptures in a complex fashion. Often he used the Creed as a way of integrating and elucidating the Scriptures: sometimes, as a searchlight to sweep rapidly across the biblical landscape; other times, as a focused beam to illuminate a key biblical episode. This in turn set up a complex dialectic: that is, while the Creed would light up the Scriptures, the Scriptures in turn would demonstrate the truth of credal claims. As Cyril said just before he recited the Creed to his candidates:

"For the present, just listen and memorize the creed as I recite it, and you will receive in due course the proof from Scripture of each of its propositions. . . . And just as the mustard seed in a small grain contains in embryo many future branches, so also the creed embraces in a few words all the religious knowledge in both the Old and the New Testament."[108]

Theodore of Mopsuestia also used the Creed as a key part of his curricular outline (1–10), but also added expositions on the Lord's Prayer (11) and on baptism (12–14). (I will take up in the next section why he explained the secret baptismal rite *before* the vigil). Theodore listed quite different reasons for focusing on the Creed: (a) "that you might learn what to believe, and in the name of whom you are baptized"; (b) that the Creed is *"our part* in the mysteries" (presumably, he means that candidates would need to be able to understand the three credal questions asked them during the baptismal rite itself); and (c) that the words have so "much power hidden in them" and are so condensed that they need exposition to tease out their subtle and potent mysteries.[109] Theodore was, at heart, a mystagogue, and felt that the Creed

---

the article "one baptism for the forgiveness of sins" because "we have spoken in earlier lectures of baptism and repentance."

107. Cyril, *Procatechesis* 11 (Stephenson, 79).
108. Cyril, *Catechesis* 5.12 (trans. Stephenson, FC 61:146).
109. Theodore, *Catechetical Homily* 12.1; 1.7; and 1.13. For the Syriac text, with a French translation, see *Les homélies catéchétiques de Théodore de Mopsueste,*

gave one access to otherwise ineffable mystery. He justified an exposition on the Lord's Prayer by claiming that, while the Creed provided knowledge of mystery, the Lord's Prayer contained "teaching of good works."[110] Together these, along with the "mysteries" themselves (baptism and Eucharist), were "symbols" that initiated one into eschatological living so that "we might gradually approach our future hope . . . while cultivating a conduct that is in harmony with the new world."[111]

Chrysostom's pre-baptismal instructions follow no systematic framework. He mentions other teachers, so that it is possible that he left more systematic instruction to others.[112] In any case, his concern—always passionate—was moral formation. Thus while his talks may be hard to outline, his admonitions were crisp and his directives, clear. In particular, he denounced many of the same vices Tertullian had denounced: oaths; public games; women's makeup; tinkering with omens, charms, and incantations.[113] He, like Tertullian, saw these as pomps of the devil. But his moralism focused not on the renunciations, as Tertullian's had, but on the new life made possible by baptism: "Those who administer the affairs of state are clad in robes bearing the imperial images. . . . How much more should this be the case with you who are about to put on Christ himself!"[114]

Noting the framework of these instructions gives one little flavor for their actual dynamism. These were emotionally charged ad-

---

Studi e Testi 145, ed. Raymond Tonneau and Robert Devreesse (Vatican: Biblioteca Apostolica Vaticano, 1949) 342–45. The only complete English translation of this is that of A. Mingana in Woodbrooke Studies, vol. 5 (for 1–10) and vol. 6 (for 11–16). I have followed the custom of English-speaking commentators on Theodore in using the paragraph numbering of the Tonneau-Devreesse edition while using the translation of Mingana. These passages are found in Woodbrooke Studies 6:17; 5:21; and 5:24.

110. Theodore, Catechetical Homily 11.1 (Mingana, 6:1).

111. Theodore, Catechetical Homily 1.4 (Mingana, 5:20). For a summary of Theodore's sense of mystery, see Johannes Quasten, "The Liturgical Mysticism of Theodore of Mopsuestia," Theological Studies 15 (1954) 431–39.

112. Chrysostom, Baptismal Instruction 10.2.

113. Chrysostom denounces spectacles in Baptismal Instruction 1.43 and 12.52; women's adornment in 1.34–38 and 12.42–47; superstitions in 1.39–40 and 12.53–60. Oaths remain his most passionate topic: e.g., 9.36–47; 10.18–29.

114. Chrysostom, Baptismal Instruction 1.45 (Harkins, 41). See also 1.46; 2.11 and 27; 11.7.

dresses. For instance, Cyril in the *Procatechesis* greeted the new *photizomenoi* with great warmth:

"Already, my dear candidates for enlightenment, scents of paradise are wafted towards you; already you are culling mystic blossoms for the weaving of heavenly garlands, already the fragrance of the Holy Spirit has blown about you. Already you have arrived at the outer court of the palace: may the King lead you in!"[115]

Chrysostom opened one of his addresses with a similar warmth ("How I have loved and longed for the throng of my new brethren!") and paid court to his candidates as people of great dignity ("I will do what people do when a man is going to acquire ruling power").[116] While these catecheses are called "instructions," they are rarely abstract or didactic. They instruct more with earthy proverbs, striking analogies, or terse biblical exempli. Teachers like Chrysostom would draw on everyday scenes and images—from civil service, judicial proceedings, medical practice, business, crafts, sports, war, marriage, slavery—to give a vividness and poignancy to their message.

(3) *Exorcism.* Egeria noted that in Jerusalem exorcisms were part of the daily Lenten routine.[117] Cyril, too, alluded to their frequency, and in the *Procatechesis*, explained their meaning: "Submit to the exorcisms devoutly. . . . Imagine virgin gold alloyed with various foreign substances: copper, tin, iron, lead. What we are after is the gold alone."[118] Chrysostom (who also mentions these more routine cleansings) and Theodore both stressed a major exorcism that took place some time before the vigil.[119] In Mopsuestia—and in Hippo, as we will see later—candidates stood barefoot on a sackcloth of goat's hair (the *cilicium*), with their heads veiled, their outer cloak stripped off, and their arms outstretched. Then the exorcist would approach and speak "in a loud and prolonged voice" denouncing Satan. To explain the meaning of this rite, Theodore used a courtroom analogy: the candidate was the accused; the devil, the plaintiff; and the exorcist, the defense

115. Cyril, *Procatechesis* 1 (Stephenson, 69–70).
116. Chrysostom, *Baptismal Instruction* 9.1 (Harkins, 131).
117. Egeria, *Peregrinatio* 46.
118. Cyril, *Procatechesis* 9 (Stephenson, 77).
119. Finn, *The Liturgy of Baptism,* 74. See, for example, Chrysostom, *Baptismal Instruction* 9.11.

lawyer. By his words, the exorcist showed that the candidate was innocent, that he had suffered a form of cruel slavery, and that the devil "had forcibly and unjustly brought him under his rule."[120] Chrysostom described the exorcists' role in a quite different way: "as if they were preparing a house for a royal visit, they cleanse your minds by those awesome words."[121]

MYSTAGOGY: TRENDS IN THE GREEK EAST

One finds two quite different traditions on the timing of mystagogy. Cyril typifies one of these: that the "mysteries" (baptism, chrismation, Eucharist) can be explained only *after* initiation. He gave his rationale for this in his opening words to the newly baptized:

"It has long been my wish, true-born and long-desired children of the Church, to discourse to you upon these spiritual, heavenly mysteries. On the principle, however, that seeing is believing, I delayed until the present occasion, calculating that after what you saw on that night I should find you a readier audience. . . ."[122]

In other words, Cyril believed that the discipline of secrecy (*disciplina arcani*) simply enshrined a good pedagogical principle: that in matters of mystery, experience must precede explanation. Cyril trusted that being stripped naked, dunked, then oiled from head to foot was itself splendid catechesis. Only after his initiates had drunk in and savored the rich, elusive power of such symbols did instruction assume its proper place. Only then would the resonances of theological reflection have sufficient poignancy. Because of these views, Cyril delivered his five *Mystagogical Catecheses* during Easter Week.[123] Ambrose, Augustine's mentor, would follow this same approach.

120. Theodore, *Catechetical Homily* 12.22–23 (Mingana, 6:31). See also Johannes Quasten, "Theodore of Mopsuestia on the Exorcism of the Cilicium," *Harvard Theological Review* 35 (1942) 209–19.

121. Chrysostom, *Baptismal Instruction* 2.12 (Harkins, 47–48). In 2.14, Chrysostom draws on an analogy from the way prisoners of war were treated.

122. Cyril, *Mystagogical Catechesis* 1.1 (trans. Stephenson, FC 64:153). There has been some dispute over Cyril's authorship of these catecheses. It is now generally accepted, though some feel the catecheses as we now have them may have been reworked by Cyril's successor, John. For a discussion of this, see Stephenson, "Introduction," FC 64:143–49.

123. For a more extensive treatment, see Riley's excursus, "Ambrose and Cyril: The Mystagogical Problem," *Christian Initiation*, 253–61. Two lengthy

Chrysostom and Theodore worked from a very different tradition. As they saw it, it was important to explain the rites of baptism *just prior* to the vigil. On one occasion, Chrysostom cited his reasons for "anticipating the event": (1) "that you might be carried on by the wings of hope and enjoy the pleasure before you enjoyed the actual benefit"; and (2) that "you might . . . see the objects of bodily sight more clearly with the eyes of the spirit" since the rite's real dynamic is the invisible work of God.[124] Thus, Chrysostom's two mystagogical instructions on baptism were delivered prior to initiation (probably on Holy Thursday); we have, in addition, six other addresses by him given to neophytes during Easter Week. Theodore, too, explained the rites of baptism *prior* to initiation and for reasons similar to Chrysostom's. As Theodore saw it, baptism was the "representation of unseen and unspeakable things through signs and emblems"; thus one must learn "the reason for all of them" that one might "receive the things that take place with great love."[125] However, Theodore did maintain a strict silence about Eucharist itself—until after the candidates' initiation.[126] Thus Theodore gave his three catecheses on baptism during Lent and his two catecheses on Eucharist during Easter Week.

Egeria's account of mystagogy in Jerusalem offers some fascinating details about setting and audience. She noted that in the days between Easter and its octave the neophytes (along with any of the faithful) would hear the mysteries; catechumens were, as

---

studies on fourth-century mystagogy have been published recently: Kilian McDonnell and George Montague, eds., *Christian Initiation and Baptism in the Holy Spirit: Evidence from the First Eight Centuries* (Collegeville, Minn.: The Liturgical Press [A Michael Glazier Book] 1991) focuses on theology of the Spirit in baptism but also offers quite useful portraits of Cyril and John Chrysostom and their respective churches; Enrico Mazza's *Mystagogy: a Theology of Liturgy in the Patristic Age* (New York: Pueblo Publishing Co., 1989) is a rather technical study which deliberately, but unfortunately, sidesteps treating these documents for what they are—catecheses—and focuses instead on the sacramental theology and terminology of Ambrose, Chrysostom, Theodore, and Cyril.

124. Chrysostom, *Baptismal Instruction* 2.28 (Harkins, 53-54).

125. Theodore, *Catechetical Homily* 12.1-2 (Mingana, 6:17).

126. Ibid., 14.29; 15.1. Chrysostom did not maintain such studied reserve, but his remarks about Eucharist during Lent were meant more to tantalize than to explain: e.g., *Baptismal Instruction* 2.27 and 10.2.

before, barred from entering. Whereas the Lenten instructions had been given in the church on Golgotha, the mystagogical ones were given, aptly enough, in the Anastasis, the Church of the Resurrection. She also noted the great enthusiasm with which the hearers greeted these addresses: "While the bishop is discussing and explaining each point, so loud are the voices of praise that they can be heard outside the church."[127]

A rich affective tone pervades these mystagogical addresses— much as it did the Lenten ones. However, their tonal register is brighter. For instance, Chrysostom opened one sermon by comparing the neophytes' robes to bright stars: "Blessed be God! Behold there are stars here on earth too, and they shine forth more brilliantly than those in heaven!"[128] In another address, he modulated rapidly from joy to awe: "See how many children this spiritual mother has brought forth suddenly and in a single night! . . . Spiritual child-bearing is such that it needs neither time nor a period of months."[129]

Fourth-century mystagogical catecheses typically wove together three common elements: (1) gestures and words drawn from the liturgies of the vigil, (2) scriptural themes and images, (3) analogies drawn from nature or the local culture. These common threads, however, received their unique shape depending on (1) local ritual practices, (2) the mystagogue's theological stance, (3) his natural temperament, and (4) the local culture and environment. Let me illustrate briefly how both these common elements and individuating strains come together in the works of Cyril, Theodore, and Chrysostom.

Both Cyril and Theodore used the liturgical rite itself for their outline and sequence of topics. In fact, they traced the rites— bodily gesture, sacramental sign, spoken word—in such detail that liturgists have been able to reconstruct the course and movement of their respective liturgies. Cyril's catechesis on the *apotaxis* (the "turning away" from Satan) serves as a good example of his basic method. First, he had the neophytes recall what they had done during the rite: "You entered the antechamber of the baptistery and faced towards the west. On the command to stretch out your

127. Egeria, *Peregrinatio* 47 (Gingras, 125).
128. Chrysostom, *Baptismal Instruction* 3.1 (Harkins, 56).
129. Ibid., 4.1 (Harkins, 66).

hand, you renounced Satan as though he were there in person."[130]
Cyril then set this gesture within the drama of salvation history.
First he retold the Exodus story, accenting how the Jewish people
had suffered under "that tyrannous and cruel despot, Pharaoh."
He then shifted to Jesus noting that "Moses' mission was to lead
out from Egypt a persecuted people; Christ's, to rescue all the
people of the world who were under the tyranny of sin." Finally
Cyril explained the liturgical gesture itself:

"Allow me to explain the reason of your facing west, for you
should know it. Because the west is the region of visible darkness,
Satan, who is himself darkness, has his empire in darkness—that
is the significance of your looking steadily towards the west while
you renounce that gloomy Prince of night."[131]

Cyril thus combined natural symbol (west as the place of darkness), bodily gesture (facing west), spoken word (formula of
renunciation), and biblical story (Exodus, the Christ event).
Together these unfolded and illuminated the mystery of the neophytes' conversion: their bodily turning mirrored their interior
one; their words of renunciation annulled their "ancient league
with hell"; and these both derived their power and their meaning
from the events of salvation history.[132] Moreover, because Cyril
spoke in the very places where these events of salvation history
took place, his words would have had an added poignancy.

   Theodore's method was similar, but his accent was different.
Whereas Cyril stressed salvation history enacted in the *present*
through liturgical sign, "Theodore's genius" was, as Riley notes,
"to take the same liturgical signs and move them in an arc pointing to the future."[133] In other words, Theodore gave them an eschatological edge—something we will see repeated in Augustine.
For instance, Theodore stressed that by the "awe-inspiring"
Eucharist: ". . . we are led through it to the future reality, because it contains an image of the ineffable economy of Christ our

130. Cyril, *Mystagogical Catechesis* 1.2 (Stephenson, 153-54). See the fine discussion of this in Riley, *Christian Initiation*, 22-25, 35-48, 54-63, 139-42.
   131. Ibid., 1.2-4 (Stephenson, 154-55).
   132. Ibid., 1.9 (Stephenson, 158).
   133. Riley, *Christian Initiation*, 454. See also Finn, "Baptismal Death and
Resurrection. A Study in Fourth Century Eastern Baptismal Theology,"
Worship 43 (1969) 175-89.

Lord, in which we receive the vision and shadow of the happening that took place."[134]

Chrysostom's mystagogy, by contrast, focused less on liturgy and more on morals.[135] Chrysostom again and again used the neophytes' "gleaming" robes as a point of departure: since their robes had "imperial emblems," neophytes were to maintain a "godly conduct and strict discipline"; their "marriage robes" were to last not only the seven days of the "bridal feast" but for all time; and the "gleam" of their robes was to be a light to guide others.[136] Chrysostom also urged his hearers to imitate certain biblical neophytes such as Paul ("Imitate him, I beg you, and you will be able to be called newly baptized not only for two, three, ten or twenty days, but you shall deserve this greeting after ten, twenty, or thirty years") and Cornelius ("who had each day a thousand things to distract and to bother him," yet who scorned drinking bouts and gluttony and attended instead to "prayer and almsgiving").[137] Chrysostom drew especially on cultural images to illustrate his points. In one talk he took up a wrestling image and, with a characteristic twist, showed how wrestling contests in the spiritual arena differ from those in the athletic:

"In the Olympic combats the judge stands impartially aloof from the combatants, favoring neither the one nor the other, but awaiting the outcome. He stands in the middle because his judgment is impartial. But in our combat with the devil, Christ does not stand aloof but is entirely on our side: . . . He anointed us as we went into the combat, but He fettered the devil."[138]

Thus while Chrysostom continued to exhort his hearers, he also stressed that the sacraments had given them new powers and these would enable them to begin living in the arena of the everyday with an uncanny moral flair.

In the fourth century, as in the third, neither the rigor of the process nor the quality of catechesis guaranteed results. Thus one finds Chrysostom complaining:

134. Theodore, *Catechetical Homily* 15.24 (Mingana, 6:85).
135. See Riley's excursus, "Chrysostom's Mystagogical Approach," *Christian Initiation*, 266–71.
136. Chrysostom, *Baptismal Instruction* 4.18 and 6.24 (Harkins, 73 and 102–3).
137. Ibid., 4.7–10 and 7.28 (Harkins, 68–70 and 116–17).
138. Ibid., 3.9 (Harkins, 58).

"I see many after their baptism living more carelessly than the uninitiated, having nothing particular to distinguish them in their way of life. It is, you see for this cause, that neither in the market nor in the Church is it possible to know quickly who is a believer and who an unbeliever; unless one be present at the time of the mystery, and see the one sort dismissed, the others remaining within—whereas they ought to be distinguished *not by their place, but by their way of life.*"[139]

139. Chrysostom, *In s. Matthaei evangelium*, Homily 4.14 (trans. George Prevost, NPNF 10:26).

Chart 2
The Catecheses of John Chrysostom

I. THE CATECHUMENATE: PASSING REFERENCES

Sermon	Text	Trans	Topic
In s. Johannis, Sermon 18	PG 59	FC 41	Denounces delays
In s. Johannis, Sermon 25	PG 59	FC 41	Denounces delays
In ep. 2 Cor, Sermon 2	PG 61	NPNF 12	Commentary on prayer for dismissal of catechumens
In s. Matthaei, Sermon 4	PG 57	NPNF 10	Baptized vs. catechumens

II. LENTEN INSTRUCTIONS

Harkins's Numbering	Manuscript Numbering	Text	Trans	Delivered
1	Stavronikita 1	SC 50	ACW 31	10 days, 390
2	Stavronikita 2	SC 50	ACW 31, MF 5	Just before Easter, 390
9	Papadopoulous-Kerameus 1 = Montfaucon 1	PG 49	ACW 31	10 days into Lent, 388
10	Papadopoulous-Kerameus 2	P-K2	ACW 31	20 days into Lent, 388
11	Papadopoulous-Kerameus 3	P-K3	ACW 31	Holy Thursday, 388
12	Montfaucon 2	PG 49	ACW 31	20 days into Lent, 390(?)

Topics	
1	Spiritual marriage: mystery, contract, gifts; belief in Trinity; yoke of Christ; portrait of meek and humble heart; adornment of women; against omens, oaths, spectacles; "Christian"
2	Baptism; Adam; eyes of faith; exorcisms; sponsors; renunciation; adherence to Christ; anointing; immersion; baptismal formula
9	Deathbed baptisms; bath of regeneration; baptism and Jewish baths; training of photizomenoi; sins of speech; avoid swearing
10	Swearing; Easter; baptism as death/resurrection; three days in tomb; exorcism; oaths; Herod
11	Spiritual marriage; wedding garb; "faithful"; renunciation; covenant with Christ; anointing; baptism; pray for Church; sacred kiss
12	"Faithful"; "Newly-illumined"; excellent conduct; evil habits; recruits; contest with Satan; adornment of women; renunciation; omens, charms, incantations

III. EASTER WEEK INSTRUCTIONS

Harkins's Numbering	Manuscript Numbering	Text	Trans	Delivered
3	Stavronikita 3 = Sermo ad neophytos	SC 50	ACW 31	Just after baptism, 388–390

Chart 2 *(cont.)*
The Catecheses of John Chrysostom

Harkins's Numbering	Manuscript Numbering	Text	Trans	Delivered
	=Papadopoulous-Kerameus 4			
4	Stavronikita 4	SC 50	ACW 31	Easter Sun or Mon 390
5	Stavronikita 5	SC 50	ACW 31	Easter Tues 390
6	Stavronikita 6	SC 50	ACW 31	Easter Wed 390
7	Stavronikita 7	SC 50	ACW 31	Easter Fri 390
8	Stavronikita 8	SC 50	ACW 31	Easter Sat 390

Topics	
3	Neophytes greeted; graces of baptism; Blood of Christ; baptism and exodus
4	Neophytes as joy of Church; Paul as model of neophyte; new creation; conduct
5	No laxity; drunkenness; danger of relaxing; Paul vs. Simon Magus; conversion to regain innocence
6	Christians at spectacles; do all for God's glory; fraternal correction; a neophyte for life
7	Tombs of martyrs; martyrs as physicians; martyrs as models; be dead to world; almsgiving; Cornelius
8	Welcome to countryfolk; Abraham as model; vanity of world; neophyte's daily program

Chart 3
The Catecheses of Theodore of Mopsuestia

I. CATECHESES GIVEN DURING LENT

Tonneau's Number/Text	Trans	Topic	Subjects Covered
1	Mingana	Creed	Reason for creed; One God
2	Mingana	Creed	Faith; Father; Creator
3	Mingana	Creed	Son: only-begotten
4	Mingana	Creed	Son: true God, *homoousios*
5	Mingana	Creed	Son: incarnation
6	Mingana	Creed	Son: two natures
7	Mingana	Creed	Son: death, resurrection, second coming
8	Mingana	Creed	Son: two natures
9	Mingana	Creed	Spirit: divinity
10	Mingana	Creed	Spirit: consubstantial, proceeds; remission of sin; resurrection of flesh
11	Mingana	Our Father	Commentary on prayer
12	Mingana	Baptism	Prebaptismal exorcism
13	Mingana, Yarnold	Baptism	Renunciation; prebaptismal anointing
14	Mingana, MF 5 Yarnold	Baptism	Immersion, consignation

II. CATECHESES GIVEN AFTER THE VIGIL

Tonneau's Number/Text	Trans	Topic	Subjects Covered
15	Mingana, Yarnold	Eucharist	Preparation of altar; dialogue of anaphora
16	Mingana, Yarnold	Eucharist	Anaphora; communion

Syriac Text: *Les homélies catéchétiques de Théodore de Mopsueste*, Studi e Testi 145. Eds. R. Tonneau and R. Dovreesse.

Translation: A. Mingana, *Woodbrooke Studies 5-6* (Cambridge).

Translation: Edward Yarnold, *The Awe-Inspiring Rites of Initiation: Baptismal Homilies of the Fourth Century*.

Chart 4
The Catecheses of Cyril of Jerusalem

Number	Text	Trans	Topic	Subjects Covered
I. LENTEN CATECHESIS				
Pro-catechesis	Cross	FC 61	Opening of Lent	Greeting, suspect motives catechesis, daily exorcism, secrecy
1	PG 33	FC 61	[Creed]	One baptism for the forgiveness of sins
2	PG 33	FC 61	[Creed]	Repentance
3	PG 33	FC 61	[Creed]	Meaning of baptism
4	PG 33	FC 61	Ten Doctrines	God, Christ, virgin birth, cross, resurrection, ascension, judgment, Spirit, soul/body, Scriptures
5	PG 33	FC 61	Faith	Abraham, in Gospels, assent, receive Creed
6	PG 33	FC 61	Creed	Unity of God
7	PG 33	FC 61	Creed	God the Father
8	PG 33	FC 61	Creed	Omnipotent
9	PG 33	FC 61	Creed	Creator
10	PG 33	FC 61	Creed	One Lord Jesus Christ
11	PG 33	FC 61	Creed	Only-begotten Son of God
12	PG 33	FC 61	Creed	Made Flesh
13	PG 33	FC 64	Creed	Crucified and buried
14	PG 33	FC 64	Creed	Rose from dead, ascended
15	PG 33	FC 64	Creed	Judge of living/dead; kingdom without end
16	PG 33	FC 64	Creed	Spirit
17	PG 33	FC 64	Creed	Spirit
18	PG 33	FC 64	Creed	Church, resurrection of flesh, eternal life, hand back Creed
II. MYSTAGOGICAL CATECHESES (DURING EASTER WEEK)				
1	Cross	FC 64, MF 5 Yarnold	Baptism	Renunciation, profession
2	Cross	FC 64, MF 5 Yarnold	Baptism	Immersion
3	Cross	FC 64, MF 5 Yarnold	Baptism	Chrism
4	Cross	FC 64, MF 7 Yarnold	Eucharist	Body and Blood of Christ
5	Cross	FC 64, MF 7 Yarnold	Eucharist	Liturgy: Kiss, dialogue, sanctus, epiclesis, Our Father, Communion

Greek Text: F. L. Cross, *St. Cyril of Jerusalem's Lectures on the Christian Sacraments*

Chapter 3

Augustine and the Catechumenate in Milan

In the last chapter I assembled a mosaic gathered from fragments of the third- and fourth-century catechumenate to serve as a backdrop for viewing Augustine's work in North Africa. Here the portrait will become more focused: on a single catechumenate—Milan—and on a single candidate—Augustine. I will not trace out a full portrait of Augustine's conversion; my concern, strictly speaking, is not Augustine the convert, but rather Augustine the catechumen. Thus I will pass lightly over the ebbs and flows of his other conversions: to "Wisdom," to Manicheism, to neo-Platonism. I will also ignore, for the moment, Augustine's personal theory of conversion, that subtle mix of biblical and neo-Platonic images and themes. Nor will I do more than touch upon the pivotal moment of that conversion, his graced experience in the garden. All of these form part of that larger portrait, and they have been traced—brilliantly—by a number of biographers (Pierre Courcelle, John O'Meara, Gerald Bonner, Peter Brown) and, of course, by Augustine himself.[1] Here I wish to highlight only a single thread

---

1. See Pierre Courcelle, *Recherches sur les Confessions de saint Augustin* (Paris: E. de Boccard, 1950); John J. O'Meara, *The Young Augustine: The Growth of St. Augustine's Mind up to His Conversion* (London: Longmans, Green, and Co., 1954); Gerald Bonner, *St. Augustine of Hippo: Life and Controversies*, 2d ed., (Norwich: The Canterbury Press, 1986); and Brown, *Augustine of Hippo*. I should also note the fine summary by Henri Marrou, *Saint Augustine and His Influence through the Ages*, trans. Patrick Hepburne Scott (London: Longmans, 1957); Marrou is especially good on Augustine as a rhetorician. For an excellent summary of the question of the historicity of the *Confessiones*, see O'Meara, *The Young Augustine*, 4–18. He notes that while the *Confessiones* gives historically accurate information, it is a work shaped by definite points of view and by a definite manner of presentation: (1) the retrospective view, (2) a selectiveness dictated by Augustine's themes and purposes, (3) a moralizing overlay, and (4) rhetorical figures (fondness for the indefinite expressions, literary allusions). It is also shaped by definite Plotinian and biblical themes

of that complex conversion: the intentional formation he received in the catechumenate in Milan. For this, I will draw on Augustine's works, especially the *Confessions,* as well as the works of his mentor, Ambrose. My purpose is equally restricted: to set a backdrop for Augustine's own work as a director of a catechumenate, so as to highlight in what ways he taught others as he had been taught and in what ways he simply followed his own lights.

AUGUSTINE THE CATECHUMEN

Augustine became a catechumen while still a child. By his own account, he was, "as a catechumen, . . . blessed regularly from birth with the Sign of the Cross and was seasoned with God's salt."[2] These two rites—a cross traced on the forehead, a taste of blessed salt—not only marked his entrance into the catechumenate, but were, as he says, repeated regularly. These rites, in the popular mind at least, were believed to help ward off attacks from demonic forces. Thus children routinely received this signing and salt as a sort of inoculation—much as children today are inoculated against invisible and dangerous viruses.[3] But parents usually stopped short of having their children baptized. Augustine's mother, Monica, was typical in this regard, and refused to have him baptized, even when he fell seriously sick. She sensed—and rightly—that her son would inevitably sow his wild oats, and she had no wish to leave him vulnerable to the rigors of public penance. Augustine, writing of this years later, looked back with regret, but admitted her sagacity: "My mother well knew how many great tides of temptation threatened me before I grew up, and she chose to let them beat upon the as-yet-unmolded clay rather than upon the finished image which had received the stamp of baptism."[4]

Augustine would drift with those tides for a long while. For instance, while studying in Carthage (the college town of North Africa), he indulged in the usual student vices: he attended bawdy theater productions, befriended some in a rowdy fraternity

and images. See Robert J. O'Connell, *St. Augustine's Confessions: The Odyssey of Soul* (Cambridge, Mass.: Harvard University Press, 1969).

2. *Confessiones* 1.11 (trans. R. S. Pine-Coffin, *The Confessions* [New York: Penguin Books, 1961] 31).

3. Brown, *Augustine of Hippo*, 41.

4. *Confessiones* 1.11 (Pine-Coffin, 32).

nicknamed the Wreckers, chased women, dabbled with astrology.[5] Such behavior was permitted catechumens. According to Augustine, the conventional wisdom was: "Leave him alone and let him do it; he is not yet baptized."[6] Still he continued to go to church, though he was moved less by piety and more by a desire to spy women.[7] Sometime during this same period he began living with a woman. She was a lower class than he, so marriage was out of the question—in fact, it was forbidden by law.[8] But it was a common arrangement among social-climbers like Augustine—at least until one could secure a marriage appropriate to one's status. The two lived together some fifteen years, and she bore him a son, Adeodatus. It was during this same period that Augustine would drift into the Manichees, becoming a "hearer" among them much as he had been a "hearer" among the Catholics. He would remain with them for nine years.[9]

The young Augustine made his living as a teacher of rhetoric, first in Carthage, later in Rome.[10] The skills he taught were highly valued, for rhetoric was considered a prerequisite for all who sought fame and fortune. According to the proverbial view, "This is the school where men are made masters of words; this is where they learn the art of persuasion, so necessary in business and debate."[11] Not only was public speaking a highly cultivated art in those days; it also was a form of popular entertainment. People went to hear great rhetoricians with the same enthusiasm some today bring to concert-going; they were as appreciative of the

5. Ibid., 3.1-4.

6. Ibid., 1.11 (Pine-Coffin, 32).

7. Ibid., 3.3.

8. Ibid., 4.2 (Pine-Coffin, 72). For valuable perspectives on this aspect of Augustine's life, see O'Meara, *The Young Augustine*, 128-29, and Brown, *The Body and Society*, 387-95; for a survey on late Roman marriage, see Brown, "Late Antiquity," in *A History of Private Life* 1:297-311.

9. *Confessiones* 3.6-12. For an excellent overview of Manicheism and of Augustine's contact with it, see Bonner, *St. Augustine: Life and Controversies*, 58-71, 157-92.

10. *Confessiones* 4.2 and 5.12. See also his complaints about students in Carthage (5.8) and in Rome (5.12).

11. Ibid., 1.16 (Pine-Coffin, 36-37). On rhetorical education, see Henri Marrou, *Saint Augustin et la fin de la culture antique* (Paris: Bibliothéque des Écoles Françaises d'Athènes et de Rome, 1938); Marrou, *History of Education in Late Antiquity*, 194-205; Paul Veyne, "The Roman Empire," in *History of Private Life*, 1:19-23, 102.

subtleties of rhetorical style and phrasing as some today are of a concert pianist's virtuoso technique or of a guitarist's improvisational runs.

Augustine had won prizes for his oratory: first, as a student; later, in a competition in Carthage where the powerful proconsul crowned him victor.[12] While in Rome, he won an even more significant competition: he was chosen to be the teacher of rhetoric for Milan.[13] Since Milan was the seat of the imperial court, this appointment meant Augustine would be able to rub shoulders with the empire's elite. In fact, he received this appointment from one of most powerful of these: Symmachus, the pagan cousin and fierce political rival of Ambrose.[14]

In the Confessions, Augustine underplays this dramatic turn in his career and says instead: "To Milan, I came, to Ambrose the bishop."[15] That was how he viewed this pivotal moment years later—seeing his journey from the point of view of a Christian convert and bishop. But that would not have been his view at the time: he was still a Manichee (admittedly a disgruntled one) and had come to Milan as a protégé of Symmachus. However, as a matter of courtesy, he paid a visit to Ambrose, one of the city's preeminent and most powerful figures. To his surprise, he was warmly received:

"This man of God received me like a father and, as bishop, told me how glad he was that I had come. My heart warmed to him, not at first as a teacher of the truth, which I had quite despaired of finding in your Church, but simply as a man who showed me kindness."[16]

12. Confessiones 4.3.

13. Ibid., 5.13. On the significance of this appointment, see Brown, Augustine of Hippo, 69–71.

14. Confessiones 5.13. Symmachus may well have chosen Augustine precisely because he knew him to be a member of an anti-Catholic religious group. In the intricate politics of the empire's upper echelon, his choice would have been construed as a subtle snub of Ambrose, who had earlier blocked Symmachus's attempt to restore public funding of pagan cults. See Brown, Augustine of Hippo, 70; O'Meara, The Young Augustine, 92–93, 115.

15. Confessiones 5.13 (trans. O'Meara, Young Augustine, 116). O'Meara (117) notes how Augustine's retrospective perspective dominates this scene. See also Paula Fredriksen, "Paul and Augustine: conversion narratives, orthodox traditions, and the retrospective self," Journal of Theological Studies n.s. 37 (1986) 3–34.

16. Confessiones 5.13 (Pine-Coffin, 107).

After this initial meeting, Ambrose would touch Augustine through a more public medium: his sermons. (In fact, the two never became intimate, even after Augustine's baptism.)[17] Augustine says that he went every Sunday to the service of readings, psalms, and prayers that preceded the Eucharist (what later became known as the Mass of the Catechumens).[18] There he would have mixed in not only with the faithful and catechumens, but also with pagans and heretics of every stripe. These liturgies were sometimes noisy affairs. "What a job it is," Ambrose would complain, "to procure silence when the lessons are read."[19] After the readings, Ambrose would preach, probably at considerable length. This task, he believed, was essential to one who "sat at the helm" and had to "pilot" the Church in "stormy seas."[20] After the sermon, Augustine, together with all other unbaptized, would be dismissed. Only the faithful remained for Eucharist, for Ambrose, more than most, deeply respected the tradition of the *disciplina arcani*.[21]

Considerable effort has been expended to try to determine precisely what sermons Augustine heard. Courcelle, in an exhaustive study, claims that Augustine must have heard Ambrose's *Hexaemeron*, *On Isaac*, and *Death as a Good*.[22] However, Courcelle's claims

17. O'Meara, *The Young Augustine*, 116.

18. *Confessiones* 6.3; see also 5.13. For a summary of the structure and atmosphere of this service of the Word, see F. Homes Dudden, *The Life and Times of St. Ambrose* (Oxford: Clarendon Press, 1935) 2:447-48. Augustine may well have attended various Liturgies of the Hours as well; note that in *Confessiones* 8.12 he quotes Ambrose's *Deus Creator omnium* word for word, a hymn that was part of the Ambrosian *lucernarium* (the Vespers service); on the Liturgy of the Hours in Ambrose's church, see Homes Dudden, 2:442-46. Augustine clearly notes that his mother traditionally attended such services, "twice every day, each morning and evening" (6.9) and that she faithfully went to hear Ambrose when she arrived in Milan (6.1).

19. Ambrose, *Explanatio psalmi* 1.9 (trans. Homes Dudden, 2:447).

20. Ambrose, *Epistola* 2.1 (trans. Melchior Beyenka, FC 26:76).

21. Ambrose, *De mysteriis* 55; *De Cain et Abel* 1.37; *Expositio psalmi* 148 2.26-28. See also Homes Dudden, *Life and Times of St. Ambrose*, 2:453-54.

22. Courcelle, *Recherches sur les Confessions*, 93-138. Courcelle's focus on these is tied to his basic thesis: that Augustine never went through a "neo-Platonist" phase; instead he first encountered the neo-Platonism of Plotinus and Porphyry in the sermons of Ambrose; in other words, he found in Ambrose's sermons a ready-made synthesis of Christianity and neo-Platonism. For an assessment of this, see below. When Courcelle described *De Isaac uel anima* as a series of sermons, he moved against the scholarly view of his time.

have been seriously disputed.[23] As Brown notes, "It is impossible to date Ambrose's surviving sermons (a small proportion of those he actually preached) with sufficient certainty."[24] But as O'Meara points out, it is not necessary to determine the exact sermons "since almost any of Ambrose's explanations of the Old Testament would illustrate that method of his which so appealed to Augustine."[25]

At first, Augustine listened to these sermons for merely professional reasons—to see if Ambrose measured up to his reputation as a rhetorician:

"My purpose was to judge for myself whether the reports of his powers as a speaker were accurate, or whether eloquence flowed from him more or less readily. So while I paid the closest attention to the words he used, I was quite uninterested in the subject-matter and was even contemptuous of it."[26]

Ambrose consciously cultivated a polished style. In a letter to a new bishop, he once advised: "Let your sermons be flowing, let them be clear and lucid so that by suitable disputation you may pour sweetness into the ears of the people."[27] The sweet flow of Ambrose's own sermons affected Augustine in ways he could not have foreseen:

"For although I did not trouble to take what Ambrose said to heart, but only to listen to the manner in which he said it . . .

On this point, scholars now apparently accept his view; e.g., Brown, *Augustine of Hippo*, 126.

23. For a review of Courcelle's *Recherches sur les Confessions*, see Christine Mohrmann, in *Vigiliae Christianae* 5 (1951) 249–54; W. Theiler, *Gnomon* 25 (1953) 113–22. Mohrmann notes that it is impossible to date these Ambrose sermons with such precision. Theiler argues that Ambrose absorbed a "stock-in-trade" Platonism from his basic sources—Origen, Basil, Gregory of Nyssa—and that there is no reason to dispute the traditional view of Ambrose's basic opposition to "philosophy." O'Meara, *The Young Augustine*, 14–18 and 118–19, gives an excellent summary of the strengths and weaknesses of Courcelle's key theses. Brown, *Augustine of Hippo*, 126 note 1, concludes that Courcelle successfully demonstrates the Plotinian influence on these particular sermons; what he sees as uncertain is the dating. On this point, Courcelle's essential thesis stands or falls.

24. Brown, *Augustine of Hippo*, 86.

25. O'Meara, *The Young Augustine*, 118.

26. *Confessiones* 5.13 (Pine-Coffin, 107).

27. Ambrose, *Epistola* 2.5 (Beyenka, 78).

nevertheless his meaning, which I tried to ignore, found its way into my mind together with his words, which I admired so much. I could not keep the two apart, and while I was all ears to seize upon the eloquence, I also began to sense the truth of what he said, though only gradually."[28]

As we read Ambrose's sermons today, we too are liable to be impressed. In the *Hexaemeron*, for instance, he would catalogue the marvels of creation with the eye and ear of a poet: "the surging white caps" and "rhythmic wave-beats" of the ocean; "the islands which adorn the seas like jeweled necklaces"; the tricks crabs play to hunt oysters.[29] We are also likely to be drawn to Ambrose's prophetic side:

"Do your spacious reception-rooms fill you with pride? They ought rather to fill you with compunction, for though they take in whole peoples, they shut out the voice of the poor. . . . You adorn your walls, but strip people down. A naked man cries in front of your house, and you are engrossed in choosing marble to adorn your floors. . . . People weep bitterly, and you finger your jeweled goblet. Wretch, you who have the power of rescuing so many souls from death, but lack the will! The gem in your finger might have saved the life of a whole people."[30]

What impressed Augustine, however, were quite different matters. First, he was struck by Ambrose's learned manner.[31] Ambrose, unlike Augustine, read Greek fluently. Thus, as Brown notes, Ambrose "could comb the books of a brilliant new generation of Greek bishops and a whole tradition of Greek Christian scholarship, to give his congregation some of the most learned and up-to-date sermons in the Latin world."[32] He would quite literally ransack the sermons of Origen and the Cappadocians for his material, sometimes translating, sometimes paraphrasing,

28. *Confessiones* 5.14 (Pine-Coffin, 108).

29. Ambrose, *Exaemeron* 3.5.21; 3.5.23; 5.8.22 (trans. John J. Savage, FC 42:73–74, 177). On themes in Ambrose's preaching, see Homes Dudden, *Life and Times of St. Ambrose* 2:461–76 and Angelo Paredi, *Saint Ambrose: His Life and Times* (Notre Dame: University of Notre Dame Press, 1964) 257–77.

30. Ambrose, *De Nabuthe Iezraelita* 56 (trans. Homes Dudden, 2:467–68—altered).

31. *Confessiones* 5.13.

32. Brown, *Augustine of Hippo*, 83.

sometimes expanding, sometimes condensing.[33] Some scholars see in this a lack of originality. But that is to judge Ambrose by a single standard: theological creativity. It would be more accurate to say that he invested his creativity elsewhere, that is, in teaching, and that he was what all good teachers are: a creative and discriminating popularist. As such, he kept his hearers abreast of the best scholarship he knew.

Second, Augustine was struck by Ambrose's use of allegorical exegesis. With this method Ambrose figuratively explained one passage after another from the Old Testament, teasing out "their spiritual meaning," and in so doing "vindicated . . . passages [which] had been death to me when I took them literally."[34] As time went on, this had a telling effect:

"Every Sunday I listened as he preached the word of truth to the people and I grew more and more certain that it was possible to unravel the tangle woven by those who had deceived both me and others with their cunning lies against the Holy Scriptures. . . . I was pleased to hear that in his sermons to the people Ambrose often repeated the text: 'The written law inflicts death, whereas the spiritual law brings life' [2 Cor 3:6], as though this were a rule upon which he wished to insist most carefully. And when he lifted the veil of mystery and disclosed the spiritual meaning of texts which, taken literally, appeared to contain the most unlikely doctrines, I was not aggrieved by what he said. . . ."[35]

Ambrose had picked up this allegorical method from Origen (and the Jewish exegete Philo), and used it for a combination of theological, apologetic, and pedagogical reasons.[36] Like Origen, he would take care to reinterpret any passages which portrayed God in anthropomorphic terms or which described morally reprehensible behavior among the Patriarchs. Like Origen, Ambrose used allegory to safeguard the unity of the Testaments while at the

33. M. J. Buck, "Introduction," in Ambrose, De Helia et ieiunio, PS 19:7.
34. Confessiones 5.14.
35. Ibid., 6.3 and 4 (Pine-Coffin, 114–16). See also Augustine's autobiographical comments in De utilitate credendi 8.20.
36. For an excellent treatment of Origen's allegorical methods, see Henri Crouzel, Origen, trans. A. S. Worrall (San Francisco: Harper & Row, 1989) 61–84; also Trigg, Origen, 120–28 and 172–200. On Ambrose's use of allegory, see Homes Dudden, Life and Times of St. Ambrose 2:457–59.

same time insisting that the Old Testament was only a type and shadow of Christ and the Church. Ambrose apparently preferred to preach on the Old Testament, partly because it posed difficulties for his hearers, partly because the better commentaries at his disposal treated Old Testament books, and partly because the allegorical method delighted both him and his hearers. Generally he gave his sermons in series which focused on a single Old Testament figure: Job, Isaac, Jacob, Joseph, David. In his hands they appeared, as Brown notes, like "a stately procession of authentic 'philosophers,' each one symbolizing the state of a soul purified by wisdom."[37]

Ambrose typically distinguished three levels of meaning: "All divine scripture is either natural or moral or mystical."[38] By "natural," he meant a passage's literal meaning; by "moral," its import for daily life; by "mystical," its foreshadowing of the "mysteries" (Christ, the kingdom, the Church). Sometimes in explaining passages, he would modulate rapidly between these various layers.[39] In other words, for Ambrose, the scriptural word was polyphonic, a cluster of hidden voices and subtle counterpoint. As interpreter, his task was to draw these out—much as a musicologist or a conductor might do. Moreover, Ambrose presumed that every word, every detail, no matter how trivial it seemed, held religious and moral significance. So he would focus on the symbolism of numbers or on the etymology of names—a practice that Augustine would later imitate to great effect. Beneath this was Ambrose's sense that the scriptural word—God's word incarnated in human speech—had untold depths and astonishing density:

"Holy Scripture is a sea which has within it profound meanings and the mysterious depths of the Prophets. Into this sea many rivers have entered. Delightful and clear are these streams; these fountains are cool, springing up into life everlasting; there, too, are pleasant words, like honey-comb, and courteous conversation which water souls with the sweetness of moral commands."[40]

Ambrose's awe for the enigmas of Scripture rubbed off on Augustine who would make this a mainstay of his own catechesis.

37. Brown, *Augustine of Hippo*, 84.
38. Ambrose, *Explanatio psalmi 36* 1 (trans. my own).
39. For example, *De Isaac uel anima*, esp. 4.23–31.
40. Ambrose, *Epistola* 2.3 (Beyenka, 77–78).

There was one final feature of Ambrose's preaching that impressed Augustine: the neo-Platonic metaphysics. In an early work, *The Blessed Life,* Augustine wrote to a fellow Christian Platonist, Manlius Theodorus: "I have noticed frequently in the sermons of our bishop . . . that when speaking of God, no one should think of Him as something corporeal; nor yet of the soul, for of all things the soul is nearest to God."[41] Ambrose may have absorbed a Platonic strain from his Christian sources like Origen and the Cappadocians.[42] Also, sometime in his career (exactly when is a matter of dispute), he appropriated the thought of two pagan neo-Platonists: Plotinus and Porphyry.[43] In his sermons, Ambrose would treat their works the same way he treated his Christian sources: sometimes lifting whole passages from them, other times subtly altering them.[44] Neo-Platonism, no doubt, appealed to Ambrose's ascetical and otherworldly bent. It also offered him a potent antidote to Manichean attacks on Christianity. The Manichees, it seems, enjoyed poking fun at the supposedly crude Christian conception of God. They would claim: since Catholics believed that human beings were "made in the image and likeness" of God (Gen 1:26), then Catholics therefore believed that God, like human beings, had a body. Educated ancients would have found this a potent argument and could be, as Augustine was, taken in by it.[45] Ambrose, for his part, was conscious of such arguments and repeatedly insisted that Christians held no such view: that the Genesis passage had to be taken figuratively; that only the soul was made in the image and likeness of God.[46] Ambrose's counter-argument apparently had its in-

41. *De beata vita* 1.4 (trans. Ludwig Schopp, FC 1:47–48).

42. O'Meara, *The Young Augustine,* 119 note 2.

43. Courcelle, *Recherches sur les Confessions,* esp. 106–20, establishes Ambrose's dependence on Plotinus. See note 23 above on the problems of dating the relevant sermons.

44. Brown, *Augustine of Hippo,* 95, 126–27.

45. Celsus attacks Genesis 1, especially 1:26, on grounds similar to those given by the Manichees—stressing how crudely anthropomorphic the Christian conception of God was. See his comments quoted in Origen, *Contra Celsum* 6.60–81; 7.62.

46. Courcelle, *Recherches sur les Confessions,* 98–103, has unearthed examples of this polemic in Ambrose's extant works. For example, in *Exaemeron* 3.32, Ambrose explicitly mentions the Manichees and their objections; in *Exaemeron* 6.40–46, Ambrose gives a lengthy commentary on Genesis 1:26 detailing precisely the points which so struck Augustine.

tended affect on Augustine, for he admitted how surprised he was to find that Christians "did not teach the doctrines which I so sternly denounced" and that they "had no liking for childish absurdities."[47]

Initially these sermons moved Augustine in small, but significant ways. First, he resolved to sever his ties with the Manichees. Second, he decided to adopt a watch-and-see attitude—suspending himself between belief and disbelief after the fashion of the philosophers of the New Academy. Finally, he resolved "to remain a catechumen in the Catholic Church . . . at least until I could clearly see a light to guide my steps."[48] As O'Meara has noted, this final decision "has been very much underestimated by biographers."[49] This was a decision affected in large measure by Ambrose's pedagogical aptitude, for he had done for Augustine what teachers must often do: debunk false preconceptions and offer an intellectually credible alternative.

Still Augustine remained an ambitious man: "I was eager for fame and wealth and marriage."[50] He knew that enormous success lay within his grasp: "I have many influential friends, and if I press for nothing more, I may at least obtain a governor's post."[51] Meanwhile, his mother had arrived and had begun playing matchmaker. She soon secured her talented son an acceptable marriage prospect: a wealthy Catholic heiress who would bring him a good dowry.[52] This also meant that the lower-class woman he had been living with had to be dismissed.[53] In other words, Augustine the catechumen must have appeared, to a man like

47. *Confessiones* 6.4 (Pine-Coffin, 115).

48. Ibid., 5.14 (Pine-Coffin, 109). The same comment is found in *De utilitate credendi* 8.20, a work written soon after his conversion.

49. O'Meara, *The Young Augustine*, 121.

50. *Confessiones* 6.6 (Pine-Coffin, 118). For an analysis of Augustine's social ambitions, see O'Meara, *The Young Augustine*, 126–30.

51. Ibid., 6.11 (Pine-Coffin, 127).

52. Ibid., 6.13.

53. Ibid., 6.15 (Pine-Coffin, 131). Brown, *Augustine of Hippo*, 88–90, sets this episode in the social context of the time, noting how extraordinary it was that Augustine even mentions the woman he lived with, let alone how pained he was by the experience. Ambrose, in *De Abraham* 1.3, offers some quite harsh views on such affairs between social unequals; Augustine—who is unusually touchy about sexuality—has more lenient views (given his time, not ours): in *De bono coniugale* 5.5, he allows that such living-together can constitute a legitimate marriage, if the couples are faithful; in *De fide et operibus* 35, he allows a

Ambrose, as the typical political opportunist—exactly the sort Ambrose denounced in no uncertain terms:

"Many, for the sake of having a wife, have faked faith for a time, but are shown to have denied inside what they confessed outside. . . . [And] here comes one to Church looking for honors under the Christian emperors; with a counterfeit reverence he feigns requesting [baptism]; he bows, he prostrates himself, but has not bent the knee of his heart."[54]

Augustine may well have heard such denunciations. He also may have heard Ambrose's exhortations to catechumens. Like the Cappadocians, Ambrose used the feast of Epiphany as a time to rally the catechumens, to induce them to turn in their names.[55] His campaigns, however, did not always meet with success. Once, in a sermon soon after Epiphany, Ambrose noted that the apostles had once spent a whole night fishing and, despite their work, had come up empty-handed; he then remarked that "No one has given in his name; it is still night for me. I cast the net of the Word at Epiphany, but I have caught nothing."[56] Could Augustine have been roused by such calls? Perhaps—for one finds him at a crucial juncture meditating on his own delays: "Time was passing and I kept delaying my conversion to you, my God. Day after day I postponed living in you, but I never put off the death which I died each day in myself."[57]

Augustine's movement from being a politic catechumen to a catechumen in earnest was slow. The factors, as he records them and as his biographers show, were varied and complex. They included: conversations with friends; pressure from his mother; a weariness with teaching and ambitious pursuits; his discovery of neo-Platonist books; his reading of St. Paul; his own restless interior meditation on matters philosophical and practical; even a potent religious experience.[58] These factors, so essential to his con-

woman who has been dismissed by her lover to be a suitable candidate for baptism.

54. Ambrose, *Expositio psalmi 148*, Sermon 20.48–49 (trans. my own).

55. Homes Dudden, *Life and Times of St. Ambrose* 1:336; Leonel Mitchell, "Ambrosian Baptismal Rites," *Studia Liturgica* 1 (1962) 242.

56. Ambrose, *Expositio evangelii secundum Lucam* 4.76 (trans. my own).

57. *Confessiones* 6.11 (Pine-Coffin, 128).

58. Ibid., 6.7–7.21.

version, subtly mixed with and filtered the formation he, as a catechumen, was slowly gaining from Ambrose's sermons. In other words, the ordinary catechesis he received, while crucial, was only one strand among many and, in all probability, not the most decisive.

At a crucial juncture, however, Augustine received a potent catechetical lesson. It came, not from a public sermon by Ambrose, but rather from a private interview with Simplicianus, an elderly presbyter whom Ambrose revered as a "spiritual father" (presumably, because he had catechized Ambrose).[59] Augustine approached Simplicianus and laid bare the driftings of his journey. In the course of their conversation, Augustine mentioned reading some philosophical treatises translated into Latin by Victorinus. Simplicianus seized on this. He explained that he had known Victorinus personally and had played a role in his conversion:

"Victorinus . . . had read the Holy Scriptures . . . and made the most painstaking and careful study of all Christian literature. Privately as between friends, though never in public, he used to say to Simplicianus, 'I want you to know that I am now a Christian.' Simplicianus used to reply, 'I shall not believe it or count you as a Christian until I see you in the Church of Christ.' At this Victorinus would laugh and say, 'Is it then the walls of the church that make the Christian?' He often repeated his claim to be a Christian, and each time Simplicianus gave the same answer, only to receive the same rejoinder about the walls."[60]

One day Victorinus was moved by a powerful fear: that Christ would denounce him at the Last Judgment. Soon after he approached Simplicianus for baptism. He was then "instructed in the first mysteries of the faith" and "gave in his name to be reborn through baptism." The climax of the story, as Augustine recounts it, was Victorinus's formal profession of faith at the *redditio symboli* (the rite of handing back the Creed):

"At Rome those who are about to enter into your grace [O God] usually make their profession in a set form of words which they

59. Ibid., 8.1 and 2.
60. Ibid., 8.2 (Pine-Coffin, 160). Rufinus also notes the prominence of this ceremony within the Roman rite of initiation; see his *Expositio symboli* 3.

learn by heart and recite from a raised platform in view of the faithful. . . . [Victorinus turned down an offer to recite it privately, saying he] preferred to declare his salvation in full sight of the assembled faithful. For there was no salvation in the rhetoric which he taught, and yet had professed it in public. . . . So when he mounted the platform to make his profession, all who knew him joyfully whispered his name to their neighbors. There can have been none who did not know him, and the hushed voices of the whole exultant congregation joined in the murmur, 'Victorinus, Victorinus.' They were quick to let their joy be heard when they saw him, but just as quickly came a hush as they waited to hear him speak. He made his declaration of the true faith with splendid confidence, and all would gladly have seized him in their arms and clutched him to their hearts."[61]

The story moved Augustine powerfully: "I began to glow with fervor to imitate him; this, of course, was why Simplicianus had told it to me."[62] Simplicianus had indeed chosen his catechetical lesson carefully, for Augustine and Victorinus had much in common: both were Africans; both, rhetoricians; both had come to Italy to earn fame and fortune; and both held powerful public positions. Simplicianus added that Victorinus had retired from public life once Julian the Apostate had banned Christians from holding such prestigious teaching posts. The moral was clear: throw off all delay; profess the Christian faith; remember the Last Judgment; abandon ambition, even at the cost of retirement.

Within a few months, Augustine would act on this advice, but not before a Christian friend, Ponticianus, told him other dramatic stories of converts: of Anthony the Egyptian peasant who had sold all he had and became a hermit in the desert; and of two imperial officials who, moved by the story of Anthony, decided to imitate him. Augustine too was moved. The rest of the story—the inner turmoil, his wandering into a garden, the tears, the mysterious voice of a child, the refrain of "*tolle, lege,*" the reading from St. Paul—was grace.[63]

61. *Confessiones* 8.2 (Pine-Coffin, 160–61).
62. Ibid., 8.5 (Pine-Coffin, 164).
63. Courcelle, *Recherches sur les Confessions*, 188–202, has raised a number of questions regarding the historicity of this scene; he demonstrates a number of literary techniques and allusions at work in Augustine's account (doublets;

During early autumn of 386, Augustine wrote to Ambrose and petitioned for baptism. He also asked for advice: to find "which books of Scripture it would be best to study, so that I might be better prepared and more fitted to receive so great a grace."[64] Ambrose wrote back and suggested the Book of Isaiah. However, he misdiagnosed the catechetical needs of his advisee: Augustine found the opening chapters unintelligible and soon laid it aside.

In the *Confessions*, Augustine passes over his final preparation for baptism in a few sentences: "When the time came for me to hand in my name for baptism, we left the country and went back to Milan." He adds that Adeodatus, his fifteen-year-old son, and Alypius, his closest friend, joined him: "Together we were ready to begin our schooling in your ways."[65] Augustine makes no mention in the *Confessions* of what this "schooling" involved. However, in an early work, *The Greatness of the Soul*, he remembers, and can quote word for word, what he learned of the Christian doctrine of God and of right worship (and its correlative—the rejection of polytheism and idolatry):

"It has been the divinely inspired and categorical teaching of the Catholic Church that no creature is to be adored by the soul (I prefer to use the very words by which these things were taught to me), but that he alone is to be adored who is the Creator of all things that are, from whom all things come, by whom all things are made, in whom all things exist. . . ."[66]

Here Augustine seems to be citing Ambrose's instruction on the Creed (the *traditio symboli*), and was able, probably because of the rhythmic parallelism, to memorize the phrase easily. Also, in another treatise, *On Faith and Works*, Augustine mentions the high-pitched excitement he felt:

---

echoes of the story of Heracles's choice between Virtue and Pleasure; echoes of Plotinus). O'Meara, *The Young Augustine*, 178–84, has offered a strong defense of the scene's substantial historicity, while acknowledging Augustine's literary artistry at work in its portrayal; see also Bonner, *St. Augustine: Life and Controversies*, 91 note 5, for a critique of Courcelle's position.

64. *Confessiones* 9.5 (Pine-Coffin, 188).
65. Ibid., 9.6 (Pine-Coffin, 190).
66. *De quantitate animae* 34.77 (trans. Joseph M. Colleran, ACW 9:106).

"Do we silence the testimony of our own experience, do we go so far as to forget how intent, how anxious, we were over what the catechists taught us when we were petitioning for the sacrament of the font—and for that very reason were called *'competentes'* "?[67]

To learn more about Lenten formation in Milan, we must turn to other sources. First, according to Ambrose's deacon and biographer Paulinus, Ambrose himself handled the instruction of the petitioners (*competentes*).[68] These Lenten instructions were one part of a worship service that also included readings and psalms and that was held twice daily, Monday through Friday, at the third and ninth hours.[69] Ambrose, unlike Cyril and Theodore, did not use the Creed as his Lenten syllabus. In fact, as we shall see, he gave only a single instruction on it. Rather he used the same curriculum he used on Sundays: sermons, often in series, focused on exemplary Old Testament figures or books.[70] In his *On the Mysteries*, Ambrose (belatedly) explained to the neophytes the rationale that had guided his Lenten pedagogy:

"We have given a daily sermon on morals, when the deeds of the Patriarchs or the precepts of the Proverbs were read, in order that, being informed and instructed by them, you might become accustomed to enter upon the ways of our forefathers and to pursue their road, and to obey the divine commands, whereby renewed by baptism you might hold to the manner of life which befits those who are washed."[71]

In other words, Ambrose saw Lent as a time for moral education. He was, of course, concerned that the *competentes* had orthodox views, but that apparently was not his focus—at least to the degree that it was for Cyril and Theodore. Moreover, he recognized that in order to learn this way of life, the *competentes* needed two

67. *De fide et operibus* 6.9 (trans. my own).

68. Paulinus, *Vita sancti Ambrosii* 38.

69. Leonel Mitchell, "Ambrosian Baptismal Rites," 242, calls this service a "pro-anaphora." Homes Dudden, *Life and Times of St. Ambrose* 1:337, uses the term *missa catechumenorum* (but this latter term dates from a period later than Ambrose).

70. On Ambrose's Lenten catechesis, see Homes Dudden, *Life and Times of St. Ambrose* 2:682–83. Ambrose's *De Abraham* (book 1 only), *De Helia et ieiunio*, *Explanatio psalmi 36–40* are three extant examples. I will survey *De Helia* below.

71. Ambrose, *De mysteriis* 1 (trans. Roy J. Deferrari, FC 44:5).

things: (1) appropriate models to imitate, and (2) basic moral principles. For both, he turned to the Scriptures: the Patriarchs provided the models, while Proverbs provided the moral principles. Moreover, both could be given in an easy-to-remember medium: story (the Patriarchs) and aphorism (Proverbs).

To get a sense of this, let us examine Ambrose's *On Elijah and Fasting*. This sermon (or sermons) was delivered at the beginning of Lent, sometime between 387–390 (meaning that it is possible that Augustine actually heard it). On this occasion, Ambrose inaugurated Lent by exhorting the whole assembly—faithful, catechumens, and *competentes*—to adopt a proper fast. First he set out Elijah as a model of true fasting and listed the benefits that Elijah enjoyed from his forty-day fast—and that, by implication, his hearers, especially the *competentes*, would also enjoy: Elijah "raised the widow's son from the dead" (just as the *competentes* would rise from the dead at baptism); "he drew down fire from heaven" (just as the *competentes* would draw down the fire of the Spirit); "while fasting he was snatched in a chariot to heaven and . . . gained the presence of God" (just as the *competentes* would be swept, after baptism, into the presence of heavenly mysteries).[72]

After extolling the benefits of fasting, Ambrose entertained his audience by lampooning the feasting and drinking habits of the Milanese elite. He described, for example, a steward from a wealthy household who would frantically comb the markets for the finest wines, oysters, and pheasant; a rich man's kitchen which resembled a slaughterhouse where "a battle was being fought, not a dinner being prepared"; a mock military funeral in which drunken soldiers were carried out on their shields.[73] He then set Christian ideals in stark contrast by quoting Isaiah 58: that one should distribute "bread to the hungry and bring the needy and harborless into your house," that "if you see one naked, cover him."[74] For Ambrose, true fasting was inseparable from the work of justice.

Ambrose directed his closing remarks to the *competentes*. He compared them to wrestlers and insisted that, like all such athletes, they were to follow a rigorous discipline: train daily; adhere to a strict diet; and—interestingly—abstain from sex. He

72. Ambrose, *De Helia et ieiunio* 2.2 (Buck, 47).
73. Ibid., 8.24–25; 13.50 (Buck, 61, 81).
74. Ibid., 10.34 (Buck, 67–69).

admitted the discipline was hard, but encouraged them to perse-vere: "When you have come into the wrestling place, . . . the heat is severe, but the victory is sweet."[75]

Sometime during Lent, *competentes* went through an exorcism (or exorcisms), what Ambrose called "the mysteries of the scrutinies." Unfortunately, he gives no specifics about the rite, except that, interestingly, it included a physical examination: "There was a search—lest anything unclean still cling to the body of anyone of you. Using exorcism we sought and brought about a sanctifying not only of your body, but of your soul as well."[76]

On the Sunday before Easter, after the readings and dismissal of the catechumens, Ambrose and the *competentes* would retire to the baptistery. There he would personally deliver the Creed to them and give a brief instruction on it.[77] We can discern something of what Augustine may have heard by looking at Ambrose's *Explana-tion of the Symbol*, a sermon delivered sometime in the late 380s or early 390s. At the outset Ambrose announced the reason for this special instruction: "It is now the time and the day for us to hand over the Symbol: a Symbol which is a spiritual seal, a Symbol which is our heart's meditation and, as it were, an ever-present guard, a treasure within our breast."[78] Here Ambrose touches in rapid succession upon images and themes that would run through the address: that the Creed was something precious; that it had to be interiorized; that it guarded one against error. Ambrose then used an analogy from fourth-century finance to explain the mean-ing of the Greek term *symbolum* to his Latin-speaking audience:

"First then we must have an explanation of the name itself. *Sym-bolum* is a Greek word which in Latin means 'contribution.' Busi-ness people especially are used to speaking of their *symbola* when they contribute their money, which—when it is lumped together, so to speak, into one sum from their individual contributions—is kept whole and inviolable, so that no one may attempt any fraud, neither with the sum contributed nor in his business dealings.

75. Ibid., 21.79 (Buck, 103–5).
76. Ambrose, *Explanatio symboli* 1 (trans. my own). For the text and a trans-lation, see the edition by R. H. Connolly, Text and Studies 10 (Cambridge: Cambridge University Press, 1952).
77. Ambrose, *Epistola* 20.4.
78. Ambrose, *Explanatio symboli* 1 (trans. my own).

Finally, among such business people this is the custom: that if anyone has committed fraud, he is tossed out as a cheat."[79]

This analogy may rely on a suspicious confusion of Greek terms— *symbolum* ("password," "token") with *symbola* ("contribution"), but it is a fine pedagogical device. It apparently impressed Augustine, for he would later use it to emphasize that the Creed committed the *competentes* to a shared venture. Ambrose's accent, however, was more ominous: to warn the *competentes* that credal fraud resulted in expulsion from the community. This analogy also allowed him to introduce a popular legend—that the Creed had been a joint composition of the twelve apostles: "The holy Apostles gathered as one and made a brief summary of the faith, so that it might always be held in memory and be remembered."[80]

After this, Ambrose had his hearers sign themselves with the Sign of the Cross. He then recited the Creed, first alone, then once more with the *competentes* joining him—apparently to impress its wording on their memory. Interestingly, in neither instance did the stenographer who recorded this address give the actual wording of the Creed, so much was its secrecy respected.[81]

Ambrose then explained the Creed phrase by phrase. He stressed the orthodox view of Trinity, that theological synthesis which had been forged by the Cappadocians he so admired and which had been ratified just a few years before at the Council of Constantinople: "We are to believe equally and alike in the Father and the Son and the Holy Spirit. For where there is no distinction in majesty, neither should there be any distinction in our belief."[82]

The address also displays Ambrose's pedagogical aptitude. For instance, he picked up the story of the Creed's joint composition and with it suggested a mnemonic device to aid memorization:

79. Ibid., 2 (Connolly, 19-20—altered). Connolly (19 note 4): "The apparent confusion of *symbolum*, a token or watchword, with *symbola*, a money contribution, found also in Rufinus and Cassian, was doubtless motivated by the tradition that the Symbol was a joint composition of the twelve Apostles." See Rufinus, *Expositio symboli* 2; Kelly gives a fine discussion of this in *Early Christian Creeds*, 52-61.

80. Ambrose, *Explanatio symboli* 3 (trans. my own). The legend is given in fuller form in Rufinus, *Expositio symboli* 2; see also Kelly, *Early Christian Creeds*, 1-6.

81. See the scribal notes in *Explanatio symboli* 4 and 5.

82. Ambrose, *Explanatio symboli* 4 (Connolly, 20).

"For just as there are twelve Apostles, so are there twelve phrases."[83] To make this clear, he broke down its constituents into groups of four: (1) Father, Son, incarnation, death/burial; (2) resurrection, ascension, seating at the right hand, judging the living and dead; (3) Spirit, Church, remission of sins, resurrection of the body.[84]

At the end, Ambrose stressed that the Creed should not be written down and that the *competentes* should say it over every day. In this way, they would enjoy its power to ward off shocks to mind and body and to shield one from demonic temptation.[85] Finally, he asked them to recite it silently so that no catechumen would hear it. We need to remember that ancients both read and prayed out loud; Ambrose, on the other hand, read silently—a habit unusual enough to merit remarks by Augustine.[86] Here he would recommend what must have seemed equally surprising: to pray silently.

AUGUSTINE THE NEOPHYTE

At the Easter Vigil, the night of 24–25 April 387, Augustine was baptized. In the *Confessions*, he touches on this event only briefly. He mentions nothing of the ceremonial, but only the stirrings of his heart:

"We were baptized, and all anxiety over the past melted away from us. The days were all too short, for I was lost in wonder and joy, meditating upon your far-reaching providence for the salvation of the human race. The tears flowed from me when I heard your hymns and canticles, for the sweet singing of your Church moved me deeply. The music surged in my ears, truth seeped into my heart, and my feelings of devotion overflowed, so that the tears streamed down. But they were tears of gladness."[87]

83. Ibid., 11 (trans. my own).
84. Ibid. It is somewhat difficult to discern precisely how these groups of four break down because the text is rather corrupt at this point.
85. Ibid., 12 (Connolly, 26–27). See also Rufinus, *Expositio symboli* 2.
86. *Confessiones* 6.3.
87. Ibid., 9.6 (Pine-Coffin, 190). Interestingly, Augustine makes no mention in the *Confessions* that it was Ambrose himself who baptized him (though such silences are almost characteristic of this work). He does, however, mention it explicitly in *Epistola* 147.52.

This interior perspective is, of course, a hallmark of the *Confessions*, but Augustine's reticence here may also have come from his deep respect for the *disciplina arcani*. He does, however, emphasize how much the music moved him. Ambrose, it seems, had recently introduced Eastern-style antiphonal chants into his Church's worship, leaving his congregation enthralled by their exotic melodies.[88] In fact, the effect was so notable that Ambrose's opponents accused him of "bewitching" his congregation; he did not deny it, but attributed the power of such hymns to their Trinitarian lyrics by which "all have become teachers, who were scarcely able to be learners."[89] The year before, Ambrose had even used these hymns as a political instrument: when the Arian empress Justina had sent troops to take possession of his basilica, he had the people chant so as to revive their flagging spirits through the long sit-in protest.[90] These chants would haunt Augustine not only at his baptism, but long after. The words of one, "Deus Creator omnium," a Vespers hymn composed by Ambrose himself, would well up in Augustine's memory on the night after his mother's death. As Augustine lay in bed sleeplessly, he suddenly tasted the truth of its words: "that sleep may restore wearied limbs, . . . soothe the careworn breast and lull our anxious griefs to rest."[91] He saw in retrospect how, at this moment and at his baptism, such hymns had subtly catechized him. Not surprisingly, Augustine would follow Ambrose's lead and make music a favorite catechetical tool.

During Easter Week, Augustine and his companions would have continued to wear their baptismal robes and gather each day to hear Ambrose's talks on the sacraments. We can discern something of what they may have heard from Ambrose's two sets of mystagogical catecheses: *The Sacraments* and *The Mysteries*. The first is a series of six sermons delivered during Easter Week; these were probably recorded by a shorthand stenographer (*notarius*)

88. *Confessiones* 9.7.

89. Ambrose, *Sermo contra Auxentium* 34 (trans. Homes Dudden 1:294). For a discussion of Ambrose's hymns, see Homes Dudden, *Life and Times of St. Ambrose* 1:293–97.

90. *Confessiones* 9.7 (Pine-Coffin, 191). For Ambrose's account of this event, see *Epistola* 20, to his sister Marcellina; for a detailed study, see Homes Dudden, *Life and Times of St. Ambrose* 1:270–93.

91. *Confessiones* 9.12 (Pine-Coffin, 202).

and published without any revision by Ambrose.[92] The second is a similar series; however, Ambrose probably re-edited it for public consumption and thus alludes only obliquely to many details of the rites (e.g., using scriptural references) so as to protect their secrecy. Apparently these talks took place within a liturgical setting, for on several occasions Ambrose alludes to the readings they had just gone over.[93] If the later Ambrosian Rite is any indication, these were held during daily Eucharistic services reserved especially for the neophytes.[94]

Ambrose's mystagogical works display many of the trends cited earlier, though in a configuration unique to his milieu, temperament, theology, and rite. First, Ambrose shared Cyril's philosophy on the timing of such catechesis: that the sacraments could be discussed only *after* initiation. Ambrose gave two reasons: first, to speak to the uninitiated about the sacraments would be to "betray" rather than "portray" them; second, the rites themselves had an inherent pedagogy, not so much in the visible play of symbols as in the inner light which "infuses itself better in the unsuspecting."[95] Also, like Cyril, Ambrose used the liturgical rites to organize the sequence of topics. For instance, in *The Sacraments*, he devotes sermons 1–3 to the baptismal liturgy; 4–5 to the Eucharistic liturgy; he also adds an instruction on personal prayer (6). (See chart 6).

92. Homes Dudden, *Life and Times of St. Ambrose* 2:705-7, following an earlier view, considered their Ambrosian authorship as questionable. However, Otto Faller, in his preface to CSEL 70, has strongly defended their Ambrosian authorship. Scholars now regard them as authentic. See Deferrari, "Introduction," FC 44:265-67; and Botte, "Introduction," SC 25:7-24. These sermons retain all the earmarks of a dynamic oral Latin; see Christine Mohrmann, "Le style oral du *De sacramentis* de saint Ambroise," *Vigiliae Christianae* 6 (1952) 168-77. Other helpful discussions of these mystagogical works include: Mohrmann, "Observations sur le *De sacramentis* et le *De mysteriis* de saint Ambroise," *Ambrosius Episcopus* (Milano: Universitá Cattolica del Sacro Cuore, 1976) 103-23; Edward J. Yarnold, "The Ceremonies of Initiation in the *De Sacramentis* and *De Mysteriis* of St. Ambrose," *Studia Patristica* 10 ed. F. L. Cross (Berlin: Akademie-Verlag, 1970) 453-63.

93. For example, *De sacramentis* 2.3; *De mysteriis* 16. For a discussion of the links between these instructions and the readings found in later Ambrosian lectionaries, see Botte, "Introduction," 30-31.

94. Homes Dudden, *Life and Times of St. Ambrose* 1:341.

95. Ambrose, *De mysteriis* 2 (trans. Deferrari, FC 44:5).

When speaking of the rites, Ambrose stressed not their sensuousness—something that tends to impress us—but their inner dynamic: the invisible action of God. For instance, he repeated a theme found in Tertullian—the disappointment of candidates on seeing the font—and gave it a Platonic twist:

"You entered; you saw the water. . . . Lest, perchance, someone say: 'Is that all?'—yes, this is all, truly, where there is all innocence, where there is all piety, all grace, all sanctification. You have seen what you were able to see with the eyes of the body, with human perception; you have not seen those things which were effected but those which are seen. Those which are not seen are much greater than those which are seen."[96]

Elsewhere, he used an epigram with a chiastic rhyme scheme to drive home his point on the play of visible and invisible:

Uidisti	You see
aquam,	the water,
sed non aqua omnis sanat,	but not all water heals;
sed aqua sanat	but water heals
quae habit gratiam	that has the grace
Christi.	of Christ.
Aliud est elementum,	One is an element,
aliud consecratio,	the other, a consecration.
aliud opus,	the one [is] a work,
aliud operatio.	the other, the worker.[97]

Such techniques made his message memorable—aptly framed to impress itself on the oral memory. As we will see, Augustine, even more than his mentor, would cultivate such wordplay. Ambrose's stress on the invisible also allowed him to describe baptism as an event whose true setting was eternity itself: that angels observed the neophytes approaching the altar and mar-

---

96. Ambrose, De sacramentis 1.10 (trans. Deferrari, FC 44:272). See also De mysteriis 15 and 19. There does not seem to have been any literary dependence of Ambrose on Tertullian; Paredi, Saint Ambrose, 131, mentions that Ambrose did not use Western sources; however, Botte, "Introduction," SC 25:40–41, suggests that Ambrose is dependent on oral tradition for the themes found in these sermons.

97. Ambrose, De sacramentis 1.15 (SC 25:58–59; trans. my own).

velled at the fresh, "bright-shining whitewash" accomplished at the font; that the neophytes themselves had become "eagles renewed by the washing" and were ready to soar heavenward.[98]

Like Cyril, Ambrose explained the meaning of the rites by drawing on biblical themes and imagery. For example, it was customary in Milan that when the newly baptized emerged from the font, the bishop would wash their feet. Ambrose interpreted this unique Milanese rite not only as an imitation of the humility Jesus demonstrated at the Last Supper; he also saw it as a way of cleaning out the venom left by Satan, that serpent whose bite had caused Adam to trip and fall.[99] Ambrose also drew heavily on traditional biblical types: the Spirit hovering over the waters at creation; the flood at the time of Noah; the Red Sea; Moses sweetening the desert spring; the cure of Naaman the Syrian. As Botte has noted, the pedagogical effect Ambrose achieved was "not so much a harmonious synthesis as a series of tableaux . . . to be engraved on the memory of the neophytes"; the interplay of images gave "them a rich, living idea of baptism" more vital than abstract theories.[100]

Yet Ambrose used these figures to draw out two points. First, "the sacraments of the Christians are more divine and earlier than those of the Jews":[101] the waters at creation and the flood at the time of Noah prove the antiquity of baptism, while the sacrifice of Melchisedech, that "king of justice, king of peace" (who therefore must be Christ), preceded Abraham and Moses.[102] This might seem an odd emphasis, but to a conservative society like the Romans, the novelty of Christianity made it suspect. Thus Christian apologists felt compelled to create for it a more ancient lineage.[103] Second, Ambrose held the idiosyncratic theory that biblical precedents were only signs and not sacraments in the true

98. Ibid., 4.5–7 (Deferrari, 298–99).

99. Ibid., 3.7. Ambrose was quite aware that Rome had no such rite; still he insisted on its legitimacy: see *De sacramentis* 3.5–6.

100. Botte, "Introduction," 37.

101. Ambrose, *De sacramentis* 1.11 (Deferrari, 273). See also *De mysteriis* 47.

102. On the antiquity of baptism, see *De mysteriis* 9, and *De sacramentis* 1.23; on the antiquity of the Eucharist, see *De mysteriis* 45–46.

103. For a summary of this apologetic theme, see Pelikan, *The Emergence of the Catholic Tradition*, 34–36.

sense: signs did not require faith, for the divine action was visible for all to see; sacraments, on the other hand, required faith.[104]

Ambrose sometimes drew on images from the culture. Thus in speaking of the first anointing, he drew on athletic imagery: "You are anointed as an athlete of Christ, as one slated to compete in the bout that is this world."[105] Similarly, he compared the renunciation to a down-payment on a loan and warned of the perils of defaulting.[106] But his favorite tableau was the marriage feast, and this he joined with lush sensual images drawn from the Canticle of Canticles: kisses, "breasts . . . better than wine," "myrrh with aromatic spices," a "bedchamber" that is at the same time "a pantry" full of "good libations, good odors, sweet honey, diverse fruits, various dishes."[107] In treating this festal imagery, Ambrose did what we saw Chrysostom do—show the ways the spiritual world paradoxically inverted the everyday:

"You are inebriated in spirit. . . . For the one who is inebriated with wine totters and sways; the one who is inebriated with the Holy Spirit is rooted in Christ. And so, glorious is the inebriation which effects sobriety of mind."[108]

Also, like Chrysostom, Ambrose used the rite as a springboard for suggesting an appropriate moral style. For instance, Ambrose took an image Tertullian had used—Christians as "fish"—and gave it a Stoic turn:

"Imitate the fish. . . . A tempest rages in the sea, storms shriek, but the fish swims [beneath]. . . . So even for you this world is a sea. It has diverse floods, heavy waters, severe storms. And, you, be a fish, that the water of the world may not submerge you."[109]

Finally, like Cyril, Ambrose reserved instruction on the Lord's Prayer for mystagogy and treated it in the course of his comments on the Eucharist. For Ambrose, the Lord's Prayer, like the Creed,

104. Ambrose, *De sacramentis* 2.4 paraphrases Paul: "Signs for the incredulous, faith for those who believe." See Yarnold, *Awe-Inspiring Rites*, 110 note 10; *De civitate Dei* 22.8.
105. Ambrose, *De sacramentis* 1.4 (trans. my own).
106. Ibid., 1.5.
107. Ibid., 5.5–11 (Deferrari, 311–12).
108. Ibid., 5.17 (Deferrari, 314—altered).
109. Ibid., 3.3 (Deferrari, 290).

had a dazzling brevity: "You see how brief the prayer, and how full of all virtues." He explained it the same way he had explained the Creed: phrase by phrase. Because of baptism, the neophytes could now enjoy a new intimacy with God: they could now turn their eyes to heaven and, "as if a son, . . . call Him Father"; "there is no arrogance here but devotion." Ambrose sometimes applied his allegorical method to the prayer. For instance, he claimed the phrase "give us our daily bread" referred to Eucharist: "not the bread that enters the body, but . . . the bread of eternal life, which supports the soul."[110] Similarly, Ambrose allegorized Jesus' command to shut the door and pray inside: that inside room referred to "the interior person," "the recesses of your breast"; thus "you have your solitude everywhere."[111] Augustine, a man who later made such interiority his trademark, apparently took such advice to heart.

Augustine emerged from Ambrose's catechumenate a changed man: he had retired from his prestigious post; he had set aside any prospect for a comfortable marriage and had committed himself to a celibate life. A year later, in 388, he would leave Milan and return to Africa to set up a quasi-monastic community on his family farm in Thagaste. Meanwhile, he wrote, speculating—often in formal philosophic terms—about the meaning of this new life made possible by baptism. As Peter Brown notes:

"The theme of 'putting off the old,' of 'putting on the new,' of rebirth and rising again from death, of the consequent ascent of the soul to heaven made possible by the descent of Christ to earth, reverberated in Augustine's imagination. In the next years, he wove his own, refined Platonic doctrine of the ascent of the soul from the 'old man' of the sense, around this elemental and mysterious action."[112]

---

110. Ibid., 5.18-24 (Deferrari, 314-16). Ambrose goes on to cite Greek terms found in the Lord's Prayer and may well be relying on Origen's treatise *De oratione* for some of his comments; see Henry Chadwick, "Introduction," *Alexandrian Christianity*, LCC 2:231.

111. Ambrose, *De sacramentis* 6.12-15 (Deferrari, 322-25).

112. Brown, *Augustine of Hippo*, 124-25. Cf. *De quantitate animae* 3.4; *Contra Academicos* 3.41-43. Such neo-Platonic speculations led scholars early in this century to venture the view that Augustine had converted not to Christianity, but to neo-Platonism. This is now recognized as a false dichotomy. Moreover, it fails to recognize Augustine's contacts in Milan. In Milan Augustine had

Once settled in Thagaste, Augustine and his companions began their distinctive new life—consciously styling themselves as "servants of God." Augustine had grand hopes for them: that they would "grow god-like in retirement."[113] Such dreams proved short-lived. His son, Adeodatus, and his close friend, Nebridius, would die within the year. In the meantime, Augustine had begun to acquire a reputation: he debated Manichees on the meaning of Genesis; he authored the brilliant pamphlet *On True Religion*. In 391, he ventured to Hippo in hopes of recruiting a new man for his community. While there, he happened to attend church—just when the bishop, Valerius, expressed his need for a new presbyter. According to Augustine's biographer, Possidius, the crowd immediately "seized him and, as is customary in such cases, brought him to the bishop for ordination."[114] Such forced ordinations were not uncommon: similar violence had led to the ordinations of Cyprian, Chrysostom, Ambrose. Now as a presbyter of Hippo, Augustine would suddenly find himself once more in a familiar role: as a teacher. And his first students would be what he and his companions had been a few year earlier: *competentes*.[115]

---

mixed with an adventurous circle of Christians determined to integrate Christianity with the best philosophic framework they knew: neo-Platonism. This circle included such intellectual notables as Manlius Theodorus, Zenobius, Simplicianus, even Ambrose himself. And these Christian neo-Platonists insisted—to the horror of their pagan colleagues—that this philosophic inheritance could in no sense undermine or tamper with the central Christian realities: the incarnation, crucifixion, and resurrection of the body. See Pierre Courcelle, "Anti-Christian arguments and Christian Platonism," in *The Conflict between Paganism and Christianity in the Fourth Century*, 151–92.

113. Augustine, *Epistola* 10.2 (trans. Brown, *Augustine of Hippo*, 133). See George Folliet, " 'Deificari in otio,' Augustin, *Epistula X*," *Recherches augustiniennes* 2 (1962) 225–36.

114. Possidius, *Vita* 4 (trans. Mary Magdeleine Muller, FC 15:77). See also Augustine's own account of the incident in *Sermo* 355.2.

115. *Sermo* 216.1–2.

Chart 5
The Catecheses of Ambrose of Milan

Work	Text	Trans	Topics Covered
I. THE CATECHUMENATE: PASSING REFERENCES			
De Cain et Abel	CSEL 32.1	FC 42	*Disciplina arcani*
Exp. ps 148, Sermon 2	CSEL 32	---	*Disciplina arcani*
Exp. ps 148, Sermon 20	CSEL 32	---	Suspect motives
Exp. ev. Luc, Sermon 4	SC 45	---	Call to put in names
Epistola 20	PL 16	FC 26	Timing of *traditio*
II. LENTEN SERMONS (TO THE WHOLE ASSEMBLY)			
De Helia et ieiunio	PS 19	PS 19	Begin Lenten discipline
De Abraham I	CSEL 32.1	---	Abraham: faith, marriage
Exp. ps 136–140	CSEL 44	---	Senses of Scripture; exhorts *competentes*
[Paulinus, *Vita* 38	PS 16	FC 15	Ambrose as catechist]
III. *TRADITIO SYMBOLI* (TO THE *COMPETENTES*)			
Expositio symboli	Connolly	Connolly	Hands over, explains Creed phrase by phrase
IV. MYSTAGOGICAL WORKS (TO NEOPHYTES DURING EASTER WEEK)			
De Sacramentis			
1 (Tues)	SC 25	FC 44, MF 6	Ephephtha; first anointing; renunciation
2 (Wed)	SC 25	FC 44, MF 6	Baptism: OT figures; font as "crucifixion"
3 (Thurs)	SC 25	FC 44, MF 6	Washing of feet; Chrism
4 (Fri)	SC 25	FC 44, MF 7	Eucharist: Roman canon; consecration; Amen
5 (Sat)	SC 25	FC 44, MF 7	Eucharist: sober intoxication, Lord's Prayer
6 (Sun)	SC 25	FC 44	Prayer: where, how, order
De Mysteriis	SC 25	FC 44	

Topics: Rationale of Lenten pedagogy; *disciplina arcani; ephephtha; apotaxis;* water: OT figures, invisible powers, anointing; washing of feet; new robes; seal; "ancient" sacraments; consecration; Amen; Eucharist.

Chapter 4

Evangelization: Unrolling the Scroll

Sometime around 400, Deogratias, a deacon from the Church in Carthage, sent Augustine a request: "to write something on the catechizing of inquirers."[1] Deogratias, it seems, had to handle those "to be grounded in the rudiments of Christian faith" and had been assigned this ministry because he had both theological know-how and good delivery. But his popularity left him feeling flat. His teaching had become "commonplace and wearisome," even to himself. He felt he talked too long and with too little enthusiasm. So he wrote Augustine for advice on method: "how suitably to present that truth . . . which makes us Christians."

In North Africa, the teaching inquirers received was limited: they might attend only a single lecture before becoming catechumens. Deogratias wanted to make this one-time lecture more effective and sought Augustine's advice on several points: (1) where the "narrative" (*narratio*) on Scripture should begin; (2) how much of the biblical story it should cover; and (3) "whether, at the end of the narrative, an exhortation should be added, or precepts

---

1. *De catechizandis rudibus* 1.1 (trans. my own). There has been some dispute over the dating of this work. See L. J. Van der Lof, "The date of the '*De catechizandis rudibus*'," *Vigiliae Christianae* 16 (1962) 198–204. Useful commentaries on *De catechizandis* include: Van der Meer, *Augustine the Bishop*, 453–67; Adolfo Etchegaray Cruz, "El *de Catechizandis Rudibus* y la metodologia de la evangelización agustiniana," *Augustinus* 15 (1970) 349–68; B. Capelle, "Prédication et catéchèse selon saint Augustin," *Questions liturgiques et paroissiales* 33 (1952) 55–64; Trevor T. Rowe, *Saint Augustine: Pastoral Theologian* (London: Epworth, 1974) 41–43; for philological background, Joseph P. Christopher, *De catechizandis rudibus liber unus: Translated with an Introduction and Commentary*, PS 8; for liturgical aspects, R. De Latte, "St. Augustin et le baptême," *Questions liturgiques* 56 (1975) 178–91. Unfortunately none of these pays significant attention to the social context of Carthage nor to the Christian mood in the late 390s (though Van der Meer handles these matters elsewhere in his book).

only."[2] Augustine answered with a small treatise, *On Catechizing Inquirers* (*De catechizandis rudibus*).[3] In it, he addressed Deogratias's queries about method. But Augustine considered the deacon's complaints about weariness and boredom a problem at least as important as technique, and so offered remedies to reignite his zest for teaching.

This brief treatise has helped shape the pedagogy and programs of influential Christian educators: Alcuin in the eighth century; Erasmus and the Protestant reformers in the sixteenth; Jungmann and the kerygmatic movement in this century.[4] Again and again, educators have been struck by Augustine's pedagogical acumen and psychological sensitivity. Perhaps for this very reason there has been a tendency to highlight his more generalizable insights at the expense of his original, and quite specific, focus: the evangelization of inquirers. Certainly some of his insights can be generalized.[5] But this work also needs to be seen within the fabric of its

2. *De catechizandis rudibus* 1.1 (trans. Joseph P. Christopher, ACW 2:13). As we will see, *narratio* is a technical rhetorical term and possesses different connotations in Latin than its English equivalent.

3. The word *rudes* in everyday Latin meant "unpolished," "ignorant," or "illiterate." However, in Christian parlance, it referred to anyone, even someone highly educated, who happened to be ignorant of things Christian. It thus became the technical term for those whom we now call "inquirers." See Ambrose, *Expositio psalmi 118* 18.26; Pontius, *De vita Cypriani* 2; Cyprian, *Epistola 70.2*—which Augustine cites in *De baptismo contra Donatistas* 5.21.29. Moreover, the verb *catechizare* had a somewhat different range of meaning than we today tend to give the verb *to catechize*. Our understanding has been shaped by modern scholars who routinely distinguish *kerygma* from *didache*, evangelization from catechesis. However, Latin authors—from Tertullian and Victorinus to Jerome and Augustine—tended to lump together under the single word *catechizare* what we tend to distinguish: evangelizing and catechizing. See Tertullian, *De idolatria* 9; Victorinus, *In epistolam Pauli ad Galatas* 2.6.6; Jerome, *Commentarius in epistolam S. Pauli ad Galatas* 2.4; 3.6; Augustine, *De catechizandis rudibus* 1.1; 8.12; 10.14; also *Contra Faustum* 13.7.

4. Christopher, "Introduction," ACW 2:8-9. On Alcuin, see also Jean-Paul Bouhot, "Alcuin et le 'De Catechizandis Rudibus' de saint Augustin," *Recherches augustiniennes* 15 (1980) 176-240; on the kerygmatic movement and the influence of *De catechizandis rudibus* on it, see Boys, *Biblical Interpretation in Religious Education*, 91 and 113-15; and Boys, *Educating in Faith: Maps and Visions* (San Francisco: Harper & Row, 1989) 93-102.

5. Standard treatments of this type are found in Eugene Kevane, *Augustine the Educator: A Study in the Fundamentals of Christian Formation* (Westminster, Md.: Newman Press, 1964) 212-17; and George Howie, *Educational Theory*

original and intended setting: the fourth/fifth-century catechumenate. In this treatise, Augustine was concerned with a quite specific group—inquirers—and a quite specific genre of instruction—a *first* catechesis. These limits need to be appreciated. His concern was not to set forth a comprehensive program of catechesis, nor even of evangelization, but rather a small, but critical, aspect of such evangelizing: a first systematic proclamation of the good news of Christ.

In the extant literature from the ancient catechumenate, Augustine's *On Catechizing* stands out as a unique document. Certainly, in the earlier survey, we saw nothing quite like it. Admittedly, Hippolytus had indicated something about how one interviewed newcomers but made no mention of presenting them a summary of the Christian message. And admittedly there are apologetic works—Clement of Alexandria's *Exhortation to the Greeks*, Minucius Felix's *Octavius*, Eusebius of Caesarea's *Preparation for the Gospel*—which summarize the Christian message and defend Christianity against its detractors.[6] And there is Gregory of Nyssa's *Catechetical Oration*, which offers teachers a philosophic arsenal for defending major Christian doctrines.[7] But all these works, while emblematic of Christian evangelization, do not address what Augustine addresses: how to present the "good news" to one who now wishes to become a Christian. Moreover, this document, while unique, should not be made to testify to more than it does: one should

---

and Practice in St. Augustine (London: Routledge & Kegan Paul, 1969) 150–53. Both discussions are marred by their neglect of the original context. A much more sensitive treatment—still accenting the generalizable—is that of Walter Burghardt, "Catechetics in the Early Church: Program and Psychology," *Living Light* 1 (1964) 100–118.

6. For a helpful anthology of these works, together with commentary, see Robert D. Sider, *The Gospel & Its Proclamation*, MF 10 (Wilmington, Del.: Michael Glazier, 1983) 40–175.

7. See Gregory of Nyssa, *Oratio catechetica magna*, praefatio. Gregory envisions his work for "leaders 'of the mystery of our religion' " and uses the views of "Jews" and "Hellenists" as foils for Christian views. He also notes that one must adapt to one's audience: e.g., Anomoeans, Manichees, Marcionites, Valentinians, Sabellians. Jungmann, in "Catechumenate," *New Catholic Encyclopedia* 3:239, sees it as an Eastern parallel to *De catechizandis rudibus*; however, I have found no reference in it to the teaching of catechumens. It seems a more general work: for apologetic debate and for teaching all sorts of Christians.

not assume, as Jungmann and Dujarier do, that introducing the kerygma in a single address was a fourth-century concoction; nor can we assume, as Jungmann does, that this was done in "the Church" as a whole (as opposed to just North Africa).[8] As for what went on elsewhere and what went on before, it seems more prudent to say that we do not know.

Augustine's treatise has two parts. In the first he spells out principles for doing this first evangelical catechesis. These principles constitute not so much a theory in any abstract sense, but rather reflections culled from his own experience in this ministry. Here he treats three topics: the candidate (chapters 5–6, 8–9); the catechesis (chapters 3–4, 7); and the catechist (chapters 2, 10–16). In the second part he puts principle into practice and offers two sample talks: the first (chapters 16–25) is lengthy; the second (chapters 26–27), quite brief.

8. Jungmann, *The Early Liturgy*, 249, claims that *De catechizandis* is an example of the reconfiguration of the third-century catechumenate, a part of "a plan" by the fourth-century "Church" "to make provision for the great majority who put off baptism" and "devised to give the most necessary spiritual equipment for those wishing to become Christians [which] was supplied immediately at the beginning of the catechumenate." Frankly this is pure speculation; also, his assumptions seem questionable: (1) it is better to speak of the churches, not the "Church," when describing ancient ritual practice—something that Jungmann is careful about elsewhere; (2) this document only testifies to practice in Hippo and Carthage, and it seems better to simply say we do not know what went on elsewhere; (3) we simply have no idea to what extent this represents a shift from earlier practice or simply a continuation of older ways; (4) Augustine in this work makes not the slightest mention of those who delay baptism. Dujarier, *History of the Catechumenate*, 94, says the following regarding the two-hour address Augustine recommends and the rite of entrance which followed it: "How could a pre-catechesis that was reduced to a meeting that did not exceed two hours work an effective transformation? The situation had certainly changed with respect to the preceding century. If, despite the great amount of patristic literature we have from the fourth century, we have so few witnesses to a serious admission examination for the catechumenate, it is because, from this time on, the rite was conferred too readily. It was used as a lure, while it should have sanctioned a conversion! And without a true conversion, it was an empty gesture." Here Dujarier combines his questionable thesis—that the third century represents the ideal—with a questionable argument from silence. Had evangelization, in fact, been reduced? If so, how does one account for the conversion of Caecilius at the end of Minucius Felix's *Octavius*? This *third-century* document—admittedly a fictional account—portrays an authentic conversion after an oration of similar length.

110

From an early date North Africa had been a Christian strong-hold, not only in the cities but in the countryside as well. In Hippo, according to Augustine, Christians were already a decided majority:

"In this city may be found many houses in which there is not even one pagan; but no house can be found where there are not Christians. And when it is thoroughly investigated, no house can be found where there are not more Christians than pagans."[9]

Between 390 and 410, the alliance of Church and State witnessed a highwater mark. With it came the gradual, sporadic, and some-times violent suppression of public pagan practice. Imperial edicts in 391, 395, and 399 officially banned sacrifices, though festivals were allowed to continue; they also forbade the destruction of temples which were now to serve only as "museums." Such edicts tended to be erratically enforced, but around 399—according to Augustine's report in the *City of God*—two imperial officials, Gaudentius and Jovius, came to Carthage and "demolished the temples of the false gods and broke up their images."[10] More likely, this was the work of Christian mobs who, in an iconoclastic frenzy, overstepped the law and took things into their own hands.

When Augustine preached in Carthage in 401, the assembly would enthusiastically break in and shout: "Down with Roman gods, down with Roman gods."[11] This was a victory celebration with violent overtones. Augustine, like other Christian thinkers, was for a time swept up in this high-pitched atmosphere. He saw in the demise of paganism a fulfillment of ancient prophecies: that

9. *Sermo* 302.19 (trans. M. M. Getty, *The Life of North Africans as Revealed in the Sermons of Saint Augustine*, PS 15:113). Some locales—it is unclear how large these were—seem to have been almost entirely Christian; a few of the nobility were the only hold-outs: *Enarrationes in psalmos* 54.13. On the possible religious and social reasons for the inroads made by Christianity in North Africa, see W. H. C. Frend, *The Donatist Church*, 87-111.

10. *De civitate Dei* 18.54 (trans. Henry Bettenson, *City of God* [New York: Penguin Books, 1972] 841). For an excellent survey of the erratic suppression and widespread survival of paganism, see Jones, *The Later Roman Empire*, 1:938-43.

11. *Sermo* 24.6 (trans. Brown, *Augustine*, 321). The *notarii* recorded the crowd's triple acclamation: "Dii Romani"; they were so loud that Augustine had to ask for quiet.

God was uprooting the idols of the nations; that "the whole world has become a choir praising Christ."[12] Meanwhile, Christian propagandists like Prudentius could sing of these "Christian times" as the dawn of a new day: "Rome fled from her old errors and shook the dark mist from her wrinkled face; her nobility now ready to enter on the way of eternity and to follow Christ at the calling of her great leader."[13]

This was more wishful thinking than fact. Many aristocrats in Rome clung tenaciously to their ancestral faith.[14] And their resistance to Christianity touched North Africa. They owned large tracts of land there, and the tenant farmers who worked these lands, it seems, were wary of converting for fear of reprisal from their powerful patrons.[15] Paganism remained a force to be reckoned with. Pagans continued to occupy positions of power, and intellectual centers like Madaura, where Augustine had done studies as a youth, resisted changing age-old ways. Maximus, a pagan grammarian from Madaura, could write to Augustine and boast:

"We behold the marketplace of our town occupied by a crowd of beneficent deities; . . . with pious supplications we openly worship our gods, gaining their favor by acceptable sacrifices and taking pains that these things be seen and approved by all."[16]

Pagans too could be violent. In 399, in Sufes, when a statue of Hercules was overturned, a pagan mob responded by murdering sixty Christians. Meanwhile the town council sat back and

12. *Enarrationes in psalmos* 149.7 (trans. R. A. Markus, *Saeculum: History and Society in the Theology of St. Augustine*, 2nd ed. [Cambridge: Cambridge University Press, 1989] 30). See also *Enarrationes in psalmos* 46.5 and 62.1; *Sermones* 22.4; 346A.2 (=Caillau 2, 19); 97A.2 (=Bibl. Casin. 2, 114). On the mood of this period and Augustine's later more skeptical assessment of it, see Markus, *Saeculum*, 30–44.

13. Prudentius, *Contra Symmachum* 1.506–10 (trans. Markus, *Saeculum*, 28).

14. Jones, "The Social Background of the Struggle between Paganism and Christianity," 31–37; Herbert Bloch, "The Pagan Revival in the West at the End of the Fourth Century," in *The Conflict between Paganism and Christianity in the Fourth Century*, 193–218; Peter Brown, "Aspects of the Christianization of the Roman Aristocracy," *Journal of Roman Studies* 51 (1961) 1–11; James J. O'Donnell, "The Demise of Paganism." *Traditio* 35 (1979) 45–88.

15. Van der Meer, *Augustine the Bishop*, 29; Macmullen, *Christianizing the Roman Empire*, 65. See *Epistola* 136.3; *Enarrationes in psalmos* 54.13.

16. *Epistola* 16.1–3 (trans. Mary Emily Keenan, *The Life and Times of St. Augustine as Revealed in His Letters*, PS 45:108).

demanded that Christians pay reparations for the damaged statue. Augustine would write them: "If you say Hercules is your god, we can take up a collection from everybody and buy you a god from the stone-cutter; [but] you must give back the lives which your fierce hand wrested from us."[17]

This political and social ferment at the turn of the fifth century forms the backdrop for *On Catechizing*. Yet it is only a wide-angle view. These larger forces and news items touched the mass of people in curious and complex ways—much as the ferment surrounding the Vietnam War touched ordinary American families in a myriad of ways. Often more immediate personal dynamics—older social traditions, educational experience, contacts with friends and neighbors—came into play and shaped conversions to Christianity. One gets a glimmer of this complexity in Augustine's reflections on the motives and types of candidates.

In chapters 5 and 6 of *On Catechizing*, Augustine takes up how to handle the interrogation of inquirers. We saw earlier that Hippolytus laid great stress on this interrogation and that his questions focused on lifestyle and profession. Augustine, by contrast, was more concerned with motive:

"It is certainly helpful to be informed beforehand by those who know [the candidate]: what his disposition of heart might be, what causes may have induced him to come and embrace religious observance. But if there is no one else from whom we may learn this, we may question the candidate directly."[18]

Augustine's focus on motive should be not surprising: he believed, as he told Deogratias, that "there is no voice to reach the ears of God save the emotion of the heart."[19] And in the *Confessions*, written about this same time, Augustine would scrutinize his own subtly divided will and curious complexity of heart. Augustine's procedure mirrored Hippolytus's in one respect: he questioned not the candidates (unless necessity dictated) but rather those who brought them. Yet Augustine used this traditional examination in

17. *Epistola* 50 (trans. Wilfrid Parsons, FC 12:237). Pagans also rioted in 408 in Calama, where Augustine's friend and later biographer, Possidius, was bishop. In the riot, a monk was killed, and Possidius barely escaped with his life. Augustine recounts the incident in *Epistola* 91.
18. *De catechizandis rudibus* 5.9 (Christopher, 25—altered).
19. Ibid., 9.13 (Christopher, 33).

untraditional ways: "that from these responses we may fashion the introduction [*exordium*] for our talk."[20] In other words, he saw this procedure less as a test and more as a way to ensure that one's catechesis played into the experience of the inquirer.

The motives that prompted conversion then were not the sort one finds today. For example, Augustine noted that most candidates were driven by fear—not fear of political authorities, but of God: "For very rarely, no, never, does it happen that any one comes to us with the desire to become a Christian, who has not been struck by some fear of God."[21] Augustine and his contemporaries believed that such fears might well be divinely prompted. Fear of the Last Judgment had spurred Victorinus's conversion. And Augustine, even as a politic catechumen, had worried: if death should "steal upon me, shall I be in a fit state to leave this world . . . [or] is it not more probable that I should have to pay a heavy penalty for my negligence?"[22] Africans, both pagan and Christian, were prone to such fears. The old pagan high-god of Africa, Saturn, was a fearsome character. Even "the God of the African Christians," as Peter Brown notes, "was very much the awe-inspiring Judge."[23]

A second inducement was dreams. Trust in the revelatory power of dreams touched the religious consciousness of pagans and Christians alike. As Robin Lane Fox has noted, "In their dreams, pagans of all classes and backgrounds kept the closest company with the gods."[24] Pagans had even developed special technologies to conjure up such "great dreams": potions, diets, sleeping cham-

20. Ibid., 5.9 (trans. my own). Note Augustine's use of the word *exordium* here. I will take up the meaning of this technical term in the next section.

21. Ibid. (Christopher, 24). Courcelle, *Recherches sur les Confessiones*, 21–22, gives a helpful list of motives he finds both in *De catechizandis rudibus* and in the *Confessiones*. However, he takes these parallels too far when he argues that the design of *De catechizandis* provides the structure for understanding the *Confessiones*. There are indeed striking parallels in the motives cited in these two works. However, the pattern of fears, dreams, miracles, etc., seems to form only one motif among many in the *Confessiones*. O'Meara, *The Young Augustine*, 14–16, strongly criticizes Courcelle's claim that *De catechizandis* gives the organizational principle for the *Confessiones*.

22. *Confessiones* 6.11 (Pine-Coffin, 127).

23. Brown, *Augustine of Hippo*, 196; see also Frend, *The Donatist Church*, 97–99.

24. Fox, *Pagans and Christians*, 150. On the dreams of pagans, see 150–63; on Christian dreams, 419–92.

bers, intricate rites. One pagan, Artemidorus of Daldis, had produced a remarkable handbook on dream interpretation; and in the work of the orator Aelius Aristeides, a long-time client of the cult of Asclepius, the great healing god of the ancient world, we can see the intimate relationship of dreams and faith-healing.

Christians—and Africans, in particular—shared this trust in the divinatory power of dreams. For instance, Perpetua, a young neophyte who was a contemporary of Tertullian, had, while in prison, dreamt of a great gladiatorial combat. This she interpreted as a divine revelation: that on the day of her martyrdom she would enjoy victory over Satan.[25] Similarly, Cyprian, the bishop of Carthage in the 250s, had had a dream the year before his martyrdom: he beheld himself on trial and saw his ultimate fate enacted in pantomime.[26] Augustine's own mother, Monica, placed great confidence in dreams and felt that "by some sense, which she could not describe in words, she was able to distinguish between [divine] revelations and her own natural dreams."[27]

A third inducement came from miracles, especially healings.[28] For instance, in one of his letters, Augustine tells the story of Dioscorus, a public health official, who "would never have bowed his neck or subdued his tongue except for some miraculous event":

"His only daughter, the joy of his life, fell ill and her cure was completely despaired of. Even her father had given up hope . . . The old man turned at length to implore the mercy of Christ,

25. *Passio Sanctarum Perpetuae et Felicitatis* 10.

26. Pontius, *De vita et passione S. Cypriani* 12.

27. *Confessiones* 6.13 (Pine-Coffin, 130). Augustine records one of her dreams in 3.11.

28. Macmullen, in *Christianizing the Roman Empire*, highlights, perhaps too strongly, the significance of such miracles. Nonetheless, his insistence is a helpful corrective to us who are guided by post-Enlightenment views and bring a skeptical outlook to such matters. His remarks on page 62 have important historiographical implications: miracles "might, of course, all be discounted on the grounds that the laws of nature could never have been really suspended, first, and second, that no sane or candid person could ever have thought so. . . . Inhabitants of the empire by and large took it for granted that the law of nature had always been and always would be suspended. They had come to terms with that fact, as they saw it; therefore they acted accordingly."

binding himself by a vow to become a Christian if he saw her cured. It happened.''[29]

This miracle may have prompted Dioscorus to become a catechumen—Augustine does not say—but he continued to "put off his vow" (baptism) until struck by blindness. Dioscorus then made a second vow: that he would seek baptism if he recovered his sight. When this second miraculous healing occurred, he put in his name for baptism. Augustine himself had witnessed miracles in the months prior to his conversion:

"It was at that time too that you [O God] revealed to your bishop Ambrose in a vision the place where the bodies of the martyrs Protasius and Gervasius were hidden. . . . Several persons who were tormented by evil spirits were cured, for even the devil acknowledged the holy relics. But this was not all. There was also a man who had been blind for many years, a well-known figure in the city. . . . He asked to be allowed to touch the bier with his handkerchief. . . . No sooner had he done this and put the handkerchief to his eyes than his sight was restored. The news spread.''[30]

Such events were heralded in Christian evangelical campaigns, for Christians, like their pagan confreres, routinely made reports of cures part of cult propaganda.[31] Such reports did not necessarily convince. Augustine, both as a catechumen and in his early years as bishop, treated these reports with a measured skepticism (though late in life he took a much greater interest in them).[32] Similarly, pagans could write off such cures as "sorcery" and would extend the same critique to the deeds of Jesus. As Augustine says in one sermon, "There are those unbelievers who reject Christ, saying that all that he did had been done through the

29. *Epistola* 227 (Parsons, 32:140—altered).
30. *Confessiones* 9.7 (Pine-Coffin, 192).
31. See A. D. Nock, *Conversion: The Old and New in Religion from Alexander the Great to Augustine of Hippo* (Oxford: Oxford University Press, 1961) 83–98; E. R. Dodds, *Pagan & Christian in an Age of Anxiety* (New York: W. W. Norton & Co., 1965) 124–26.
32. See Peter Brown, *The Cult of the Saints: Its Rise and Function in Latin Christianity* (Chicago: University of Chicago Press, 1981) 27–28, 77–78.

magic arts."[33] In fact, they could dismiss Jesus' deeds as unspectacular compared to the wonders wrought by Apollonius of Tyana or the great local wizard, Apuleius of Madaura.[34]

These inducements—fears, dreams, miracles—had once prompted conversion to pagan cults. Now they prompted conversion to Christianity. Yet there was a difference. What distinguished Christianity, according to Ramsay Macmullen, was that "it destroyed belief as well as creating it": that is, if a miracle was associated with a pagan god, the person would simply add one more god to his or her personal pantheon; if a miracle was associated with Christianity, the person would "now deny the pantheon entirely. . . . It was this result, destruction, that non-Christians of the time perceived as uniquely Christian."[35]

Augustine advised that one use a gentle finesse in handling candidates spurred by such motives:

"If by chance [the candidate] answers that his becoming a Christian is the result of a warning or dread inspired from on high, he affords us a wonderful opportunity for opening our remarks on [the theme of] God's great care for us. We should direct his thoughts from the guidance of wonders or dreams of this kind to the more solid path and the more trustworthy oracles of the scriptures. . . . He should not seek visible miracles but accustom himself to hope for those that are invisible and should receive warnings not when sleeping but when awake."[36]

In other words, Augustine did not deny that dreams, fears, or wonders might be "oracles," but hoped to divert attention to more trustworthy sources: the Scriptures, and oral teachings given on them. Augustine had tasted the oracular power of Scripture in

33. *Sermo* 43.5 (trans. my own). This appears again and again in the works of Augustine: *De consensu evangelistarum* 1.9.14; 1.8.13; 1.14.22; *Sermones* 71.5; 229J.4 (= Guelf. App. 7).

34. Marcellinus brought this up to Augustine as a typical attitude in his circle: *Epistola* 136.1. Augustine's response is in *Epistola* 138.19. See the discussion of this in Pierre Courcelle, "Propos antichrétiennes rapportés par S. Augustin," *Recherches augustiniennes* 1 (1958) 155 and in Robert L. Wilken, *The Christians As the Romans Saw Them* (New Haven: Yale University Press, 1984) 98–101.

35. Macmullen, *Christianizing the Roman Empire*, 108–9. On the exclusivity of Christian faith, see O'Donnell, "The Demise of Paganism," 45–88.

36. *De catechizandis rudibus* 6.10 (Christopher, 26—altered).

his own conversion. In the garden in Milan he had obeyed the call of *tolle, lege* as a "divine command" and read the first passage on which his eyes fell.[37] Augustine not only saw the Scriptures as an oracle, but thought that the catechist could be one as well. One finds this again and again in passing remarks in *On Catechizing*: that "God may . . . speak through us"; that the candidate "listens to us, or rather is listening to God through us."[38] Augustine interpreted his own experience in such terms. When writing *The Confessions,* he looked back on Ambrose as a "holy oracle"; and in one of his letters, he characterized a piece of Ambrose's practical advice—that one should follow the liturgical practice of one's locale—as "a heavenly oracle."[39]

The candidates Augustine dealt with did not usually harbor high political ambitions. Hippo was too much a backwater town for such types. Reports—and denunciation—of politic conversions came from those, like Eusebius and Ambrose, who moved among the elite circles of the imperial court. Still Augustine had met his share of opportunists:

"If [someone] wants to become a Christian in the hope of getting some benefit from people whom he thinks he could not otherwise please, or to escape from some injury at the hands of people whose displeasure or enmity he dreads, he really does not want to become a Christian so much as he wants to feign being one. . . . If he has come with a counterfeit motive, desirous only of temporal advantages, or thinking to escape some loss, he will, of course, lie."[40]

Note Augustine's emphasis here: while he knew of opportunists who sought "temporal advantages," he was equally conscious that many feared "enmity," "injury," and "loss." These may well have been either townspeople frightened by the government crack-down on paganism or poor farmers whose powerful landlord had become Christian. For such cases, Augustine advised prudence and compassion:

"You must derive your opening [remarks] from the very lie he tells. You must not do this, however, with the intent of unmask-

---

37. *Confessiones* 8.12.
38. *De catechizandis rudibus* 11.16 (Christopher, 41). See also 7.11.
39. *Confessiones* 6.3; *Epistola* 54.3.
40. *De catechizandis rudibus* 5.9 (Christopher, 24–25—altered).

ing his false pretense, as though sure of it; but if he says that he came with an intention that is really praiseworthy, whether he is speaking the truth or not, we should nevertheless so approve and praise the intention he says he came with so as to make him take delight in actually being such as he desires to seem."[41]

Augustine knew from self-examination the complex layers of his own interiority: that inside him were the "vast cloisters" and "spacious palace" of memory; that his inner self could be "a house divided against itself"; that he could become "a question to himself."[42] Augustine presumed that others too had this complexity of heart. Thus he advised Deogratias to presume the best and to recognize the mystery of those he dealt with: "It is hidden from us when the one whom we now see present in body does really come in spirit; nevertheless, we should deal with him in such a way that this desire may come to birth in him even though it does not as yet exist."[43] Augustine also suggested that God might use the catechist as a graced instrument: "Undoubtedly the mercy of God is often present through the ministry of the catechist, so that a person—swept up by [our] teaching—now wishes to become in reality what he had decided to feign."[44]

This lenient attitude led Augustine to defend even suspicious conversions. For example, in Carthage—where politic conversions were more likely—Augustine once defended a banker named Faustinus who, people believed, had his eye on the office of magistrate. When presenting Faustinus to the wary Carthaginian congregation, Augustine said:

"We cannot see into the human heart nor put it on display. . . . You cannot inspect the heart of a new Christian. . . . You say: 'But [Faustinus] believes because he felt he had to.' That can be said also of . . . [St. Paul] who was at first a blasphemer, a persecutor, a scoffer. This one too . . . was knocked down by a heavenly voice. . . . [It used to be said]: 'Who was the one guilty of such-and-such?' 'Faustinus.' 'Who used to be opposed to Christ?' 'Faustinus.' [Now it can be said:] 'Who has come to fear Christ?' 'Faustinus.' Christ came to call the sick, as we have heard

41. Ibid. (Christopher, 25—altered).
42. *Confessiones* 10.8; 8.8; 10.33.
43. *De catechizandis rudibus* 5.9 (trans. my own).
44. Ibid. (Christopher, 24–25—altered).

in the gospel. . . . Teach [Faustinus] the right path; let him find the right path in you. . . . The future will tell whether his life and his zeal for the faith of Christ will prove worthy."[45]

This example—admittedly extreme—points to what lengths Augustine would go to presume the best in candidates.

In chapters 8 and 9 of *On Catechizing*, Augustine takes up the question of different classes of inquirers. He mentions three types: the unlearned; the well educated; and "those from the ordinary schools." Concerning the unlearned, he says almost nothing, but interestingly his two sample talks—and most of his sermons—are fitted to their needs. In this section he reserves his remarks to the latter two. These types, while few in number, were an influential elite. Thus it is not surprising that he devoted such attention to them and to the challenges they presented catechists. Augustine described the well-educated inquirer in this way:

"Should someone refined in liberal studies come to you to be catechized and, having already decided to become a Christian, come with the express intention of becoming so: it is most unlikely that this person has not acquired a considerable knowledge of our Scriptures and literature, and thus has come already trained so as to be made a partaker in the sacraments. For such people tend to investigate carefully every point beforehand, and not at the very hour in which they become Christians; typically they make known beforehand the stirrings of their own hearts to such others as they can and discuss these with them."[46]

This portrait is reminiscent of a case Augustine would cite in *The Confessions:* Victorinus. With such candidates, Augustine advised that "we be brief and not dwell with annoying insistence upon things which they know." Still he advised that one do a quick review, but in a such a way that the person "may not have to listen to it as from a teacher." He also advised an interrogation of a quite specific sort: to see if the person "has been moved to that decision by books, whether the canonical Scriptures or those of good writers." Again this probe was less a cause to accept or reject candidates, as it had been in Hippolytus, and more a tool for

45. *Sermo* 179.1–3 (trans. my own). This sermon was given in June 401, i.e., roughly contemporary with the writing of *De catechizandis rudibus*.
46. *De catechizandis rudibus* 8.12 (trans. my own).

sizing up their unique catechetical needs. Thus, if they mentioned books that influenced their decision, the catechist might begin by saying something about these. Augustine also noted that since such inquirers were outsiders, they could have indiscriminately picked up apocryphal or heterodox books or older Christian authors who, while orthodox in their own lifetime, held views out of step with contemporary standards. These questions were to be handled in a "discreet conference"; one was not to use any more of a "magisterial tone" than was necessary.[47]

Augustine then took up how to handle those trained in grammar and rhetoric. Such men—and only men would have enjoyed such schooling—styled themselves as "educated." Augustine held no such opinion of them. He thought of them as prickly elitists, ill-equipped to deal with "serious questions." He knew their ilk well, for he had had exactly the same sort of education as they: largely literary and rhetorical.[48] Such men might know only a smattering of philosophy, science, or history. Instead they would have studied—memorized, might be more accurate—a few classics: Vergil, Cicero, Ovid, Terence. More importantly, they spoke "proper" Latin and not like that of a commoner. They had been trained—at the cost of beatings from the schoolmaster's cane—to purge from their speech all barbarisms or slang and to sprinkle their speech with phrases and allusions lifted from the classics.[49] The ideal embodiment of this education was the orator, one who exercised magisterial control over his tongue and who could sway any audience with the force of his words. In other words, schooling in the ancient world had been shaped not by the educational ideals of Plato but by those of the sophist Isocrates, and these had been passed to the Latin-speaking world by Cicero.[50] As Brown has noted:

"The great advantage of [this] education . . . was that, within its narrow limits, it was perfectionist. The aim was to measure up to the timeless perfection of an ancient classic. . . . [A man with such an education] had been taught to maneuver, with infinite

47. Ibid. (Christopher, 30–32).
48. For what follows, see Marrou, Saint Augustin et la fin de la culture antique, 3–83; and History of Education in Antiquity, 194–205; 242–313.
49. See, for instance, Confessiones 1.13; 1.18; De utilitate credendi 6.13.
50. Marrou, History of Education in Antiquity, 194.

precision, in the cramped but supremely well-charted environment of an age-old tradition. Such a man could communicate his message to an educated Latin at the other end of the Roman world, merely by mentioning a classical figure, by quoting half a line of a classical poet. It is not surprising that the group of men who had, by their education, come to conform so successfully to this rigidly-defined traditional standard of perfection, should have come, by the fourth century, to stand apart as a caste of their own."[51]

When such men came as inquirers, they came the way Augustine had when he first went to hear Ambrose: more attuned to style than content. Moreover, they, like the young Augustine, would have been put off by the crude, uncultivated language found in the Old Latin translation of the Bible.[52] For such types, one sought wisdom only in classics with a proper eloquence.

With this backdrop, one can appreciate Augustine's impatience. First, he advised Deogratias to warn these aesthetes: they were to cease preferring "the trained tongue" to "the pure heart," to cease turning up their noses at "faults of diction" and worry more about "faults of character." Augustine then encapsulated his advice in an elegant epigram:

Ex quo fit ut	It follows that
ita malle debeant	they ought to prefer
ueriores quam disertiores	to hear true rather than
audire sermones,	eloquent discourses,
sicut malle debent	just as they ought to prefer
prudentiores quam formosiores	to have wise rather than
habere amicos.	handsome friends.[53]

Second, Augustine advised that they be admonished not to scoff at the unpretentious diction of the Bible. Instead they should learn to pierce through its "fleshly coverings" to taste "the power of these concealed oracles." In fact, the catechist ought to give them some taste of how "something which failed to stir them when set plainly before them is brought to light by the unraveling of some allegory."[54] In other words Augustine suggested treating these

51. Brown, *Augustine of Hippo,* 37.

52. See Marrou, *Saint Augustin et la fin de la culture antique,* 473–77.

53. *De catechizandis rudibus* 9.13 (CCSL 46:135; Christopher, 33).

54. Ibid. People who had been trained in grammar and rhetoric would have been exposed to allegorical exegesis before: for this was how Homer and

men the way Ambrose had treated him: pique curiosity with scriptural riddles.

THE CATECHESIS: PRINCIPLES

When members of the kerygmatic movement rediscovered Augustine's *On Catechizing* in the 1950s, they found its emphasis on the story of salvation history a breath of fresh air. It offered welcome relief from the dry abstractions of the Tridentine catechism. But that was to see it within—or set against—the modern horizon, and not within the patristic. Augustine's readers would have seen his advice on catechesis against a very different horizon: the tradition of classical rhetoric and the modifications it had undergone in Christian circles. We can scarcely imagine how rich and intricate this horizon was for ancients.[55] For us, "rhetoric" means "style" at best and "extravagant artifice" at worst. And rhetoric, if it remains in our curriculum at all, has been reduced to written composition and shorn almost completely of its original oral dimension. But, for ancients, being educated meant being a trained orator. And the educated elite had spent literally years refining performance skills and had at their fingertips an intricate and highly codified analytical vocabulary for measuring their own and others' performances. The closest parallel we have to such education is that which classical musicians undergo—except that the performance and analysis of classical music is not our cultural ideal, whereas rhetorical performance and analysis was in the ancient world the standard against which one was measured. Thus to appreciate *On Catechizing* we must digress a moment and undertake an all-too-brief overview of ancient rhetorical practice.

1) *The Classical Background.* Augustine had, of course, been trained in and had taught in these schools of rhetoric. There he would have mastered, if not memorized, Cicero's *On Invention*, a

---

Virgil were routinely interpreted within the schools. Thus such people would have readily understood it as a hermeneutic method; the novelty would have come from seeing it applied to the Christian Scriptures.

55. Marrou, *Saint Augustin et la fin de la culture antique*, 4: "C'était une culture essentiellement littéraire, fondée sur la grammaire et la rhétorique et tendant à réaliser le type idéal de l'orateur." For the points which follow, see Marrou, *History of Education in Antiquity*, 194-205 and 243-313, and *Saint Augustin et la fin de la culture antique*, 3-83.

textbook on how to construct set speeches.[56] (Augustine quotes this work a number of times and had probably taught from it and from Victorinus's commentary on it; in fact, one of Augustine's former students, Eulogius, once dreamed that his old teacher suddenly appeared and elucidated one of its baffling passages.[57]) In this textbook Cicero focused on one type of oration, the "judicial," the sort delivered during a lawsuit or criminal case.[58] Following a long-standing Greek tradition, he insisted that a proper legal speech had six parts:

a) The introduction (*exordium*), which should render the jury "well-disposed, attentive, and receptive."

b) The narrative (*narratio*), which is "an exposition of events that have occurred," what we would call "the facts of the case."

c) The division (*partitio*), which lays out where "we agree with our opponents and what is left in dispute."

d) The proof (*confirmatio*), which analyzes the evidence and "marshals arguments" that "lend credit, authority, and support to our case."

e) The refutation (*reprehensio*), which is "used to impair, disprove, or weaken the . . . proof in our opponents' speech."

f) The conclusion (*peroratio*) which includes:
   i) the summing-up (*enumeratio*) of one's case;
   ii) the denunciation (*indignatio*)—that is, "the stirring up of ill-will against one's opponent";

56. Marrou, *Saint Augustin et la fin de la culture antique*, 50. See also the discussion of *De inventione* in George A. Kennedy, *Classical Rhetoric and Its Christian and Secular Tradition from Ancient to Modern Times* (Chapel Hill: University of North Carolina Press, 1980) 90–96.

57. *De cura pro mortuis gerenda* 11.13. Here Augustine refers to *De inventione* by the title that ancients from Quintilian on had used: *Rhetorici libri*. Augustine lifts phrases or sentences word for word from it throughout his whole career: *De libero arbitrio uoluntatis* 1.13.27; *De moribus ecclesiae catholicae* 1.6.9; *Sermo* 150.8; *Enarrationes in psalmos* 83.11; *De doctrina christiana* 4.5.7; 4.25.55; *De trinitate* 14.11.14; *Contra Iulianum*, 4.3.19. For a list for these parallels, see Harald Hagendahl, *Augustine and the Latin Classics*, Studia Graeca et Latina 20 (Guteborg: Acta Universitatis Cothoburgensis, 1967) 1:157–59; see his valuable discussion of Augustine's use of Cicero's rhetorical ideas, 2:553–69.

58. Cicero, *De inventione* 1.7 (trans. H. M. Hubbell, Loeb, 15–17).

iii) the impassioned appeal (conquestio)—that is, "the rousing up of pity and sympathy" for one's client.[59]

Such a speech, like any rhetorical endeavor, had a dual aim: both to convince the mind and to arouse the emotions. This shaped both the tone and flow: the speech's introduction (exordium) and conclusion (peroratio) were directed toward winning the audience's heart, while the body of the speech (the narratio and the confirmatio) was directed at establishing the credibility of one's case.[60]

This six-part speech is, of course, only a textbook version. In actual practice, classical orations were much more complex, and the movement from one part to another was not so crisply articulated. In fact, to show the architecture of one's address too clearly was considered pedantic and artless. Yet this outline shaped standards and expectations. It, of course, guided the arrangement of actual legal speeches. But it had broken free from its moorings in the world of law many years earlier and had become a standard outline for formal debates and controversies of all sorts.[61] Moreover, this terminology formed the standard vocabulary that ancients used to analyze their own declamations.

Set against this classical backdrop, the evangelical address that Augustine describes takes on a new slant[62] (see chart 6.) First, Deogratias's questions—where to begin the "narrative" and where to end it—were in fact questions about the structure of a set speech. And Deogratias even used a technical term, narratio, and Augustine, an ex-teacher of rhetoric, would have recognized it as such. Second, Deogratias's questions concerned only a single part

59. Cicero, De inventione 1.20, 27, 31, 34, 78 (Hubbell, 41, 55, 63, 69, 123).

60. Cicero, De partitione oratoria 1.4–5 (trans. H. Rackham, Loeb, 313).

61. Christians, from an early date, took over the six-part scheme and adapted it as a vehicle for apologetics. Minucius Felix's Octavius follows the controversia format fairly strictly, though, interestingly, he makes little use of Scripture. See the commentary on the Octavius by G. W. Clarke, ACW 39:28–30. Clement of Alexandria's Exhortation to the Greeks, likewise, follows this arrangement; see Sider, The Gospel & Its Proclamation, MF 10:74.

62. For a treatment of the way Augustine used and altered the traditional six-part outline in other of his works, see Marrou, Saint Augustin et la fin de la culture antique, 59–69. For its place in De catechizandis rudibus, see Etchegaray Cruz, "El de Catechizandis Rudibus y la metodologia de la evangelización agustinina," 361–65, and Christopher, ACW 2:95; Cruz does not draw out as clearly as he might the degree to which Augustine and other Christians transfigured traditional canons to suit their own needs.

of a much larger oration. In other words, he had not asked, for instance, about the refutation or the denunciation. Still, Augustine's advice would touch not only on the narrative but on other parts as well. As we saw in the last section, Augustine offered passing advice on how to craft the introduction (*exordium*): that is, he stressed that it should draw on or take its cues from the candidate's motives, whether these be fears or dreams or books.[63]

2) *The Narrative: Making the Case for Christianity.* In response to Deogratias's questions on the narrative, Augustine's answer was brief, and to the point: "The narrative [*narratio*] is complete when the beginner is first catechized from the text, 'In the beginning God created heaven and earth,' down to the present period of Church history."[64] This advice, at first sight, seems overwhelming: that the catechist should have to survey the whole of biblical and Church history in a single speech. Not surprisingly, Augustine turned from scope to method. He counselled—obviously, tongue-in-cheek—against taking his suggestion too literally: "That does not mean, however, we ought to repeat verbatim the whole" of the Scriptures, even "if we have learned them by heart."[65] Augustine insisted that the catechist be selective: on the one hand, give a comprehensive survey, and on the other, highlight "certain of the more remarkable facts." Augustine, echoing Cicero, suggested two principles of selection: (a) those things which were heard with greater pleasure and (b) those events which constituted the pivotal moments. To explain this, Augustine offered an analogy: one's narrative should flow as though it were a valuable parchment being carefully unrolled and spread out to view that the audience might both examine it and admire its beauty. What guided this was a commonsense pedagogy:

63. Augustine mentions the term three times: that one fashion the *exordium* from what one has learned from the interrogation (*De catechizandis* 5.9); that if a candidate had been moved by fears or dreams, the *exordium* should stress God's care (6.10); that if an educated candidate happened to be influenced by books, the catechist should begin by saying something about them (8.12).

64. *De catechizandis rudibus* 3.5 (Christopher, 18—altered).

65. Ibid. The final phrase might strike us as astounding—that one might have committed the entire Bible to memory. But such prodigious feats were more routine in the ancient world. Pagans often knew their Homer and Virgil by heart, and Augustine would routinely quote the Christian classic from memory. See Marrou, *Saint Augustine and His Influence through the Ages*, 61.

"In this way not only are the points which we desire to emphasize brought into high relief by keeping others in the background,
but also the one whose interest we are anxious to rouse by the
narrative (*narratio*) does not come upon them with a mind already
exhausted nor with a memory confused."[66]

In other words, the criterion was audience response: what might
excite interest, what might enlighten the mind, what would not
burden the memory.

It is important to recognize that neither Augustine nor Deogratias would have thought of declaiming the *narratio* simply as "telling the story." The paradigm they worked from was judicial, and
in that paradigm the *narratio* was a presentation of the facts of the
case. For Augustine, the "case for Christianity" was best proved
by the history of salvation. Augustine's suggestion was, for the
most part, a traditional one. Presenting the sweep of salvation history had long been a way Christian teachers made their case, for
they were also heirs to another rhetorical tradition: that of Judaism.[67] And in that tradition, one way of arguing was to appeal to
history, specifically covenantal history, for that history held
authority: it traced the sequence of God's wondrous deeds and
thus was a vehicle of God's self-expression. Christian apologists,
from the New Testament on, had taken over this traditional Jewish mode of argument and would even turn it against mainstream
Judaism. They asserted that, in Jesus, history received its definitive configuration: Jesus' death and resurrection marked a water-
shed and created a complex discontinuity-in-continuity within the
history of the acts of God.[68] One finds historical recitals of this
sort in the Acts of the Apostles and in the works of apologists

66. *De catechizandis rudibus* 3.5 (Christopher, 18–19—altered). See Cicero, *De
partitione oratoria* 3.10.

67. For a suggestive overview of the blending of Jewish and Greek rhetori-
cal styles in Christian preaching, see Thomas K. Carroll, *Preaching the Word*,
MF 11 (Wilmington, Del.: Michael Glazier, 1984) esp. 9–37. On the Jewish rhe-
torical tradition and its use of covenantal history, see Richard J. Clifford, *Fair
Spoken and Persuading: An Interpretation of Second Isaiah* (New York: Paulist
Press, 1984).

68. The great early formulator of this is, of course, St. Paul; see Leander E.
Keck, *Paul and His Letters* (Philadelphia: Fortress Press, 1979) 32–81; see also
Pelikan, "The Turning Point in History," *Jesus through the Centuries: His Place
in the History of Culture* (New Haven: Yale University Press, 1985) 21–33;
Pelikan, *Emergence of the Catholic Tradition*, 12–27.

ranging from Justin and Irenaeus down to Eusebius.[69] Augustine's one innovative twist was in his final phrase: that this recital should also include Church history. Augustine believed the Christian era also had a place on the map of salvation history, for it marked the time when ancient biblical prophecies came to fulfillment.[70]

Augustine then spelled out the hermeneutic governing this narrative:

". . . for no other reason were all the things that we read in the holy Scriptures written before our Lord's coming than to announce his coming and to prefigure the Church to be. . . . Therefore, in the Old Testament the New is concealed, and in the New the Old is revealed."[71]

This statement—one of Augustine's most famous—encapsulates in the briefest terms the principles that Augustine had learned from Ambrose: that the Old Testament was "prophecy," "type," "shadow." This method enabled Augustine, as it had enabled Ambrose, to prove the "antiquity" of Christianity: that it had existed, albeit in hidden form, prior to and within Judaism. Thus, as Arnaldo Momigliano notes, Augustine, like other Christian teachers, could "silence the objection that Christianity was new, and therefore not respectable."[72]

Seeing the Old Testament fulfilled in the New was, of course, traditional. Christian apologists, from the New Testament on, had cited fulfilled prophecies as proofs of Christian claims. Moreover, in rhetorical theory, prophecies and oracles constituted what Cicero had called "divine evidence" and were considered a standard way to defend one's case.[73] Augustine knew from experience

69. For an excellent study of the divergence between pagan and Christian views of history, see Arnaldo Momigliano, "Pagan and Christian Historiography in the Fourth Century A.D.," in The Conflict between Paganism and Christianity in the Fourth Century, 79–99; on Augustine's debt to this tradition, see Markus, Saeculum, 7–9; on the early development of this tradition, see Grant, Greek Apologists of the Second Century (Philadelphia: Westminster Press, 1988).

70. Markus, Saeculum, 32. Markus (22–44) traces the different shifts in Augustine's thought on this, particularly the way he distances himself from the notion of a Christian empire.

71. De catechizandis rudibus 3.6 and 4.8 (Christopher, 2:19 and 23).

72. Momigliano, "Pagan and Christian Historiography," 83.

73. Cicero, De partitione oratoria 2.6.

the pedagogical effectiveness of this appeal to prophecy. In *Against Faustus* he describes how the average inquirer responded:

"Hearing these prophecies, and seeing their actual fulfillment, I need not say that the person would be affected; for we know from experience how the hearts of believers are confirmed by seeing ancient predictions now receiving their accomplishment."[74]

Such "divine evidence" touched something deep in pagan religious consciousness: people would now respond with wonder at the fulfillment of biblical prophecies just as they had once marvelled at the fulfillment of oracles given at the pagan shrines.

Augustine then suggested a guiding thread for this recital of salvation history: "charity . . . a standard to which we should make all that we say refer."[75] Augustine believed that God's love formed the bedrock beneath the shifting sands of salvation history. To justify this view, he appealed first to Scripture itself: that love was the fulfillment of the Law and that on the great commandment of love of God and neighbor depend the whole Law and the Prophets. He then pointed to the experience of human love: that even a "callous heart" is set "aflame . . . the moment it learns it is loved in return." Augustine then joined this basic human experience with the biblical and argued that in the incarnation lay the answer to people's deepest yearnings and the model of what it meant to be truly human:

". . . Christ came mainly for this reason: that we might learn how much God loves us, and might learn this to the end that we might begin to glow with love of him by whom we were first loved, and so might love our neighbor at the bidding and after the example of him who made himself our neighbor by loving us."[76]

This was, for Augustine, the Christian message in a nutshell. And it was a message that newcomers very much needed to hear. He therefore recommended that this theme bind together the catechist's speech "like gold which holds together in harmonious arrangement the jewels of an ornament—[yet] *without it becoming*

74. *Contra Faustum* 13.7 (trans. R. Stothert, NPNF 4:202). See the hypothetical interview that Augustine creates in *Contra Faustum* 13.7–16.
75. *De catechizandis rudibus* 3.6 (Christopher, 19).
76. Ibid., 4.7–8 (Christopher, 21–24—altered).

unduly conspicuous."[77] His final phrase might seem surprising: why should this theme of love *not* be conspicuous? The reason, according to Augustine and his contemporaries, was that one's oration was a work of art; that pedagogy, in part, followed aesthetic criteria. And their aesthetic dictated a measure of subtlety. The classical maxim was: "to conceal the art *is* the art" (*ars est celare artem*).[78] This meant that transitions should be disguised, that the address as a whole should, like a fugue, be a seamless flow of hidden threads. In other words, the theme of God's love was to undergird whatever one said, but subtly, without having undue attention drawn to it.

3) *Exhortation and Endtime.* Augustine then took up Deogratias's final question: whether the narrative should close with an exhortation. Augustine's answer was: yes, the duty of admonition and exhortation should indeed follow upon and flow from the narrative.[79] Cicero, as we have seen, did not include an exhortation as a formal element within a set speech—though exhortatory digressions were both common and expected.[80] However, the type of exhortation Augustine recommended had several elements, and each of these both resembled and transfigured standard rhetorical turns.

First, Augustine advised that the narrative, focused on the scriptural past and the ecclesial present, should flow into an exhortation, focused on the Christian vision of the future. This resembles Cicero's formula for a political speech: that the orator should first

77. Ibid., 6.10 (Christopher, 27—altered).
78. On this ancient aesthetic, see O'Connell, *St. Augustine's Confessions*, 10; Van der Meer, *Augustine the Bishop*, 417–18.
79. *De catechizandis rudibus* 2.4.
80. Cicero, *De inventione* 1.97. However, Kennedy (*Classical Rhetoric*, 94) notes that "ironically ethical digressions [between the 'reprehensio' and the 'peroratio'] . . . are very characteristic of his greatest judicial speeches." A whole speech could be an "exhortation"; one genre bears a certain resemblance to the oration described in *De catechizandis rudibus*: the protrepticus. The protrepticus was an introductory lecture given by a pagan philosopher calling his hearers to make a conversion to the philosophic way of life. The most famous example of this was Aristotle's *Protrepticus* (one of his works that has been lost). Clement had adapted this genre to Christian purposes, making his *Protrepticus* (or *Exhortation to the Greeks*), a call to enter the Christian way of life. See the discussion of this in Sider, *The Gospel & Its Proclamation*, 73–85. Cicero had also composed such a work, the *Hortensius*—the work that had such a powerful effect on Augustine. See Marrou, *History of Education in Antiquity*, 206–7, Hagandahl, *Augustine and the Latin Classics*, 2:486–97.

present a narrative (*narratio*) outlining the political facts, whether past or present; then he should make a persuasive argument (*suasio*) setting out his vision of the future.[81] The future Cicero had in mind was political, one that would come about if the state adopted the policy the orator was arguing for. The future Augustine had in mind was, by contrast, eschatological: the cate- chist was to speak of "the Last Judgment to come, with its good- ness towards the good, its severity toward the wicked, its certainty in relation to all."[82] In that future, praise and blame would come not from the orator's judgment, but from God's. The Christian idea that history would end with a Last Judgment—with salvation for some and damnation for others—would have been alien for pagans. While they—some at least—harbored notions of immortality, such views remained on the periphery of actual pagan religiosity.[83]

Augustine then suggested a second element in this exhortation: "In this discussion we should . . . combat the vain scoffings of unbelievers about the resurrection of the body."[84] This element was, in essence, a Christian equivalent of the refutation (*reprehen- sio*) of the opponent's case. Augustine knew that the resurrection of the flesh was *the* stock objection of pagans: "In no other thing is the Christian faith challenged so vehemently, so tenaciously, so vigorously and combatively as [is the belief] in the resurrection of the flesh."[85] Not surprisingly, Christian apologists as early as Athenagoras had forged a repertoire of arguments to defend it, and their rebuttals were passed on and sharpened by later Chris- tian teachers like Cyril of Jerusalem and Ambrose so that these arguments formed a stock element of Christian apologetic.[86] Au-

81. Cicero, *De partitione oratoria* 4.13 (Rackham, 321). Etchegaray Cruz, "El *de Catechizandis Rudibus* y la metodologia de la evangelización agustiniana," 366, cites this parallel, but fails to note the distinctive transformations this took in Christian hands.

82. *De catechizandis rudibus* 7.11 (Christopher, 28).

83. See Macmullen, *Christianizing the Roman Empire*, 11, as well as his more detailed treatment in *Paganism in the Roman Empire* (New Haven: Yale Univer- sity Press, 1981) 53-57.

84. *De catechizandis rudibus* 7.11 (Christopher, 27-28).

85. *Enarrationes in psalmos* 88.5 (trans. my own). For the range of problems concerning the resurrection that Augustine reports dealing with, see Cour- celle, "Propos antichrétiens rapportés par saint Augustin," 163-69.

86. For a summary of this theme in patristic thought, see J. N. D. Kelly, *Early Christian Doctrines*, rev. ed (New York: Harper & Row, 1978) 459-79.

131

gustine routinely treated this doctrine in his sermons and would later address it at length in his great apologetic work *City of God*.[87] In his advice to Deogratias, Augustine stressed that the resurrection of the flesh was an issue to be handled from the outset: (a) because it could well be a stumbling block for newcomers, and (b) because it held such significance in the Christian vision of history and human destiny.

At the close of the exhortation, one should, according to Augustine, "arm" candidates "against trials and offenses, whether outside the Church or inside it: outside, as against pagans or Jews or heretics; inside, as against the chaff of the Lord's threshing floor."[88] This turn resembles the traditional denunciation (*indignatio*) of one's opponents at the close of one's speech. But Augustine's suggestion here was not simply rhetorical, but pastoral. He knew new converts needed encouragement to face opposition from outsiders. As he noted in one sermon, Christians were not only persecuted in the past: "It continues even to this very day. Whenever [pagans] come upon a Christian, they habitually insult him, harass him, mock him, call him stupid, witless, heartless, and utterly devoid of worldly experience."[89] Pagan jibes could be caustic. They included: "adorer of a dead scoundrel"; "worshipper of a crucified man" (i.e., a criminal); "corruptors of morals; perverters of discipline" (i.e., because Christians taught that sins were forgivable).[90] When rains failed to fall at planting time, the cry was, "Blame the Christians"; when floods came at harvest time, the cry was again, "Blame the Christians."[91]

While such outside pressures were still formidable, it was inside problems that most concerned Augustine. He was alert, as few North Africans were, to the scandalous behavior of Christians, and offered Deogratias a litany of their vices:

87. This theme appears frequently in Augustine's sermons: *Enarrationes in psalmos* 84–87; *Sermones* 241.1; 242.4; 264.6. Augustine devotes the last half of the last book of *De civitate dei* (22.11-30) to it; in other words, this topic forms the climax of the book.

88. *De catechizandis rudibus* 7.11 (Christopher, 28—altered).

89. *Enarrationes in psalmos* 34.2.8 (trans. Scholastica Hebgin and Felicitas Corrigan, ACW 30:216).

90. *Enarrationes in psalmos* 68.1.12; *Enarrationes in psalmos* 101.10 (trans. my own). For an excellent summary of such popular sentiments, see Courcelle, "Anti-Christian Arguments and Christian Platonism," 151–57.

91. *Enarrationes in psalmos* 80.1 (trans. my own).

"[Those] depraved persons who in mobs fill the churches in a bodily sense only: . . . drunkards, covetous, extortioners, gamblers, adulterers, fornicators, lovers of shows, wearers of idolatrous charms, soothsayers, astrologers, or diviners employing vain and unholy arts."[92]

When pagans saw such types, they resorted to irony: "Behold the Christians"; and Augustine could complain in one sermon, "If anyone exhorts [a pagan] to believe, the answer comes back: 'Do you wish me to be like so-and-so?' "[93] Augustine's idea that one should warn inquirers about scandalous Christians may strike us as both honest and realistic. It was, nonetheless, unconventional—at least for North Africa. His Donatist rivals did not speak this way. They spoke of the Church in the purist language they had picked up from Cyprian (and Ephesians): that the Church is the bride of Christ without wrinkle or spot. For Augustine, such purity was only an eschatological reality; the Church that one would encounter here and now was a "mixed group" (corpus permixtum), or as he more often put it, an unsifted mix of "wheat" and "chaff."[94]

Exhortation—whether from pagan or Christian orators—did not focus only on the negative: it included praise as well as blame, summons to do good as well as to avoid evil. And according to Cicero, an oration was to end with a final impassioned plea meant to rouse the audience and lead them to decision (conquestio). In the same way Augustine advised that this evangelical exhortation end on a positive note: one should set forth "examples of the good, . . . not that we may be justified by them, but that we may know that, if we imitate them, we also shall be justified by [God] who justified them."[95]

THE CATECHIST: CULTIVATING DELIGHT

Deogratias thought his most pressing problem lay in inadequate method. Augustine, by contrast, considered the catechist's affec-

92. De catechizandis rudibus 7.11 (Christopher, 28).

93. Sermo 5.8; Sermo 15.6 (trans. my own). See also Enarrationes in psalmos 25.14.

94. For an excellent treatment of Donatist ecclesiology, see Bonner, St. Augustine: Life and Controversies, 276–89; also Carole E. Straw, "Augustine as Pastoral Theologian: The Exegesis of the Parables of the Field and Threshing Floor," Augustinian Studies 14 (1983) 129–51.

95. De catechizandis rudibus 7.11 (Christopher, 29).

tions a greater concern: "It is not a tough job to spell out in what ways beliefs might be instilled. . . . But . . . that one enjoy catechizing: that is [my] greatest concern."[96] Augustine admitted that he too was "nearly always dissatisfied" with his talks. His first impulse was to blame this on the gap between his inner intuition, that "sudden flash of light" which "floods the mind," and his self-expression, which, of necessity, had to trickle out in a slow, drawn-out stream of words. To combat discouragement, he relied on others' judgment: that "often the enthusiasm of those who desire to hear me shows me that my speech is not as dull as it seems to me." Augustine thus advised Deogratias to see his own case in a similar light:

"In the same way you too—from the very fact that those who are to be steeped in faith are so often brought to you—ought to be convinced that your talk is not as dissatisfying to others as it seems to you."[97]

Towards the end of the first part, Augustine would pursue this topic in greater detail and suggest "ways to be of good cheer."[98] Here he would cite five more reasons that might lead to burn-out: (1) boredom, (2) fear of making a mistake, (3) facing an apathetic audience, (4) upset at being interrupted, and (5) grief of heart. To counteract each, he exhorted Deogratias to keep certain aims in view. First, Augustine noted why he got bored:

"Because the topics that candidates have to be introduced to are now so familiar to us and no longer necessary for our own progress, it irks us to go back to them so often. And our heart, having outgrown them, no longer moves with pleasure along such well-worn and, as it were, childish paths."[99]

Augustine suggested that, to counteract this, one take Paul's advice to heart: that one should imitate Christ who took the form of a servant and emptied himself and who "became a little child in the midst of us, like a nurse cherishing her children." Augustine then drew on everyday examples for his exhortation: Be like the father who finds it "a pleasure to murmur into [an infant's] ear

96. Ibid., 2.4 (trans. my own).
97. Ibid., 2.3-4 (trans. my own).
98. Ibid., 2.4 (trans. my own).
99. Ibid., 10.14 (trans. my own).

broken and mutilated words." Be like a mother who would rather "chew morsels small and put them into her tiny son's mouth than to chew and consume large morsels herself." Be like "the hen . . . who with her drooping feathers covers her tender brood, and with tired cry calls her peeping chicks to her side" to rescue them from birds of prey. Augustine admitted Platonic spirituality might have its place: that it was fine for one's intellect to soar and penetrate the very essence of things. But he insisted that Christian values took precedence: that one's heart should first "delight in . . . graciously descend[ing] to the lowliest station."[100]

Augustine was concerned that the catechist not simply condescend but do so with *delectatio*, with "delight." To suggest how, he drew on a familiar experience—taking a friend on a tour:

"Is it not common that when we show certain beautiful, spacious locales, whether in town or out in the countryside, to those who have never seen them before, we—who have been in habit of passing them by without any enjoyment—find our own delight renewed by their delight at the novelty of it all? . . . How much more then ought we to rejoice when people now approach to study God himself . . . and how much more ought we to be renewed in their newness, so that if our preaching—now a matter of routine—has cooled off, it may get fired up because of our hearers for whom it is all new."[101]

Augustine would also use familial images to describe this evangelical work: that one ought to approach catechizing with "a brother's, a father's, and a mother's love." Augustine took seriously the traditional theme of Christian community as the household of God. As he saw it, Christians needed to be held together by such powerful bonds; and he would use such familial imagery to tap these powerful feelings.

Moreover, he insisted that love was infectious and that, in the dynamic of catechesis, it created an unexpected effect:

"For so great is the power of sympathy, that when people are affected by us as we speak and we by them as they learn, we dwell each in the other and thus both they, as it were, speak in us what

100. Ibid., 10.15 (Christopher, 37–38).
101. Ibid., 12.17 (trans. my own).

they hear, while we, in some way, learn in them what we teach.''[102]

For us, the idea that the student can teach the teacher is a more commonplace insight (albeit, one not always acted on). But in Augustine's time such a view was novel and, given the premises of his culture, foreign. Since social relations were regulated according to a strict and stratified hierarchy, few would have expected to learn anything from "lessers"; and given the presuppositions of the Platonic hierarchy of knowledge, few would have expected to learn anything from those who lack knowledge of the higher realms—or in the case of Christian Platonists, knowledge of the mysteries of Scripture and sacrament.[103] Yet Augustine took this reciprocity between teacher and learner seriously and made it a routine theme in his catechesis.[104]

A second cause of anxiety was fear of failure or of rejection. As noted earlier, inquirers with schooling could have quite high standards and were prone to mock anything but the most pristine speech. This could well provoke stage-fright. Thus Augustine suggested that if a slip of the tongue betrayed less-than-perfect oratory, the very error itself might teach that it was truth, and not eloquence, that mattered. Others might fear not oratorical fumbling, but doctrinal imprecision, even error. Augustine advised that one accept this as a test from God: "to see whether we can endure correction with calmness of mind"; should someone take this as an opportunity for fueling rumors, "let them furnish us an occasion for the practice of forbearance and compassion." Finally, even if one's speech was adequate and one's theology exact, one might still fear rejection: the Christian message, because of its very novelty, could appear harsh and might well offend the hearer. Such rejection was not without precedent: Christ too had seen his catechesis rejected.[105]

---

102. Ibid., 12.17 (Christopher, 41—altered).
103. We saw this earlier in some of Chrysostom's and Cyril's remarks. It is most obvious in Pseudo-Dionysius, *De ecclesiastica hierarchia* 3.6: Together with the possessed and penitents, catechumens are among "those who are stone deaf to what the sacred sacraments teach." See also Maximus Confessor, *Mystagogia* 15 and 23.
104. *Sermo* 216.1–2; *De doctrina christiana* 4.29.62.
105. *De catechizandis rudibus* 11.16 (Christopher, 39–40).

A third problem was having to cope with an unresponsive audience: "But in truth it is a hard thing to continue speaking up to the point determined upon beforehand, when we do not see our hearer moved."[106] Ancient audiences were noisier than many today and would express "approval either by word or by some gesture." This approval might include vigorous applause or cheers. Like the "Amen" one hears in a Baptist church, this applause could signal either agreement or understanding (that hearers followed the train of thought) or simply appreciation (that they enjoyed a clever turn of phrase).[107] Thus ancient orators could gauge their effectiveness more immediately than we. In this milieu, it was natural that an orator might feel that an unresponsive (i.e., silent) audience meant disapproval, that one's talk was worthless.

Augustine, drawing on long experience, warned against this hasty interpretation. There could well be other reasons: perhaps inquirers were held by "religious awe" or were held back by natural shyness; perhaps they did not understand what was said or they were simply weary. After all, he counselled, one could not see into their mind; to be sure, effort had to be made to "dislodge" them from their "hiding place." To do so, one had to switch methods: from lecture to question and answer. If they were shy, one should introduce the idea of fellowship. If they already knew all this, one should be brief. If they did not understand, one should speak more clearly and simply. If a person happened to be "slow-witted," one "should bear with him in a compassionate spirit, and . . . say much on his behalf to God, than say much to him about God." If they were tired, one should say something using a spicy turn of phrase; or one might offer something "calculated to arouse great wonder and amazement" (i.e., dazzle them with allegory); or one should simply offer them a chair.[108] This final suggestion seems strange from our perspective: why was the

106. Ibid., 13.18 (Christopher, 42–43).
107. See Van der Meer, *Augustine the Bishop*, 427–28. Enthusiastic responses from the congregation appear again and again; Augustine was frequently interrupted by applause and acclamations. Sometimes, the *notarii* who transcribed his sermons record the shouts of the audience. For examples of this, see *Sermones* 67.1; 151.8; 163B.5 (= Frang. 5); 313B.3 (= Denis 15). I will take this up in more detail in chapter 5.
108. *De catechizandis rudibus* 13.18–19 (Christopher, 42–44).

audience not seated in the first place? In antiquity, however, the procedure was the exact opposite of our own: usually it was the teacher who sat and the audience who stood.[109] Thus Augustine's suggestion, however pragmatic it seems to us, was certainly un-traditional. He thus took pains to justify it: (1) with an ecclesial argument—churches elsewhere in the empire had their audiences seated; (2) with a biblical argument—that Mary sat at the feet of Jesus when he taught.[110]

A fourth problem was the upset that came from being inter-rupted. He admitted such feelings were natural: it was hard to set aside some other task that might seem, at the moment, more im-portant. He also admitted: good pastoring demanded planning; but as God's servants, one should presume providence in all mat-ters, that it was God's schedule, not one's own, that counted:

"If then we are able to carry out [our plans] in the way we in-tended, let us rejoice, not because it was our will, but because it was God's will that they should be so done. But if anything un-avoidable happens to disturb our order, let us bend readily to it, lest we be broken; so we may make our own the order which God has preferred to ours."[111]

Augustine presumed life was mysterious: that "we can surmise only by the slenderest and most uncertain guess" the long-term value of our labors; that what might seem to be one more annoy-ance could in fact be a token of God's loving order.[112] Thus he advised: treat interruptions as providential and act accordingly.

One final source of discouragement was bad timing: that one was at that moment "troubled by some scandal" or by the defec-tion of some Christian.[113] During his career Augustine had his share of scandals and defections to cope with: wealthy landowners who extorted double the going tax-rate from poor tenants;[114] one

109. *Sermo* 355.2. See further discussion of this in the next chapter.
110. *De catechizandis rudibus* 13.19.
111. Ibid., 14.20 (Christopher, 46).
112. Ibid.
113. Ibid., 14.21.
114. *Epistola* 247. This incident is discussed in Van der Meer, *Augustine the Bishop*, 262. This and the other scandals and defections I cite are simply some of the most newsworthy; Augustine also was troubled by more ordinary scan-dals (drunken feasts at the tombs of martyrs, Christians at the public amuse-

of his presbyters who disobeyed house rules by retaining property on the sly;[115] a subdeacon who had secretly been a Manichee for years;[116] and some from his congregation who, on one occasion, had even lynched a corrupt commander of the local garrison.[117] As Augustine saw it, no matter what the discouragement, one should seize the moment at hand: that a candidate would even come to the door ought to "alleviate and dispel our grief"; and that one let the "joy over [new] gains alleviate grief over losses." Augustine advised against suppressing the sorrow; instead one should let "grief supply the fuel"—that one's words have "more fervor" and that the "emotions of our hearts not pass away without bearing fruit."[118]

At the end of the first part of the treatise, Augustine appended a disclaimer: that his sample addresses had "a future reader in view" and were a far cry from "catechizing with a listener actually present." He thus reminded Deogratias of things an orator took for granted. First, one had to suit the words to the audience—to their education, age, sex, social standing, place of origin—and that if the audience was mixed, one had to intuit their unique chemistry "since they themselves mutually affect one another . . . by their mere presence." Second, different settings dictated different styles of discourse: that what was appropriate to a one-on-one chat was inappropriate to a public sermon, and vice versa. Augustine indicated, in passing, the range of settings he used: sometimes this first catechesis took place privately; sometimes with a single candidate but overheard by others who "judge and endorse a subject familiar to them," presumably with applause and acclamations; and sometimes *de loco superiore* (literally, "from an elevated place")—in other words, with the catechist seated on the raised *cathedra* in the basilica while "a silent throng gazes with rapt attention."[119] Third, one should "bear a certain

---

ments) and more ordinary defections, usually to the Donatists; see Frend, *The Donatist Church*, 251.

115. *Sermones* 355-56. Brown, *Augustine of Hippo*, 409-11, discusses the details of the incident.

116. *Epistola* 236.

117. *Sermo* 302.10-20. On this incident, see Van der Meer, *Augustine the Bishop*, 142-43; Markus, *Saeculum*, 94-96.

118. *De catechizandis rudibus* 14.21 (Christopher, 47-48).

119. Ibid., 15.23 (Christopher, 49-50).

facial expression, as it were, disclosing the frame of mind of the speaker and should affect the audience in various ways."[120] Here Augustine alludes to one of the stock items found in rhetorical handbooks: the delivery (*pronuntiatio*). This art included not only control of voice (*vocis figura*) but also of gesture and facial expression (*corporis motus*).[121] Great care was taken that one's body complimented, indeed choreographed, the play of words and emotions. Finally, Augustine, who trusted living models more than rule books, offered to apprentice Deogratias: that "you might learn this [art of improvisation] better by seeing me in action than by reading what I dictate."[122]

THE CATECHESIS: EXAMPLES

In the second half of *On Catechizing*, Augustine gives two sample addresses: the first of considerable length and intricacy; the second, a bare-bones summary. Both lack, as he is at pains to insist, the improvisational touch he relied on when he had a flesh-and-blood inquirer before him. Augustine designed both with a specific candidate in mind: "one of the *uneducated* class, . . . a townsman such as you must come across in great numbers"; moreover, one who had come not with illicit motives, but sought only "the rest which is hoped for after this life."[123] This point is critical, and often overlooked by commentators: Augustine geared his sample catecheses to Deogratias's typical addressee and *not* the sort that he had discussed in detail earlier (e.g., those with suspect motives or those from the educated elite).

The first address opens with a lengthy *exordium*. In fact, Augustine displays little hurry in getting on to the narrative. Earlier, he had suggested that the *exordium* take the candidate's background and motives into account. Here he puts this principle into practice. His opening words mix warmth with warning (and include a pun on Deogratias's name—a touch he, no doubt, found amusing):

"Thanks be to God, brother (*Deo gratias, frater*)! I congratulate you with all my heart and rejoice with you that amid the great and

120. Ibid. (Christopher, 50).
121. Kennedy, *Classical Rhetoric*, 98; also Marrou, *History of Education in Antiquity*, 200, especially his comments on chironomy ("hand-play").
122. *De catechizandis rudibus* 15.23 (trans. my own). The same sentiment is repeated in *De doctrina christiana* 4.3.4. Cf. Cicero, *De oratore* 2.22.90.
123. *De catechizandis rudibus* 16.24 (Christopher, 52).

perilous storms of this world, you have thought of the one true and sure refuge. For even in this life people seek rest and repose from great labors, but because of their twisted desires, they do not find it. For they wish to be at rest amid restless things and because in the course of time these objects are withdrawn and pass away, they vex their victims with fear and anguish and allow them no rest."[124]

Augustine then illustrates his point with quick snapshots of the "cauldron" that was ancient Carthage.[125] He traces, for instance, how simple men might, on a lark, squander their meager savings. Then to escape poverty, they plunge into a life of crime, becoming burglars or highwaymen. This, of course, offers no peace. At night, fears haunt them, and "they who a little earlier were singing in the tavern now dream of the sorrows of prison." Even more telling, according to Augustine, is the behavior seen in the stadium. There "frantic mobs" cheer "poor wretches" pitted against each other or against wild animals. The fury of the crowd stirs up the fury of the gladiators who then vent their wrath against one another. This, in turn, raises the crowd's fury to a new, more frenzied pitch. Augustine then draws the moral: the pursuits of city life—whether wealth or fame, whether alcohol or sex—are in the end vanity: "mad pleasures are no pleasure," for it takes only "one little fever" and "all these things vanish"; all that is left is "a void and a wounded conscience."[126] Augustine then turns his attention to the townsman and commends his wisdom for seeking to abandon such follies: "But you, inasmuch as you are seeking that true rest which is promised to Christians after this life, shall taste its sweetness and comfort even here. . . ."[127] He goes on to praise him for seeking to enter the Church not for "temporal advantage" nor with a "feigned heart" like "the chaff" who may dwell in the Church "until the time of winnowing" but who will be separated from the "everlasting rest."[128]

In this *exordium*, Augustine fulfills Cicero's classic requirements: to make the listener "well-disposed, attentive, and receptive" by

124. Ibid. (Christopher, 52–53—altered).
125. *Confessiones* 3.1. In calling it a "seething caldron [*sartago*]," he was punning on the city's Latin name, *Carthago*.
126. *De catechizandis rudibus* 16.25 (Christopher, 53–55—altered).
127. Ibid. (Christopher, 55).
128. Ibid., 16.24–17.25 (Christopher, 55).

commending his wisdom and purity of purpose.[129] And Augustine uses one of the tactics Cicero had recommended for winning this goodwill: showing one's opponents as "base, haughty, cruel, or malicious" and as deserving contempt for "their laziness, carelessness, sloth, indolent pursuits or luxurious idleness."[130] And Augustine has held it all together with a single theme: true rest.

Augustine takes this theme of rest as his point of entry for the narrative:

"Now concerning this rest Scripture declares and does not keep silent, that from the beginning of the world wherein God made heaven and earth and all the things that are in them, He worked six days and on the seventh day He rested."[131]

Immediately Augustine anticipates objections: if God is indeed all-powerful, why did it take six days to create the world? and why, in any case, should God have to labor at all? Augustine then asserts: "He could have made all things even in a single instant"; moreover, "He had not labored to rest" for "He spoke and they were made; He commanded and they were created." Instead, Augustine argues, the seven days of creation foreshadow the structure of salvation history: these "signify that after the six ages of this world, in the seventh age as on the seventh day, [God] would be at rest in His saints."[132]

In his recital Augustine gives the rich detail found in Genesis short shrift. The story of the creation and fall is sketched in a few quick strokes. Augustine's focus is less on the story and more on what it says about God and about us: that God is "almighty and good and just and merciful"; that we are made in his own image and thus reign over the earth as God reigns over the whole of creation. Once more, he anticipates objections: why would an all-knowing God create an imperfect creature? and how could such a God be all-powerful if the devil had the power to seduce the first couple? Against these objections, Augustine insists that human beings were created to be like God—that is, free; that the first couple fell freely; and that God foresaw the fall and, like a just judge, meted out just deserts by the "laws of His wondrous dis-

129. Cicero, *De inventione* 1.20—cited in Augustine, *De doctrina christiana* 4.4.6.
130. Cicero, *De inventione* 1.22 (Hubbell, 45).
131. *De catechizandis rudibus* 17.28 (Christopher, 56–57).
132. Ibid. (Christopher, 57).

pensation."[133] Clearly, this account is not so much a narrative in our sense of it (i.e., a story); it is rather a narrative in the traditional rhetorical sense: an argument framed, positively, in defense of Christian views and, negatively, in opposition to possible detractors.

Earlier, Augustine had suggested two threads to shape the narrative: (1) foreshadowings of the New Testament, and (2) the love of God. Again and again, one finds Augustine portraying Old Testament events as "spiritual mysteries closely associated with Christ and the Church."[134] For instance, he notes that the righteous in Noah's time were saved from the great flood by the wood of the ark. According to Augustine, this anticipates the fact that the righteous in the Church have been "buoyed up" by the wood of the Cross and thus saved from the flood "in which this world is submerged."[135] Later, when speaking of the Exodus, he notes that in the Red Sea the Egyptians drowned while Israel crossed over. He then adds: this foreshadows "baptism, in which the faithful pass into new life but their sins like enemies are totally blotted out." Similarly, the Jewish rites of Passover foreshadow later events: the sacrifice of the paschal lamb anticipates Christ's passion, while the marking of the doorpost with lamb's blood anticipates the rite of entering the catechumenate: that is, "with the sign of his passion and cross, you today are to be signed and sealed upon your forehead, as it were upon a doorpost."[136] Towards the end of the narrative, he points out Christ's own predictions and their fulfillment in the history of the Church: the spread of the gospel; persecution and martyrdom; heresies and schisms. As Augustine puts it, "All these things, foretold long before, have come to pass exactly as we read."[137] Finally, he gently tries to move the inquirer—as he had said he would—from trust in miracles to trust in Scripture: that while the first Christians witnessed miracles and so came to faith, people in his own day hear the Scriptures and, seeing its prophecies fulfilled, likewise come to faith.

133. Ibid., 18.29-30.
134. Ibid., 19.33 (Christopher, 63).
135. Ibid., 19.32 (Christopher, 62).
136. Ibid., 20.34 (Christopher, 65).
137. Ibid., 24.45 (Christopher, 76).

The theme of God's love appears, but in muted tones. Early on, Augustine notes that God "made all things through his Word; and his Word is Christ himself" and that thus "we are saved by believing that He would come—that we might love God, who so loved us that He sent His only Son."[138] It is not until his thumbnail sketch of Church history that the motif of love reappears. There it winds its way through the recital linking various threads: the love poured forth by the Spirit into the hearts of the disciples; the Decalogue reduced to the two-fold commandment of love; the "concord of Christian love" expressed in the redistributing of goods "to everyone according to need."[139]

These two themes—fulfilled prophecies and God's love—appear more in brief digressions and passing remarks. It is two other themes that shape the main flow of the narrative: (1) the two cities and (2) the seven ages. Early on, he introduces the first of these:

"Two cities—one of the wicked, the other of the just—have been swept along [through history]: from humankind's birth to time's end. At this moment they [journey] joined in body, but divided in will; judgment day will see them at long last sifted in body as well."[140]

This theme was one of Augustine's favorites. He had probably picked it up from Tyconius, a Donatist exegete whose work he admired.[141] But this sort of dualism had long held pride of place in the catechesis of new converts. The *Didache*, perhaps the earliest Christian document outside the New Testament, had counseled teachers to set out for converts the stark polarities of the "two ways"—the "way of life" and "the way of death."[142] Seeing these two ways played out in human history had also been integral to Augustine's thought for a long while: it appears in his early pamphlet, *On True Religion*.[143] And later this theme would serve as the blueprint for the *City of God*.[144]

138. Ibid., 17.28 (Christopher, 57—altered).

139. Ibid., 23.41.

140. Ibid., 19.31 (trans. my own).

141. On Augustine's probable dependence on Tyconius, see Bonner, *St. Augustine: Life and Controversies*, 287–89; Markus, *Saeculum*, 115–16.

142. *Didache* 1–6.

143. *De vera religione* 27.50.

144. For a summary of the "two cities" theme, its development in Augustine's thought and the nuances he gave it, especially in *De civitate dei*, see A. Lauras

In *On Catechizing*, this "two cities" theme—their intermingling and division—receives its clearest rendering when Augustine describes the two great archetypal cities: Jerusalem and Babylon. Both have names whose etymologies reveal their inner character: Jerusalem "is interpreted 'vision of peace'" while Babylon is "interpreted 'confusion.'"[145] Moreover, just "as Jerusalem signifies the city and fellowship of the saints, so Babylon signifies the city and fellowship of the wicked." For Augustine, the key point is that historically Jerusalem "was made captive and a great part of it led away into Babylon." This he interprets allegorically: "Now all this was a figure signifying that the Church of God, with all the saints who are citizens of the heavenly Jerusalem, was to be in bondage under the kings of this world."[146] This bondage and exilic experience of the saints reverberates down to the present era: Christians pay taxes; they submit to the vagaries of the Roman state and the inequities of the social order. Augustine then transposes Christian submissiveness here and now into an eschatological horizon: that "Christian servants" may now serve "temporal masters" but in the last days they will judge them "if they find them wrong" and, if just, will reign with them "as equals." Augustine here digresses on a favorite theme: even now "earthly kings" are "forsaking idols for the sake of which they once persecuted Christians," thus fulfilling ancient prophecies. These kings—the Christian emperors—have "given the Church . . . temporal quietude for the spiritual building of houses and planting of gardens and vineyards"—echoing Jeremiah's exhortation to the exiles in Babylon to build houses and plant gardens since the restoration of the kingdom still lay far off.[147]

Here the "two cities" stands at center stage. More often, it lies in the background, subtly shaping the flow of thought. For instance, Augustine portrays Abraham as one of the early "citizens of that holy city," who serves all later ages as archetype and model.[148] And later he would stress that Christ "was born in the city of Bethlehem, which among all the cities of Judea was so in-

---

and H. Rondet, "Le thème des deux cités dans l'oeuvre de saint Augustin," *Études augustiniennes* 28 (Paris: Aubier, 1953) 97–160; Markus, *Saeculum*, 45–71.

145. *De catechizandis rudibus* 20.36; 21.37 (Christopher, 66–67).
146. Ibid., 21.37 (Christopher, 67–68).
147. Ibid., 21.37 (Christopher, 68–69).
148. Ibid., 19.33.

significant, that today it is called a village." This detail had moral import: God "did not want anyone to glory in the exaltation of an earthly city."[149]

The other motif—the seven ages—also figures prominently. This idea was likewise a traditional one.[150] According to Augustine's (and the traditional) framework, the Old Testament recorded five ages: (1) from Adam to Noah; (2) from Noah to Abraham; (3) from Abraham to David; (4) from David to the Babylonian captivity; (5) from the return of the exiles to the incarnation. Augustine's concern is the sixth age, the age of the coming of Christ and the Church. As he saw it, it marked a caesura in the map of salvation history. In this sixth age "the human mind is renewed in the likeness of God, even as on the sixth day human beings were made in the likeness of God."[151]

It is within his description of the sixth age that Augustine summarizes the good news of Christ. His focus is less the gospel story and more its meaning. This he maps out with a long series of paradoxes. The following is an excerpt—charted so as to highlight the intricate verbal sonorities:

Esuriuit qui omnes pascit,	He hungered, he who feeds all,
situit per quem omnis potus,	He thirsted, he who created all we drink,
et qui spiritaliter	He who spiritually is both
panis est esurientium	the bread of the hungering and
fonsque sitientium . . .	the wellspring of the thirsting.
uelut obmutuit	He became as one dumb
et obsurduit	and deaf
coram conuiciantibus,	in the presence of revilers,
per quem mutus locutus est	He through whom the dumb spoke
et surdus aduiuit:	and the deaf heard.
uinctus est,	He was bound,
qui de infirmitatum,	he who freed [us] from
uinculis soluit:	infirmities' bonds.

149. Ibid., 22.40 (Christopher, 71–72).
150. On this traditional scheme, see Danielou, *The Bible and the Liturgy,* 278–95. On Augustine's use of it, see Markus, *Saeculum,* 17–18.
151. *De catechizandis rudibus* 22.39 (Christopher, 70–71).

146

flagellatus est,	He was scourged,
qui omnium dolorum	he who drove out
flagella de hominum	every scourge of pain
corporibus expulit:	from peoples' bodies.
crucifixus est,	He was crucified,
qui	he who put an end
cruciatus nostros finiuit:	to all our crosses.
mortuus est,	He died,
qui	he who raised
mortuos suscitauit.	the dead to life.[152]

Reveling in paradox had long been integral to the language of Christian hymns and liturgy, and appears repeatedly from the earliest Christian writers (Ignatius of Antioch, Melito of Sardis) to Augustine's older contemporaries (Ephrem the Syrian, Gregory of Nazianzus).[153] Such language set the central Christian mysteries in high relief and could be easily memorized—an urgent need if one had an illiterate audience. Augustine here exploits this tradition to great effect. He weaves an intricate combination of rhetorical figures and verbal sonorities so that in his hands the language of the Christian kerygma verges on poetry.

Narrative then shifts unobtrusively to exhortation. First, Augustine turns—as he said he would—to the Last Judgment, joining it to his "two cities" motif: on the "last day of judgment . . . all the citizens of both these cities shall receive again their bodies and shall render an account of their life before the judgment seat of Christ, the Judge."[154] Second, he defends the doctrine of bodily

152. Ibid., 22.40 (CCSL 46.165; trans. my own).
153. On this language in Ignatius and Melito, see Pelikan, *Emergence of the Catholic Tradition*, 177. There is a remarkable similarity between the passage quoted above from Augustine and ones in Ephrem the Syrian, *Hymn on the Nativity* 11.7-8 and in Gregory of Nazianzus, *Theological Oration* 3.20. Augustine did not apparently know about Gregory's third oration until some fifteen years later. Rufinus did a translation of nine of Gregory's sermons around the year 400, but this was not one of them. See the discussion of this in Eugene TeSelle, *Augustine the Theologian* (New York: Herder & Herder, 1970) 294-96. Augustine's pattern of kerygmatic paradoxes was more likely a standard sequence passed on orally.
154. *De catechizandis rudibus* 24.45 (Christopher, 76). Note that Christopher, in his outline in ACW 2, has mismarked the beginning of the *exhortatio*: it should begin at 24.45, not 25.46. See Augustine's comments in 7.11.

resurrection—again as he had announced. But the ploys he uses are subtle. He begins as though his hearer already sided with him: "And so, brother, strengthen yourself, in the name and help of Him in whom you trust, against the tongues of those who mock at our faith." He then puts forward arguments for the resurrection of the body—not by direct rebuttal, but by a series of rhetorical questions:

"For where was that mass of your body and where that form and structure of your limbs a few years ago—before you were born or even before you had been conceived in your mother's womb? Where was this present mass and stature of your body? Did it not come forth into the light from the hidden recesses of this creation, secretly fashioned by the Lord God, and rise by a regular growth through various stages to its present size and shape? Is it, then, too difficult a thing for God—who even in a moment brings together from their hiding places the cloudbanks and overcasts the sky in the twinkling of an eye—to restore that substance of your body as it was before?"[155]

Augustine then recapitulates themes from both the introduction and the narrative: the two cities; the seven ages; the wheat and chaff; love of God and neighbor; eternal rest. Yet he does more than simply sum up. He also appeals to the hearer's heart—just as Cicero had advised. First, he encourages the candidate to "be on fire with love and longing for the everlasting life of the saints" that he may taste the rewards of the seventh age, the promised rest. Here Augustine sketches the topology of endtime: in the city of God there will be "no weariness of mind, no exhaustion of body, . . . no want"; "God shall be the whole delight and contentment of the holy city"; most importantly, "we may . . . see what we believe," the Trinity, not "in a babble of words, but may absorb this by a most pure and most fervent contemplation in that heavenly silence."[156] Augustine then warns: avoid heretics and schismatics; bear with the "chaff" who must be endured "until the season of winnowing," the "drunkards, covetous, defrauders, gamblers, adulterers," "those crowds" which "fill the church on the feast days of the Christians which likewise fill the theatres on

155. *De catechizandis rudibus* 25.46 (Christopher, 77–78—altered).
156. Ibid., 25.47 (Christopher, 78–79).

the ritual days of the pagans."[157] Finally he begs the new candidate—as he said he would—to "associate with the good, whom you see loving your King with you" and "to love those who are not yet just, that they may become so."[158]

We who have heard the Christian view of things for so long are liable to underestimate how striking such an address would have been to the average pagan hearer. First, as Momigliano points out, Jewish and Christian history was not common knowledge, even among many educated pagans, so that "conversion meant literally the discovery of a new history from Adam and Eve to contemporary events."[159] Second, the Christian view that history had an inner direction and meaning meant that the convert not only acquired a new history, but also a history that contained an implicit philosophy of history.[160] Third, as Macmullen notes, pagan worship was not generally motivated by love. As pagans saw it, the gods certainly deserved service because human beings needed benefits only gods could offer (good health, rain for crops, freedom from earthquakes, plagues, and social upheavals); but not love, "since a god (as Aristotle had long taught) could feel no love in response."[161] Thus the idea that God loves us, that God took flesh out of love, would have been astounding, perhaps even absurd. Fourth, while pagans might have been shocked by the idea of a Last Judgment and might have thought the idea of resurrected bodies a bit crude, still, as Macmullen notes, "no pagan cult held out promise of afterlife for the worshipper as he knew and felt himself to be. Resurrection of the flesh was thus a truth proclaimed to the decisive advantage of the Church."[162] Finally, Momigliano has stressed that seeing history with Christian eyes—from Genesis to the Last Judgment—meant that "the convert, in abandoning paganism, was compelled to enlarge his historical horizon: he was likely to think for the first time in terms of universal history."[163]

157. Ibid., 25.48 (Christopher, 79–80).
158. Ibid., 25.49 (Christopher, 81).
159. Momigliano, "Pagan and Christian Historiography," 82.
160. Ibid., 83. See also Charles Norris Cochrane, *Christianity and Classical Culture: A Study of Thought and Action from Augustus to Augustine* (London: Oxford University Press, 1968) 456–516.
161. Macmullen, *Paganism in the Roman Empire*, 53.
162. Ibid., 136.
163. Momigliano, "Pagan and Christian Historiography," 83.

Augustine reminded Deogratias that, after such catechesis, candidates be asked whether they "believe these things and desire to observe them"; if so, they were to be "signed with due ceremony" and "handled according to the custom of the Church."[164] This ceremony—the entrance into the catechumenate—included several rites: perhaps, a laying-on of hands; certainly, a signing of the cross on the forehead and a taste of salt. Augustine considered the salt "a sacrament" which, in some sense, "preserved" and "seasoned" the candidate. In fact, in his treatise *On Merits and the Remission of Sins*, he says that this salt was considered "holier than any food which constitutes our ordinary nourishment."[165]

Augustine saw this succession of rites as a momentous step. In his sermons, he frequently reminded his congregation that the Sign of the Cross had been "tattooed" on their foreheads, that they had thus been set apart and now belonged to Christ.[166] And

164. *De catechizandis rudibus* 26.50 (Christopher, 82). We should not assume that the reaction to such an address and its closing question would be a muttered "yes." Minucius Felix, in *Octavius* 39 (trans. Clarke, ACW 39:125), gives the following reaction to a lengthy oration directed to a pagan: "Thus Octavius completed his oration. For some time afterwards we were so stunned that we could say nothing but kept our eyes fixed on him. So far as I was concerned, I was completely lost in profound amazement at the wealth of proofs, examples, and authoritative quotations he had used to illustrate matter easier to feel than to express. . . . He had shown the truth to be so simple as well as so attractive." Admittedly, this work is a fictionalized drama and is 150 years before Augustine; yet it offers an intriguing picture of the desired audience response to such an oration.

165. Augustine mentions the sacrament of salt explicitly in *De catechizandis rudibus* 26.50; cf. *Confessiones* 1.11. He alludes to three elements—Sign of the Cross, laying on of hands, and apparently a taste of salt—in *De peccatorum meritiis et remissione* 2.26.42. Van der Meer, *Augustine the Bishop*, 354, thinks there was also an *exsufflatio* (a breathing on the candidate to exorcise the devil); he justifies this claim by citing *Contra Cresconium* 2.5.7, but Augustine here refers not to Catholic, but to Donatist practice. Van der Meer's claim has some warrant since both the Donatists and Catholics followed the same ritual traditions. Van der Meer also suspects that the "sacrament of salt" may refer to "salted bread"; the idea of "salted bread" has been seriously challenged by Bernard Botte, "Sacramentum catechumenorum," *Questions liturgiques* 43 (1963) 322–30. For a good summary of this question, see R. De Latte, "Saint Augustin et le baptême," 181–91.

166. See, for example, *Sermones* 32.13; 97A.3 (=Bibl. Casin. 2.214); 301A.8 (=Denis 17); *Tractatus in evangelium Ioannis* 3.2.

in a sermon he once addressed to neophytes, he interpreted these first rites as a shadow and foretaste of the sacraments of initiation; by these, candidates were conceived in the womb of mother Church.[167] Henceforth, according to Augustine, candidates could count themselves as "Christians"; henceforth, they belonged to "the great household."[168] They were now catechumens.

THE MESSAGE AND THE MESSENGER

I have given Augustine's *On Catechizing* close scrutiny. Yet it is important not to lose sight of wider evangelical efforts. For example, Augustine used to correspond with sympathetic pagans such as Longinianus, a Platonist philosopher, or Volusianus, a prominent aristocrat.[169] These writings were more like open letters than private correspondence. Augustine knew, for instance, that Volusianus would circulate these among the elite circles he moved in. Thus Augustine took great care in the way he handled the subtle and politically volatile objections raised by Volusianus and his circle: e.g., that Jesus had simply been a magician; that the God of the Christians, in abrogating the Mosaic Law, showed a fickle nature; that the Lord of the universe could not possibly have "hidden within the tiny body of a wailing infant"; that the Christian doctrine of turning the other cheek threatened the very welfare of the empire.[170] Besides such letter-writing campaigns, Augustine expended enormous effort in composing *City of God*—meant to defend Christianity against those who charged that the abandonment of the old pagan rites had led to the Goths' sack of Rome in 410.[171] This massive apologia was, of course, read in elite circles. But others had access to it. We know, for instance, that

167. *Sermo* 260C.1 (=Mai 94) (trans. my own).
168. *Sermo* 301A.8 (=Denis 17); *Tractatus in evangelium Ioannis* 11.4. See also *Tractatus in evangelium Ioannis* 44.2; *Sermones* 46.31; 97A.3 (=Bibl. Cas. 2.114).
169. For the correspondence with Longinianus, see *Epistolae* 233–35; for the correspondence with Volusianus, see *Epistolae* 132, 135–39. Marcellinus, an imperial delegate and friend of Augustine, served as an important intermediary in this exchange.
170. *Epistola* 135.2, Volusianus to Augustine (Parsons, 20:14); also *Epistola* 136, Marcellinus to Augustine.
171. *De civitate Dei* 1.1. On circumstances and milieu of its writing, see Brown, *Augustine of Hippo*, 287–329.

enthusiastic intellectuals once spent three successive afternoons listening to a public reading of Book 18.[172]

More difficult to document is the evangelization carried on by ordinary Christians. In quiet ways they worked to pass on the Christian message to pagan friends, family, and neighbors. As Augustine noted in one sermon, just as the Samaritan woman had proclaimed Christ to those in her village, "so it is done today with those who are outside and not yet Christian. Christ is announced through Christian friends."[173] Encounters of this sort, so critical to the spread of Christianity among the mass of ordinary people, are exactly the sort rarely preserved in the historical record. Still we saw glimmers. Why, for instance, would pagans like Dioscorus pray to Christ for healing? Because ordinary Christians had spread the word of Christ's healing powers. Why were pagans having dreams about Christ? Because ordinary Christians had spread word concerning Christ's divinity. Moreover, ordinary Christians would accompany inquirers and would know enough of their religious experience to act as witnesses in the initial interrogation.

Within this wider sweep, the evangelization described in *On Catechizing* held a limited, but critical, place. Formal catechesis was modest: a single, though often lengthy, address. And this catechesis was, in essence, an overture: both a prelude and an overview. Its contours—at least as Augustine described it—both relied on and modified the outline used in traditional orations. The introduction (*exordium*) took its point of departure from the motives that sparked the inquirer's interest in Christianity—whether these had come from books, oracles, or dreams. In the body of the address, the catechist "unrolled the scroll" of salvation history. Yet this involved not so much storytelling as it did making the case for Christianity. The Christian narrative would draw on salvation history for both the facts of the case (as in a legal *narratio*) and the evidence (as in a legal *confirmatio*). In this recital, the catechist not only tried to convince inquirers' minds, but also to evoke delight

172. *Epistola* 2*.3 (trans. Robert B. Eno, FC 81:20). This is from one of Augustine's letters recently discovered by Johannes Divjak. On this discovery and collection, see Henry Chadwick, "New Letters of St. Augustine," *Journal of Theological Studies*, n.s. 34 (1983) 425–52.

173. *Tractatus in evangelium Ioannis* 15.33 (trans. John W. Rettig, FC 79:99). See Macmullen, *Christianizing the Roman Empire*, 36–42; while he is speaking of the pre-Constantinian era, many of his comments are relevant.

and amazement—whether by pointing to prophecies fulfilled or by uncovering hidden allegorical meanings. According to Augustine, two overarching principles governed this recital. First, the catechist was to show both the unity of the Testaments and the priority of the Christian dispensation. Second, the jewel-like episodes taken from Scripture were to be set within the golden message of love, the love of God and of neighbor. At the close of the address, narrative shifted to exhortation—from a scriptural past to an eschatological future. The Christian exhortation—at least as Augustine described it—drew on traditional rhetorical turns. It had a *reprehensio*: the pagan case against the resurrection of the flesh was to be dismantled. It had an *enumeratio*: earlier threads (e.g., true rest, the two cities) would be drawn together by setting them within the framework of the Last Judgment. It had an *indignatio*: the catechist would arm inquirers not only against Christianity's detractors but also against the chaff within the Church. And finally it had a *conquestio*: the catechist would encourage inquirers to imitate the wheat within the Church and to love those who were not yet righteous that they might become so.

For Augustine evangelical catechesis was essentially an oral art. It demanded an improvisational touch—attuned to the mood of the moment and to the experience and education of the inquirer. It also demanded respecting the face-to-face dynamic: that by the very nature of oral teaching, no clear line could be drawn between the Christian message and the Christian who bore that message. Inevitably, the bearing of the messenger affected the bearing of the message. Thus Augustine insisted that what Deogratias needed was not method, but good cheer. A glum Deogratias would have proved a poor spokesman for the awe-inspiring love of God. Moreover, evangelical catechesis involved more than methods or message; it also—and perhaps ultimately—involved forming a relationship. Augustine expected, for example, that a sympathy would spring up between catechist and inquirer so that supposedly clear lines between the two would blur. And he thought it only natural to compare the experience of evangelization to the experience of one friend giving another a tour through the countryside.

Finally, Augustine believed that the heart of the matter lay in the heart. This certainly meant keeping an eye on what excited inquirers and playing to that interest. But this also meant that one respect their less-than-pure motives, that one presume the best—even in the most suspicious of conversions—and that one hope for God's grace to make up for what seemed lacking. Augustine stressed the affective dynamic within evangelization because he believed that no voice reached the ears save the emotion of the heart. And as he saw it, the core of Scripture was a message aimed at the human heart: the love of God and love of neighbor, for God, in Christ, had shown how much he loved us and, in Christ, had made himself our neighbor. This message shaped the pedagogy: inquirers needed to have a first taste of this love of God and of neighbor. Yet they needed only a first taste. During the catechumenate, there would be ample time for purifying motives, for learning the range and depth of the Christian message, and for working out a way of life appropriate to those who bore on their forehead the cross of Christ.

Chart 6
Augustine's Opening Catechesis and the Classical Juridical Oration

Cicero's Outline for Oration	Function	Augustine's Outline for First Catechesis
1. Exordium	Opening: render audience well disposed, attentive and receptive	1. Exordium: play on motives raised in inquiry; touch on books read by educated inquirer
2. Narratio	Facts of the case	2. Narratio: recite cardinal points of salvation history from Genesis to present Church; charity as thread
3. Partitio	Where agree with opponents and where disagree	[No equivalent given]
4. Confirmatio	Arguments that support one's own case	Narratio: Cite fulfilled prophecies
5. Reprehensio	Arguments that weaken the opponent's case	In exhortatio, respond to objections against resurrection of the flesh
6. Peroratio	Conclusion:	3. Exhortatio:
a. Enumeratio	Sum up one's case	Case summarized within perspective of Last Judgment
b. Indignatio	Arouse ill will against opponents	Arm inquirer against pagans, heretics, Jews; and against "chaff" within the Church
c. Conquestio	Arouse pity and sympathy for one's client	Encourage inquirer and exhort to imitate the good within the Church

Chapter 5

Catechumenate:
Breaking Open the Bread of The Word

In his treatise *On Faith and Works,* Augustine touched briefly on the dynamic of the long catechumenate phase. First, he mentioned its raison d'être: "What is all that time for, during which they hold the name and place of catechumens, except to hear what the faith and pattern of Christian life should be?"[1] He then admitted: while "study becomes far more earnest and intensive" during Lent, still "this training actually goes on during all that time which the Church has beneficially appointed" for the catechumenate.[2] Finally, he noted that in his sermons he presented a "cross-weave" of doctrine and of moral admonition and that "both were given to catechumens, both, to the faithful"; in this way, the "catechumens were instructed," while the "faithful were roused from forgetfulness."[3] Augustine gives no further specifics here; he presumed readers would know what these were. These passages—at once tantalizing and vague—do at least provide a vocabulary for our questions: What was the faith and pattern of Christian life presented to catechumens? Where and when did they hear it? How specifically were they instructed? In what sense was this training?

To answer these questions is not easy. Why? Because the catechumenate phase lacks—from our vantage point—the easy visibility of the other phases. Catechumens were not generally the center of attention. Nor, it seems, did they receive special instruction, at least the sort *competentes* and neophytes received.[4] Instead

1. *De fide et operibus* 6.9 (trans. Marie Liguori, FC 27:231).
2. Ibid.
3. Ibid., 7.11 (trans. my own).
4. Busch, "De modo quo sanctus Augustinus descripserit initiationem christianam," *Ephemerides Liturgicae* 52 (1938) 425–26; De Latte, "Saint Augustin et le baptême," 190.

catechumens seem to have simply blended in with the baptized, with penitents, with any who might attend the Liturgies of the Word. There all would have pondered the same Scriptures, sang the same psalms, heard the same sermons. In other words, what catechumens heard did not seem to have differed from what other groups in the assembly heard. Some modern commentators—Dujarier and Jungmann, for instance—presume that this style of catechumenate meant no catechumenate.[5] Even Van der Meer, normally an astute observer of Augustine, says as much:

"There was no further instruction [beyond that described in *On Catechizing*]; they were dependent on what they could learn from ordinary sermons. . . . No doubt they listened, but they did not understand; they were *audientes,* not *intelligentes* [i.e., 'hearers' not 'understanders']."[6]

This last statement is astounding, for it contradicts Van der Meer's own portrait of Augustine's brilliance as a preacher. These low estimates rely—apparently—on two unspoken assumptions: (1) only talks directed *exclusively* to catechumens would be truly instructive; (2) ordinary sermons would be either too short, too infrequent, or too insubstantial to meet their needs. Such assumptions may or may not be true: much depends on the form, length, frequency, content, and style that a preacher brings to the medium. Earlier we saw how much Ambrose's quite ordinary sermons affected Augustine: they dismantled his deep-seated biases against Scripture; they provoked him to question his social-climbing ways; they dazzled him with a new vision of God. In this chapter, we will see that Augustine's sermons could be equally potent: they were frequent, lengthy, substantive, moving, and memorable; and equally important, he would often gear them precisely to those least likely to understand—whether poorly instructed faithful or

5. Dujarier, *History of the Catechumenate,* 94–97: "The catechumenate, properly speaking, no longer existed. . . . The Church seemed to be more preoccupied with 'pushing' spiritless candidates to baptism." Jungmann, *The Early Liturgy,* 249: "The entire preparation for Baptism was therefore, condensed into two sessions: the opening catechesis and the catechesis in Lent." See chapter 4, note 8, on my reaction to these unsubstantiated views.

6. Van der Meer, *Augustine the Bishop,* 356–57. I believe that this seriously distorts the evidence. Van der Meer's assertion is accurate in only one area: the catechumens' ignorance of the sacraments (because of the *disciplina arcani*). See the discussion of this below.

simple catechumens. In any case, to understand Augustine as an instructor of catechumens, one must understand Augustine the preacher.

A moment ago, I noted that the catechumenate, from our vantage point, lacks easy visibility because catechumens simply blended in with the larger worshipping assembly. In the main, this is true. But every so often they become visible; that is, whenever Augustine in the course of an ordinary sermon would turn and speak to them directly. In the sermons that have come down to us (only a fraction of those he gave), he makes at least twenty-two of these turns.[7] (For a list of these, see chart 7; for other passing references, see chart 8.) These turns basically take one of four forms: (1) Augustine would beg catechumens to live in a manner that respected the cross they bore on their foreheads; (2) he would remind them of their ignorance of the "secrets" (i.e., baptism and Eucharist); (3) he would single out their behavior to illustrate a point; (4) he would exhort them to complete their initiation. These turns, while of considerable interest, are usually brief. If we were to study only these isolated moments, we would certainly see some ways Augustine taught catechumens; but we would also ignore much of what they actually heard. After all, they were present not just for those brief moments, but for the *whole* sermon, and it was the whole sermon which served as their instruction. But even if we were to examine these twenty-two sermons, not just the momentary turns but the whole sermon, we would still get a quite fragmented picture. It would not give us any sense of what a group of catechumens may have heard over time. For that, one needs a sequence of sermons. Only in that way can one get any sense of Augustine's curriculum. It happens that scholars have isolated one such sequence: an intertwining series of sermons on the Psalms (*Enarrationes* on Ps 119–133 and 95) and on the Gospel of John (*Tractates* 1–12) (see charts 9–11).[8] This series was

7. This is a conservative count, that is, those moments when Augustine explicitly mentions the catechumens. There are many other implied ones, especially when he discusses the "sacrament" of the Cross on the forehead. In addition, I have found four letters Augustine wrote to catechumens.

8. I have cited only those sermons considered here. There are others: perhaps *Tractatus in epistolam Ioannis ad Parthos* 1–6, possibly also 7–8 (given during Easter Week), and certainly *Tractatus in evangelium Ioannis* 13–16 (sometime after Easter Week). The Maurists, in their classic edition of Augustine's

given between December and the opening of Lent of a single liturgical year (probably 406–407, though this remains a matter of dispute).[9] What makes this sequence especially relevant is that within it are six explicit (and several implied) turns to the catechumens; and the climax of the sequence, *Tractate 11*, is devoted almost entirely to the catechumens: there Augustine begs them to turn in their names for the Lenten training.[10] Thus this sequence seems to offer a glimpse into Augustine's approach to a curriculum for catechumens—at least what he did with one group of them during one-third of one liturgical year.

Thus, to examine Augustine as a teacher of catechumens, we will need to look at Augustine the preacher. This chapter will take a more wide-angle view. Here the emphasis will be on three matters: the where of his catechesis (physical setting, liturgical context, audience);[11] the how (rhetorical techniques, affective tenor,

---

works, had noted several of the interconnections between these two sets of sermons. The path-breaking study was done by Maurice LeLandais, "Deux années de prédication de saint Augustin: Introduction a la lecture de l'*In Joannem*," *Études augustiniennes* 28 (Paris: Aubier, 1953) 1–95. I have translated and reproduced his summary chart as chart 11. While scholars have unanimously agreed with LeLandais that these sermons form a single series, his dating has been seriously challenged. See next note.

9. The current consensus was established by A.-M. LaBonnardière, *Recherches de chronologie augustinienne* (Paris: Études augustiniennes, 1965). Other have confirmed her dating of these using other methods: M.-F. Berrouard, "La date des Tractatus I–LIV *In Iohannis evangelium* de saint Augustin," *Recherches augustiniennes* 7 (1971) 105–68; Eugene TeSelle, *Augustine the Theologian* (New York: Herder and Herder, 1970) 234–37 and 256–60. However, LaBonnardière's dating on the Tractates beyond the first sixteen has been widely challenged by Berrouard and others. For a good summary of these questions, see Rettig, "Introduction," FC 78:23–31.

10. Suzanne Poque "Trois semaines de prédication à Hippone en février-mars 407," *Recherches augustiniennes* 7 (1971) 169–87. She has demonstrated that *Tractatus in evangelium Ioannis* 11 was not delivered just prior to Easter, but near the beginning of Lent, probably the first Sunday of Lent: her precise dating for the remaining sermons is intriguing, but highly speculative.

11. There are a number of fine works on Augustine's habits as a preacher: Maurice Pontet, *L'exégèse de s. Augustin prédicateur* (Paris: Aubier, 1946); Christine Mohrmann, "Saint Augustin prédicateur," *La Maison Dieu* 39 (1954) 83–96; Brown, *Augustine of Hippo*, 244–69; M.-F. Berrouard, "Introduction," *Homélies sur Évangile de saint Jean*, BAug 71:1–124; Van der Meer, *Augustine the Bishop*, 388–452. On the extemporaneous character of the sermons, the classic articles remain those of Roy J. Deferrari, "St. Augustine's Method of Compos-

language), and the why (rhetorical aims and principles, view of Scripture).[12] I will treat these matters in some detail for they are relevant not only for this chapter, but for the next three as well. The next chapter will take a more close-up view—focusing on the intertwining sequence of sermons on John and the Psalms. There we will look at the what (specific topics) and the how (specific teaching methods). From these two chapters, we should see how Augustine's ordinary sermons served as instructions for the catechumens and how Augustine's turns to the catechumens formed only one pedagogical thread within a much broader and richer catechetical enterprise.

FEEDING THE HUNGRY: THE LITURGY OF THE WORD

The earliest known portrait of Augustine is a fresco dating from about the year 600. It captures him in the classic pose of the ancient preacher: seated on an episcopal *cathedra*, his hands clasping a codex of the Scriptures. This icon, while artistically crude, is at least apt, for it portrays Augustine as he wanted himself remembered: as a servant of the Word. As he saw it, his task involved much more than merely explaining the Bible. Rather it demanded that he do with the Word of God what Christ did with bread— break it open, multiply it, feed the hungry:

"When I unpack the holy Scriptures for you, it is as though I were breaking open bread for you. You who hunger, receive it. . . . What I deal out to you is not mine. What you eat, I eat.

_____

ing and Delivering Sermons," *The American Journal of Philology* 43 (1922) 97–123, 193–219; "Verbatim Reports of Augustine's Unwritten Sermons," *Transactions and Proceedings of the American Philological Association* 46 (1915) 35–45. Also helpful: Michele Pellegrino, *The True Priest: The Priesthood as Preached and Practised by St. Augustine,* trans. Arthur Gilson (New York: Philosophical Library, 1968) esp. 89–104; G. W. Doyle, "Augustine's Sermonic Method," *Westminster Theological Journal* 39 (1977) 213–38.

12. See especially Christine Mohrmann, "Augustine and the Eloquentia," *Études sur le latin des Chrétiens* (Rome: Edizioni di Storia e Letteratura, 1961) 1:351–70; Hagendahl, *Augustine and the Latin Classics,* 1:156–67 and 2:553–69; J. Oroz, "La retórica agustiniana: clasicismo y christianismo," *Studia Patristica* 6, ed. F. L. Cross (Berlin: Akademie-Verlag, 1962) 484–95; Marrou, *Saint Augustin et la fin de la culture antique;* Ernest Fortin, "Augustine and the Problem of Christian Rhetoric," *Augustinian Studies* 5 (1974) 85–100; Gerald A. Press, "The Subject and Structure of Augustine's *De doctrina christiana,*" *Augustinian Studies* 11 (1980) 99–124.

What you live on, I live on. We have in heaven a common store-house, for from it comes the Word of God."[13]

This image appears again and again in his sermons. Another time, on the anniversary of his ordination, he remarked: "From that which I feast on—from that I feed you. I am a table-servant, not the master of the house. From that which I set before you—from that I too draw my life."[14] For Augustine, this complex of images and associations—Scripture as "bread," the teacher as "table-servant," preaching as "feeding the hungry"—was more than clever metaphor. For him and for his hearers, the words he served up *were* life, for they broke open a truth beyond words: the divine life itself.

Augustine handed out this "bread" at public liturgies. In Hippo, both Eucharist and Vespers seem to have been held daily, or al-most daily.[15] Augustine may not have always preached at both, but did so sometimes. Outside of Easter, he preached at least four times a week; during Lent, daily; and during Easter Week, twice a day. We know that large crowds attended not only every Sunday, but at many other times as well: on feast days and their vigils, on fast days, on the numerous and ever-popular "birthdays" (*natalitia*) of martyrs.

On these occasions, crowds would stream into Augustine's church, the *Basilica Pacis*.[16] It was an imposing edifice—some

13. *Sermo* 95.1 (trans. my own). See *Sermo* 229E.4 (=Guelf. 9); *Tractatus in evangelium Ioannis* 34.1; the same thought underlies the prayer that opens *De doctrina christiana* 1.1.1.

14. *Sermo* 339.4 (trans. my own). See also *Sermones* 101.4; 260D.2 (=Guelf. 18); 179A.8 (=Wilmart 2). On the idea of servant, see Pellegrino, *The True Priest*, 57–88.

15. On daily Eucharist, see *Epistola* 54.2; *Sermo* 58.12. On daily Vespers, *Epistola* 29.11; cf. *Sermo* 308A.7 (=Denis 11), preached in Carthage. For a dis-cussion of the frequency of liturgy and preaching in Augustine's church, see Van der Meer, *Augustine the Bishop*, 172–75.

16. For an extremely detailed study of the archeological excavations in Hippo, see Marec, *Monuments chrétiens d'Hippone*, esp. 15–30 and 215–34. Marec's study includes a number of helpful maps, photographs, and illustra-tions. For an examination of the literary evidence concerning the basilica, see Othmar Perler, "L'Eglise principale et les autres sanctuaires chrétiens d'Hippone-la-Royale d'après les textes de saint Augustin," *Revue des études augustiniennes* 1 (1955) 299–343. For a summary of Marec's work, see Marrou, "La basilique chrétienne d'Hippone," *Revue des études augustiniennes* 6 (1960)

twenty meters wide and fifty meters long (making it one of the largest churches thus far uncovered in North Africa). It lay on the outskirts of the center of town, away from the forum with its bustling marketplace and old pagan temples. When people entered the basilica, they would find the glare of the North African sun replaced by a softer light: the flicker of gold flames in small oil lamps. (This lamplight impressed Augustine: he thought of it as a symbol of Christ's light shining forth in the darkness of the world.)[17] The basilica's interior, divided into three naves, was open, spacious. Its floors were inlaid with colorful mosaics.[18] There were no pews, so people stood: women on one side, men on the other.[19] "The great numbers crowd right up to the walls," Augustine once said; they "annoy each other by the pressure and almost choke each other by their overflowing numbers."[20] These crowds included people from all levels of provincial society—artisans and fishermen, merchants and magistrates—but the majority seem to have been poor townspeople.[21] Among this assembly were, of course, the baptized. But given the widespread delay of baptism, the number of catechumens was probably sizeable. Even pagans, Jews, Donatists, or Manichees might mingle among the crowd, for this celebration—according to conciliar decree—was open to all comers.[22]

The liturgy began with a solemn procession.[23] Augustine would follow an entourage of subdeacons, deacons, and presbyters up to

109-54; and Adolar Zumkeller, *Augustine's Ideal of the Religious Life*, trans. Edmund Colledge (New York: Fordham University Press, 1986) esp. 32-48. See also the photographs of ancient churches, including Hippo, in Van der Meer and Christine Mohrmann, *Atlas of the Early Christian World*, trans. Mary F. Hedlund and H. H. Rowley (London: Thomas Nelson and Sons Ltd., 1958).

17. *Sermo* 221.1-2.

18. Marec, *Monuments chrétiens d'Hippone*, 35-95; Marrou, "La basilique chrétienne d'Hippone," 127-30.

19. *De civitate Dei* 2.28.

20. *Enarrationes in psalmos* 39.10 (trans. LF 25:142).

21. See Brown, "Christianity and Local Culture in Late Roman North Africa," *Journal of Roman Studies* 58 (1968) 85-95.

22. Fourth Council of Carthage, *canon* 84.

23. For an imaginative reconstruction of Augustine's Liturgy of the Word, see Van der Meer, *Augustine the Bishop*, 388-97; also G. G. Willis, *St. Augustine's Lectionary* (London: SPCK, 1962) 1-5. In my reconstruction, I have tried to limit myself to what can be derived explicitly from Augustine's own writings.

the raised apse at the far end of the church.[24] The apse itself was semi-circular. Around its walls was a two-tiered set of stone benches where the presbyters would sit. And at the center of these, set against the back wall and elevated up a few steps, was the episcopal *cathedra* (both a "professor's chair" and a "judgment-seat").[25] A precious tapestry was draped over it to mark it off as a place of honor.[26] It was from this perch that Augustine would preside over things, "overseeing" the assembly's "coming in and going out."[27] Once the procession had made its way to the apse, Augustine would position himself on the top step in front of the *cathedra*. There, flanked by his presbyters and deacons, he would proclaim the traditional greeting: "The Lord be with you." "And with your spirit," the assembly would shout back. As Augustine once noted in a sermon: "We traditionally say these words when we greet you from our place in the apse . . . because we need the Lord to be with us always, since without him we are nothing."[28]

After the greeting, the reader—often enough, a young boy—would "stand on the raised platform in the sight of all" and proclaim an excerpt from the Old Testament or from an apostle.[29] On the feasts of martyrs, another reading would be added: from the martyrs' *acta*, the record of their trial and death.[30] (Reading was a much harder task in those days: ancient codices lacked punctua-

24. On Augustine's clergy, see *Sermones* 355 and 356; Van der Meer, *Augustine the Bishop*, 199-234.

25. Augustine mentions the steps that led up to the cathedra in *De civitate Dei* 22.8. He frequently refers to it as a "locus superior" (a "high spot"): *De catechizandis rudibus* 15.23; *Sermones* 339.8; 151.4; *Enarrationes in psalmos* 126.3; *Epistola* 29.8. For a description, see Marec, *Monuments chrétiens d'Hippone*, 27-29; photographs of this are found on page 14 and in Marrou, *Saint Augustine and His Influence through the Ages*, 64.

26. *Epistola* 23.3.

27. *Enarrationes in psalmos* 126.3 (trans. my own).

28. *Sermo* 229A.3 (= Guelf. 7) (trans. my own). "Peace be with you" was also used: *Enarrationes in psalmos* 124.10; cf. *Epistolae* 42.31; 53.3; the deacon may also have given the greeting.

29. *De civitate Dei* 2.28 (Bettenson, 85). For a thorough study on readers, see Elisabeth Paoli-Lafaye, "Les 'lecteurs' des textes liturgiques," in *Saint Augustin et la Bible*, 59-74. On the tendency to drop the Old Testament readings, see Willis, *St. Augustine's Lectionary*, 4-5.

30. See, for example, *Sermones* 274; 275.1; 280.1; 299D.7 (= Denis 16); Third Council of Carthage (397 A.D.) Canon 36.

tion and ran words together, making it crucial that the reader know how to break apart the words [*distinguere*] and to mark out the phrases with proper inflection [*pronuntiare*]. As Marrou has noted, "for ancients, just to read a text was to begin interpreting.")[31] After the reading, Augustine would send word to the cantor which psalm he wanted sung. Then as now, liturgical planning could backfire: on one occasion, the cantor sang the wrong psalm; undaunted, Augustine preached on the psalm that was sung rather than the one he had prepared, "choosing to follow the will of God in the cantor's mistake."[32] Normally, the psalm was sung using a responsorial style: the cantor intoned the verses, while the assembly joined in the refrain. After this, a deacon would read the gospel.[33] When finished, the deacon would come over to Augustine and hand him the codex so that he might refer to it while preaching.[34]

NOISY IMPROVISATIONS: THE SERMON AND ITS HEARERS

After the readings, Augustine would begin the sermon. From all accounts, he was a dazzling public speaker. Even his opponents acknowledged as much. For instance, a Manichee named Secundicus once quipped that he had never been able "to discern a Christian in [Augustine], but on all occasions, a born orator, a veritable god of eloquence."[35] When the crowds came to hear him, they came not just for instruction, but also for entertainment—to be dazzled by the flow and music of his words. Certainly Augustine, who so often railed against pagan theaters, was quite conscious

31. Marrou, *Saint Augustin et la fin de la culture antique*, 21; also, *History of Education in Antiquity*, 165–66. Cf. *De doctrina christiana* 3.2ff.

32. *Enarrationes in psalmos* 138.1 (trans. LF 39:191). The same thing happens in *Sermo* 352.1.

33. *Sermo* 139A.1 (=Mai 125). On the gospel as the last of the readings, see *Sermo* 49.1.

34. See the remarks of the *notarius* who recorded *Sermo* 356. *Epistola* 29 gives a fascinating picture of the way Augustine would have codices with different books of the Bible brought to him in the course of a sermon. *Tractatus in evangelium Ioannis* 40.1: Augustine notes that he is preaching with the gospel book in hand; *Tractatus* 35.9: Augustine mentions at the end of the sermon that he will now lay aside the codex he has in his hand.

35. Secundinus, *Ad sanctum Augustinum epistula* 3 (trans. Van der Meer, *Augustine the Bishop*, 412). See also *Epistola* 16, written by Maximus, a pagan grammarian from Madaura, to Augustine.

that Christianity had its own theatrics: the liturgy itself, the biblical drama of salvation, even his own verbal wizardry. As he once put it: "Do not think, brothers, that the Lord our God has sent us away without theatrical extravaganzas; for if there are no extravaganzas, why have you come together today?"[36]

(1) *Written Text and Oral Performance.* When we today encounter Augustine the orator-showman, we meet him only through the sermon-texts which have come down to us. Interestingly, he worked neither from notes nor from a text first written out, then memorized; he prepared only by prayer and study.[37] In other words, the texts we have record his on-the-spot improvisations. His words were preserved thanks to scribes known as *notarii*. These *notarii*, like the contemporary court stenographer, were masters of a special shorthand which enabled them to record a speaker's every word. In one sermon, Augustine alluded to them: "What we are saying is being taken down, as you see, by the *notarii* of the church; what you say is being taken down too. [That way,] neither my words nor your shouts fall uselessly to the ground."[38] Sometime later, other scribes known as *librarii* would transcribe these stenographic notes to create the texts we now have. Churches in the ancient world routinely employed such people, the same way that businesses, large households, and government offices did. Augustine's own *notarii* were not the only

36. *Tractatus in evangelium Ioannis* 7.6 (Rettig, 78:159—altered). This theme appears again and again: *Sermones* 51.1-2; 301A.7 (=Denis 17); 313A.3 (=Denis 14); *Enarrationes in psalmos* 39.9; 80.22.

37. See Deferrari, "St. Augustine's Method of Composing and Delivering Sermons," 97-123 and 193-219. Deferrari gives an enormous body of evidence that shows how extraordinarily spontaneous Augustine's sermons were. He concludes that they fall into two classes: "extempore" (those "given after some previous meditation on the subject, but with no extensive preparation") and "strictly extempore" ("given unexpectedly and without any preparation of any kind"); the majority are of the first class; *Enarrationes in psalmos* 138 is a classic example of the latter. In *De doctrina christiana* 4.10.25, Augustine notes that working from a prepared or memorized text hindered the ability to keep one's rapport with the audience; in 4.15.32, he says that he prepared with prayer. He had, of course, worked on some texts long and hard in his study.

38. This sermon is preserved in *Epistola* 213.2 (Parsons, 32:55—altered). On the training and importance of *notarii*, see Marrou, *A History of Education in Antiquity*, 312-13. On the different classes of scribes, see Deferrari, "St. Augustine's Method of Composing and Delivering Sermons," 106-7. Augustine refers to their special shorthand in *De doctrina christiana* 2.26.40.

ones scribbling down his sermons. Sometimes, according to Possidius, members of the congregation—"whoever wanted and was able"—would bring along their own "*notarii* to take down what was said."[39] Their speed and accuracy were proverbial. That reputation is borne out by *Sermon* 37: it has come down to us via two completely independent transcripts, yet the two texts are identical.[40]

In working with such texts, we must constantly bear in mind that they contain only a faint residue of Augustine's living speech. As Van der Meer has noted:

"What is true of all good speakers is certainly true of Augustine, namely, that the bare text which has been reconstructed from the notes of stenographers does not even give an approximate idea of the reality. That stream of words that ceaselessly rushes on, sparkling and shimmering as it goes, has been reduced to a shadow of its true self."[41]

What has been lost, stripped away, is the very thing that gave his living speech its dynamism, its punch: the cadence of delivery, the accents and pauses, gestures and facial expressions. We need only compare a transcript of Martin Luther King's "I Have a Dream" with the film to appreciate how striking this gap is between text and oral performance. Certainly Possidius, Augustine's biographer and longtime friend, sensed the difference: "Those who read what he has written on the things of God profit from them; however, I think that greater profit came to those who were able to see and hear him speak in church."[42]

Sermons frequently lasted about an hour, and on occasion, even more.[43] That may seem long by our standards, particularly given that Augustine's audience was standing. Yet his hearers expected

39. Possidius, *Vita* 7 (trans. my own).

40. Bonner, *St. Augustine: Life and Controversies*, 145. On occasion, the *notarii* lacked the skill to keep pace; see Augustine's description of their note-taking during a spirited debate in *Epistola* 44.

41. Van der Meer, *Augustine the Bishop*, 412. See also Berrouard, "Introduction," BAug 71:10–11.

42. Possidius, *Vita* 31 (trans. my own).

43. More precisely, the time alloted was an *hora*—one twelfth of the time between sunrise and sunset; it could thus vary depending on the season. Many sermons are shorter, and the reasons vary considerably: the mood of

nothing less. As Van der Meer has noted, prolixity, not brevity, was the fashion of the day:

"*Copia,* or amplitude, was in those days considered an essential mark of genius. . . . Brevity was accounted as the sign of a poor and ill-furnished mind and was looked upon as a mark of weakness. A single idea must be made to sparkle in a hundred forms."[44]

Often Augustine would be so swept up by the flow of his words that the hour would pass without his completing even a fraction of what he had intended to say:

"I have forgotten how long I have been talking. . . . I guess I have given quite a long talk—but because of your enthusiasm, it has not been enough. You are too excitable. O, that with this fervor you would snatch up the kingdom of heaven."[45]

Van der Meer has noted an often overlooked correlative to this fashionable long-windedness: "This age of interminable speeches seems to have been blessed with a gift of interminable listening."[46] Despite this, Augustine was always alert to signs of his hearers' ebbing attention and would break off abruptly if he sensed them fatigued.[47]

He typically remained seated when preaching.[48] Sitting in such a prominent spot—and the honor it implied—left him uneasy:

"Do not think just because we speak to you from this elevated spot—that for that reason, we are your teachers. There is One who is the teacher of all, the One whose *cathedra* is above the

---

the audience, Augustine's own exhaustion, a martyr's feast day (because the *acta* of the martyr were read). Some are considerably longer.

44. Van der Meer, *Augustine the Bishop,* 419; see also Marrou, *Saint Augustin et la fin de la culture antique,* 70, 75–76. The tradition of beautiful long-windedness dates back at least to Cicero and Quintilian: see Kennedy, *Classical Rhetoric,* 101.

45. *Enarrationes in psalmos* 72.34 (trans. my own).

46. Van der Meer, *Augustine the Bishop,* 176.

47. See *Tractatus in evangelium Ioannis* 19.20; cf. 4.16; 8.13. In *Enarrationes in psalmos* 89.1.29, he senses people were tired and so tells them to go home and eat; he would finish his remarks when they got back.

48. *Sermones* 17.2; 95.2; 355.2. Sometimes Augustine did stand: *Tractatus in evangelium Ioannis* 19.17; cf. *Sermo* 94A.5 (= Caillau 2, 6).

heavens. Under that One we come together as one school; and we and you—we are all classmates."[49]

Despite his discomfort with sitting high up, the arrangement was still quite intimate. People could press up quite close so that the front row might stand only a few yards away.

Not only did Augustine preach in close physical proximity to his audience; he also stayed close to them emotionally. He had a sharp eye for the subtle hues of the human heart and brought this fine-tuned sense to his preaching. It allowed him to read the emotions of his hearers—and to let them read his. As Peter Brown notes, Augustine always spoke *ex pectore*: "He made his first concern to place himself among his hearers, to appeal to their feelings, to react with immense sensitivity to their emotions, and so, as the sermon progressed, to sweep them up into his own feeling."[50] On some occasions, Augustine could get quite worked up: he might weep or utter loud groans.[51] As he saw it, some feelings were simply too deep for words: "A man can express nothing which he cannot also feel, but he may feel something which he cannot express."[52] Most of the time, however, he had an uncanny ability to find words for his feelings. And with these words, he would share his great yearnings, his sense of delight and wonder, his anguish and fears. Augustine focused so intently on the heart—both his own and his hearers'—because he believed the heart to be the privileged locus of faith. As he told Deogratias, "there is no voice to reach the ears of God save the emotion of the heart."[53]

(2) *Audience Response.* Augustine's audience responded to his appeals with gusto—with thunderous applause, shouts, cries. In his day, churchgoing was a raucous, noisy affair. The assembly would applaud whenever they recognized a favorite Scripture verse.[54]

49. *Sermo* 301A.2 (=Denis 17) (trans. my own). See also *Enarrationes in psalmos* 126.3 and *Sermo* 340A.4 (=Guelf. 32).

50. Brown, *Augustine of Hippo*, 251.

51. *Epistola* 29.5 and 7.

52. *Sermo* 117.7 (trans. R. G. MacMullen, NPNF 6:461). The same theme appears in *Enarrationes in psalmos* 99.5. See Henry Chadwick, *Augustine*, Past Masters (New York: Oxford University Press, 1986) 48–50.

53. *De catechizandis rudibus* 9.13 (Christopher, 33).

54. *Sermones* 19.4 and 163B.5 (=Frang. 5); *Enarrationes in psalmos* 120.12; *Tractatus in evangelium Ioannis* 3.21. On the variety of audience reactions, see Van der Meer, *Augustine the Bishop*, 270–72, 339–41 and 427–32; Pontet, *Exégèse*, 37–38.

They would even interrupt and shout out the remainder of a verse he had begun to quote.[55] They loved to show off their biblical expertise. Once, Augustine obliquely alluded to a man who, while "coming to marry a foreign-born wife," met a "roaring lion" and "strangled" it. The crowd immediately shouted, "Samson," before he could give the name.[56] They also would try to outguess him, and when they saw him winding his way towards a favorite theme, they would begin shouting in anticipation.[57] Other times, when they felt chastised—either by the reading from Scripture or by what Augustine said—they would fill the church with loud sighs or groans or would "beat their breasts" like workmen "laying pavement stones."[58] Often they applauded his musical turns of phrase, much as we might applaud a jazz clarinet's improvisational flurries. Once, for instance, Augustine began rattling off some rhythmic phrases:

"Loved is the world: but let [your love] prefer the One by whom the world was made.
Vast is the world; but more vast is the One by whom the world was made.
Beautiful is the world; but more beautiful is the One by whom the world was made.
Alluring is the world; but more alluring is the One by whom the world was made."[59]

As the emotional pitch of this sequence mounted, the assembly began to cheer. Augustine seemed surprised by the outburst: "What have I said? What is there to cheer about? We are still battling with the problem and you have already started to cheer."[60] Clearly Augustine brought something to his preaching—a style, a flair, a passion—that made these sermons not monological preachments, but engaging dialogues. This did not mean his hearers always agreed with him: they would, on occasion, heckle. Nor did

55. *Sermo* 52.13.
56. *Enarrationes in psalmos* 88.1.10.
57. *Sermones* 131.5; 169.7; 313B.3 (=Denis 15).
58. *Sermo* 332.4 (trans. my own). They also beat their breasts when saying the Lord's Prayer: *Sermo* 67.1. On sighing, see *Sermo* 151.8; on groaning, *Enarrationes in psalmos* 127.9.
59. *Sermo* 96.4 (trans. my own).
60. Ibid. (trans. Van der Meer, *Augustine the Bishop*, 429).

they hang on his every word: sometimes a point he raised might set them off chit-chatting among themselves.[61]

Usually when the assembly shouted or applauded, they were signaling that they understood, that they had followed the train of thought or appreciated the cogency of argument. In fact, so ingrained was this pattern that Augustine used it as a barometer of his pedagogy. As he says in *On Christian Doctrine:*

". . . the teacher should be especially careful to assist the silent learner. An attentive crowd eager to comprehend usually shows by its motion whether it understands, and *until it signifies comprehension* the matter being discussed should be considered and expressed in a variety of ways."[62]

Over and over again one sees in the sermons the way he made this principle a part of his practice. For example, in one sermon, he noticed shouts from only one part of the assembly: "Those of you who have cheered have understood; but you who have understood, bear with me a little longer for the sake of those who have not, that I might open it up to them."[63] Or as he says in another sermon: "Those of you who have foreseen my drift in your minds, think of those who walk a little slower. Slow your pace down a bit—that you do not leave behind your slower companions."[64]

(3) *The Disciplina Arcani.* Caring for those who "walked a little slower" was his working pedagogical principle. There was, however, one important exception: how to handle the catechumens' ignorance of sacraments. On other matters, he would speak as long as was needed to win their applause. But the sacraments posed a unique pastoral and pedagogical problem. In Augustine's church, like everywhere else, the *disciplina arcani* was still in force. As Augustine put it in one sermon: "What is hidden, and not in the Church's public square? The sacrament of baptism, the sacra-

61. *Tractatus in evangelium Ioannis* 37.7; 19.5; *Sermo* 23.8.

62. *De doctrina christiana* 4.10.25 (trans. D. W. Robertson, *On Christian Doctrine* [Macmillan Publishing Co., 1958] 134–35).

63. *Sermo* 335A.2 (=Frang. 6) (trans. my own). See *Sermones* 52.20; 101.9; 163B.5 (=Frang. 5); 164.3.

64. *Sermo* 169.7 (trans. my own). See also *Sermo* 101.9; *Enarrationes in psalmos* 90.2.1.

ment of the Eucharist."[65] Problems arose whenever a Scripture passage with baptismal or Eucharistic overtones was read; for instance, mention of the Red Sea, of manna, of the sacrifice of Melchizedek, of the pool of Siloam. At that moment the congregation would split: the baptized would cheer the instant they spotted these foreshadowings of the sacraments, while the catechumens would be left silently wondering what all the fuss was about. This left Augustine in a quandary: on the one hand, his pedagogical instincts dictated that he turn and explain things to the catechumens; on the other, his respect for Church tradition dictated that he not violate anything as venerable as the *disciplina arcani*. Augustine presumed such liturgical traditions held some inner wisdom; and as he saw it, the wisdom of the *disciplina arcani* lay in its ability to prick the curiosity of the catechumens. As he once noted in his *Tractates on the Gospel of John*: "The sacraments of the faithful are not divulged to [catechumens] . . .: that they may be more passionately desired by them, they are honorably concealed from their view."[66]

This judgment shaped how Augustine handled the divide in the congregation. For example, in a sermon on psalm 80, he mentioned the Red Sea, noting that it meant "nothing else but the sacrament of the baptized." He then turned to the catechumens:

"You who have not yet come, why are you afraid of coming to the baptism of Christ, of passing through the Red Sea. . . . You shall hear a language you do not know, one which those in the know hear and recognize—bearing witness and knowing. You shall hear where you ought to have your heart. [He evidently pauses because of the cheering.] Just now when I said these things, many understood and answered by cheering. The rest of you stood mute because you heard a language you did not know. So come, cross over, learn."[67]

He used the same tactic in *Sermon* 132, delivered on the first Sunday of Lent or just before. The gospel that day was from John 6, the discourse on the bread of life. Augustine knew that the call to eat the Lord's flesh and drink his blood would make no sense to

---

65. *Enarrationes in psalmos* 103.14 (trans. my own).
66. *Tractatus in evangelium Ioannis* 96.3 (trans. my own).
67. *Enarrationes in psalmos* 80.8 (trans. LF 32:118–19—altered).

those who had never seen the Eucharist. So he turned first to the baffled catechumens:

"Not all who heard these [words] have understood them. Those of you who have been baptized—the faithful—know what [Christ] meant. But those among you who are called catechumens, or hearers: you might have been hearers when the reading was read; but were you able to understand it?"[68]

Then using one of his favorite devices, the soliloquy, he spoke as though he were a catechumen: "Perhaps right now, while the gospel was being read, you said in your hearts: 'What is it he said: "My flesh is true food and my blood true drink"? How is the flesh of the Lord eaten and the blood of the Lord drunk? Did I get that right?' "[69] Augustine then made his pitch:

"There is a veil over this, but if you want, the veil will be removed. Come make your profession and you will have solved the riddle. . . . You are called a catechumen, a hearer, [but] you are deaf. . . . *Easter approaches! Give in your name for baptism!* If the festival does not rouse you, let curiosity lead you. . . . Knock and it will be opened—that you may know *with me* what has been said. . . . So I knock. Open up to me! When I speak aloud to your ears, I knock at your breast."[70]

Here he touched on a spectrum of emotions: he toyed with their curiosity; he prodded them with sarcasm; he played on their enthusiasm for festivals; he promised that he and they would enjoy a new common bond. Augustine was certainly willing to exploit this divide, if only to get the catechumens to end their procrastinating. Ultimately, though, he yearned only to share with them the *gnosis* the Church reserved for the baptized. As a rule, he disdained anything that smacked of elitism: he scoffed at cultured snobs and railed against the Donatist quest to create a Church of the pure. So this division within his own congregation bothered him: thus, the rousing appeals. He wanted to dismantle the barriers such readings created, but he knew he could pull down the walls only if they heard him "knocking" and so enrolled for the Lenten training.

68. *Sermo* 132.1 (trans. my own).
69. Ibid.
70. Ibid.

A SEASONED RHETORIC: THE METHOD

In his sermons, as in all his works, Augustine remained a verbal virtuoso. Yet he subjected that virtuosity both to the demands of the liturgical setting and to the needs of his noisy and diverse audience. His sermons thus display a distinctive rhetorical style and approach. Here he consciously flaunted the dictates of orthodox rhetoric, those cumbersome rules and canons promoted by the schools of his day. As he put it in one sermon, "What do the rules of schoolmasters matter to us? Better you should understand . . . than be left high and dry on the heights of our eloquence."[71] Augustine knew that the rhetorical fineries of the schools—the arcane vocabulary, the subtle allusions to the classics, the studiously correct diction—would mar the directness he needed to touch the uneducated and the catechumens within his assembly. As he says in *On Christian Doctrine*, "Of what use is a gold key if it will not open what we wish?"[72] And what Augustine wished to open was his hearers' minds and hearts, open them to both the dazzling mystery of God and the weighty demands of Christian life. He thus sought "clarity," not "cultivation," and adopted—in a phrase he lifted from Cicero's *The Orator*—"a kind of studied neglect."[73] This did not mean he was careless; nor did he, as a rule, resort to street Latin. Instead he retained the elegant Latin of the elite but pruned it down to such simplicity that even the least educated could follow him with ease.[74] Brown notes that this "superbly unaffected 'Christian' style was in reality a simplicity achieved on the other side of vast sophistication."[75]

This did not mean that Augustine avoided rhetorical ornaments. Far from it: his language, despite its simplicity, is studded with musical figures and wordplays. As he once put it, speech like "food—without which life is impossible—must be seasoned."[76] And the spices he pulled from his rhetorical pantry were especially suited to the tastes of his uneducated audience, "the kind of thing," as Van der Meer notes, "we can at all times find in nursery rhymes, proverbs, and popular song": assonance, alliteration,

---

71. *Enarrationes in psalmos* 36.3.6 (trans. my own). On this, see Marrou, *Saint Augustin et la fin de la culture antique*, 47–84 and 505–40.
72. *De doctrina christiana* 4.11.26 (Robertson, 136).
73. Cicero, *Orator* 78, quoted in *De doctrina christiana* 4.10.24 (trans. my own).
74. Mohrmann, "Saint Augustin prédicateur," 89.
75. Brown, *Augustine of Hippo*, 268.
76. *De doctrina christiana* 4.11.26 (Robertson, 136).

antitheses, puns, paradoxes, jingling rhymes.[77] These ornaments made his ideas at once entertaining and memorable, for he knew his people had fine-tuned oral memories and would easily snap up and retain his catchy phrases.[78] These ornaments—it should also be remembered—were not written out beforehand, but were improvised on the spot. Such feats may seem astonishing to us, yet improvisation of ornaments was part of the art, much as it is in jazz. However, as Marrou notes, such improvisation, whether in oratory or in jazz, comes "from a well-stocked memory" of traditional turns and devices.[79] From our vantage point, these ornaments give Augustine's language a sort of baroque extravagance. His verbal style might seem spicy to our taste; yet in his own time, the second sophistic movement was the rhetorical rage, and some Christian preachers in the Greek East, like Gregory of Nazianzus and John Chrysostom, would cook up even spicier fare for their congregations. Augustine did not share their taste: what mattered was "food," not "spice."[80]

Augustine knew the perils of rhetoric: that it was an art in itself indifferent, that it could be of equal service "in urging evil or urging justice." Yet he lamented that too often "defenders of truth are ignorant of the art." Thus he asked: "If the evil usurp it for winning vain and perverse causes, why should it not also be exploited for use by the good?"[81] Thus in the final book of *On Christian Doctrine*, Augustine adapted for Christian usage several key principles from classical rhetoric.[82] He hoped that Christian

---

77. Van der Meer, *Augustine the Bishop*, 427. See Mohrmann "Augustine and the Eloquentia," 363–68. She points out that Augustine's favorite figures—the parallelism, paratactic cola, antithesis, climax, and dialecticon—are precisely the ones he emphasizes in his rhetorical analysis of Scripture texts in *De doctrina christiana* 4.7.11ff. She roots Augustine's use of rhyme and word-play in popular parlance. For a complete list of Augustine's rhetorical ornaments, see Barry, *St. Augustine the Orator*, PS 6.

78. Mohrmann, "Augustine and the Eloquentia," 367.

79. Marrou, *History of Education in Antiquity*, 200.

80. *De doctrina christiana* 4.14.30–31. On Augustine and the second sophistic movement, see Marrou, *Saint Augustin et la fin de la culture antique*, 511–14; Mohrmann, "Augustine and the Eloquentia," 359–62.

81. *De doctrina christiana* 4.2.3 (Robertson, 118–19). Augustine here is simply repeating one of the truisms of the standard rhetorical textbooks: in 4.5.7, he quotes Cicero's *De inventione* 1.1, to the same effect.

82. There has been considerable dispute over the structure of this treatise. For a summary of the debate, see Press, "The Subject and Structure of *De*

174

teachers and preachers too might be eloquent, but hoped even more that their eloquence be in harmony with their specific task. He admitted his brief commentary would not serve as a substitute textbook.[83] He also admitted that some of what the standard textbooks contained had value, but warned, much as Cicero did, that the widespread obsession with rules was futile. No performing orator, in the heat of the moment, had the luxury of remembering rules. More importantly, great orators "fulfilled [rules] because they were eloquent; they did not apply them that they might be eloquent." Augustine did not think much of rhetorical schooling. He shared Cicero's views: that to learn the art, one simply needed raw talent, much practice, and good models, for "those with acute and eager minds more readily learn eloquence by reading and hearing the eloquent than by following the rules of eloquence."[84]

Thus in this brief book (really an essay) Augustine tried to cut through the morass of ancient rhetorical theory and zero in on what he had found, from a lifetime of preaching and teaching, to

doctrina christiana." Marrou, *Saint Augustine et la fin de la culture antique,* reads books 1–3 as an outline for a Christian "grammar" and book 4 as the outline for a Christian "rhetoric." He thus makes two extravagant claims (repeated and expanded in the work of Eugene Kevane): (1) that *De doctrina christiana* offers a program for forming a Christian culture (Marrou, 381); (2) that it represents a major departure from the classical rhetorical tradition, "quelque chose de nouveau" (Marrou, 519; repeated by Van der Meer). Hagendahl, *Augustine and the Latin Classics,* 559–69, challenges (successfully, I believe) these two claims. Against the first, he shows from numerous passages that Augustine's goal is quite limited and is aimed at a practical end: giving principles for those who interpret and expound publicly on the Bible, i.e., for clergy. Against the second, he demonstrates by careful comparison that Augustine's sentiments and language are thoroughly Ciceronian "in the general conception of rhetoric and even in words: in the division, terminology and other technicalities"; *De doctrina* "cannot make a substantial claim to novelty and originality . . ., [but] at most a slight modification of this or that point." Both Press and Hagendahl conclude (apparently independently—their work appeared at the same time) that the whole *De doctrina* may be seen simply as a rhetorical work: books 1–3 offers principles for "invention"; book 4, principles for "elocution." In other words, Augustine has written exactly on the two subdisciplines of rhetoric that most occupied Cicero (classical rhetoric had three others).

83. *De doctrina christiana* 4.1.2. See J. Oroz, "La retórica agustiniana," 489; and Hagendahl, *Augustine and the Latin Classics,* 567.

84. *De doctrina christiana* 4.3.4 (Robertson, 119–20). This paraphrases Cicero's dictum in *De oratore* 1.146 and 2.90.

be indispensable.[85] He devoted his attention mainly to two matters: (1) the three aims of the orator and (2) the three styles. Concerning the first, Augustine, like Cicero, insisted that the one "who is eloquent should speak so as to teach, to delight, and to motivate."[86] Of these three, teaching came first—both logically and temporally. If one looks at Augustine's sermons, it is clear this teaching moment could last from a few seconds to a few minutes—just long enough to explain some morsel of truth. He admitted that, in theory, merely teaching (i.e., instructing the mind) might suffice: people "may be so moved by the knowledge . . . that it is not necessary to move them further by greater powers of eloquence."[87] This, while theoretically possible, was not the usual case: only a "few of the most studious . . . learn what is taught no matter how abjectly and crudely it is presented."[88] More often, one needed to entertain, since "listeners have to be delighted if they are to be retained as listeners."[89] Augustine's sermons bear this out: rare are the passages in which he does not indulge in at least a few verbal fireworks. Still, of these three aims—teaching, delighting, motivating—Augustine, like Cicero, gave the greatest weight to the third: "It is necessary . . . for the ecclesiastical orator, when he urges something be done, not only to teach that he may instruct and to please that he may hold attention, but also to persuade that he may be victorious."[90] Augustine knew that too often a gap existed between knowing a truth and doing it. Thus merely instructing the mind missed the mark.

85. Hagendahl, *Augustine and the Latin Classics*, 567: "In line with his declaration of principles, Augustine leaves out what can be learnt elsewhere or is considered as immaterial for the ecclesiastical orator, and focuses his attention on what he holds to be absolutely necessary. . . . Augustine's procedure is that of elimination and concentration." Book 4 of *De doctrina christiana* was not written until 427—that is, some thirty years after books 1-3, and after some forty years as a preacher.

86. *De doctrina christiana* 4.12.27 (trans. my own). Augustine here cites Cicero, *Orator* 69, but with a difference: where Cicero has *probare* ("prove"), Augustine has *docere* ("teach"). The difference comes from their respective settings: Cicero is referring to an orator in front of a court; Augustine has an ecclesial context in mind. See Hagendahl, *Augustine and the Latin Classics*, 1:163 note 4.

87. *De doctrina christiana* 4.12.28 (Robertson, 137).

88. Ibid., 4.11.26 (Robertson, 135-36—altered).

89. Ibid., 4.12.27 (Robertson, 136).

90. Ibid., 4.13.29 (Robertson, 138); adapting a passage from Cicero, *Orator* 69.

Education meant doing more: it meant "moving the minds of listeners, not [simply] that they may know what is to be done, but that they may do what they already know should be done."[91]

Augustine then inquired: if the ultimate goal is persuasion, how does one persuade? This led to his second topic: the three styles. Augustine repeated the standard textbook view, that there exist three styles: the subdued (*summissa*); the moderate (*temperata*); and the grand (*grandis*).[92] By subdued, he and his contemporaries did not mean colloquial—their language was far too stylized to be that—but rather straightforward, prosaic. The moderate, by contrast, meant ornamented, adorned with musical figures and word-plays. The grand—at least as Augustine understood it—sometimes involved ornaments, sometimes not: the difference lay not in ornamentation, but in "the furor of feelings," not only those of the orator, but of the audience as well.[93] Traditional commentators like Cicero had spelled out when to use each style: "He therefore will be eloquent who can speak of small things in a subdued manner, of middling things in a moderate manner, and of grand things in a grand manner."[94]

Augustine felt this principle needed adjusting, for in preaching "everything we say is of great importance" since it touched on people's "eternal welfare." For instance, one had to speak of a trivial amount of money when preaching on the story of the widow's mite; but this did not dictate using the subdued style since "justice is not small."[95] On the other hand, simply because matters of faith were always weighty, one did not necessarily speak about them in the grand style. Rather: ". . . concerning one and the same thing, [the orator] speaks in a subdued manner if he teaches, in a moderate manner if he is praising it, and in a grand manner if he is moving an adverse mind to conversion."[96]

In addition, the speaker, like the musician, had to modulate: to remain in one style too long loses the listener; rather one had to blend the three so one's "speech ebbs and flows like the sea."[97]

91. *De doctrina christiana* 4.12.27 (Robertson, 137).
92. Kennedy, *Classical Rhetoric*, 87.
93. *De doctrina christiana* 4.20.42 (trans. my own).
94. Cicero, *Orator* 69 quoted in *De doctrina christiana* 4.17.34 (Robertson, 143—altered). See Hagendahl, *Augustine and the Latin Classics*, 164–67.
95. *De doctrina christiana* 4.18.35 (trans. my own).
96. Ibid., 4.19.38 (Robertson, 145).
97. Ibid., 4.22.51 (Robertson, 159).

Augustine's practice bears out the principle. In his sermons he began, often enough, in the moderate style to draw in his listeners, to render them—according to Cicero's dictum—"benevolent, attentive, docile."[98] Then he would dip to the subdued: listing arguments, role-playing both sides of a heated debate, launching into a staccato rhythm of question and answer. Then he would shift to the moderate, now praising, now denouncing, all the while piling up image upon image, ornament upon ornament. Then he would shift again, either returning to the subdued or leaping to the grand; and if he leapt, his voice would grow fervent, infusing musical figures—whether parallelisms, alliterations, or antitheses— with passion, until finally he would snap the cadenza to a close with a flurry of rhymed admonitions. Here he might end, or more often, change registers, slipping back to the subdued, to begin a new theme.

Cicero had taught that there was a link between the three aims and the three styles: in teaching, one used the subdued; in delighting, the moderate; in persuading, the grand.[99] Augustine agreed—but with certain reservations. He found, for instance, his subdued style could be equally delightful:

"Frequently the subdued style, when it solves difficult riddles and demonstrates things in unexpected ways—especially if . . . a few rhythmic closings are used, not for show but, as I say, as if necessary, arising from the things being discussed—that it excites such applause that it is hardly recognized as being subdued."[100]

Similarly, Augustine did not always resort to the grand style when he wanted to persuade. Rather he tended to reserve it for one urgent case: whenever "the hard heart" needed "to be bent to obedience."[101] He thus remarked:

"If a speaker is applauded frequently and vigorously, he should not think that for that reason he is speaking in the grand style; for the acumen revealed in the subdued style and the ornaments of the moderate style may produce the same result. For the grand style frequently prevents applauding voices with its own weight

98. Ibid., 4.23.52 (Robertson, 159). 4.4.6 alludes to Cicero, *De oratore* 2.80.
99. *De doctrina christiana* 4.17.34.
100. Ibid., 4.26.56 (Robertson, 163—altered).
101. Ibid., 4.26.58 (Robertson, 164).

. . . [People] do not show [its success] through applause but rather through their groans, sometimes even through tears, and finally through a change of their way of life."[102]

To illustrate this, Augustine cited a personal experience. Once he journeyed to Caesarea in Mauretania to convince the citizens there to abandon an ancient custom. Apparently, for a few days each year, these people would carry on a sort of ritualized civil war: they would divide into two camps and then stone, even murder, anyone from the other side. To these people, Augustine gave an impassioned appeal, and its passion won not their applause, but their tears and, more importantly, their abandoning of the brutal custom.[103]

Thus Augustine acknowledged that while the facile parallelism between the three aims and the three styles had a certain validity, one could not press the matter too far. Rather "it is the universal office of eloquence, in any of the three styles, to speak in a manner leading to persuasion."[104] For Augustine, persuasion was the bottom line—and by persuasion, he meant not nodding assent, but moral living. While he certainly wanted people both informed and fervent, he wanted, even more, people who enfleshed their faith, embodied its charity, and enacted its justice. As he remarked in one sermon: "See—you are Christians. You come to church regularly; you hear the word of God; you are swept away by God's word. [The assembly had been cheering.] You praise the preacher. I want your actions to match it."[105]

Augustine insisted that good living was itself eloquent speech. This was true of the teacher: that "the life of the speaker has greater weight in determining whether he is obediently heard than any grandness of eloquence."[106] Similarly, hearers who enfleshed the preached word acquired an eloquence all their own.[107] This view shaped how Augustine sometimes exhorted the baptized: he would beg them to lead masterful lives, ones that catechumens, like budding orators, might rightfully imitate: "[You who are bap-

---

102. Ibid., 4.24.53 (Robertson, 160–61).
103. Ibid.
104. Ibid., 4.25.55 (Robertson, 161).
105. *Sermo* 178 (trans. my own).
106. *De doctrina christiana* 4.27.59 (Robertson, 164).
107. Ibid., 4.29.62; *Sermo* 216.1.

tized:] be exhorters, not by words, but by your way of life, that
they who have not been baptized may rush to follow you—but in
such a way that they do not perish by imitating you [who live
badly]."[108]

SCRIPTURE AND ITS RIDDLES:
THE CORE CURRICULUM

In the end, Augustine saw verbal finesse simply as a useful tool.
He reminded readers of *On Christian Doctrine* of an often-ignored
truism from the rhetorical tradition: that eloquence, if left to itself,
was either frivolous or destructive; that eloquence, to be of value,
needed to root itself in wisdom.[109] And for Augustine the Christian bishop, the only wisdom worthy of the name was Scripture.[110] Thus he insisted that the Christian orator was ultimately
"an expositor and teacher of Divine Scripture."[111] "Expositor"
(*tractator*) seems too neutral, too detached, a term to communicate
the urgency Augustine brought to this task. As he said in a letter
to Jerome, the foremost biblical scholar of the age: "I neither have
nor can have as much knowledge of the Divine Scriptures as I see
abounds in you—and if I do gain any stock of knowledge, I pay it
out immediately to the people of God."[112]

Augustine again and again used such monetary metaphors to
explain his task: he was a debtor; by preaching he paid off his
debts; and the coinage he used was God's word. As he put it in
one sermon: "We give what we receive. . . . The money is the
Lord's: we are the dispensers, not the donors."[113]

---

108. *Sermo* 132.2 (trans. my own). Cf. *Sermo* 392.5 in which he asks the
catechumens to imitate those among the baptized who are worthy of imitation.

109. *De doctrina christiana* 4.5.7. Augustine here quotes Cicero, *De inventione*
1.1.

110. *De doctrina christiana* 4.5.8.

111. Ibid., 4.4.6. See Mohrmann, "Praedicare—tractare—sermo," *Études sur le
latin des Chrétiens*, 2:63–72.

112. *Epistola* 73.5 (trans. Brown, 252, Parson, FC 12:336). On the correspondence between Augustine and Jerome, see Robert J. O'Connell, "When
Saintly Fathers Feuded: The Correspondence between Augustine and Jerome," *Thought* 54 (1979) 344–64; and Joseph Trigg, *Biblical Interpretation*, MF 9
(Wilmington, Del.: Michael Glazier, 1988) 250–95.

113. *Sermo* 260D.2 (= Guelf. 18) (trans. my own). The same idea appears in
Sermo 179A.8 (= Wilmart 2). Preachers remain in their hearers' debt until they

The catechumens in Augustine's assembly would have received this coinage in abundance. In his sermons, Augustine let the biblical text—its structure, its mood, its vocabulary—control everything. We saw in the last chapter the way he took the traditional six-part outline for orations and modified it for the teaching of inquirers. In his sermons, that traditional outline all but disappears. At most one finds an *exordium* or a *peroratio*, and these are typically brief. Instead, Augustine let a biblical text—usually a pericope sung or proclaimed that day—hold sway. Moreover, he did not look for some connecting thread within it, nor did he reduce it to "three points" as some modern preachers do. Rather he read it verse by verse, even word by word, straining each phrase, each word, for its submerged resonances, its mystical glimmerings and moral import. As Van der Meer notes:

"This had been the manner in which the *grammaticus* had for centuries dealt with Homer and Vergil in the routine of the schools, and for centuries more than this was the way the learned bishops were unconsciously to follow their example in the expounding of their pericopes and their exegesis of the biblical books. The texts had changed; the method remained the same."[114]

This grammatical method led Augustine and his contemporaries to focus on terse snippets of Scripture, on minutiae, on odd or beautiful turns of phrase. At a deeper level, it reflected their mode of perception, what Marrou has called "a sort of psychological atomism."[115] Ancient commentators tended to locate truth—or rather, the experience of it—in brief fleeting insights, in the sudden breakthroughs that came from contemplating such small fragments. This did not mean they neglected synthesis. Far from it—but their construction techniques differed from those of later ages. They did not create vast theological systems like the medievals; they had no theological Gothic cathedrals. Instead their syntheses were smaller, denser, more jagged—a theological equivalent of the brilliant mosaics of their day. And these commentators treated their materials—the words and phrases of

---

pay off with their words: *Enarrationes in Psalmos* 88.2.1; 95.1; *Tractatus in evangelium Ioannis* 6.1.

114. Van der Meer, *Augustine the Bishop*, 440; see also Marrou, *Saint Augustin et la fin de la culture antique*, 10-26 and 428-30.

115. Marrou, *Saint Augustin et la fin de la culture antique*, 25-26.

Scripture—the same way mosaic artists treated their tesserae: as jewel-like fragments to be plucked up, admired, and patiently pieced together. The end result tended to spark.

Augustine's sermons are literally studded with scriptural tesserae. For instance, in his sermon on psalm 119, he ranged quite literally from Genesis to Revelation, quoting or echoing thirty-seven different verses—not counting those from the psalm he was commenting on. As Brown notes: "This method of exegesis, which involved creating a whole structure of verbal echoes, linking every part of the Bible, was particularly well-suited to teaching [a] hitherto quite unknown text, to an audience used to memorizing by ear."[116] This quote-and-echo technique was both venerable and stylish. Late Roman orators were trained to lace their speeches with phrases snatched from the pagan classics. Not surprisingly, Augustine and his fellow Christian preachers mined their classic the same way.[117]

Educated catechumens would have found the technique familiar. What would have struck them as odd, perhaps gauche, was applying it to the Bible. After all, the Latin Bible prior to Jerome's Vulgate was too crude to merit the status of a classic: it had too much jargon, too many neologisms, too many awkward turns of phrase.[118] As a youth, Augustine had been put off by this diction, presuming what all educated people presumed: how could something be wise that was not also eloquent?[119] Thus as we saw in the last chapter, Augustine never failed to address this issue with educated inquirers. But in his sermons he displayed a different attitude. He made few apologies. Instead, he repeated biblical phrases again and again, as though he were chewing on them, as

116. Brown, *Augustine of Hippo,* 254.

117. Marrou, *Saint Augustine and His Influence through the Ages,* 61: "The historian who tries to reconstruct the methods of work which [Augustine] used . . . must be especially struck with Augustine's astounding memory, whose operation he has described in words which have justly remained classical, evoking the extent, the 'vast palaces' of that memory of his, with its innumerable and ever-present treasures. He has the whole of Scripture by heart, as he has the classics, and this enables him to recall without effort a whole chain of verses, associated by ideas or images, taken from the most diverse corners of the Bible." Marrou notes that Augustine in his extant works cites the Scriptures 42,816 times—often enough from memory.

118. See Marrou, *Saint Augustin et la fin de la culture antique,* 473-77.

119. *Confessiones* 3.5.

though savoring their sweetness. The melody of Jewish thought intrigued him—much as the simple and exotic melodies of the gypsies intrigued Bartok. And like Bartok, Augustine let his own classical harmonies be shaped by these simple, exotic melodies. Moreover, his repetition of biblical phrases was part of a conscious pedagogy: by it, vital matters got "pounded into the memory, as gravel is pounded into a path, to make sure that they do not pass out of the mind."[120]

Augustine found the wisdom of Scripture a paradoxical mix. As he said in a letter to Volusianus, the pagan aristocrat:

"The very language in which holy scripture is expressed is easy for all, although understood by very few. In its easily understood parts it speaks to the heart of the unlearned and learned like a familiar friend who uses no subterfuge, but in those truths which it veils in mystery, it does not raise itself aloft with proud speech. Thus, the backward and untutored mind dares to draw near to it as a poor person to a rich one, because it invites all in simple language, and feeds the mind with its teaching in plain words, while training it in the truth by its hidden message, having the same effect in both the obvious and the obscure. But should the obvious cause disgust, the hidden truths arouse longing; longing brings renewal; renewal brings sweet inner knowledge."[121]

It was these hidden truths that fascinated Augustine. In his sermons, he moved from one "knotty problem" to another, from one "mystery" to another. His usual attitude was: *Factum audivimus, mysterium requiramus* ("We've heard what happened; let's delve into the mystery").[122] Augustine did not deny that Scripture recorded history. On the contrary, he solemnly warned that if the events Scripture described had not taken place, then one "would be building castles in the air."[123] Yet he focused on mysteries because he found these best nourished the "hungry." As he once

120. *De civitate Dei* 22.8 (Bettenson, 1045). Here Augustine is not talking about Scripture, but reading miracle stories in liturgy; still it shows his understanding of the pedagogy of repetition.

121. *Epistola* 137.18 (Parsons, FC 20:34—altered). Cf. *Confessiones* 6.5.

122. *Tractatus in evangelium Ioannis* 50.6 (trans. my own).

123. *Sermo* 2.7 (trans. my own). For a translation and discussion of this, see Trigg, *Biblical Interpretation*, 239–49.

noted, there was something about people's psychological make-up that somehow made hidden truths more compelling:

"All those truths which are presented to us in figures tend in some manner to nourish and arouse that flame of love, an impulse which carries us upward and inward toward rest; and they stir and enkindle love better than if they were set before us unadorned, without any symbolism of mystery. It is hard to explain the reason for this; nevertheless it is true that any doctrine suggested under an allegorical form affects and pleases us more, and is more esteemed than one set forth explicitly in plain words."[124]

Augustine's hearers keenly enjoyed the way he would untie the "scroll-covers" and "unroll" what lay hidden within.[125] In fact, the more subtle his allegories, the more they cheered. It intrigued them much as detective stories or courtroom dramas intrigue us. In fact, Augustine's approach was not unlike that of a detective or a lawyer. (After all, his rhetorical training had been, in part, training for the law courts.[126]) Thus like a good detective or lawyer, Augustine always had his eye out for odd clues, for things "covered with a dense mist":[127] exotic place names, strange animals, numbers, double entendres, quirky metaphors. These he would put under his magnifying glass, for he presumed they opened up unexpected mysteries. Then he would scour the Scriptures from end to end, searching for clues that might unravel the knot, that might crack open the case. Sherlock Holmes used to tell Dr. Watson that some things were elementary; Augustine had a similar view: "Hardly anything may be found in these obscure places which is not found plainly said elsewhere."[128]

Typically Augustine turned to "things that are obvious"—usually passages from Paul or the Gospels—"to illuminate those things which are obscure."[129] Yet to dig up these more illuminating passages required an "expert investigator," one who had read all the Scriptures and committed much to memory.[130] But such an

---

124. *Epistola* 55.21 (Parsons, 12:277). Cf. *De doctrina christiana* 2.6.8; 4.7.15.
125. *Enarrationes in Psalmos* 147.23 (trans. my own).
126. Marrou, *A History of Education in Antiquity*, 287–89.
127. *De doctrina christiana* 2.6.7 (Robertson, 37).
128. Ibid., 2.6.8 (Robertson, 38).
129. Ibid., 2.9.14 (Robertson, 42—altered). See also 3.26.37.
130. Ibid., 2.8.12 (Robertson, 40).

encyclopedic memory was just the beginning. One needed other knowledge and other skills: mastery of rules for valid inference; ability to read biblical languages to check errors in translation; knowledge of history, the arts, even minutiae such as weights and coinage.[131] And then there were rules that applied to interpreting any text, such as checking the context of a passage; and, of course, there were two foundational rules that applied specifically to Scripture: consult the rule of faith, and read things in light of the commandment of love of God and of neighbor.[132] In the first three books of *On Christian Doctrine*, Augustine spelled out these rules, knowledges, and principles in some detail. In so doing, he created for Catholic teachers of his generation what the Donatist exegete Tyconius had done a generation before: he set out "mystic rules so that the one who walks through [Scripture's] immense forest of prophecy [can be] led by these rules as if by pathways of light."[133]

To carry on this sort of investigation, Augustine made certain presumptions. As Brown notes:

"For Augustine and his hearers, the Bible was literally the 'word' of God. It was regarded as a single communication, a single message in an intricate code, and not as an exceedingly heterogeneous collection of separate books. Above all, it was a communication that was intrinsically so far above the pitch of human minds, that to be made available to our senses at all, this 'Word' had to be communicated by an intricate game of 'signs.'"[134]

Augustine believed the obscurity of Scripture befitted the nobility of its origin: "The higher in honor anyone is, the more veils are suspended in his palace."[135] But Scripture's veils and riddling ways held a deeper purpose: they served as a built-in moral pedagogy. As he noted in *On Christian Doctrine*, this "healthy and useful" obscurity served a dual purpose: on the one hand, "exer-

---

131. Ibid., 2.32.50–37.55; 2.11.16–15.22; 2.25.38–30.47.

132. Ibid., 3.2.2; 3.10.14–15.23.

133. Tyconius, *Liber regularum*, prologue; quoted by Augustine, *De doctrina christiana* 3.30.3 (Robertson, 105). For a translation of Tyconius, see Karlfried Froelich, *Biblical Interpretation in the Early Church* (Philadelphia: Fortress Press, 1984) 104–32.

134. Brown, *Augustine of Hippo*, 252.

135. *Sermo* 51.5 (MacMullen, 247).

cising and sharpening, as it were, the minds of readers and destroying disdain and stimulating the desire to learn"; and on the other, "concealing their intention in such a way that the minds of the impious are either converted to piety or excluded from the mysteries of faith."[136] In other words, Scripture itself discerned: it both spurred on the genuine seeker and denied entry to the counterfeit.

At its core, Scripture's pedagogy was a pedagogy for wisdom—that is, "wisdom" as the ancients understood it: skilled living. By its very language, Scripture "cleanses" one for the "journey home" to God, a journey made not "by moving from place to place, but by good endeavor and good habits."[137] Augustine believed that Scripture had a moral core—despite the welter of detail, despite any indications to the contrary—that ultimately it "teaches nothing but charity, nor condemns anything except cupidity, and in this way shapes people's way of life."[138] In other words, "the plentitude and end of the Law and of all the sacred Scriptures" was the "double love of God and of neighbor."[139] And this love demanded more than fervent feelings; it demanded action. As Augustine insisted to one noisy audience: "What I have said you have praised, cheered, and loved. . . . I want [to see] it in your way of life, not your voices. Praise wisdom in your living—not through making noise, but through harmonizing [with God's wisdom]."[140]

Augustine knew it was easier to win applause than to form a community that lived in harmony with God's wisdom. He also knew his natural temptation was to glory in the applause. In sober moments, it left him with a divided heart. This he once shared with his people:

"It would be dangerous for me to pay attention to the way you praise me and shut my eyes to the way you live. . . . I do not want praise from those who live evil lives. That I abhor, that I detest. It causes me pain, not pleasure. But, if I were to say that I

136. *De doctrina christiana* 4.8.22 (Robertson, 132—altered). See also *Sermo* 51.5. On this theme of the *exercitatio animi*, see O'Connell, *St. Augustine's Confessions*, 15–18; Marrou, *Saint Augustin et la fin de la culture antique*, 299–327.

137. *De doctrina christiana* 1.10.10 (Robertson, 13).

138. Ibid., 3.10.15 (Robertson, 88).

139. Ibid., 1.35.39 and 36.40 (Robertson, 30).

140. *Sermo* 311.4 (trans. my own).

do not wish to be praised by those who live well, I would be lying. Yet if I were to say that I want it, I fear that I might be craving something more hollow than solid. What then should I say? I neither fully wish to have it nor be without it. I do not fully want it—that people's praise might place me in danger. I do not altogether want to be without it—lest it be unrewarding to those I preach to."[141]

Augustine felt the stark clash between the applause he received and Scripture's demanding wisdom. He knew that the same people who came to church on the great feasts would later fill the bawdy theaters and bloody arenas;[142] that many used the feasts of martyrs as an excuse to get drunk;[143] that his congregation daily brought their petty squabbles before his courtroom;[144] that upper class men kept mistresses, as he once had, and were annoyed whenever he preached against it;[145] that the rich were greedy, always ready to wrest away property from their poor neighbors just to get a little more light into their already sprawling villas;[146] that his catechumens would delay and delay, more fearful of future sins than present ones,[147] and say to themselves, "Let me live the way I want a little longer." Augustine knew that the weight of habit too often overwhelmed desire for conversion: that "those who say, 'I intend to start a new life tomorrow,' . . . when tomorrow comes, you will say the same again."[148]

Such lethargy of habit deeply troubled him. He thus turned to Scripture to define his own role. On these occasions he saw himself, like Ezekiel, called to be a "sentinel for the house of Israel"; he, like Ezekiel, was compelled to preach judgment as well as

141. *Sermo* 339.1 (trans. my own). For a complete translation of this important sermon, see Audrey Fellowes, *"We are Your Servants": Augustine's Homilies on Ministry* (Villanova: Augustinian Press, 1986) 56–77.

142. *Sermo* 301A.8 (=Denis 17); *Enarrationes in psalmos* 39.10.

143. On Augustine's campaign against the drinking at these feasts, see *Epistola* 29; Bonner, *St. Augustine: Life and Controversies,* 116–20.

144. On Augustine as a judge, see Possidius, *Vita* 19; see also Augustine's complaints about the experience: *Enarrationes in psalmos* 25.2.13–14 and 118.24.3–4; cf. *Epistola* 24*.1 (Divjak). For the background on this, see Bonner, *St. Augustine: Life and Controversies,* 123.

145. *Sermo* 223.4.

146. *Sermo* 50.7.

147. *Sermo* 97A.3 (=Bibl. Casin. 2, 114). Cf. *Sermo* 16A.6 (=Denis 20).

148. *Sermo* 339.8 (Fellowes, 74–75).

mercy, repentance as well as joy. It went against the grain of his temperament: "To have to preach, to convict, to rebuke, to edify, to feel responsible for every one of you—it is a heavy burden, a great weight, hard labor."[149] The biblical message of judgment deeply troubled him:

"What am I to do? Can I erase such words? I am afraid that they may erase me. Should I just be silent? I am afraid to be silent. They force me to preach. I instill fear because I am afraid. Be afraid *with me* so you may rejoice *with me*."[150]

As Brown notes, "the moments when Augustine stands outside his flock and threatens them in this way are rare."[151] Yet even in these, the phrase "with me" appears again and again. Augustine may have had ascetic leanings, but he was no solitary. He, unlike Plotinus, had no wish to soar alone to the Alone. Instead, he wanted companions, but like St. Paul, his model, he always sought a companionship that was "in Christ":

"Why do I preach? Why do I sit up here? What do I live for? For this one thing alone: that together we may live with Christ! This is my passion, this is my honor, this is my fame, this is my joy, this is my one possession! . . . But I do not want to be saved without you!"[152]

Scripture was the standard he set before catechumens and baptized alike; but it was a standard he first set before himself: "When I exhort you, I [first] peer into myself. For one is a hollow preacher of God's word on the outside if one is not [first] a hearer on the inside."[153] In fact, the hour before Augustine preached, he did just this sort of inner hearing: he prayed. Thus in *On Christian Doctrine*, Augustine insisted that the preacher "is a petitioner before he is a speaker," that he "should raise his thirsty soul to God in order that he may give forth what he drinks, that he may pour out what fills him."[154]

---

149. *Sermo* 339.4 (trans. my own).
150. *Sermo* 339.8 (trans. my own).
151. Brown, *Augustine of Hippo*, 250.
152. *Sermo* 17.2 (trans. my own).
153. *Sermo* 179.1 (trans. my own).
154. *De doctrina christiana* 4.15.32 (Robertson, 140—altered).

CONVERSI AD DOMINUM: DISMISSAL

Augustine not only prepared his sermons by praying; he also ended them this same way—in this case, by praying aloud. The formula he used was so commonplace that the *notarii* usually recorded only its opening words: "Turning to the Lord" ("*Conversi ad Dominum*").[155] At this moment, all present may well have turned to the east and lifted up their hands in the traditional orant position.[156] Augustine would then have recited a prayer laced with florid, courtly formulae:

"Turning to the Lord God, Father Almighty, let us, with a pure heart—as best our weakness can—give him our deepest and richest thanks; praying with all our being to his extraordinary gentleness: that by his good pleasure he would deign to hear our prayers favorably; that by his power he would drive the enemy from our deeds and thoughts; that he would increase our faith, steer our minds, grant us spirit-filled reflections, and carry us over into his blessedness, through his Son Jesus Christ. Amen."[157]

After this came the dismissal (*missa*) of the catechumens.[158] We do not know exactly what this involved. Perhaps the catechumens received a blessing. We know penitents did: they lined up and, one by one, came forward to have Augustine lay hands on them.[159] Catechumens may also have received the "sacrament of salt" at this time.[160] In any case, they were dismissed. The liturgy they attended would have lasted around an hour and a half. During it, they heard—actually heard, sang, cheered, prayed—God's Word. As Augustine insisted: through it all, through a chorus of voices—the reader, cantor, preacher, even the assembly itself— "God speaks; all this is the voice of God [echoing] throughout the

155. See *Sermones* 15A.9 (=Denis 21); 16A.13 (=Denis 20); 16B.4 (=Mai 17); 18.5; 23A.4 (=Mai 16); 26.15; etc.

156. Van der Meer, *Augustine the Bishop*, 397.

157. *Sermo* 67 (trans. my own). Two other complete versions are found in Augustine's sermons: *Sermones* 223A.5 (=Denis 2) and 362.31. Augustine discusses it in *Sermo* 348A.3.

158. *Sermo* 49.8.

159. On Augustine's complaints on the length of dismissing penitents, see *Epistola* 149.6 and *Sermo* 232.7-8. The dismissal of penitents did not occur at this time, but just before Communion. See the discussion of the *missa* structure in both East and West in Kavanagh, *Confirmation*, 3-38.

160. Third Council of Carthage, *canon* 5.

round world."[161] Once the catechumens left, the doors would be closed. They would not be allowed to witness the mysteries that followed—not until they had passed through the waters. Nor did they know that sometime later those who remained would be "exhorted to pray . . . for the catechumens that [God] may breath into them a desire for regeneration."[162]

161. *Enarrationes in psalmos* 93.9 (trans. LF 32:357). See also *Sermo* 17.1.
162. *Epistola* 217.2 (Parsons, 32:76).

Chart 7
Sermons and Works Addressed to Catechumens

Sermon	Verbraken #	Text	Trans	Scripture/Feast
1. Cross on the Forehead				
*32	32	BAC 7	---	Ps 143
*107	107	BAC 10	NPNF 6	Lk 13:13-21
*302	302	BAC 25	---	St. Lawrence
Bibliotheca Cas 2, 114	97A	BAC 10	---	Luke 5:31-32
Denis 17	301A	BAC 25	---	Luke 14:28-33
*En in Ps 68,1	---	CCSL 39	LF 30	Ps 68
*En in Ps 141	---	CCSL 40	LF 39	Ps 141
*Tract Jn 3	---	CCSL 36	FC 78	John 1:15-18
Tract Jn 11	---	CCSL 36	FC 79	John 2:22-3:5
*Tract Jn 50	---	CCSL 36	NPNF 7	John 11:55-12:11
*Tract Jn 53	---	CCSL 36	NPNF 7	John 12:37-43
2. Catechumens Ignorance of "Secrets"				
131	131	BAC 23	NPNF 6	John 6:54-56
132	132	BAC 23	NPNF 6	John 6:56-57
235	235	BAC 24	FC 38	Luke 24:13-35
307	307	BAC 25	---	St. John the Baptist
En in Ps 80	---	CCSL 39	LF 32	Ps 80
En in Ps 109	---	CCSL 40	LF 37	Ps 109
Epistola 140	---	CSEL 44	FC 20	---
Tract Jn 11	---	CCSL 36	FC 79	John 2:22-3:5
3. Catechumens as Examples to Illustrate a Point				
46	46	BAC 7	---	Ezek 34:1-16
232	232	BAC 24	FC 38	Luke 24:13-35
Denis 20	16A	BAC 7	---	Ps 38:13
Tract Jn 4	---	CCSL 36	FC 78	John 1:19-23
Tract Jn 5	---	CCSL 36	FC 78	John 1:33
Tract Jn 13	---	CCSL 36	FC 79	John 3:22-29
Tract Jn 44	---	CCSL 36	NPNF 7	John 9:1-41
4. Admonition to Seek Baptism				
132	132	BAC 23	NPNF 6	John 6:56
135	135	BAC 23	NPNF 6	John 9:1-41
392	392	BAC 26	---	---
Bibliotheca Cas 2, 114	97 A	BAC 10	---	Luke 5:31
En in Ps 80	---	CCSL 39	LF 32	Ps 80
En in Ps 109	---	CCSL 40	LF 37	Ps 109
Epistola 151	---	CSEL 44	FC 20	---
Epistola 258	---	CSEL 57	FC 32	---
Epistola 2* (Divjak)	---	CSEL 88	FC 81	---
Lambot 10	136 B	BAC 23	---	John 9:1-41

Chart 7 *(cont.)*

Sermons and Works Addressed to Catechumens

Sermon	Verbraken #	Text	Trans	Scripture/Feast
Lambot 26	335 H	BAC 25	---	Martyrs
Tract Jn 10	---	CCSL 36	FC 78	John 2:12-21
Tract Jn 11	---	CCSL 36	FC 79	John 2:22-3:5
Tract Jn 12	---	CCSL 36	FC 79	John 3:6-21
Tract Jn 44	---	CCSL 36	NPNF 7	John 9:1-41

* = Reference to catechumens is implied.
Note: Some sermons touch on elements from more than one category.

Chart 8
Passing References to Aspects of the Catechumenate

Sermon	Verbraken #	Text	Trans	Topic
19	19	BAC 7	---	Catechumens during earthquake
46	46	BAC 7	---	Catechumens as Christians
49	49	BAC 7	---	Dismissal of catechumens
181	181	BAC 23	---	Lord's Prayer not for catechumens
229	229	BAC 24	FC 38	Catechumenate as "observation"
295	295	BAC 25	---	Catechumens as Christians
Confessiones 1	---	CCSL 27	Pine-Coffin	Sacrament of salt
De catechizandis rudibus	---	CCSL 46	ACW 2	Cross on forehead; Sacrament of salt
De coniugiis adulterinis	---	CSEL 41	FC 27	Divorced catechumens
De fide et operibus	---	CSEL 41	FC 27	Meaning of catechumenate
De octo Dulc. quaestionibus	---	CCSL 44A	FC 16	Story of Celticchius
De peccatorum et meritiis	---	CSEL 60	NPNF 5	Sacrament of salt
De sancta uirginitate	---	CSEL 41	FC 27	Lord's Prayer not for catechumens
Enarratio in Ps 36, 2	---	CCSL 38	ACW 30	Cross on forehead
Enarratio in Ps 41	---	CCSL 38	LF 32	Ps 41 as theme song of catechumen
Enarratio in Ps 103, 1	---	CCSL 39	LF 37	Disciplina arcani
Epistola 126	---	CSEL 34	FC 18	Dismissal of catechumens
Epistola 217	---	CSEL 57	FC 32	Prayers made for catechumens
Etaix 1	65A	BAC 10	---	Catechumens part of the Church
Guelf 3	218C	BAC 24	---	Cross on forehead
Mai 94	260C	BAC 24	---	Entrance rites as conception in womb
Tract Jn 36	---	CCSL 36	NPNF 7	Cross on forehead
Tract Jn 96	---	CCSL 36	NPNF 7	Disciplina arcani
Tract Jn 116	---	CCSL 36	NPNF 7	Cross on forehead

Chapter 6

Catechumenate: The Eagle and the Staircase

In Augustine's time the bishop had the right to choose the lections during certain periods of the liturgical year. Augustine used this freedom to guide people through certain of his favorite biblical books, or parts of them, on a *lectio continua* basis.[1] Beginning in December (c. 406), he embarked on a special series which intertwined sermons on John with others on the psalms. Over the next four months he preached on these two books at a pace of two to three sermons per week (with a month break somewhere in the middle).[2] During this same period he apparently preached on other texts as well, for he refers on several occasions to giving a "rain of daily exhortations."[3] His audience included the usual mix: merchants and beggars; married and ascetics; freeborn and slaves; baptized and, of course, the catechumens.[4] For the next

1. *Tractatus in evangelium Ioannis* 2.1. Peter Cobb, "The Liturgy of the Word in the Early Church," in *The Study of the Liturgy*, ed. Cheslyn Jones et al. (New York: Oxford University Press, 1978) 185. In Augustine's case, see Willis, *St. Augustine's Lectionary*, 5–9; Poque, "Trois semaines de prédication," 178. Augustine mentions that the readings for Holy Week and the Octave of Easter were fixed (*Tractatus in evangelium Ioannis* 6.17; *Sermo* 232.1).

2. The texts themselves give a number of indications. See chart 11. For attempts to reconstruct the dates when individual sermons were given, see LaBonnardière, *Recherches de chronologie augustinienne*, 46–53, and Poque, "Trois semaines de prédication," 183–87. While both have to rely on a variety of hypotheses, they represent the best attempts to date to deal with the welter of time indications found in the series. Concerning the translation of sermons in this intertwining series: the only complete translation of the *Enarrationes in psalmos* is an accurate, but rather stilted one in the Library of the Fathers which dates from the 1850s; as a result, I have retranslated most of these passages. Rettig in FC 78 and 79 has produced a careful up-to-date translation of *Tractatus in evangelium Ioannis* 1–27; his rendering is very literal, so that I have sometimes amended it to give it a more fluent style.

3. *Tractatus in evangelium Ioannis* 3.1 (Rettig, 78:75). See also 12.14.

4. For a carefully documented look at the various groups present in the audience, see M.-F. Berrouard, "Introduction," BAug 71:36–54.

194

several months the psalms and John would be Augustine's curriculum for his assembly and thus for his catechumenate. Catechumens would receive his direct attention from time to time: and that attention would increase as the series progressed and drew nearer to Lent. Augustine would mention the catechumens by name six times in the series, and there are a number of other implied references to them. Most often, however, what Augustine said, he said to all, and the catechumens were numbered among that all. Throughout, the care he took for those who "walked a little slower" is evident—and the catechumens would be among those who walked a little slower.

John's Gospel and the psalms were two of Augustine's favorites. Over the course of his life, he commented on the whole of both. He loved John's Gospel for its sublimity: ". . . the evangelist John soars to greater heights like an eagle; he transcends the murky darkness of earth; he looks upon the light of truth with a steadier gaze."[5] What John had gazed on was the Word—at once the divine Word and the Word made flesh—and the unfathomable paradox of this captivated Augustine as it had so many before him: Origen, Athanasius, the Cappadocians. But there was another facet of the Gospel that attracted him: whereas the Synoptics focused mainly on Jesus' concrete words and deeds, John probed their inner meanings.[6] This appealed to Augustine's taste, for he was fascinated less by the facts of history than by its deeper rhythms and undercurrents.

In this four-month series Augustine would work his way through the first three chapters of John: e.g., the lofty prologue, the baptism of Jesus, the encounter with Nicodemus. These episodes led Augustine to explore facets of the mystery of Christ: his divinity and humanity, his role in creating the world and recreating humankind. Throughout, Augustine challenged opponents—Manichees, Arians, Donatists—and waged what Berrouard has called "a combat for the honor of Christ."[7] By treating these issues Augustine gave the catechumens (among others) an understanding of key facets of Christian doctrine, and his frequent com-

5. *Tractatus in evangelium Ioannis* 15.1 (Rettig, 78:78—altered). See also *Tractatus* 19.5; 36.1; 40.1.

6. *Tractatus in evangelium Ioannis* 36.1; see also Rettig, "Introduction," FC 78:11–12; Berrouard, BAug 71:55–63.

7. Berrouard, "Introduction," BAug 71:78–113.

ments on baptism—its meaning, its responsibilities, its joys—did much to prepare the catechumens for the weighty step that lay before them. Also, his polemics against various opponents sharpened the catechumens' sense of Catholic identity and gave them tools to defend themselves against the polemics of those outsiders they met daily in the streets.

The psalms were equally dear to Augustine's heart. At his baptism, the "sweet singing of the Church" had left him in tears.[8] This music continued to cast a spell over him: "I realized that when they are sung these sacred words stir my mind to greater religious fervor and kindle in me a more ardent flame of piety than . . . if they were not sung."[9] Their language became part of the air he breathed: almost every page of the *Confessions* quotes or echoes one of the psalms. Not surprisingly, he worked to pass on this spirituality to catechumens and others. As he told one correspondent, he used singing to fill in the transition moments within the liturgy:

"Is not any time appropriate for singing sacred hymns when the brethren gather in the church (except when there is reading or discussion or praying aloud by the bishop, or prayer in common, led by the voice of the deacon)? I know of nothing better or more holy for Christians to do. . . ."[10]

His efforts met with only mixed success: many in the African Church remained lackadaisical when it came to singing.[11] Yet Augustine did not simply want passionate singers; he wanted thoughtful ones. After all, he insisted, human beings must not be like "blackbirds, parrots, ravens, and magpies" who mimic things "they cannot understand."[12] As he saw it, the psalms touched the "inward ear"; they drew one to an "inner place of sanctity"; there a "seductive loneliness" took hold as though one were drawn to "someone softly strumming an instrument."[13] In addition, Augustine insisted that the voice of the psalmist was the

8. *Confessiones* 9.6.
9. Ibid., 10.33 (Pine-Coffin, 238).
10. *Epistola* 55.35 (Parsons, 12:290).
11. *Epistola* 55.34 (Parsons, 12:290).
12. *Enarrationes in psalmos* 18.2.1 (Hebgin and Corrigan, 29:182); see also *Tractatus in evangelium Ioannis* 13.3.
13. *Enarrationes in psalmos* 41.9 (trans. my own).

passionate voice of Christ—by turns, the voice of the Risen Lord and the voice of his body, the Church on earth: "It is his voice in all the psalms: now strumming gently, now moaning, now rejoicing in hope for what will be, now sighing about things as they are."[14] Augustine, a man who loved to probe his own powerful feelings, was drawn, as Peter Brown notes, to the psalms' "immensely rich deposit of human emotions."[15] By mining this vein, Augustine would give the catechumens tools to explore their own affectivity and would pass on to them a repertoire of religious emotions he considered vital to Christian life.

In this four-month series, Augustine focused on the psalms of ascent, (Pss 119–133 in the old Latin numbering), those songs pilgrims had once sung on their way up to the Temple in Jerusalem. As he saw it, the title affixed to these psalms determined their meaning: that each was a "song of steps" (canticum graduum); that while on staircases one can either go up or down, on the psalms' staircase he and they were to act "as people resolved to go up."[16] And he would cite Psalm 83:6 as his guide for interpreting them: that God had "set steps of ascent in the heart." This meant that the journey upward to God was in fact a journey inward through the heart. Thus, according to Augustine, these psalms would lead him and his fellow pilgrims, both catechumens and faithful, to explore the heart's depths and to gain a foretaste of the heavenly Jerusalem. These psalms thus seemed both a map for the catechumens' and faithfuls' journey to God and a spirituality for their sojourn. It would be a journey into the ineffable:

"Singers at harvest or in vineyards or at some other arduous toil express their rapture by beginning with songs set to words; then, as if bursting with a joy so full that they cannot give vent to it in set syllables, they drop the words and break into the free melody of pure jubilation. . . . And to whom does that jubilation rightly ascend, if not to God who is ineffable? Truly God is ineffable. You cannot give voice to Him in words. And if you cannot give voice to Him in words—yet you ought not remain silent—what else can you do but break into jubilation? In this way the heart rejoices

14. Ibid., 42.1 (trans. my own).
15. Brown, Augustine of Hippo, 257.
16. Enarrationes in psalmos 119.1 (trans. my own).

without words, and the boundless expanse of rapture is not bound in by syllables.''[17]

It was this passion that Augustine wanted both catechumens and baptized to taste.

TWO SESSIONS: DECEMBER 406

To appreciate Augustine's catechumenate, it is important to have some taste for the dynamic of individual sessions. Let us therefore focus on two sermons from this sequence: *Tractate* 1 on John 1:1-5 and *Enarratio* on Psalm 121. In the first Augustine used the Gospel text to explore the meaning and import of Christ's divinity; in the second, he used the psalm text to explore the feelings that ought to guide one's pilgrimage to the City of God. These two sermons (the third and fourth of the sequence) were given in early December—apparently within a few days of one another. In treating these I will put the camera into motion, so to speak, tracing step by step the language he used, the themes he touched on, and the moods he evoked. In this way we will be able to view at closer range some important ways Augustine used Scripture to catechize the catechumens.

TRACTATE 1: In the *exordium* rhetoricians traditionally proclaimed their poor ability for speaking on the issue at hand. This was, of course, mere posturing.[18] Here Augustine seems to echo the convention: ''I am very much at a loss how, even with the Lord's largesse, I may say or explain in my small measure what has been read from the gospel.'' Yet his complaint was justified. On this day, he found himself having to speak on John's prologue, a text that had inspired some of his own and his contemporaries' most subtle theological thinking. He had his audience very much in view: ''Among you, my beloved people, there are many who think only in human ways and who are not yet able to raise themselves to a spirit-imbued understanding.''[19] He had in mind apparently the uninitiated, especially catechumens. Despite his ambivalence, he insisted he had no wish to cheat any who might profit from his words.

17. Ibid., 32.2.8 (Hebgin and Corrigan, 30:112—altered).
18. H. M. Hubble, ''Chrysostom and Rhetoric,'' *Classical Philology* 19 (1924) 268.
19. *Tractatus in evangelium Ioannis* 1.1 (trans. my own).

198

First, he quoted a verse from Psalm 120 "which we sang a little while ago": "I have lifted my eyes to the mountains, from which help shall come to me." For Augustine, the evangelist "John [was] one of those mountains." Augustine then shifted into the moderate style and gave a brief encomium on John the mountain:

"This mountain . . . was contemplating the divinity of the Word. What kind of mountain was he? How high? He had risen beyond all the mountain peaks of the world. He had risen beyond all the fields of the sky. He had risen beyond all the heights of the constellations. He had risen beyond all the choirs and legions of angels."[20]

Augustine the neo-Platonist presumed that John had ascended to the divine by passing from the visible to the invisible, from the created to the uncreated. He wanted his hearers to make a similar ascent, to follow the path of John the mountain. So before speaking of the Word itself, he traced the scope of what the Word had created—the things of earth, the earth itself, the whole visible universe—and insisted that the Word simply spoke and it was created.

Augustine then paused—apparently wary of embarking on any explanation of the inner life of God. First, he called people to imitate John, noting that at the Last Supper the apostle "reclined upon the breast of the Lord." According to Augustine this meant that John "drank from the breast of the Lord that which he might give us to drink." (This image—drinking in wisdom from the heart of the Word—has almost maternal overtones, as if John had nursed at the breast of the Word.)[21] Augustine then exhorted the catechumens and baptized to imitate John:

"[John] has given you words to drink; you, however, ought to receive understanding from that [same] source . . . so that you may lift your eyes to the mountains from which help will come to you, that from there you might receive the chalice, as it were, that is, the Word given [as] drink. . . ."[22]

20. Ibid., 1.5-6 (Rettig, 78:44-45).
21. The maternal overtones of this are drawn out explicitly in *Enarrationes in psalmos* 119.2; 130.8-13; cf. *Tractatus in evangelium Ioannis* 1.17; 36.1.
22. *Tractatus in evangelium Ioannis* 1.7 (Rettig, 78:46-47). See also 36.1.

At last, Augustine embarked on an explanation of the divine Word. In so doing, he would pass on insights that appear in his subtle and brilliant book *The Trinity*. As Van der Meer notes, this was vintage Augustine: "He withholds nothing from his people of his profound, daring, and grandiose thought; he gives the best he has; but he is at pains to say it all as simply as possible, and to explain it in the greatest possible detail."[23] First, Augustine called attention to the words he himself spoke, noting that they boomed out, then drifted away into silence. The divine Word too "sounds forth" but it, unlike human words, "does not drift away"—and so keeps all creation rolling. With this simple antithesis, Augustine hoped to communicate the idea of the Word's never-ending creativity. He then asked his hearers to turn within themselves and note the dynamic: that, before they spoke, an inner word would echo within their hearts. He then explained: "If you can have a word in your heart, as if a design born in your mind, so that your mind gives birth to a design, the design may be present there, an offspring of your mind, so to speak, a son of your heart."[24]

Note his simple, yet subtle word-choice: just as the human mind "gives birth" to an inner word, so too the divine Mind "begets" an inner Word. In this way Augustine linked quite disparate concepts: "Word" and "Son." At the same time he laid the groundwork for claiming that human beings were made in the image and likeness of God, that the structure of human consciousness mirrored the structure of the divine. Moreover, that inner word, whether human or divine, was a "design." Augustine then invoked an analogy: an architect would envision building a magnificent structure; yet until it was built, one would not be able to see into the architect's mind to glimpse the inner blueprint. But when the project was complete:

"People look at a fine building and admire the design of the builder; they are amazed at what they see and delight in what they do not see, for who is there who can see a design? . . . A human design is praised because of some great building: Do you

23. Van der Meer, *Augustine the Bishop*, 442. Mohrmann, "Saint Augustin prédicateur," 94–95, insists on this with equal force.
24. *Tractatus in evangelium Ioannis* 1.8–9 (Rettig, 78:47–49).

wish to see what a design of God is the Lord Jesus Christ, that is, the Word of God?"[25]

With this, Augustine began a panegyric on the brilliant design of the universe: he pointed to the "splendor of sky," the "fertile earth," the rhythmic "variation of seasons." In the course of this he digressed and attacked the Arian claim that the Word was not divine in the way that the Father was. To do this Augustine used a stock technique, the diatribe: that is, he first offered a mock challenge, as if there were actually Arians standing in his audience ("Let some one of the unbelieving Arians come forward now and say that the Word of God was made"); then Augustine pummelled his invisible opponent with questions, as if the Arian case were on trial.[26] Also in the course of this digression, Augustine would make, in passing, an appeal to the catechumens: "You have already been made through the Word, but you need to be made anew through the Word."[27] He then continued his survey of the wonders of creation, "from the angel to the grub worm," in hopes that his hearers might peer through this visible magnificence and glimpse the invisible magnificence which "the nature of the Word is."[28]

He then relaxed from such philosophic high-flying to tell a little fable. Augustine was not usually a storyteller. While his sermons teem with images from the life around him—and in this way stay close to his hearers' experience—only rarely did he tell stories. In this sermon he broke from his usual habits. He spoke of a man annoyed by flies. Flies buzzing around one's face were, of course, a part of everyday life, given both the heat and unsanitary conditions in North Africa. One day, a Manichee noticed the man's distress. "Who made them?" the Manichee asked; "the devil," the man had to admit. With this, the Manichee then led him, step by step, to concede that the devil must have made other creatures—bees, locusts, lizards, birds, sheep, elephants, even human beings—until "that wretched fellow, when annoyed at flies, became himself a devil-possessed fly"; in other words, a servant of Beelzebub, the lord of the flies.[29] This simple-humored folktale

25. Ibid., 1.9 (Rettig, 78:49).
26. Ibid., 1.11 (Rettig, 78:50).
27. Ibid., 1.12 (Rettig, 78:51).
28. Ibid., 1.9–13.
29. Ibid., 1.14 (Rettig, 78:54).

was meant to delight. Yet with it, Augustine got across a simple point—that all creation, even flies, are God's good gift—and at the same time warned his people, both catechumens and faithful, of a snare that had once snared him: Manicheism.

Augustine then returned to the text and noted John 1:3: that "all things were made through [the Word]." This idea lay at the heart of the Christian vision of creation: it appears, of course, in the Nicene Creed; it also figured as a key theme in an address on the Creed that Augustine once gave to a council of North African bishops.[30] Not surprisingly, Augustine took care to explain this idea to the catechumens and faithful. First, he, like a grammarian, noted how the text should be punctuated (as we saw above, ancient codices lacked punctuation) and that incorrect punctuation could lead to misinterpretation. Then to explain the verse, Augustine invoked the analogy of a carpenter making a chest. It was the carpenter's invisible design that gave "life" to the visible chest. In the same way, it was the Word's invisible design that gave "life" to the whole visible universe (John 1:4): "You see the earth; there exists an earth in [the Word's] artistic mind [ars]. You see the sky; there exists a sky in his artistic mind. You see the sun and the moon; these, too, exist in his artistic mind."[31]

Augustine would take up this same analogy once more in his next sermon on John, and there give it a paradoxical twist: that while a carpenter works on his creation from the outside, "God constructs while infused in the world; he constructs while situated everywhere."[32] In other words, in Tractate 1, Augustine showed how the artistry of the Word and the carpenter were similar; in Tractate 2, he would show how they were dissimilar. In this way, Augustine would communicate in simple terms the Christian doc-

30. De fide et symbolo 4.5.
31. Tractatus in evangelium Ioannis 1.17 (trans. my own). It is difficult to translate Augustine's terminology here. Rettig translates ars as "creative knowledge" and notes "neither 'design' nor 'theory' nor 'art' nor 'idée' precisely express what Augustine is trying to say. Ars in Latin often designates a kind of knowledge of some particular sort . . . and especially a knowledge of precepts that leads to some concrete end. . . . When this Latin concept is combined with Platonic concepts, then the artist possesses a knowledge, gained through intellection, of the perfect form or idea involved in his artistic work" (78:56 note 40).
32. Ibid., 2.10 (Rettig, 78:69).

trine of creation as well as his own mystical sense of the Word's omnipresence.

At the sermon's close, Augustine exhorted the assembly to seek the wisdom of the Word, that "life" which is "the light of humankind" (John 1:4), a life and light whose existence some fail to see. According to Augustine, just as the light of the sun shone on those whose eyes were blind, so the wisdom of the Word shone on those whose hearts were blind. Then, using a medical analogy, Augustine begged his hearers to seek the Word:

"If [a man] were not able to see because of dirty and sore eyes, the doctor would say to him, 'Cleanse from your eye whatever muck is there.' Dust, muck, smoke: sins and iniquities are just like these. Remove them all from the eye [of your heart] and you will see the Wisdom that is always there—for God is that Wisdom; and as the saying goes, 'Blessed are the clean of heart, for they shall see God.'"[33]

This whole presentation reveals Augustine's pedagogical mastery: beneath its simplicity lay great philosophic complexity. Its turns and insights were frequently those of Plotinus, but with a difference: as Brown notes, "What Plotinus had struggled to convey to a select classroom in Rome, the Christians of Hippo . . . could hear any Sunday in the sermons of Augustine."[34]

ENARRATIO ON PSALM 121: Augustine opened this sermon by comparing the human heart to a bird: if mired in muddy loves, it would flap like a bird trapped in birdlime; if purged, it too could take flight on its "two wings": the love of God and love of neighbor. Augustine hoped to coax his hearers to take wing. It was the psalm's joyous opening verse that served as the catalyst: "I rejoiced when I heard them say, 'Let us go to the house of the Lord.'" Augustine heard in this the shouts of the saints, those "companions . . . who have already seen [Jerusalem] itself and summon us to run towards it." Their shouts echoed across the centuries, "from a distant age to [us] their descendants."[35]

The fervor in the verse reminded him of the fervor that surrounded the feasts of North African martyrs. These were celebra-

---

33. Ibid., 1.19 (trans. my own).
34. Brown, *Augustine of Hippo*, 245.
35. *Enarrationes in psalmos* 121.2 (trans. my own).

tions as riotous as Mardi Gras. People would gather at the martyrs' shrines, and there pray, banquet, dance until frenzied, and drink themselves into a "holy stupor."[36] While sometimes an excuse for self-indulgence, these were in fact mantic rituals whose agitations served as a vehicle for inducing religious visions and ecstasy. Early in his career, Augustine had campaigned against them. In this sermon, he uttered not a word of protest, but instead tapped on them as an emotional analogy for the fervor catechumens and baptized would need for true pilgrimage:

"Friends, recall: . . . how on such a day crowds stream in together to celebrate: how the crowds fire each other up, how they exhort each other, and say, 'Let us go, let us go.' And some ask, 'Where are we to go?' And others call back: 'To that place! To the holy place!' So they call out to each other, back and forth, igniting one by one until they become like one fiery blaze; and this one blaze, fueled by back-and-forth calls, sweeps itself off to the holy place."[37]

This is typical of Augustine the word-painter: in a few quick strokes he captures a scene. The emotion in the psalm's opening verse certainly grabbed him, but its highly alliterative sounds—*In domum Domini ibimus*—did as well. Augustine took this melodic phrase and made it a theme for his own fugal variations (even in English the music can be heard):

"So let us run: run! For we shall go to the Lord's house. Let us run, for we shall arrive there, there where we shall not grow weary. Let us run to the Lord's house, let our soul be swept into rejoicing by those who say these words to us. For they who speak to us have seen that country before us and cry from a distant age to their descendants, 'We will go to the Lord's house: Walk! run!' The apostles have seen it, and say to us, 'Run! walk! follow! We will go to the Lord's house!' And what does each of us reply? Let me rejoice in those who said to me, 'We will go to the Lord's house.' Let me rejoice in the Prophets! Let me rejoice in the

36. On the character of these feasts, see especially Frend, *The Donatist Church*, esp. 174–75; on the world view that underlay such enthusiasm, see Brown, *The Cult of the Saints*; on Augustine's campaign against them, Bonner, *St. Augustine: Life and Controversies*, 116–19.
37. *Enarrationes in psalmos* 121.2 (trans. my own).

Apostles! For they all said to us, 'We will go to the Lord's house.' "[38]

Here one sees Augustine's grand style. He does not want to instruct; he wants to persuade. And such a passage, while musical, is more notable for its furor of feeling: it is the voice of one trying to bend the hard heart to obedience. Augustine's refrain of *In domum Domini ibimus*, like Martin Luther King's "I have a dream," was meant to build a crescendo of feeling; its alliterative tones were meant to echo in his hearers' ears long after the sermon's end. Augustine wanted to make it, quite literally, unforgettable, to implant it deep within their memory, so that at some later time, perhaps a moment of flagging spirits, it might well up and console the same way Ambrose's evening hymn welled up and consoled Augustine the night his mother died.

Later Augustine noted verse 3 of the psalm: that "Jerusalem is being built as a city." In his view, the phrase had to be read as prophetic since by David's time Jerusalem had already been built; it seemed a prophetic echo of 1 Peter's image of the Church "being built" from "living stones." Augustine would thus explore the meaning of this temple of living stones. First he contrasted how spiritual construction projects differed from physical ones. He had the assembly look around and consider "this basilica, whose ample size you see": that in building the basilica in Hippo, workers had laid the foundation at the lowest point and built from the ground up. Spiritual building, he noted, was just the opposite: it began from the highest point, since Christ was the foundation of the Church of living stones. Augustine then exhorted his hearers: "Let us therefore run there—there where we may be built up." Augustine noted that if one was to be built into this temple of living stones, one had to partake of Christ, the "I Am," a mystery beyond comprehension. Then, drawing on imagery from the parable of the Good Samaritan, Augustine would stress the healing work of Christ:

"Remember what he, whom you cannot comprehend, became for you. Remember the flesh of Christ—toward which you were raised when sick and when left half-dead from the wounds of robbers—that you might be brought to the Inn, and there might be cured."[39]

38. Ibid.
39. Ibid., 121.4-5 (trans. my own).

Augustine continued exhorting. He returned to verse 2 of the psalm and reflected on what it meant to "stand in the Lord's house." As he saw it, this meant that one be humble and without guile like Nathanael, that one be a "confessor" not a "pretender." The proud were, by contrast, pretenders, frauds—like those who claimed to have musical talents though they could not play a note. Moreover, God would say to the proud what people in Augustine's day said to a musical claimant: " 'Play, let us see if you are a flutist'; he would not be able to."[40] In other words, the proud would not find themselves numbered among the "musicians" in the Lord's house. Augustine also stressed that to "stand in the Lord's house" one had to work to rectify the unjust economic order. He thus appealed to the wealthy to make the indigent their special care. Moreover, even an ordinary laborer was to do what he could: "his resources may not equal [those of a Zaccheus]; but his charity should not be unequal."[41] Finally, in the *peroratio*, Augustine would return to the earlier refrain—that "we go up to the house of the Lord"—and close the address with a final torrent of imperatives: "These overflowing and urgent words—pluck them up, chew on them, drink them; grow strong on them, run with them, seize them."[42]

These two sermons illustrate, in microcosm, dynamics that run through the larger sequence. They show, for instance, typical ways Augustine used Scripture: (a) the way he would find one text evoking echoes of others (e.g., 1 Peter's temple of living stones, the parable of the Good Samaritan); (b) the way he would play with scriptural phrases whose music intrigued him; (c) the way he let the flow of the text guide the outline of his own remarks—so that his talk moved less by logical progression and more by a pattern of theme-and-variations on God's Word. More importantly, these two sermons illustrate a pedagogical strain that runs through the sequence; that is: in his sermons on John, Augustine focused more on doctrine and on an intellectual understanding of faith; in his sermons on the Psalms, he focused more on spirituality and on an affective grasp of faith. By alternating between John's Gospel and the psalms, he created, in effect, a con-

40. Ibid., 121.8 (trans. my own).
41. Ibid., 121.10 (trans. my own).
42. Ibid., 121.14 (trans. my own).

trapuntal rhythm that aimed at educating, by turns, the mind and the heart.

MELODIC THEMES

As we saw in the last chapter, Augustine thought of himself, first and foremost, as a "expositor" (*tractator*) of Scripture. Thus it was Scripture and *not* the disciplines of systematic theology—Christology, ecclesiology, ethics—which shaped the flow of his curriculum for catechumens and faithful. Nonetheless, as one scans these sermons on John and the psalms, one finds Augustine touching, at one time or another, on each major area within what would later become systematic theology. (See chart 10 for a survey of topics.) Yet Augustine's approach to curriculum was more musical than systematic. Theological themes tended to ebb and flow: a given theme might be introduced briefly in one sermon, but left undeveloped; it might then appear again several sermons later and there be given extended treatment; often enough, it might reappear several more times, but set in harmony with or in counterpoint against other themes.[43] To get a sense of this musical approach to curriculum, let us now touch on four major themes that wind their way through the sequence. From this, we will be able to see some key theological topics Augustine taught the catechumens (among others) and some key ways he communicated these.

(1) *The Paradox of Christ.* The mystery of Christ forms perhaps the most prominent thread within the sequence. In *Tractate* 1—as we saw earlier—Augustine gave concerted attention to the doctrine of Christ's divinity. Such systematic treatment was unusual. More often, he would touch on the mystery of Christ in brief, easy-to-remember turns. For example, when teaching on Psalm 120, he noted verse 4 ("He that keeps Israel neither slumbers nor sleeps") and gave it an unexpected Christological twist:

"Christ must not sleep in you: . . . 'How,' you ask? Because if your faith sleeps, Christ sleeps in you. . . . In the one whose faith does not sleep, in that one Christ stands watch. And if perhaps your faith sleeps, . . . [then you are] like that vessel which

43. On this "musical" ordering in the *Confessiones*, see the analysis by O'Connell, *St. Augustine's Confessions*, esp. 37–40.

met a gale as Christ slept: wake Christ up, and the gales will be calmed."[44]

Augustine typically described Christ in paradoxical terms. One sees this repeatedly in passing phrases used throughout the sequence: Christ is the "human God";[45] "the man Jesus . . . the God Jesus";[46] "the Word of God, the Word made flesh, the Son of the Father, the Son of God, the Son of man, exalted that he might create us, humbled that he might re-create us";[47] "in that [Christ] was human, God died; and in that he was God, humankind was raised and arose and ascended into heaven."[48] As Brian Daley has noted, Augustine, unlike his contemporaries in the Greek East, did not usually engage in "technical speculation on the unity and inner constitution of Jesus' person"; instead he preferred "to speak of the mystery of Christ in concrete, rhetorically challenging phrases that let the believer savor the inherent paradox of preaching an incarnate God."[49]

To communicate this paradox Augustine used not only brief phrases like those cited above. He also drew on images and themes from the biblical text at hand and would give these a paradoxical turn. For example, in *Tractate 7*, he played off the words of John 1:29 ("Behold the Lamb of God who takes away the sin of the world") to show the Lamb's subversive power:

"When the time came for God to show mercy, the Lamb came. What kind of Lamb is it whom the wolves fear? What kind of Lamb is it who, though killed, kills the lion? For the devil has been called a lion, going about roaring, seeking someone to devour; by the Lamb's blood the lion has been conquered."[50]

44. *Enarrationes in psalmos* 120.7 (trans. my own). See also *Sermo* 63.2.

45. *Tractatus in evangelium Ioannis* 4.14 (trans. my own).

46. Ibid., 8.1 (Rettig, 78:180).

47. Ibid., 10.1 (Rettig, 78:212).

48. *Enarrationes in psalmos* 130.10 (trans. my own).

49. Brian E. Daley, "A Humble Mediator: The Distinctive Elements in Saint Augustine's Christology," *Word and Spirit* 9 (1987) 101. For a summary of the debate in the Greek East, see Young, *From Nicaea to Chalcedon;* Leo Donald Davis, *The First Seven Ecumenical Councils (325–787): Their History and Theology,* Theology and Life Series 21 (Collegeville, Minn.: The Liturgical Press, 1983); Aloys Grillmeier, *Christ in Christian Tradition: From the Apostolic Age to Chalcedon,* trans. J. S. Bowden (New York: Sheed and Ward, 1965).

50. *Tractatus in evangelium Ioannis* 7.6 (Rettig, 78:157–59—altered).

Similarly, in *Enarratio* on Psalm 123, Augustine noted that there was something odd about the note of joy in the psalm: that Christians sang as though they had arrived at the kingdom despite their still being on the road. Thus, Augustine insisted, Christians enjoyed a foretaste: while their joy was not yet a reality, still the hope they lived in made it one. This paradox of sentiment led him to ponder the paradox of Christ:

"Let us therefore walk as if we were on the way; for the king of our homeland has made himself the way [to it]. . . . There he is truth; here, the way. Where do we go? To truth. How do we go? By faith. Where do we go? To Christ. How do we go? Through Christ."[51]

Augustine drew his imagery not only from Scripture, but also from the local culture. One that appears repeatedly is that of Christ the physician.[52] In *Tractate* 1 Augustine had alluded to this idea; in *Tractate* 3 he drew this out further. Taking his cue from Paul, Augustine argued that Law gave the prognosis—that we need healing:

"Now the sick confess that they are sick. Let the physician come and heal the sick. The physician. Who? Our Lord Jesus Christ. . . . [On the cross] he cured your wounds where so long he endured his own; there he healed you of eternal death where he deigned to die a temporal death."[53]

According to Augustine, Christ showed the courage and compassion of a plague doctor by making himself vulnerable to the epidemics devastating humankind at every level—physical, affective, interpersonal, social. Yet Christ used an unusual pharmacology: whereas human physicians administered medicines, Christ the physician, by taking our diseases into his very being, had made himself the medicine.

51. *Enarrationes in psalmos* 123.2 (trans. my own). See also *Tractatus in evangelium Ioannis* 13.4.
52. *Tractatus in evangelium Ioannis* 1.19; 2.16 (heals eyes); 7.2 (heals insane); 12.12; *Enarrationes in psalmos* 121.5 (inn of Samaritan as clinic); 125.2 and 15 (inn of Samaritan); 130.7 (healed Paul). For a survey, see R. Arbesmann, "The Concept of *Christus Medicus* in St. Augustine," *Traditio* 10 (1954) 1–28.
53. *Tractatus in evangelium Ioannis* 3.2–3 (Rettig, 78:77–78).

Augustine did not always use paradox. One theme that appears repeatedly is that of Christ the inner teacher.[54] Playing upon a Platonic idea, Augustine claimed that within each person was the Word, the *Logos*; and for Augustine the Christian, that inner *Logos* was none other than Christ. As Augustine put it in an early treatise, *The Teacher*: ". . . it is truth that presides within over the mind itself . . . And he who is consulted, he who is said to dwell in the inner person, he it is who teaches—Christ—that is, the unchangeable power of God and everlasting wisdom."[55] This idea affected Augustine's pedagogy. As he saw it, he as "outer teacher" was not necessarily giving people something new; rather, he might be reminding them of truths Christ the "inner teacher" had already taught. Also, true listening was a dual activity: "turn your ears to us, your heart to [Christ], so that you may fill both."[56] Thus in *Tractate* 3, Augustine asked the catechumens and faithful to "ponder the lowliness of Christ" by turning within: "Let him describe it within. He who dwells within describes it better than he who shouts from without. Let him show you the grace of his lowliness, he who has begun to dwell in your hearts."[57] This idea also affected how Augustine sometimes acknowledged applause. For instance, towards the end of this same sermon, he quoted from Psalm 25: "that I may gaze on the delight of the Lord." His audience recognized the passage and cheered. Augustine then interpreted their applause in light of this concept: "My friends, why do you shout, why do you exult, why do you love except that the spark of this love is there [within]?"[58]

Augustine also drew heavily on Paul's theme of Christ as the new Adam. Typically, Augustine would frame this using rhymed antitheses. For example, in *Enarratio* on Psalm 119, he contrasted the descent of Christ with the fall of Adam:

54. This theme appears repeatedly in this sequence: *Tractatus in evangelium Ioannis* 1.7; 7.9; 10.1 and 9; *Enarrationes in psalmos* 126.2. It appears with great regularity in Augustine's other sermons: e.g., *Tractatus in evangelium Ioannis* 20.3; 26.7, 40.5; *Sermones* 102.2; 153.1; *Tractatus in epistolam Ioannis* 3.13. For a summary of its place in Augustine's sermons, see Berrouard, BAug 71:839–40.

55. *De magistro* 11.38 (trans. Joseph M. Colleran, ACW 9:177—altered). On Augustine's theory of inner illumination, see TeSelle, *Augustine the Theologian*, 100–107.

56. *Tractatus in evangelium Ioannis* 1.7 (Rettig, 78:47).

57. Ibid., 3.15 (Rettig, 78:87).

58. Ibid., 3.21 (Rettig, 78:91).

. . . *quia cecidit Adam,*	because Adam fell,
ideo descendit Christus:	Christ therefore descended:
ille cecidit,	the first fell,
ille descendit,	the other descended;
ille cecidit superbia,	the first fell from pride,
ille descendit misericordia.	the other descended in mercy.[59]

According to Mohrmann, Augustine picked up a fondness for such antithetical parallelisms from the psalms themselves; this figure of speech is "the essence of his homiletic style, and results in a way of thinking that is all his own. . . . Its fundamental rhythm dominates not only the words, but the thought itself."[60]

This Adam/Christ contrast also appears in Augustine's allegorical explorations. For example, on three occasions (*Tractates* 9 and 10; *Enarratio* on Ps 95), Augustine claimed that Adam's name had a mystical meaning: that

A = *anatole* ("east")
D = *dysis* ("west")
A = *arktos* ("north")
M = *mesembria* ("south");

that therefore in Adam the whole world was contained; and that in Christ the new Adam it was transfigured.[61] Another Adam/Christ contrast appears in *Tractate* 10. First, Augustine noted that, according to John 2:20, it had taken forty-six years to build the Temple in Jerusalem. Like Origen and Ambrose, Augustine presumed that such a minute detail held some hidden meaning. Moreover, he and his congregation shared with pagans a fascination with numbers, and like them presumed that numbers held some mystical import. According to Augustine, the forty-six years it took to build the Temple mystically referred to Adam: that in Greek, as in Latin, numbers were written as letters; and that in Greek numbering, Adam's name equaled forty-six ($A=1$, $D=4$, $A=1$, $M=40$). And what was more: in Christ's death, the old Temple (i.e., Adam) was destroyed; in Christ's resurrection three days later, a new Temple was built; since three represented Trinity, Christ the New Temple thus reconstructed the fallen

59. *Enarrationes in psalmos* 119.2 (CCSL 40:1776; trans. my own).
60. Mohrmann, "Saint Augustin prédicateur," 89.
61. *Tractatus in evangelium Ioannis* 9.14.

temple of humankind and reconsecrated it by restoring the true image of God.[62]

(2) *The Church as the Inn of the Samaritan.* Augustine often used biblical images to hold together different facets of his theology. For example, he would join Christology with ecclesiology using an image from Ephesians: that the Church was the body of Christ while the Risen Lord was its Head. In *Enarratio* on Psalm 127, Augustine would give this theme its clearest exposition:

There are many Christians and there is one Christ. Christians themselves, with their head—who ascended into heaven—are one Christ. It is not that He is one and we are many, but we many are one in that One. Christ then is one man, head and body. What is his body? His Church.[63]

Just as Augustine's Christology often took a paradoxical form, so his ecclesiology could take a paradoxical form. Thus, in *Enarratio* on Psalm 122, he used this head/body ecclesiology to explain the deeper meaning of singing "psalms" of ascent: since "the head came down and ascended with the body," Christians, even during this life, could sing joyously for they enjoyed some foretaste of life in God:

Si per caritatem	If through love
ipse nobiscum in terra est,	he himself is with us on earth,
per eamdem caritatem	then through this same love
nos cum eo in caelo sumus . . .	we are with him in heaven. . .
Ergo et ille adhuc deorsum est,	He is therefore below,
et nos iam sursum sumus:	and we are above:
ille deorsum est	he is below
compassione caritatis,	through the compassion of love,
nos sursum sumus	we are above
spe caritatis.	through the hope of love.[64]

In the course of the sequence, he would draw on other biblical images to describe the Church. For instance, he would compare it to Jacob's ladder: that just as angels had ascended and descended

---

62. Ibid., 10.10–12. On the ancient fascination with numbers, see Brown, *Augustine of Hippo*, 268–69; Pontet, *Exégèse*, 569–73.
63. *Enarrationes in psalmos* 127.3 (trans. my own).
64. Ibid., 122.1 (CCSL 40:1814; trans. my own).

on the ladder, so too the Church had both climbers and back-sliders.[65] Similarly, Augustine (like Cyprian) would describe the Church as an ark which, like Noah's, rescued one from the "flood of the world." Moreover, the Church, like Noah's ark, contained both "doves" and "ravens":

"Noah had the raven there; he also had the dove. That ark contained each kind. If the ark symbolized the Church, you see, of course, that it is necessary for the Church in this flood of the world to contain each kind, both the raven and the dove. Who are the ravens? They who seek the things that are their own. Who are the doves? They who seek the things that are Christ's."[66]

According to Augustine, the call of each bird revealed its true character: good Christians, like doves, cooed with love; evil living Christians, like ravens, were "full of loud shrieking, not cooing" and revelled "in a hollow happiness."[67]

Perhaps the most original of these biblically based images of Church is Augustine's description of the inn of the Samaritan. In *Enarratio* on Psalm 121, as we saw earlier, Augustine cited the parable of the Good Samaritan as a description of Christ's healing work. In *Enarratio* on Psalm 125, he returned to the parable, but instead stressed its implications for ecclesiology. First, Augustine exhorted his hearers to ascend to the heavenly Jerusalem by good works, not descend from it. The idea of ascending and descending from Jerusalem seemed to him an echo of Jesus' parable, for the man in the parable had come down from Jerusalem. According to Augustine the parable had hidden allegorical meanings: that the man who descended from Jerusalem and fell among thieves was Adam; that "we are all Adam"; that the priest and the Levite who passed by symbolized the Law which could not heal; that the Samaritan was Christ who healed us by lifting us upon his "beast," that is, "his flesh," and then "took us to the inn, that is, the Church"; that Christ "entrusted us to the innkeeper, that is, the Apostle," and left "two coins by which we might be healed: the love of God and love of neighbor."[68] With this allegory Augustine was thus able to teach the catechumens ecclesiology

65. Ibid., 119.2.
66. *Tractatus in evangelium Ioannis* 6.2 (Rettig, 78:131).
67. Ibid., 6.2 (Rettig, 78:130).
68. *Enarrationes in psalmos* 125.5 (trans. LF 39:16).

213

with image: that baptized Christians were not the healed, but the recovering; that the catechumens would face a lifelong convalescence; and that they, like Paul, would have to learn to glory in their weakness.[69]

(3) *Baptism and the Debate with the Donatists*. The rivalry between Catholics and Donatists was bitter and drew out Augustine's most combative instincts. This split within the African Church dated from the 310s.[70] It originated with the disputed election of Caecilian as bishop of Carthage. Opponents charged that the unpopular Caecilian had been ordained by a *traditor*—one who had "handed over" copies of the Bible to Roman authorities during the persecution of Diocletian and who had thus made himself an apostate. In some African eyes, this polluted Caecilian's ordination. Soon after, some bishops ordained a rival who was succeeded, in turn, by Donatus of Casae, the man from whom the schism gets its name. Before long, rival churches existed not only in Carthage, but throughout North Africa, and in time, in many areas, the majority of Christians were Donatist. This rivalry, always vociferous, became on occasion quite violent—much like fractures between co-religionists today in the Middle East and Northern Ireland. And as in these, political, economic, and ethnic factors came into play, hardening the division and fueling grievances.

A critical point of controversy was baptism. The Donatists worked from two principles they took from St. Cyprian: (1) there was no salvation outside the Church; (2) baptism—which made salvation possible—could only be given by one still in the Church. The Donatists thus held that since Caecilian was outside the Church all sacraments rendered by him were null and void. They extended the same claim to those rendered by his allies—the churches throughout the world that accepted his legitimacy—and by any of his spiritual descendants, such as Augustine's friend, Aurelius of Carthage, and Augustine himself. Because the Donatists regarded all Catholic sacraments as worthless, they routinely rebaptized Catholics who came to their Church. They alone,

69. See *Sermones* 131.6; 151.4–5.

70. The classic study of the schism is that of Frend, *The Donatist Church*. However, some aspects of Frend's study have received strong criticism: see Brown, "Christianity and Local Culture in Late Roman Africa," 85–95. On the theological debate, see Bonner, *St. Augustine: Life and Controversies*, 276–311.

they felt, remained the world's one true Church, the one "without wrinkle or spot."

Throughout this sequence, Augustine again and again challenged Donatist views. For instance, he would admit that the Donatists had truly received baptism, but insisted that it was of no benefit to them:

"Suppose you are a soldier. If you should have the tattoo of your general [and stay] within [your regiment], then you serve securely as a soldier. If you have it outside [your regiment], not only does that tattoo not benefit you: you will also be punished as a deserter."[71]

In the same way, the Donatists had the tattoo of baptism; but it only marked them out as deserters. Other times Augustine would lampoon them. For example, he noted that Psalm 95 was a song in which "all the earth" was called "to sing a new song." He then noted that "many barbarous nations" were Christian, that "Christ possesses regions which the Roman Empire has not yet reached."[72] This international perspective sparked one of his favorite rejoinders against the Donatists—that they were too provincial and ignored the unity of the Church across the world: "The clouds of heaven thunder out throughout the whole world in which God's house is being built; meanwhile [Donatist] frogs croak from the marsh, 'We alone are Christians.'"[73]

In *Tractate 5*, Augustine treated the Donatist question at length. He began by using one of his favorite devices, a knotty problem: the Synoptics indicated the Baptist had recognized Jesus before the baptism, while the Johannine text said he did not know Jesus until afterward.[74] Augustine then made a bold claim: that he would not only solve this contradiction, but that his solution both vindicated the truth of the Catholic position on baptism and

71. *Tractatus in evangelium Ioannis* 6.15 (trans. my own). This "character" was a brand, normally on the back of the right hand; see Jones, *The Later Roman Empire*, 2:616 and 649.

72. *Enarrationes in psalmos* 95.2 (trans. LF 32:400).

73. Ibid., 95.11 (trans. LF 32:408—altered).

74. *Tractatus in evangelium Ioannis* 5.1. Augustine first poses the dilemma in *Tractatus in evangelium Ioannis* 4.15–16, and refers to it in *Enarrationes in psalmos* 126.13. He pits Matthew 3:14 (with its clear implication of John's recognition of Jesus' true identity) and John 1:30-33 (where John says he "did not know him" until "the dove from heaven . . . remained on him").

undermined the Donatist case. His argument—stripped of its musical rhetoric, careful repetitions, and biblical citations—was simple enough: (1) "John is truthful, Christ is truth," and therefore there could be no ultimate contradiction; (2) it was not a matter of John not knowing Jesus, but rather of John learning something new, of knowing "more fully the one he already knew";[75] (3) the new thing John learned was that Christ had retained for himself the power of baptism and that, no matter whether the minister was good or bad, it was Christ who baptized; (4) this distinction between the minister of baptism and the power of baptism was what the descending dove had taught John. In other words, Augustine claimed that what John had learned from the dove was Augustine's own argument against the Donatists: that it was Christ who baptized, that the spiritual pedigree of the minister (whether the hotly disputed Caecilian or Augustine himself) was ultimately irrelevant, and that the Donatists only denigrated the power of Christ by their rebaptizing ways.

Here I have stripped away all but the core argument—in other words, exactly those elements that made Augustine's argument both entertaining and pedagogically effective. Let me now retrace several of these. First, Augustine presented the opening premise in a sing-song tongue-twister (audible even in translation):

"John is truthful, Christ is truth. John is truthful, but every truthful person is truthful from the truth. If, therefore, John is truthful and a person cannot be truthful except from the truth, from whom was he truthful except from the one who said, 'I am the truth'? Thus neither could the truth speak against the truthful, nor the truthful against the truth . . . If the truth had sent John, Christ had sent him."[76]

Second, Augustine would encapsulate key points in epigrams. For example, he played on the distinction between the divine Word and the Word made flesh to create a terse paradox: "Just as [Christ] created Mary and was created by Mary, so he gave baptism to John and was baptized by John."[77] Third, Augustine would sometimes turn his argument into drama. At one point, for

75. *Tractatus in evangelium Ioannis* 5.2 (Rettig, 78:110—altered).
76. Ibid., 5.1 (Rettig, 78:108–9).
77. Ibid., 5.4 (Rettig, 78:111).

instance, he pretended that he was John the Baptist interviewing himself:

[John as interviewer]: "Who is he?"

[John as respondent]: "The Lord. I know."

[interviewer]: "But did you already know this—that the Lord, having the power of baptizing, would give that power to no servant but would retain it for himself, so that everyone who is baptized through the ministry of the servant may ascribe it not to the servant, but to the Lord? Did you already know this?"

[respondent]: "I did not know this."

[interviewer]: "What in fact did [the Spirit] say to me?"

[respondent]: "He upon whom you will see the Spirit descending as a dove, and remaining upon him, he it is who baptizes with the Holy Spirit."[78]

Early in his career, Augustine had once written a whole book, *The Soliloquies*, in this style. Here he acted it out. Finally, he relied, as usual, on analogies. For example, he compared the corrupt minister to a conduit used for irrigation:

"Uncontaminated is the gift of Christ—it flows through him undefiled. . . . Water passes through a stone conduit; water passes on to garden plots; in the stone conduit it produces nothing; but still it brings forth plentiful fruit in the gardens."[79]

This is the heart of Augustine's polemic: what mattered was not the minister, not the conduit, but Christ the gardener and giver of the growth. As Augustine saw it, Donatist fretting about a minister's spiritual pedigree was hopelessly clericalist.

In this sermon, Augustine's focus was not on the catechumens per se; yet what he said was of vital importance to them. First, he gave them a way of understanding their own upcoming baptism: that it was Christ who would baptize them, that it was Christ's power that would recreate them. Also Augustine armed them with perspectives that would help them fend off Donatist jibes and that would perhaps prevent them from being wooed into the Donatist camp.

78. Ibid., 5.9 (Rettig, 78:116).
79. Ibid., 5.15 (Rettig, 78:122–23—altered).

(4) *A Spirituality for Exiles.* The spirituality Augustine passed on through this sequence was, in large measure, a spirituality of pilgrimage. Often he would sound a somber note: "In this life we wander as pilgrims; we sigh for the return to [Jerusalem]; so long are we wretched, so long toiling—until we go back."[80] Such melancholy sentiments were standard fare among ancients: to them, earth seemed a swirling chaos set beneath the stately order of the heavens; here demonic powers roamed about freely; here life was an *agon*, a combat.[81] Such feelings were not ungrounded. The poor in Augustine's assembly, like the poor in the Third World today, suffered terribly: from hunger, devastating plagues, high infant mortality, rigid social structures, a brutal government. Even the wealthy escaped few of these ills.

The task, according to Augustine, was to journey from this "valley of tears" to the "mountain" of Christ the divine Word; yet, Augustine would insist, to speak of life in Christ was impossible since, as Paul said, it was a life which "the eye has not seen, nor ear heard, nor has it ascended into the human heart." According to Augustine, this journey was possible only because Christ the mountain had made himself the valley:

Ipse tibi fecit patiendo	By suffering, he made himself
conuallem plorationis,	for you a valley of weeping,
qui fecit manendo	By staying put, he made himself
montem adscensionis.	a mountain of ascent.[82]

Christ was thus the model of Christian spirituality: that just as a mother would eat solid food so that through her flesh she would produce milk for her infant, so Christ the "food of angels was made flesh, was made milk." Thus Augustine would exhort his hearers: "Nurse on what he became for you, and you will grow into what he is." Moreover, he would insist, the path that Christ followed set the tone: the journey upward to God was, in fact, a journey downward: that climbing the mountain meant descending to become milk for the weakest.[83]

---

80. *Enarrationes in psalmos* 125.1 (trans. my own).

81. See *De agone christiano.* On the ancient world view, see E. R. Dodds, *Pagan & Christian in an Age of Anxiety,* 7–8; Suzanne Poque, *Le langage symbolique dans la prédication d'Augustin d'Hippone: Images héroiques* (Paris: Études augustiniennes, 1984) 1:71–84.

82. *Enarrationes in psalmos* 119.1 (CCSL 40:1777; trans. my own).

83. Ibid., 119.2 (trans. my own).

Augustine also stressed that spirituality took its cues from Scripture. He thus begged his hearers to approach God's word "as if you were hearing yourselves, as if you were looking at yourselves in the mirror of the Scriptures." The Scriptures, especially the psalms, were the voice of Christ, both head and body, a voice that had a wide register of feelings: "These members of Christ: what do they sing? For they are in love, and, loving, they sing; longing, they sing. Sometimes when troubled, they sing; other times overjoyed, they sing; when hopeful, they sing."[84] Augustine also stressed that Scripture's mysteries would give the catechumens and faithful eyes to see the mysteries at play within their everyday world. For example, in *Tractate* 9, he noted that the Gospel spoke of the marriage feast at Cana at which Christ miraculously transformed water into wine. Augustine knew his audience's fascination with the miracles; yet as we saw in chapter 4, he tended to downplay such things. In this sermon, he pitted one-time miracles like Cana against the everyday miracles of nature: that "on that day at the wedding" Christ "made wine," yet every year it "is the same Lord who does this on the vines." He then pointed out: rains come, vines sprout, grapes ripen, wine ferments; but this natural process "does not amaze us because it happens every year; by its regularity it has lost its wonderment." He then explored what diminished people's capacity for wonder:

"Because people, concentrating upon something else, have abandoned reflection upon the works of God in which they might give praise to the creator every day, God has saved for himself, as it were, certain extraordinary things to do so that by amazing events he might arouse people, as if they were asleep, to worship him. A dead man arose; people were astonished. Every day many are born and no one is amazed. If we were to reflect more wisely, it is a greater miracle that one, who was not, *is* than that one, who was, comes back to life."[85]

As Augustine saw it, people's wonder was too narrow; their sleepy eyes missed the extraordinary in the ordinary. To counter

84. Ibid., 123.2–3 (trans. my own).
85. *Tractatus in evangelium Ioannis* 8.1 (Rettig, 78:179–180—altered).

this, he recommended praise of God; praise would rouse them and sharpen their sight. By this wake-up, they too would become the stuff of miracles: "Let us knock that he may open and may inebriate us with invisible wine; for we, too, were water and he made us wines; he made us wise."[86]

Periodically, Augustine offered suggestions on prayer. For instance, he read the story of Christ's cleansing of the Temple as an instruction on prayer: that just as Christ had cleansed the Temple of Jerusalem, so the catechumens and baptized were to cleanse the temple of their heart. Moreover, he noted, Christ the inner teacher was also an inner listener:

"Do not direct your eyes to some mountain. Do not lift up your face to the stars or to the sun or the moon. Do not think you are being heard then, when you pray by the sea. Rather, . . . cleanse the chamber of your heart; wherever you are, wherever you pray, he who hears is within."[87]

Similarly, when preaching on Psalm 129, Augustine noted its opening verse: "out of the deep have I called to you, O Lord." It reminded him of Jonah who had cried from the depths: "Those waves . . . did not block his prayer from reaching God, nor could the beast's belly squelch his pleading voice. It penetrated all things; it burst through all things . . . since the ears of God were in the praying heart."[88] In the same way, the catechumens and faithful needed to see "from what depths we call out to the Lord"; like Jonah, "we cry out, groan, sigh until . . . delivered."[89] This praying with tears and groans was exactly how Augustine himself had prayed since the days he had been a catechumen under Ambrose. As he once told a correspondent: in prayer, "business is transacted more by sighs than by speech, more by tears than by utterance."[90]

According to Augustine, such sighing was the voice of the Spirit within. He drew out this theme at length in *Tractate 6*. In the *exordium*, he raised "a knotty problem": why had the Spirit at

86. Ibid., 8.3 (Rettig, 78:182).
87. Ibid., 10.1 (Rettig, 78:212).
88. *Enarrationes in psalmos* 129.1 (trans. my own).
89. Ibid., 129.1 (trans. my own).
90. *Epistola* 130.20 (Parsons, 18:391). On the way Augustine himself prayed, see *De ordine* 1.8.22; cf. *Soliloquiorum* 1.9.

Christ's baptism appeared *as a dove*? Augustine resolved this riddle by playing on the double meaning of the Latin verb *gemere* which, on the one hand, meant the "sighing" of a person and, on the other, the "cooing" of a dove. Augustine used this double entendre to explain the role of the Spirit:

". . . cooing [*gemitus*] is characteristic of a dove, as we all know. Doves coo [*gemunt*] when in love. Now hear what the Apostle says, and it will no longer surprise you that the Holy Spirit wished to be shown in the form of a dove. He says: 'For we do not know how to pray as we should, but the Spirit himself intercedes for us with unspeakable sighing [*gemitibus*, Rom 8:26]."[91]

The mention of sighing led Augustine back to a theme from his sermons on the psalms: "The Holy Spirit teaches us to sigh, for he makes known to us that we are in exile, and he teaches us to groan for our native land, and we sigh with that very longing."[92] With this one word, Augustine thus passed on to the catechumens and faithful a cluster of associations: (1) that the Spirit spoke within; (2) that the Spirit spoke not in words but in inexpressible feelings; (3) that this inner longing was in fact a way of voicing of one's love of God; and (4) that by this one discovered one's true status as an exile yearning for the kingdom.

Yet this spirituality could not be merely interior: it had to be lived out. For instance, in the inaugural sermon of the sequence, Augustine noted that in singing the psalms, what mattered was not the well-tuned voice, but the well-wrought life: ". . . to test how truly you sing . . . you [must] begin to do what you sing. . . . Begin to act, and see what we speak. Then tears flow forth at each word; then the psalm is sung, and the heart does what is sung."[93] Augustine believed that with a changed heart came changed living —and that was his ultimate concern and measure. Typically he used brief, evocative images to map out the contours of this. For instance, in *Enarratio* on Psalm 128, he stressed that living out gospel imperatives meant following the music of the Spirit: "Just as a dancer moves his arms and legs to the music, likewise those who dance God's Law follow its rhythm

91. *Tractatus in evangelium Ioannis* 6.2 (Rettig, 78:129—altered).
92. Ibid. (Rettig, 78:130).
93. *Enarrationes in psalmos* 119.9 (trans. LF 37:469–70).

by what they do."[94] On another occasion, Augustine noted verse 5 of Psalm 125: "They that sow in tears shall reap in joy." This idea of sowing in tears reminded him of the fact that local farmers planted wheat during the rainy North African winter. Thus he exhorted:

"When the farmer troops out with the plough and brings along seed: Is the wind not sometimes fierce? Do [cold] showers deter him? No—he looks up at the sky, sees it lowering, shivers with cold; and yet he goes out and sows. For he is afraid: if he were just to watch the foul weather and wait for sunshine, the time would pass away, and he would find that he has nothing to harvest. Friends, do not put things off; sow in winter, sow good works, even while you weep."[95]

This sowing good works especially meant taking care of the poor. Thus Augustine would denounce the elite: that their abounding pursuit of wealth, honor, and power produced only abounding destitution and greed; that they invested more effort in beautifying their houses than in working for justice—ignoring the obvious fact that mortality made their houses more "an inn for passing guests" than "a permanent residence."[96] On another occasion, he noted Psalm 131's mention of the Lord's Temple. For Augustine, the true temple was the heart, our one true private possession. He contrasted this with the often destructive preoccupation with physical possessions:

"Because of those things we each possess, there arise lawsuits, enmities, squabbles, wars, riots, . . . scandals, sins, inequities, murders. And for what? . . . Shall we go to court over those things we hold in common? In common we inhale this air; in common we all behold the sun."[97]

Thus he begged catechumens and baptized alike: while they did not need to dispense with private possessions, at least they were not to be so infatuated with them. He then offered an analogy: that if a senator were to come to their house and happened to spot an object that offended him, they would remove it; they

94. Ibid., 128.1 (trans. my own).
95. Ibid., 125.13 (trans. my own); see also 120.2.
96. Ibid., 122.8–11.
97. Ibid., 131.5 (trans. my own).

were to do the same for Christ who "wants to be entertained in your house."[98]

PEDAGOGY IN PRACTICE

In this survey of themes, we have seen various rhetorical techniques that Augustine used to make his message memorable: metaphors, paradoxes, antitheses, puns, tongue-twisters, knotty problems, soliloquies. There are other important aspects of his pedagogy that emerge within this sequence. First, in virtually every sermon of the series, he would begin with a review of key points from previous sermons. These reviews were sometimes lengthy, other times almost epigrammatic. Yet he considered them vital: "Why are we compelled to repeat the same things except that we are not sure about the memory of your hearts."[99]

Second, he would weave current events into his interpretation. For instance, at the very moment Augustine was delivering *Tractate 7*, there were pagans outside the church celebrating a local feast. Thus in his *exordium*, Augustine expressed his delight at seeing the large crowd who came to church rather than joining in the pagan festivities. He then noted that while there may be rowdy banquets going on outside the church, another sort of banquet was in progress inside: "But we who have assembled, let us feed at the banquets of God and let his Word be our joy. For he has invited us to his gospel; and this is our food—nothing is sweeter, but only if one has a healthy palate in the heart."[100] Later in the sermon, he noted that while the pagans were celebrating the drama of some goddess, Christians played out a drama of their own, the victory of Christ over Satan and the forces of death; thus Augustine exclaimed: "Behold the theatrical extravaganzas of the Christians!" In other words, Christians had their own theater (the basilica), their own chorus numbers (the psalms), their own epic drama (the Scriptures). And these won boisterous applause: "You have seen and shouted out; you would not shout unless you had seen" this drama of Christ.[101] On this occasion, Augustine

98. Ibid., 131.6 (trans. LF 39:94–95).
99. *Tractatus in evangelium Ioannis* 5.5 (Rettig, 78:113). See, for instance, the reviews of previous material in *Enarrationes in psalmos* 121.2; 122.1; 123.1; 124.1; 125.1; *Tractatus in evangelium Ioannis* 1.6; 2.1; 5.3; 6.6; 7.1; 9.1.
100. *Tractatus in evangelium Ioannis* 7.2 (Rettig, 78:155—altered).
101. Ibid., 7.6 (Rettig, 78:159—altered).

preached longer than the usual hour. At the end, he offered no apologies; his lengthy sermon had been a conscious ploy: "We have kept you a little too long; that was our intention: that the troublesome hours might pass by. However, those people, I believe, have by now finished their vanity."[102] This ploy was directed particularly at the catechumens. Since it was Sunday—and this sermon apparently took place before a Eucharistic liturgy—Augustine knew that the faithful would naturally be staying on; the catechumens, however, would be dismissed after the sermon. Thus, he prolonged his talk so that the catechumens would not be able to join belatedly in the pagan festivities. Once assured the pagans had finished, he let the catechumens go.

Third, Augustine tended to focus especially on scriptural images that lay close to his hearers' experience. For instance, in *Enarratio* on Psalm 125, he focused on verse 4 of the psalm: "Turn our captivity, O Lord, as the torrents in the south." To interpret this, he cited another verse, Sirach 3:17: "Sins shall melt away, even as ice in warm weather." The latter implied that "we were frozen—locked up lifeless in sins' chill."[103] This was a metaphor his hearers could feel in their bones, for at the very moment Augustine was preaching, they were suffering through a cold winter. He then reminded them that when winter ended in North Africa, a hot sirocco blows in from the south, from the Sahara; the ice melts, and the streams run in torrents. He then unlocked the spirituality within the image:

"That south wind—the Holy Spirit—has blown in; our sins have been written off; we are thawed from the frost that imbalanced us; like ice in fair weather, our sins have melted away. Let us run to our homeland, like torrents in the south."[104]

In a similar way, he used imagery from the local environment to explain scriptural themes. For example, he often invoked sea-faring images. This was not accidental: he taught in a port city; and many in his audience made their living by the sea as fishermen or merchants. It was a dangerous business: both sudden storms and the forbidding cliffs along the coast made shipwreck a constant

102. Ibid., 7.24 (Rettig, 78:177).
103. *Enarrationes in psalmos* 125.10 (trans. my own).
104. Ibid.

concern.[105] Thus, in *Enarratio* on Psalm 128, Augustine tapped on this imagery to contrast the rigors of greed with the ease of gospel justice:

"Greed orders you to cross the sea, and you obey; it orders you to trust yourself to wind and waves. I order you to give from what you have to the poor at your doorstep. You are lazy in doing a good work at your doorstep and tireless when it comes to crossing the sea. When greed commands, you snap to it; when God commands, you grumble. Why?"[106]

Similarly, to explain that John's Gospel offered a far-off truth, Augustine spoke of a shipwrecked sailor who could spot his homeland on the far horizon:

"For it is as though he could see his homeland from afar, and a sea lay in between; he sees where to go but has not the means to go. . . . The sea of this world lies in between where we are going, even though we already see where we are going. . . . And what has [God] done? He has provided the wood by which we may cross the sea. For no one can cross the sea of this world unless carried by the cross of Christ."[107]

Such imagery lay close not only to people's experience, but also to their literary imagination. Even the unschooled knew the story of Odysseus and his long voyage home and perhaps even the typical allegorizations of it: that it represented an odyssey of the mind to God. Augustine thus gave this Homeric image a Christian twist: the only ship to God was the cross of Christ.

The local world also influenced certain turns of thought. For instance, in *Enarratio* on Psalm 125, Augustine noted that the psalm spoke of the exiles returning to Jerusalem. For Augustine, Christians too were exiles, and in their journey to the heavenly Jerusalem, they would discover that Christ had already built their road home:

---

105. On sea-trade and its perils, see Jones, *The Later Roman Empire* 2:824–72; on the contours of the Barbary coast, see Frend, *Donatist Church*, 26.

106. *Enarrationes in psalmos* 128.4 (trans. my own).

107. *Tractatus in evangelium Ioannis* 2.2 (Rettig, 78:62). The same image appears later in the series: *Enarrationes in psalmos* 125.2. Shipwreck images figure prominently: *Enarrationes in psalmos* 123.9; 124.4; *Tractatus in evangelium Ioannis* 1.3. Cf. *Sermones* 63.2; 75.1–8.

"For Christ himself became our road. [But] do you not risk meeting bandits? He says to you: 'I have paved you a road home. Do not leave the road. Such a road have I built that a bandit does not dare get close to you.' Walk therefore in Christ, and sing rejoicing, sing as one comforted."[108]

Note the mention of highway brigands. In Augustine's time, travel by road could be perilous (much as it was in the Old West); in fact, on one overland trip, Augustine himself just missed being ambushed and killed by Donatist assassins.[109] Given this milieu, it was natural that he would reassure his hearers that on their road home, Christ had made things safe.

Fourth, Augustine frequently directed himself to those "who walked a little slower." For instance, he would focus on biblical exotica such as Hebrew names and places, for he knew that such words sounded foreign to catechumens and the illiterate. Thus he made the words he spoke "be their codex."[110] For instance, when commenting on Psalm 124's last verse ("But peace shall be upon Israel"), he noted: "Israel" meant "seeing God" while "Jerusalem" meant "vision of peace."[111] To drive the point home, he repeated these etymologies in three successive sentences (and twice elsewhere in the sequence). He thought the point crucial: "Israel is the same as Jerusalem: for the people of God are the city of God."[112]

Similarly, Augustine would shirk rhetorical decorum for the sake of clarity. At one point in *Enarratio* on Psalm 123, he expressed dissatisfaction with the Latin translation: it failed to capture the nuance of doubt he found in the Greek text. Yet he knew that few of his audience knew Greek (and he himself was no master of it).[113] To get across the exact nuance, he translated the phrase into Punic, the vernacular of many of his people. This apparently

108. *Enarrationes in psalmos* 125.4 (trans. my own).
109. Possidius, *Vita* 12.
110. *Enarrationes in psalmos* 121.8 (trans. my own).
111. Ibid., 124.10. In this sequence, he comments on several besides the ones cited here: *Enarrationes in psalmos* 126.1 (Solomon); 131.3 (David); 131.11 (Ephrata); *Tractatus in evangelium Ioannis* 11.3 (rabbi).
112. *Enarrationes in psalmos* 124.10 (trans. LF 37:546). See also *Enarrationes in psalmos* 120.6; 121.8. Cf. *Enarrationes in psalmos* 134.26; 136.1; 137.28; 149.3.
113. For a discussion of Augustine's knowledge of Greek, see Bonner, *St. Augustine: Life and Controversies*, 394-95.

bothered the educated in the audience: Punic was a "barbaric" tongue, utterly ill suited for public discourse. Augustine paid such standards no mind, insisting that "I often use words that are not Latin that you may understand."[114]

TURNING TO THE CATECHUMENS

From time to time in this sequence, Augustine turned to the catechumens and addressed them directly. Most of these turns were brief: e.g., in *Tractates* 3, 4, 10, and 12. Only in *Tractate* 11— given on the first Sunday of Lent, or just before—did the catechumens receive Augustine's concerted and sustained attention. These turns, while important, obviously form only one thread among the other threads—Christological, ecclesiological, sacramental, spiritual; and obviously, it was not simply these brief turns which served as the catechumens' instruction, but the whole range of topics raised in the course of the sequence. Let us now examine the most explicit of these turns and see in what ways and for what reasons Augustine made the catechumens the focus of his remarks.

TRACTATE 3: Earlier, we saw that when one became a catechumen, a cross was traced on one's forehead. In his sermons, Augustine would mention this "sacrament" frequently and for a variety of ends. Sometimes he stressed that the sign was no magical amulet, that its power could be tapped only if one laid claim to the Christian way of life:

"Many . . . find it easy to have Christ's sign on their forehead, yet do not hospitably take Christ's word into their heart. Friends, I have said—and I repeat—Christ's sign evicts the usurper [i.e. the devil] only if our hearts have Christ as lodger."[115]

Other times, he would appeal to it as a way to admonish catechumens for their loose living: "'Are you a catechumen?' 'Yes, a

---

114. *Enarrationes in psalmos* 123.8 (trans. LF 37:529). This touches on a complex question: Augustine here may be using "Punic" simply to mean native dialects; here and there he shows some grasp of the local version: for instance, in *Epistola* 19.2, he translates Punic names into Latin, and in *Enarrationes in psalmos* 136.18 notes that in both Hebrew and Punic *edom* means "blood." However, in *Epistola* 66.2, he implies that he does not understand the country dialects. See Brown, *Augustine of Hippo*, 22 and 139.

115. *Tractatus in evangelium Ioannis* 50.2 (trans. my own). See also *Sermo* 107.7.

catechumen.' 'Do you have one forehead to receive Christ's sign and another one to wear to the theater? So you want to go there? Then change foreheads before you go!' ''[116] On still other occasions, he used it in appeals to procrastinating catechumens: that by the cross on the forehead, they had become Christ's slaves and thus members of the larger household; still they could not enjoy the rights of freeborn children until they dropped their "heavy backpack of sins."[117] Most often, however, he used it to exhort both catechumens and baptized not to be ashamed of the cross of Christ. He noted, for instance, that people blushed when ashamed and that that blush was visible on the forehead:

"So far am I from blushing at the cross that I keep it, not in some hidden locale, but bear it on my forehead. Because our blushing shows on the forehead . . . [Christ] set disgrace itself—that which pagans mock—right on the spot of our shame. You have heard how people tease a shameless man—by saying: 'He has no forehead.' What does this mean: 'He has no forehead'? That he is shameless. Let me not have a bare forehead; let the cross of my Lord shield it."[118]

In *Tractate* 3, Augustine invoked this "sacrament" of the cross on the forehead to stress this latter idea:

"We are Christian people. . . . And if Christians, then necessarily, by the very name, people belonging to Christ. We should carry his sign upon our foreheads; and we do not blush about this if we also carry it in our hearts. His sign is his lowliness."[119]

In this case, Augustine wanted to speak to the whole household of Christ, to catechumens and faithful alike. He thus invoked not a symbol which could divide them—for instance, baptism or Eucharist—but rather chose one which united them—the cross on the forehead. This symbol signified both their solidarity and the humility of their path. And as he stressed here, it was a badge

116. *Sermo* 301A.8 (=Denis 17) (trans. my own). See also *Enarrationes in psalmos* 50.1.

117. *Sermo* 97A.3-4 (=Bibl. Casin. 2, 114) (trans. my own).

118. *Enarrationes in psalmos* 141.9 (trans. my own). See also *Sermones* 107.7; 218C.4 (=Guelf. 3); *Tractatus in evangelium Ioannis* 53.13; *Enarrationes in psalmos* 68.1.12.

119. *Tractatus in evangelium Ioannis* 3.2 (Rettig, 78:75-76).

that needed not only to be worn boldly on the outside, but also to be interiorized, to be taken to heart.

TRACTATE 4: In the course of this sermon, Augustine raised a knotty problem: why would Christ have submitted to baptism? According to Augustine, this was simply one more example of Christ's self-emptying:

"And was there a need for the Lord to be baptized? I quickly answer also with questioning. Was there a need for the Lord to be born? Was there a need for the Lord to be crucified? Was there a need for the Lord to be buried? So if he assumed so great a lowliness for us, would he not receive baptism? And what good did it do . . .? That you might not disdain to receive the baptism of the Lord."[120]

Augustine then claimed that Christ's action was prophetic, that he had submitted to baptism to teach humility to one genus of catechumens, the ascetics. Augustine explained that sometimes one saw unusually ascetic catechumens: they would choose celibacy; they would distribute their goods to the poor; they would know the intricacies of doctrine better than many faithful; yet for all this, they still refused baptism. After citing these supposed virtues, Augustine then played psychologist to lay bare what he believed their hidden motives to be:

" 'What more am I going to receive? Look, I am better than this one of the faithful and than that one of the faithful'—as [the catechumen] ponders the fact that some of the faithful are married, or perhaps uninstructed, or hold and own their property, while he has distributed his to the poor. [And this man,] reflecting that he is better than that one who has already been baptized, may disdain to come to baptism, saying, 'Am I to receive what this one and that one have?' And he may in his own mind review those he despises and it may seem to him of virtually no value to receive what lessers have received, because he already seems to himself to be the better man."[121]

120. Ibid., 4.13 (Rettig, 78:103).
121. Ibid. (Rettig, 78:103—altered). Augustine reviews this whole passage in *Tractatus in evangelium Ioannis* 5.3.

This type of catechumen, however foreign to our experience, was apparently not uncommon in Augustine's day. In fact, Augustine fully believed that there were likely "in church [today] some catechumens of more eminent grace" who fit this description.[122] It was quite possible. The new religious hero of Augustine's age was the ascetic, the sort who flocked in droves to the Egyptian and Syrian wastes. And we do know that among these early monks were a certain number of catechumens.[123] Augustine apparently detected in some of his ascetic catechumens the all-too-human tendency to compare oneself to one's neighbors—a tendency all the more pronounced in the gossipy little world of a late Roman town. Romans had a fierce sense of social class and typically held themselves aloof from their lessers. It was precisely this psychology that Augustine's method flushed into the open. He then turned to the catechumens and exhorted those who saw their own attitudes played out in his little one-man play. He did not dispute that such a catechumen possessed an excellence, but it was a worthless one, for "all of his sins remain with him unless he comes to saving baptism, [there] where sins are loosed." This "disdaining to receive [salvation] together with the uninstructed" ignored the self-emptying example of Christ who had received "the baptism of his servant."[124]

TRACTATE 10: The reading this day described Jesus' cleansing of the Temple. Augustine first offered an instruction on prayer—on cleansing the temple of the heart (cited earlier). He then stressed that this laboring in the Temple was not only interior; it was also communitarian. As he saw it, zeal for God's house should consume his hearers as it had consumed Christ; thus if they saw

122. Ibid., 4.13 (Rettig, 78:103).
123. Derwas J. Chitty, *The Desert a City: An Introduction to the Study of Egyptian and Palestinian Monasticism under the Christian Empire* (Crestwood, N.Y.: St. Vladimir's Seminary Press, 1966) 48 and 61 note 23. In *Catechesis* 4.24, Cyril of Jerusalem addresses monks present among his audience, but it is not clear whether these were baptized who happened to attend or were numbered among those preparing for baptism (see also *Catechesis* 12.33). The Coptic lives of Pachomius make explicit mention of catechumens as monks. On the desert movement, see also Philip Rousseau, *Ascetics, Authority, and the Church in the Age of Jerome and Cassian* (Oxford: Oxford University Press, 1978); Brown, *The Making of Late Antiquity* (Cambridge: Harvard University Press, 1978).
124. *Tractatus in evangelium Ioannis* 4.13 (Rettig, 78:104). On the fierce sense of social class, see Brown, "Late Antiquity," *History of Private Life*, 1:239-51.

backsliders: "stop those you can; hold back those you can; frighten those you can; flatter those you can; but do not keep quiet."[125] Augustine presumed that encouragement and exhortation were not his task alone; all were called to the task of teaching gospel imperatives. It was in this context that he turned to the catechumens. Using imagery from the gospel of the day, he made an appeal that they throw off their procrastinating:

"We are soon to celebrate, in annual solemnity, the destruction and rebuilding of this temple. And we urge you to prepare yourselves for it, if any of you are catechumens, that you may receive grace. Right now is the time! Right now let that be in labor which then may be born!"[126]

TRACTATE 11: In this sermon, Augustine devoted his full attention to the catechumens. It was a Sunday—probably the first Sunday of Lent—in any case, the day he gave his annual appeal that they turn in their names. It also happened that his verse-by-verse commentary on John had reached chapter 3, Jesus' encounter with Nicodemus. Augustine saw this coincidence of text and time of year as "opportune," as something "the Lord has arranged for us." He then explained: "Opportunely it has happened that you heard today from the gospel that 'unless a man be born again of water and the Holy Spirit, he will not see the kingdom of God.' For it is time for us to exhort you who are still catechumens."[127]

Augustine took the text quite literally: that without baptism, there could be no salvation. Thus he begged the catechumens to cease delaying and to receive the one thing that might save them. He compared them to people "carrying some heavy backpack, either filled with stone or wood." He thus exhorted the catechumens: "run to put down this backpack; it weighs [you] down and drowns [you]."[128]

---

125. *Tractatus in evangelium Ioannis* 10.9 (Rettig, 78:221).

126. Ibid., 10.10 (Rettig, 78:222). Some scholars have misunderstood Augustine here—presuming he was speaking only a few days before Easter. However, Suzanne Poque has shown that Augustine's language was formulaic: he was pleading that they turn in their names for the Lenten retreat. Poque, "Trois semaines de prédication," 175–83.

127. *Tractatus in evangelium Ioannis* 11.1 (Rettig, 79:9).

128. Ibid. This image is one Augustine regularly uses in his baptismal appeals: see *Sermones* 97A.3 (=Bibl. Casin. 2, 114); 335H.3 (=Lambot 26).

As usual, Augustine focused on what he saw as a knotty problem within the text of the day. In this case, he noted John 2:23: that "many believed in [Jesus'] name" but "Jesus did not trust himself to them." It was the "mystery" of these words that allowed Augustine to interpret both the Nicodemus episode and the situation of the catechumens. First, Augustine noted that Nicodemus had witnessed to his belief in the "name" by calling Jesus "teacher"; catechumens likewise believed in the "name": "If we say to a catechumen, 'Do you believe in Christ?' he answers, 'I do believe' and signs himself. He already carries the cross of Christ on his forehead and is not ashamed of the Lord's cross."[129] Because the cross on the forehead signified belief, catechumens thus fit the first phrase of John 2:23. Augustine then tried to show that they fit the second phrase as well. To do this, he cited their ignorance of sacraments: "Let us [now] ask [a catechumen], 'Do you eat the flesh of the Son of man and drink the blood of the Son of man?' He does not know what we are saying because Jesus has not trusted himself to him."[130] Thus catechumens, like Nicodemus, were in the dark.

In the course of the sermon, Augustine made appeal after appeal. First, he noted that the cross on the forehead was a sign they were slaves, not children: "Because catechumens have the sign of the cross on their foreheads, they are already part of the great house; but let them switch from being slaves to being children."[131] In other words, unlike children, slaves lacked inheritance rights; also unlike children, they did not have the run of the house. Later, Augustine used the *disciplina arcani* for a second appeal. He noted that the baptized had crossed the Red Sea and that "all their sins, like enemies pursuing them, were destroyed just as all the Egyptians perished in that sea"; they also enjoyed "manna." Augustine then chided the catechumens:

"Catechumens do not know what Christians receive! Let their faces therefore blush red because of their ignorance; let them pass over through the Red Sea; let them eat manna so that, as they believed in Jesus' name, so Jesus may trust himself to them."[132]

129. *Tractatus in evangelium Ioannis* 11.3 (Rettig, 79:12).
130. Ibid.
131. Ibid., 11.4 (Rettig, 79:13—altered).
132. Ibid. (Rettig, 79:13-14).

232

Finally, using a rhyming antithesis, he begged them to grasp the fullness of life that awaited them:

Non ex te ille maior,	He is not greater because of you,
sed tu sine illo minor. . .	but you are less without him . . .
Reficieris si accesseris,	You will be remade if you come up,
deficies si recesseris.	you will be undone if you stay back.[133]

In the course of this sermon, Augustine explained aspects of the theology of baptism. First, he noted why the Red Sea was red: it was "consecrated by the blood of Christ."[134] Second, to explain Nicodemus's ignorance, he compared baptismal birth with human birth using first an alliterated chiasm, then rhyming antitheses:

Non noverat	He knew only
iste nisi unam nativitatem	that one birth
ex Adam et Eva;	from Adam and Eve;
ex Deo et ecclesia	[that] from God and Church,
nondum noverat;	he did not yet know.
non noverat nisi eos parentes	He knew only those parents
qui generat ad mortem;	who beget for death;
nondum noverat eos parentes	he did not know those parents
qui generat ad vitam;	who beget for life;
non noverat nisi eos parentes	he knew only those parents
qui generant successuros;	who beget successors;
nondum noverat eos	he did not know those
qui semper viventes	who, living forever,
generant permansuros . . .	beget "everlasters" . . .
Una est de terra,	One is from earth,
alia de caelo;	the other from heaven;
una est de carne,	one is from flesh,
alia de Spiritu;	the other from the Spirit;
una est de mortalitate,	one is from mortality,
alia de aeternitate;	the other from eternity;
una est de masculo et femina,	one is from male and female,
alia de Deo et ecclesia.	the other from God and Church.[135]

133. Ibid., 11.5 (CCSL 36:113; trans. my own).
134. Ibid., 11.4 (Rettig, 79:14).
135. Ibid., 11.6 (CCSL 36:113–14; Rettig, 79:16—altered).

Augustine used this sequence, with its back and forth swings and sing-song rhymes, both to make things clear and to inscribe them indelibly onto the catechumens' memory. Finally, to help the catechumens rebut Donatist polemics, Augustine gave this two-births motif a new wrinkle: just as "Adam cannot beget me a second time," so "Christ cannot beget me a second time; just as the womb cannot be sought again, so neither can baptism."[136]

TRACTATE 12: Augustine gave this sermon a few days after Tractate 11—just as the routine of Lent was getting underway. At the outset, he noted with pleasure the unusually large and excited crowd in church. He thus took advantage of this to make one last appeal to the catechumens—apparently to round up any last-minute stragglers:

". . . we have encouraged and do encourage our brothers and sisters, the catechumens. . . . Let them be born again of water and the Spirit; let the Church which is pregnant with them bring them forth. They have been conceived; let them be brought forth into the light. Let them have breasts at which they may be nourished. Let them not fear that they may be choked after their birth. Let them not withdraw from their mother's breasts."[137]

This labor/birth imagery was critical to Augustine's understanding of initiation. Scripture, of course, had referred to baptism as a new birth. Augustine simply took the image one step further: that is, if the baptism given at Easter was a new birth, then Lent was time in the womb. As we will see in the next chapter, this motif would form a major thread in Augustine's sermons to the competentes.

THE THEATER OF THE WORD

In the last two chapters, I have covered much ground. Thus it seems critical to draw together some of the major threads. First,

136. Ibid., 11.6 (Rettig, 79:16).
137. Ibid., 12.3 (Rettig, 79:30). Poque, "Trois semaines de prédication," 76, notes subtle shifts in Augustine's vocabulary between Tractatus 10 and 11: "comme s'il y avait, d'un sermon à l'autre, soustraction d'un certain nombre de catéchumènes et que le second sermon s'addressât, comme à un reste, à ceux 'qui sont encore catéchumènes' "; and between Tractatus 11 and 12: "l'exhortation est présentée (au parfait) comme un fait passé, que l'on renouvelle."

Augustine's classroom was his basilica; here the rhythms of education moved to the rhythms of the liturgy itself. Every gesture, every sign, every word mattered—whether ritual greetings, sitting-and-standing arrangements, the cross people "wore" on their foreheads, or the secrecy of what followed dismissal. All these, Augustine insisted, held some import for how one believed, felt, and acted. In this classroom, silence was rare; instead, the atmosphere was rowdy, emotionally charged, more like that of a sports arena than a modern church. It offered entertainment as well as instruction, theatrics as well as worship: its drama was salvation history; its script was the Scriptures; and its actors included everyone.

It was in this milieu that Augustine held his catechumenate. Here catechumens mixed with baptized, penitents, and outsiders. Here they heard sermons that were substantive, frequent (four times a week or more), and lengthy (sometimes an hour or more). Here Augustine improvised his lessons, guiding their flow as much by the outcries of his hearers as by the inspiration he drew from the text in his hand. He believed that as preacher and catechist he could not merely instruct; he also had to tantalize and humor, to chide and encourage, for what mattered was not simply changed minds but changed hearts and changed lives. Certainly, he attended to the understanding. In fact, he would not move to his next point until satisfied that those who walked a little slower, whether catechumens or the poorly educated, understood. Still, he worried less about the architecture of the whole, whether an individual sermon or a series of them, than he did about each sentence he spoke. Each morsel mattered: that its images be potent enough, that its sounds be musical enough. The thought he used in this forum was more poetic than philosophical; it moved more by association than by logical rigor. He withheld from the catechumens nothing of his most daring thought, whether subtle views on human interiority, the generation of the Son, or divine omnipresence, but he always sought ways to wrap such thinking in some memorable garb. And for this he tapped his repertoire of rhetorical techniques: analogies, paradoxes, double entendres, soliloquies, rhyming antitheses. Despite this, he insisted that rhetorical finesse was a tool, not an end; what mattered was food, not spice.

Scripture was his catechumenate's textbook. It structured everything: whether individual sermons or a whole sequence; whether the mood he evoked or the very language he used. He focused on small fragments—single verses, even single words—presuming that within such minutiae were hidden a microcosm that hinted at a larger whole. He certainly analyzed, but his analyses more resembled a poet's than an exegete's. Like a poet, he mined Scripture's images, melted them down, and refitted them for new settings. And while he certainly explained, he did not explain away, for he preferred Scripture's rich ambiguities. He enjoyed the way its images and music allowed him to elide a cluster of meanings, sentiments, and attitudes into an imaginative whole. In particular, he focused on scriptural images that lay close to the catechumens' experience: sea-faring, highway bandits, and hot desert winds. Scripture's music became a favored pedagogical tool, whether the psalms the catechumens and faithful had sung or the melodies of his own Scripture-laced words.

The intertwining sequence on John and the Psalms offers intriguing indications of Augustine's approach to a curriculum for catechumens. He seems to have preferred depth to breadth: that with three chapters of John and fifteen psalms he could get across enough of what was vital. Moreover, by intertwining the two biblical books, he set up an unusual contrapuntal effect: in the sermons on the Psalms, he focused on educating the catechumens' *hearts*, encouraging a journey at once upward and inward; in the sermons on John, he focused on educating the catechumens' *minds*, but the intellectualism he used was less that of an academic theologian and more that of a courtroom lawyer unraveling knotty problems. Without trying to be systematic, he nonetheless wove Christology with ecclesiology, pneumatology with spirituality, doctrine with moral admonition. Without violating the *disciplina arcani*, he gave the catechumens much on baptism: that sins drowned in its Red Sea and melted in the Spirit's sirocco; that like physical birth it was unrepeatable; that ultimately the true baptizer was not the minister, but Christ the giver of the growth; that by baptism one joined the freeborn heirs who enjoyed the run of the Lord's house. Still Augustine offered his catechumens no illusions about the Church: it was an ark full of ravens and doves, an inn for lifelong convalescents. At its best, it was full of mountain climbers who descended to nurse the lowly and do justice for the indigent.

236

Through the whole sequence, Christ remained the center, appearing in many guises: the inner teacher and inner listener, the road builder and storm calmer, the Word who creates from within the fabric of creation and the undercurrent of history hidden in strange names and numbers. Most often, Christ appeared as the self-emptier: the Lamb whose death kills the lion, the mountain who becomes a valley, the King who makes himself the royal road, the plague doctor who makes himself the medicine. Admittedly this sequence illustrates only some of what Augustine did over a short period of time with one group of catechumens. Still it at least gives one some sense of the range, depth, and tenor of teachings he would expose catechumens to.

In the end, Augustine's catechumenate suffered the same ills that beset those of his contemporaries: he too had lax catechumens who preferred cheering to changing; he too had zealous catechumens who measured spiritual progress more by culture and class than by the gospel; he too had procrastinating catechumens more daunted by high baptismal standards than by threats of hellfire. It does not seem that they lacked understanding—except, of course, about sacraments. In fact, they may have understood many matters better than many baptized today. The deeper problem seems to have been the lack of a humane remedy for postbaptismal failures. Neither Augustine nor his contemporaries, for all their pedagogical gifts, created a penitential process that could alleviate such fears. Both he and they seem to have let the gospel view of baptism as new creation overwhelm the gospel message of mercy. Given this, Augustine struggled to meet his own criterion for successful education: persuasion. But year after year, he had a measured success, even with his high standards; for year after year, despite obstacles and fears, catechumens continued to turn in their names for baptism.

Chart 9

The Sequence on the Psalms and John:
Text and Order

Sermon	Text	Trans	Scripture	Turns to Catechumens
A. Sequence begins in early December				
En in Ps 119	CCSL 40	LF 37	Ps 119	
En in Ps 120	CCSL 40	LF 37	Ps 120	
Tract Jn 1	CCSL 36	FC 78	John 1:1-5	(X)
En in Ps 121	CCSL 40	LF 37	Ps 121	
Tract Jn 2	CCSL 36	FC 78	John 1:6-14	
En in Ps 122	CCSL 40	LF 37	Ps 122	
En in Ps 123	CCSL 40	LF 37	Ps 123	
Tract Jn 3	CCSL 36	FC 78	John 1:15-18	(X)
En in Ps 124	CCSL 40	LF 37	Ps 124	
En in Ps 125	CCSL 40	LF 39	Ps 125	
Tract Jn 4	CCSL 36	FC 78	John 1:19-23	X
En in Ps 126	CCSL 40	LF 39	Ps 126	
Tract Jn 5	CCSL 36	FC 78	John 1:33	X
Tract Jn 6	CCSL 36	FC 78	John 1:32-33	
En in Ps 127	CCSL 40	LF 39	Ps 127	
Tract Jn 7	CCSL 36	FC 78	John 1:34-51	(X)
En in Ps 128	CCSL 40	LF 39	Ps 128	
En in Ps 129	CCSL 40	LF 39	Ps 129	
Tract Jn 8	CCSL 36	FC 78	John 2:1-4	
Tract Jn 9	CCSL 36	FC 78	John 2:1-11	
Tract Jn 10	CCSL 36	FC 78	John 2:12-21	X
En in Ps 130	CCSL 40	LF 39	Ps 130	
En in Ps 131	CCSL 40	LF 39	Ps 131	
En in Ps 95	CCSL 39	LF 32	Ps 95	
B. Beginning of Lent (probably)				
Tract Jn 11	CCSL 36	FC 79	John 2:23-3:5	X
En in Ps 132/133	CCSL 40	LF 39	Ps 132/133	
Tract Jn 12	CCSL 36	FC 79	John 3:6-21	X
C. Easter Week				
Tract Ep 1 Jn, 1-6 (possibly 7-8)	SC 75	LCC 6	1 John 1:1-4:16	Neophytes
D. After Easter Week				
Tract Ep 1 Jn 9-10	SC 74	LCC 6	1 John 4:17-5:3	
Tract Jn 13	CCSL 36	FC 79	John 3:22-29	X
Tract Jn 14-16	CCSL 36	FC 79	John 3:29-4:53	

Chart 10

The Sequence on the Psalms and John: Topics

Sermon	Topics Covered
En in Ps 119	"Song of steps": ascent of the heart; Christ as mountain and valley; Jacob's ladder; the motherly Christ; conversion: arrows of God; true singing as tears and virtuous action; polemic against the Donatists: not seek to separate wheat and chaff
En in Ps 120	Ascent of the heart; good works as sowing seed in winter; Christ quells the storm in the heart; grammar: Pasch as "Passover" not "Passion"; knotty problem: "hand of your right hand"; St. Crispina; spiritual intoxication
Tract Jn 1	Evangelist John as mountain; the birth of the Word; Christ the inner teacher; baptism as recreation by the Word; story of the Manichee and the flies; God as creator: analogy of the carpenter; analogy of the physician
En in Ps 121	Two commandments as the wings of the soul; sighing for Jerusalem; analogy: festival of martyrs; the temple of living stones; the Christ as the Samaritan; plea to the rich to do justice; drinking word of God
Tract Jn 2	Sailing home on the wood of the cross; God as creator: the carpenter analogy; Divine adoption vs. human; Christ the physician heals eyes of heart.
En in Ps 122	Descent of Christ the Head, ascent of the Body of Christ; heaven not a place; being a son and being a servant; polemic against pursuit of money, fame, power, self-righteousness
En in Ps 123	Psalms as songs and sentiments of Christ and his Body; psalms as mirror; King of country is the Way to it; grammar: translation into Punic of verse; the shipwreck of riches; Christ breaks the snares of the fowlers
Tract Jn 3	Preaching: a rain of exhortation; the Cross on the forehead; Grace and the Law; Christ the Physician; the image of God in the mind; knotty problem: grace for grace; Inner Teacher
En in Ps 124	Allegory: the mountains around Jerusalem; putting up with unrighteous rulers; "City of God is the people of God"; unlike the Donatists, "Be Israel"
En in Ps 125	Christ as redeemer from slavery; groaning of the people of God; conversion: God turns us around; the Spirit as a hot southern wind; good works as sowing in winter; Church as inn of the Samaritan

Chart 10 *(cont.)*

The Sequence on the Psalms and John: Topics

Sermon	Topics Covered
Tract Jn 4	Christ the quiet Judge and loud Teacher; knotty problem: the contradiction between the words of Christ and of John the Baptist; the proud catechumen; polemic against the Donatists; call to mull over knotty problem
En in Ps 126	"Song of steps" by Solomon; preaching: the inner teacher; people of God: wheat/chaff; bishop as overseer of and one with people; Eve from Adam, Church from Christ; the resurrection; the Church groans to give birth; the obscurity of Scripture
Tract Jn 5	Christ as Truth, John as truthful; Christ the baptizer and the baptized; polemic against the Donatists: the minister and the power of baptism, sinful ministers; solution to knotty problem: what John learned from the dove
Tract Jn 6	Love as moaning of the dove; allegory of Noah's two birds: dove and raven; polemic against Donatists: the tattoo of the deserter; against the circumcellions
En in Ps 127	Problem: does a psalm about wife and children apply to all?; prophets speak in enigmas; digression: Christ as Head/Body; Felix the martyr; "clean fear" of God; loving Christ; Church as wife and children; the Lord's hunger for good deeds
Tract Jn 7	Pagan vs. Christian spectacles; the dangerous Lamb of God; the Son as lawyer; polemic against the use of charms and amulets; the kenosis of Christ, of Paul, and of preachers
En in Ps 128	Dancing to the rhythm of the commandments; the evils of the Church today not as bad as in past; the demands of Christ easier than those of money; creation's praise of God; against usury
En in Ps 129	Praying in the depths; a merciful God; bear burdens: image of the stags; pardoned, yet waiting for the kingdom; martyrs as models
Tract Jn 8	Water into wine: everyday miracles, Christ's renewal of us; divine and human in Jesus; the two births of Jesus: Son of Father, Son of Mary; polemic against astrologers and Manichees
Tract Jn 9	Defense of marriage; the intoxication of Scripture; theology of the Spirit; allegory: the six jars of wine as the six ages of salvation; the meaning of Adam's name

Chart 10 (cont.)
The Sequence on the Psalms and John: Topics

Sermon	Topics Covered
Tract Jn 10	Prayer and the Inner Teacher; the "brothers" of Jesus; corrupt bishops; duty of community admonition; first appeal to catechumens; the meaning of Adam's name and the forty-six years of building the Temple
En in Ps 130	Review: Head/Body; sinning as weaving a whip of cords; singing with the heart; Paul on the body of Christ; Christ the physician; John 1:1 as "bread" vs. John 1:14 as "milk"; divinization; avoid literalism; wheat/chaff
En in Ps 131	Interpretation: seek mysteries; against private possessions; entertaining Christ; tent of God/house of God; putting on Christ
En in Ps 95	Singing is building the Temple; Christ beyond the Roman Empire; Donatists build walls not temple; God beyond words; bringing a contrite spirit; Donatists as frogs; mystical name of Adam; Christ the artist; offerings to Christ the judge
Tract Jn 11	Appeal to the catechumens to enroll for baptism; knotty problem: Why does Christ not trust catechumens?; Nicodemus the catechumen; baptism and the Red Sea; the two births; polemics against the Donatists: birth is unrepeatable; allegory: the patriarchs
En in Ps 132/133	Celebrate unity; monks vs. circumcellions; allegory: Noah, Daniel, Job; *Deo gratias* vs. *Deo laudes*; St. Stephen; murmurers
Tract Jn 12	Greets excited crowd; final appeal to the catechumens; role of preacher; born of water and Spirit; voice of the Spirit; two births of Christ and ours; Paul against the Donatists; Christ the physician; call to repentance; sin as bilge water; daily preaching as discipline

Year of sequence disputed: probably 406–7 (La Bonnardière, Poque, Berrouard, Rettig, TeSelle); however, others claim 414–15 (Le Landais); 412–13 (Zarb); 416 (Maurists).

Chart 11

The Sequence on the Psalms and John:
Intertwining Themes

Chart from Maurice Le Landais, "Deux années de prédication de saint Augustin," *Études augustiniennes* 28 (1953) 35; see 15-26.

Sermon	Links between En Ps and Jn	Chronological References
En in Ps 119	---	---
En in Ps 120	4: "mountains"	13: St. Crispina, Dec 5; (cf. Tr 1.6: Ps "sang a little while ago")
Tract Jn 1	2-3 "mountains"	A Sunday (cf. Tr 2.1)
En in Ps 121	5-6 "the same"	Vigil of Tract 2 (cf. 1)
Tract Jn 2	2: "the same" 16: promises to speak of "grace and truth"	16: promises Tract 3 in a little while
En in Ps 122	---	---
En in Ps 123	14: renews promise to speak of "grace and truth"	14: Vigil of Tract 3
Tract Jn 3	1: recall promise of "grace and truth" and fulfills it	---
En in Ps 124	5: "sparrow in the mountains"	---
En in Ps 125	[This may come here or after Tract 4]	---
Tract Jn 4	11: sparrow in the mountains; 16: poses problem of "dove"	---
En in Ps 126	13: recalls promise to explain the "dove"	13: Vigil of Tract 5
Tract Jn 5	1: completes promise of explaining "dove"	17: Early January (New Year's Day?)
Tract Jn 6	19: "olive in ark"	1: "cold outside"
En in Ps 127	13: recalls "olive"	6: St. Felix [of Nola?, Jan. 6]
Tract Jn 7	10-11: the "jurist"	24: Sunday
En in Ps 128	---	---

Chart 11 *(cont.)*

The Sequence on the Psalms and John:
Intertwining Themes

Sermon	Links between En Ps and Jn	Chronological References
En in Ps 129	4: the "jurist"	---
Tract Jn 8	---	13: Tract 9 tomorrow
Tract Jn 9	14: "ADAM"	1: Tract 8 day before
Tract Jn 10	12: "ADAM" 5: "scourge of rope"	11–12: Tract 9 on day before 10: Approach of Lent
En in Ps 130	2: "scourge of rope"	---
En in Ps 131	---	---
En in Ps 95	13: "olive in ark" 15: "ADAM"	15: Mentioned "ADAM" "a little while ago": Tr 9.10
Tract Jn 11	---	1: Sunday (cf. Tr 12.1) probably on or before first Sunday of Lent
En in Ps 132/133	6: "pool" = unity	---
Tract Jn 12	9: "pool" = unity	3: third appeal to catechumens
Tract Ep 1 Jn 1–7	Prologue: notes cycle on John's Gospel interrupted (cf. Tr 13)	Prologue: Easter Week

Note: LeLandais (and LaBonnardière) presume that the mention of the approach of "Pasch" in Tractates 10 and 11 means that these were delivered sometime just before Easter. Suzanne Poque, "Trois semaines de prédication à Hippone," *Recherches augustiniennes* 7 (1971) 169–87, has corrected this and shown that these were delivered near start of Lent.

Chapter 7

Lent: Time in the Womb

Each year, a certain number of catechumens would take the momentous step of petitioning for baptism. Some would respond to Augustine's impassioned appeals: that "our friendship may be true and everlasting and unite us not only to each other, but also to the Lord himself."[1] Others would witness some miraculous healing or experience a great vision and so be moved to turn in their names.[2] For instance, in *The Care to be Taken for the Dead*, Augustine cites the case of Curma, a poor magistrate from the town of Tullium (located not far from Hippo). This "simple country fellow" had fallen into a coma and "lay almost dead for some days." During this time, he had visions of the dead (such as his namesake, Curma the smith) and the living (including Augustine himself); he also had a vision in which he was "led into Paradise and was told . . .: 'Go be baptized if you wish to be in this place of the blessed.' "[3] So he, like others from the surrounding villages, would make their way to Hippo near the beginning of Lent. They would find somewhere to lodge and stay on for about two months: through the forty days of Lent, through the vigil and Easter Week, until they had at last "fulfilled the duties of the Easter season." These countryfolk would gather with catechumens from Augustine's home church. All told, there would be enough of a crowd that Curma, "like many others," might remain "unknown to us."[4] As Augustine saw it, these catechumens had heard the voice of their own hearts voiced in the opening verse of

1. *Epistola* 258.4–5 (Parsons, 32:252). In this letter, Augustine writes to an educated catechumen named Marcianus to convince him to end his procrastinating and to "enroll his name among the *competentes*."
2. For a miraculous healing prompting the turning in of names, see *Epistola* 227.
3. *De cura pro mortuis gerenda* 12.15 (trans. John Lacy, FC 27:370–72).
4. Ibid. (Lacy, 372).

Psalm 41: "As the deer longs for flowing streams, so my soul longs for you, O God." And so with thirsty hearts, they would "rush headlong to the grace of the holy font."[5]

During Lent, these "petitioners" *(competentes)* would go through a training that included (1) a demanding penitential discipline, (2) scrutiny and exorcisms, (3) a mix of public and private catecheses. Our knowledge of this formation is fragmentary: some fragments offer rich, often detailed glimpses into the shape of the training and catechesis; others give us only the floor plan of Augustine's catechetical edifice, one whose interior and ornaments can only be guessed at. In this chapter, I will gather these fragments under five headings. In the opening section, I will examine the treatise *On Faith and Works* in which Augustine speaks—often in passing—about the contours and guiding principles for the Lenten training. Then I will focus on four sets of catecheses: (1) on the discipline and meaning of Lent (e.g., *Sermons* 205-10); (2) on the scrutiny/exorcism (*Sermon* 216); (3) on the Creed (*Sermons* 212-15; *On the Symbol*); and (4) on the Lord's Prayer (*Sermons* 56-59).

THE CROSS-WEAVE OF FAITH AND WORKS

Around 413, Augustine received some books which were written by "laypeople . . . learned in the Scriptures" and which questioned both standards for admission to baptism and the legitimacy of the traditional prebaptismal training.[6] These people were moved, in part, by pastoral concerns: they questioned why both male catechumens with mistresses and divorced-and-remarried people were barred from baptism.[7] More importantly, they buttressed their polemics with biblical texts which seemed to undermine the foundational principles on which both the catechumenate and the Lenten training had been built: namely, that formation involved both faith and morals; that it demanded long, concerted effort; and that it required the reform of the whole person. For instance, they cited stories from Acts indicating that the apostles had baptized their hearers after a simple declaration of faith: e.g., Peter's baptism of the three thousand or Philip's baptism of the Ethiopian eunuch. They also appealed to the great Old Testament

5. *Enarrationes in psalmos* 41.1 (trans. my own).
6. *Retractiones* 2.64 (trans. M. I. Bogan, FC 60:198). See also *De fide et operibus* 1.1-2.
7. *De fide et operibus* 1.1-2.

type of baptism, the Exodus, and noted that the Jewish people had passed through the Red Sea *before* receiving the Law. Thus these critics suggested that it might be more biblical for the Church to teach *competentes* only what was necessary for "faith," i.e., dogmatic truths. They felt that if these dogmas were accepted, then the Church should baptize; only afterwards should it teach the moral life required of Christians.

Augustine answered these objections with the treatise *On Faith and Works*. He admitted these people showed "a charity that is laudable"; however, he feared that their views, if accepted, would lead to "admitting all to baptism indiscriminately."[8] He thus saw them as extremists whose laxity betokened a loss of balance as perilous as that of rigorists whose praise of virginity and abstemious ways led them to condemn marriage and moderate wine-drinking.[9] Augustine insisted that orthodoxy was a balancing act and that on this issue—admittance to baptism—the Christian teacher should "neither become numbed in the name of patience nor rage under the pretext of zeal."[10] He thus tried to answer his opponents and show "not only how those reborn by the grace of Christ are to live, but also what kind of people are to be admitted to the bath of rebirth."[11] In particular, he defended the traditional formation against the charge that it might somehow be unbiblical. He thus spent the greater part of the treatise refuting his opponents' exegeses. He insisted, for instance, that Peter had told the three thousand to do penance; that the Jewish people, in leaving Egypt, had left behind their sinful ways; and that Scripture had simply passed over in silence the Ethiopian eunuch's baptismal formation.[12] What especially bothered Augustine was the glib

8. Ibid., 15.25 (Liguori, 25).

9. Ibid., 4.5 (Liguori, 226–27). Augustine also cites the Sabellians and Donatists as examples of this loss of balance. It is not clear which rigorists Augustine is referring to, whether local ascetic extremists or monks from Egypt and Syria that he has heard of. On the encratite tendency in early Christianity, see Frend, *The Rise of Christianity*, 174–75, 197, 371; Brown, *The Body and Society*, 92–101.

10. *De fide et operibus* 5.7 (trans. my own).

11. *Retractiones* 2.64 (trans. my own). Augustine cites and summarizes *De fide et operibus* a number of times in other works: *Enchiridion* 18.67; *Epistola* 205.18; and *De octo Dulcitii quaestionibus* 1.2. He apparently sensed it answered some crucial matters.

12. *De fide et operibus* 8.12–13; 11.17; 9.14.

separation his opponents seemed to make between faith and morals. He retorted that Paul did not separate things this way; that it would be absurd to suggest that those portions of Paul's letters focused on faith were addressed to catechumens and *competentes*, while those on morals were addressed to the baptized.[13] Against this, Augustine insisted that faith was much more than assent to dogmatic truths; that faith, as understood by Paul and by the Church, had always been "a faith 'laboring in love.'"[14]

In this treatise, one finds much on a Scripture-based rationale for the catechumenate and Lenten training, and little on the shape these actually took in Augustine's day. Yet here and there, some important points can be gleaned. At the beginning of chapter 5, I cited his brief remarks on the long catechumenate phase. One finds more information, though in rather piecemeal form, on the training during Lent. First, Augustine consistently distinguished ordinary catechumens from those who had put in their names for baptism. He referred to the latter either as *baptizandi* ("those to be baptized") or as *competentes*. And one finds this same distinction maintained in his sermons.[15]

Second, Augustine implied that "during the days for harvesting this grace," the Church investigated the lifestyle of those who had "given in their names."[16] Egeria, as we saw in chapter 2, had described a solemn, formal rite in which this was done: on the first day of Lent, the bishop would investigate each candidate's lifestyle by questioning sponsors and neighbors. Augustine makes no explicit mention of such a rite, but it is clear that there was some procedure for barring unworthy candidates. Nor is there any mention of questioning sponsors or neighbors. However, at some point, the candidates themselves formally declared their resolve to

13. Ibid., 7.11. Apparently his opponents had noted that Paul's letters typically closed with paraenetic sections; they thus claimed that the doctrinal body was directed at those preparing for baptism while the latter portions were for the baptized.

14. Ibid., 25.46 (trans. my own). Augustine is quoting Galatians 5:6. In *Enchiridion* 18.67, he refers to this point as the heart of the treatise's whole argument.

15. The term *baptizandi* appears in *De fide et operibus* 7.11; 8.13; 11.17; 13.19; and 20.36; *competentes*, in *De fide et operibus* 6.9; 18.33; and 19.35. This distinction between ordinary catechumens and *competentes* is made especially in *Sermo* 392.1; also *Sermones* 216.1; 228.1; 229.1.

16. *De fide et operibus* 6.8 (trans. my own).

live a life worthy of a Christian. Here and there, Augustine alludes to certain criteria. For instance, candidates agreed to live only with "their lawful and true wives."[17] Also "prostitutes and actors and all other professionals in public indecency" were refused unless they had "first loosened, or broken themselves altogether from their filthy bondage."[18] Finally, "drunkards, the greedy, the evil-tongued" were to be "rigorously disciplined" and admitted only if they "approach baptism with a change of heart for the better." The investigator was to "refuse them baptism if they resist correction and publicly declare themselves inflexible."[19] Should someone be barred, it was not a matter of "preventing willing candidates from coming to Christ" but rather of taking people at their own word: "we are [only] convicting of guilt those who, by their own public statements, do not want to go to Christ."[20]

Third, he listed prominent landmarks within the geography of Lent. At one point, he noted that people were "cleansed by abstinence, fasts, and exorcisms"; later he says that they were "catechized, exorcised, scrutinized."[21] Similar lists appear in sermons Augustine addressed to neophytes: in *Sermon 227*, he mentions "the humbling fast and the sacrament of exorcism"; in *Sermon 229*, he says that, after people had "given in their names," a "milling" process began "with fasts and exorcisms"; in *Sermon 229A*, he reminds them that "you underwent [a sort of threshing] by fasts, by observances, by all-night vigils, by exorcisms."[22] In the next two sections, we will see what precisely Augustine meant by "fasts," "observances," "scrutiny," and "exorcisms." Yet these quick reviews are revealing: ascetical practices and exorcisms are cited in each case while catechesis is cited only once. Perhaps Augustine was simply taking catechesis for granted and wanted to stress elements that made the Lenten training distinctive. On the other

17. Ibid. (Liguori, 229).

18. Ibid., 18.33 (Liguori, 283). Here it is not perfectly clear whether Augustine is referring to a Lenten interrogation or the interrogation on entrance to the catechumenate itself—but he explicitly remarks that such vices are to be denounced during Lenten catecheses.

19. Ibid. (Liguori, 283–84—altered).

20. Ibid., 17.31 (trans. my own).

21. Ibid., 6.8–9 (Liguori, 229–30).

22. *Sermo 227; Sermo 229.1* (=Denis 6); and *Sermo 229A.2* (=Guelf. 7) (trans. my own).

hand, it may indicate Augustine's priorities: that asceticism and exorcism served as the core curriculum and that catechesis, while certainly an element, may have played a subsidiary role.

Fourth, Augustine alluded to emphases in Lenten catechesis. In line with his polemic, he stressed paraenesis: that the "one catechizing those to be baptized" should "instruct on and give warnings about their way of life."[23] He also cited his own practice; namely, that no matter who his audience might be, he always joined doctrine with moral admonition:

"Quite frequently [matters of faith] come first and [admonitions] follow; still, in the cross-weave of a sermon, both are given to catechumens, both to the faithful, both to those to be baptized, both to those already baptized: that by health-giving teaching and highly crafted preaching, either the catechumens may be instructed or the faithful roused from forgetfulness, that either those to be baptized may be led to profess the art [of Christian living] or those already baptized firm up [their skills in it]."[24]

As Augustine saw it, this cross-weave of doctrine and moral admonition followed the gospel's own cross-weave: "There can be no love of God in a person who does not love his or her neighbor, nor love of neighbor without the love of God."[25]

Fifth, Augustine says that a highly charged emotional atmosphere set in during Lent:

"Do we silence the testimony of our own experience, do we go so far as to forget how intent, how anxious, we were over what the catechists taught us when we were petitioning for the sacrament of the font—and for that very reason were called 'competentes'? Do we not gaze at others who, year after year, race to the bath of rebirth, do we not see how they act during the days they are being catechized, exorcised, scrutinized: how sharp-eyed they look when gathering, with what eagerness they move along, with what care, what suspense, they hang upon it all?"[26]

Eagerness and anxiety, an edgy suspense and a sharp-eyed intensity—it was this heady mix of emotions that Augustine had

23. *De fide et operibus* 13.19 (trans. my own).
24. Ibid., 7.11 (trans. my own).
25. Ibid., 13.20 (Liguori, 246).
26. Ibid., 6.9 (trans. my own).

felt as a petitioner and had observed year after year working as a catechist. This affective sensitivity is, of course, typical Augustine. And as we will see, it was to exactly such feelings that he would pitch his own Lenten sermons: sometimes further fueling enthusiasms, other times dampening them; sometimes confirming fears, other times quelling and comforting them.

Finally, Augustine gave what he saw as the bottom line: that people must already have embarked on a "life resonating in harmony with sacred baptism."[27] Lent was thus *the* time for *competentes* to hone their skills, to plot out "a way of life [that] would square with the great sacrament they are yearning to receive."[28] Following Paul's admonition, they were to strip off the old and put on the new; following Christ's, they were not to patch new cloth on old garb nor pour new wine into old wineskins. Still—Augustine admitted—neither inquiries into lifestyle nor well-aimed catechesis nor demanding asceticism offered any guarantee: inevitably, some less-than-worthy candidates would slip through.[29] Moreover, on this side of the eschaton, the Church would inevitably be a mix of wheat and chaff, an ark full of animals both clean and unclean, a good net catching bad fish as well as good.[30] These realities, however inevitable, should give no cause that either "sternness of discipline or watchfulness should slacken or be dropped altogether."[31] For Augustine and his contemporaries, the rigorist legacy of the third century and the memory of martyrs' heroics still loomed large. Augustine shared the tradition's awe of baptism and of the new life it promised. But he had begun to edge, in carefully measured ways, towards a Church of the many, with all the uneasy compromises that that entailed. And, while he saw his unnamed opponents as radical laxists, he found himself equally repelled by other currents: first by the purist ideology of the Donatists and, later by the elitist strains and ascetical optimism of the Pelagians.[32]

27. Ibid., 26.48 (trans. my own).
28. Ibid., 6.9 (trans. my own).
29. Ibid., 19.35.
30. Ibid., 27.49; 17.31–32.
31. Ibid., 2.3 (trans. my own).
32. See the excellent recent study of R. A. Markus, "Augustine: A Defense of Christian Mediocrity," in *End of Ancient Christianity* (Cambridge: Cambridge University Press, 1990) esp. 52–55.

BOOT CAMP: THE LENTEN DISCIPLINE

During Lent, the *competentes* embraced a strict ascetical regimen. According to Augustine, they were expected to fast each day until the ninth hour (around 3 P.M.).[33] They also abstained from all meat and wine and kept their diet bland and simple.[34] On Sundays and on Holy Thursday, the fast was lifted, while on Holy Saturday, it was tightened so that they, together with all the faithful, would take neither food nor drink.[35] Moreover, the *competentes*, if married, were strictly enjoined to fast from sex.[36] They also distributed alms and, on occasion, spent all night praying.[37] The *competentes* were not the only ones who followed this discipline. According to Augustine, "in Lent, almost all, more or less, according to the choice or ability of individuals," would take on these same rigors.[38]

Finally, the *competentes* were not allowed to bathe—an ancient tradition alluded to as early as Hippolytus. This meant not only physical discomfort; it also meant breaking ties with one of the great social centers in the Greco-Roman world: the public baths. In these recreational complexes, one not only bathed; one also relaxed, mingled with friends, hosted parties, even attended lectures. The *competentes'* fast from bathing ended on Holy Thursday.

33. *Epistola* 54.9; cf. *De moribus ecclesiae* 2.13.29. Concerning the Lenten discipline in Hippo, see Poque, "Introduction," SC 116:24–25; and the excursus, "El ayuno cuaresmal," BAC 24:789–90.

34. *Sermo* 205.2; cf. *Sermones* 207.2; 209.3; 210.8–9.

35. On relaxing the fast on Holy Thursday, see *Epistola* 54.9. On Holy Saturday, see *Sermo* 210.1. On Sundays, see *Epistola* 36; Augustine treats the question at length and presses hard against rigorists who would extend the fast to include Sunday; he also defends the pluralism of practice among the African and Italian churches.

36. *De fide et operibus* 6.8; *Sermones* 206.3; 207.2; 208.1; 209.3. Augustine's attitudes towards sexuality in general and sexual renunciation in particular need to be interpreted within the context of early Christianity and its pagan and Jewish inheritance. For a careful and sensitive study of this complex and often misunderstood aspect of early Christianity, see Brown, *The Body and Society*, especially his chapter on Augustine, 387–427; also helpful is his article "Augustine and Sexuality," *Center for Hermeneutical Studies in Hellenistic and Modern Culture*, Colloquy 46 (May, 1983) 1–13.

37. On almsgiving, see *Sermones* 56.11; 58.10; 205.3; 206.2; 210.10. *Sermo* Guelf. 1.11 mentions one all-night vigil; *Sermo* 229A.2 (=Guelf. 7) uses the plural *vigiliis*.

38. *Contra Faustum* 30.5 (trans. R. Stothert, NPNF 4:330).

As Augustine told one correspondent, this came from a concern for hygiene:

"If you ask how the custom of bathing [on Holy Thursday] arose, no more reasonable explanation occurs to me than that the bodies of those to be baptized had become foul during the observance of Lent, and they would be offensive if they came to the font without bathing on some previous day."[39]

This cluster of disciplines was simply an outward indication of an inner resolve. As Augustine once told the *competentes*, penitential practices were taken up because "no one chooses a new life without having repented of the old." Moreover—he reminded them—the Church's rhythm of penance first, baptism later, followed that dictated by Peter in Acts 2: "Do penance and be baptized in the name of our Lord Jesus Christ."[40]

Augustine, echoing Joel 2:15, would "sound the trumpet" with a sermon to signal the outbreak of this "war" called Lent.[41] Six of these "trumpet blasts" have come down to us: *Sermons* 205–10.[42] All six were addressed to the assembly as a whole and not just to the *competentes*. However, *Sermon* 210 is of special interest: (1) because Augustine several times refers to "those to be baptized"; (2) because its imagery and turns of thought situate Lent, its meaning and discipline, in terms of the Easter sacraments, giving the impression that it was framed especially for the *competentes*; and (3) because it gives important clues why Augustine regarded asceticism as so vital to their preparation for baptism.

Augustine opened *Sermon* 210 with one of his favorite pedagogical devices, a knotty problem. He noted that Christ had been baptized before he fasted whereas the *competentes* were baptized after they had fasted. In other words, the Church seemed to do the

39. *Epistola* 54.10 (Parsons, 12:259–60).

40. *Sermo* 352.2 (trans. my own), quoting Acts 2:37-38. This text is one of his favorite prooftexts to explain the penitential practices of the *competentes*: *Sermo* 351.2; *De fide et operibus* 8.12; 11.17.

41. *Sermo* 208.1 (trans. Mary Sarah Muldowney, FC 38:92). Cf. Ambrose, *De Helia et ieiunio* 1.1.

42. See also the sermon *De utilitate ieiunii* (text and translation: Dominic Ruegg, PS 85). It is probably another of these inaugural Lenten sermons, though it is possible that it was delivered on some other fast day during the year. *Tractatus in evangelium Ioannis* 12 ends with exhortations similar to those found in *Sermones* 205–10; see Poque, "Trois semaines de prédication," 179–83.

very opposite of what Christ did. Augustine then made several distinctions to show that the contrast did not hold. First, he offered a liturgical argument: because of the bounty of Christ, the Church did not need to baptize after some forty-day fast; it could baptize any day if need be. However: "Because a far greater number of those to be baptized assembles on Easter, this day stands out, not because it is richer in the grace of salvation, but because the greater joy of the feast invites us."[43] Augustine then gave an exegetical argument: the baptism Christ received from John had been superseded by the baptism Christ gave his followers. John's baptism was thus numbered among the sacraments of the old dispensation, much as circumcision and Passover were. Augustine then repeated a theme presented in his sermons on John's Gospel: that Christ had submitted to baptism "to provide us an example of humility and devotion" and to "show the great devotion we should receive these sacraments with." Finally Augustine sorted out the knotty problem by using one of his common-sense exegetical principles: check the context of a passage. Thus, he argued that to understand Christ's fast, one must look not at the episode that preceded it—Christ's baptism—but rather the episode that followed it—Christ's battle with Satan. In other words, fasting during Lent meant imitating Christ, but not the way first posed by the knotty problem; rather, Christ "clearly taught by his example that we must fast anytime we clash with the tempter in a quite bitter wrestling-bout."[44] The battle Christ faced was one everyone faced: "In this world, human life is a time of testing, and in the night of this age, the 'lion goes about seeking someone to devour,' not the 'lion of the tribe of Judah,' our king, but the diabolic lion, our adversary."[45]

Here and elsewhere in the sermon, Augustine appealed to the same cluster of images Chrysostom and Ambrose had used: athletic competition and military conflict. Like them, he believed that the ascetical exercises of Lent mirrored those used for the training of athletes or soldiers. Lent was thus a sort of sacred fitness program or boot camp. It trained one for a wrestling match with Satan or for a battle against the forces of darkness. For such combat, one needed to muster all the power at one's disposal. This

43. *Sermo* 210.1 (Muldowney, 98—altered).
44. *Sermo* 210.2 (trans. my own).
45. *Sermo* 210.4 (Muldowney, 101—altered).

meant training not only one's interiority—both mind and heart—but also one's body: "One must fast . . . so that the body may fulfill its military stint by its being disciplined and the soul may gain a victory by its being humbled."[46] As Augustine makes clear here and throughout his Lenten addresses, the body was a key locus of conflict. Thus the body too had to be trained; it too had to be catechized. Since the battle was waged by the whole person, training for battle necessarily involved training the whole person. However, as Augustine noted in *Sermon* 205, this training of the body moved contrapuntally to the training of one's interiority; that is, while people "fasted in body, they feasted in spirit"; they refreshed themselves with "God's word . . . so that the inner person can get on with and keep to a robust chastening of the outer."[47]

As Augustine was at pains to point out, the asceticism of Lent had nothing to do with a Gnostic rejection of the flesh. Thus, in avoiding food and drink, one should not "by a sacrilegious error condemn a creation of God";[48] nor should one "think that the flesh is an enemy of the spirit, as if there were one creator of the flesh and another of the spirit."[49] Augustine and his orthodox contemporaries viewed the body not as the Gnostics did. Rather both he and they would speak at times more in a Stoic or Platonic accent: that the body was a headstrong horse that bucked up and threw its rider; that it was a contentious rebel plotting against the good governance of that which distinguished human beings from animals, the mind and will.[50] Lenten discipline was thus a way of bringing the body back into right relation with our interiority:

"Let us restrain our body and saddle it into service; and let us, in taming it, bridle it back somewhat from things allowed: so that we not, because of our untamed flesh, slip-slide into things not allowed. Other days, we should avoid drunkenness and carousing; these days, however, we should pull back from meals [usually] permitted. We should always swear off—and flee from—

46. *Sermo* 210.2 (trans. my own). On the theme of the *militia Christi*, see Poque, *La langage symbolique dans la prédication d'Augustin d'Hippone*, 1:37–68.

47. *Sermo* 205.1 (trans. my own).

48. *Sermo* 208.1 (trans. my own). See also *Sermo* 205.2; *De utilitate ieiunii* 3.

49. *De utilitate ieiunii* 4.4 (Ruegg, 71).

50. Ibid., 3.3 (Ruegg, 71). On interiority as the distinctive feature of the human person, see, for instance, *De fide et symbolo* 4.8.

adultery and fornication; but these days, even married people
should hold back from sex. [That way,] our flesh, which will have
gotten used to being reined in from enjoying its own rights, will
submit to you so as not to usurp someone else's."[51]

Ultimately, for Augustine, the problem was not the flesh per se;
the flesh was simply where the problem surfaced. The real culprit
was the unruly human heart which clung to the wrong things or,
more precisely, loved things in the wrong way.[52] So he would repeat Pauline views: that "for the clean, all food is clean," but, he
would add, "for no one is luxury clean."[53] The discipline of Lent
was thus a way of rooting out slovenly and self-destructive habits.
It meant purging the poisons out of one's system—not unlike the
demanding reshaping of habit that an alcoholic or drug addict
must go through.

Augustine's assessment of the body—troubling in the trajectory
it helped set the Church on once his thought was given authoritative status and was joined with other strains within patristic
thought—was, in many respects, unexceptional. He certainly had
views on sexuality, the body, the will, and the Fall which sharply
differed from the ascetical mainstream: some more moderate,
some more extreme.[54] But these do not appear in his Lenten sermons. Moreover, when one sets these sermons against the horizon of that ascetical mainstream, it becomes clear, as Brown notes
in his recent study, The Body and Society: "Augustine was content
with the most banal exhortations to restraint."[55] For instance, he
did not speak of Lent in the lyric tones that some of his colleagues

51. Sermo 207.2 (trans. my own). Cf. Sermones 205.2; 206.3.

52. Confessiones 10.31. Possidius, when writing his biography, would quote
this passage as the classic statement of Augustine's views; see Vita 22.

53. Sermo 205.2 (Muldowney, 85). See also Sermones 208.1; 209.3.

54. The ascetical mainstream linked ascetical practices with the "angelic"
life, a return to a state prior to Adam and Eve's fall into "flesh." Augustine
read Genesis differently: Adam and Eve had been created to be creatures of
flesh; they had been created to have sex and to produce children. Thus the
fall did not cause a fall into flesh; rather, it produced a fissure between the
human will and the human body. Thus asceticism was to repair the break in
"marital concord" between spirit and flesh: Enarrationes in Psalmos 140.16. On
Augustine's slow movement away from the ascetical mainstream, see Brown,
The Body and Society, 396-408, 425-27; "Augustine and Sexuality," 1-13; also
excellent is Markus, End of Ancient Christianity, 45-62.

55. Brown, The Body and Society, 424.

in the East used: as a chance for average householders to "breath
in the free air of the desert," as an opportunity to taste the
prelapsarian "angelic life" enjoyed by monks.[56] More importantly,
what Augustine meant by "reining in" the body was borne by his
own lifestyle. Both during his own time (particularly in Syria) and
during the Middle Ages, asceticism would move towards violent
extremes. John Chrysostom and others would wreck havoc on
their health by their ascetical gymnastics. Augustine, however,
chose simplicity over self-destructive austerity, as Possidius insisted:

"His clothes and shoes, and even his bedding, were simple and
appropriate, being neither overly fastidious nor slovenly. . . . His
meals were frugal and economical; at times, however, in addition
to herbs and vegetables they included meat for the sake of guests
or sick brethren. Moreover they always included wine. . . . Only
the spoons were of silver; the vessels [unlike the silver ones used
by many contemporaries] . . . were of earthenware, wood, or
marble."[57]

Moreover, Augustine refused to adopt the costly raiment some of
his episcopal colleagues had; instead he wore the same sort of
byrrhus, or cloak, worn by working-class laity. When the wealthy
sent him fine clothes as gifts, he would send them back: "Such a
gift perhaps becomes a bishop, but it does not become Augustine,
who is a poor man and born of poor parents."[58]
   When Augustine spoke of the Lenten discipline, he invoked not
only masculine imagery, such as military or athletic combat; he
also used feminine images: Lent was time in the womb. In *Sermon*
205, he noted that "a person, about to lead this [baptismal] life, is
formed in the womb for forty days."[59] In *Sermon* 210, he developed this further. First, he quoted John's Gospel: "When a
woman is in labor, she is sad because her day has come. But
when she has brought forth the child, there is great joy because a

   56. Ibid., 255.
   57. Possidius, *Vita* 22 (trans. Audrey Fellowes, *The Life of St. Augustine*
[Villanova: Augustinian Press, 1988] 91–93). On Augustine's "monastery," see
Zumkeller, *Augustine's Ideal of the Religious Life*, 24–100.
   58. *Sermo* 356.13 (trans. Bonner, *St. Augustine*, 129).
   59. *Sermo* 205.1 (Muldowney, 84).

person is born into the world." Thus during Lent, people "fast and pray since this is the day of labor"; moreover, the Spirit "stirs up in our hearts the indescribable pains of holy desire," a sort of spiritual equivalent of a woman's labor pains.[60] While the baptism of the *competentes* would mark one sort of coming to birth, it was still only a beginning; while certain labor pains ended, others continued. True rebirth would happen only with the coming of the kingdom in which "we shall be poured out from this pregnancy of faith into eternity's light."[61] For Augustine, the human condition was inevitably a paradoxical mix: of anguish and joy, toil and rest, soured dreams and heady visions. And, as he explained to the *competentes* and others, these twin threads within human life found expression in the seasons of Lent and Easter: Lent symbolized the darker one, the painful coming to birth that took a lifetime; Easter symbolized the happier one, that periodic foretaste of an eschatological birth into God.[62] Thus, in these two liturgical seasons, Christians drank in, by turns, the "not yet" and "already" of New Testament eschatology.

Analogies were not Augustine's only pedagogical tools. He also resorted to biblical typology. Like Ambrose, he would cite the fasts of Moses, Elijah, and Christ as foreshadowings of what the *competentes* and others in the assembly embraced. Sometimes, he gave these typologies an allegorical twist: Moses symbolized the Law while Elijah symbolized the Prophets; thus "both the Law and the Prophets gave testimony" to Christ.[63] He would also play to his assembly's fascination with numerology: a forty-day fast was chosen because the "mystical" number forty was the product of four times ten; four symbolized the four Gospels while ten symbolized the decalogue, meaning that "the four Gospels agreed with the ten-fold Law" and that thus "the Old and New Testaments are indispensable for us in this life."[64]

60. *Sermo* 210.5 (Muldowney, 103).

61. *Sermo* 210.2 (trans. my own). This eschatological perspective on baptism is drawn out especially in *Enarrationes in psalmos* 41.

62. *Sermones* 210.6; see also 205.1; 206.1.

63. *Sermo* 210.7 (Muldowney, 105). See also *Epistola* 55.27.

64. *Sermo* 205.1. In *Sermo* 210.6, he gave a somewhat different numerological scheme: four represented the four points of the compass (and thus the whole world) while ten represented the Decalogue, "fulfilled in the grace of charity." Cf. *De consensu evangelistarum* 2.4.8; *Epistola* 55.27.

After this, Augustine turned to the particulars of the discipline. In all six sermons, he stressed the three forms of penitential piety that Christianity had inherited from Judaism: fasting, prayer, and almsgiving. When he discussed fasting, he, like Ambrose, would entertain his audience by lampooning the wealthy. He mocked their pseudo-religiosity: they "fast, not to cut down their usual gluttony by tempering things, but to bloat their innumerable cravings by importing things from all over"; they may give up simple table wine, but instead scour the marketplace for rare liquors; they may give up meat, but instead indulge in so many lavish and heavily spiced dishes that they do little but bankrupt their patrimonies and give themselves heartburn; they may fast until afternoon, but "when the time for eating comes, they stampede to well-laden tables like cattle to troughs"; as a result, they are "loathe to have the season of Lent come to an end."[65]

On the serious side, Augustine would insist that the Lenten discipline should move people at once inward and outward: inward to quell out-of-kilter passions and outward to rectify out-of-joint social structures. He would insist that a proper fast meant that one not let the sun go down on one's anger, that one "fast from hatred and feast upon love."[66] Besides setting aside inner angers and halting public vendettas, one should help repair the broken social order through almsgiving. This was not some pious option, but a duty required by justice itself, for the "failure to share one's surplus with the needy is like theft."[67] This command lay at the heart of Augustine's view of social justice: "The surplus goods of the rich are the necessities of the poor. When you possess surplus goods, you possess the goods of others."[68] He also insisted that prayer without almsgiving was mere pretence:

"If a farmer is not justified in seeking a harvest when he knows he has sowed no seed, how much more unreasonably does one

65. *Sermo* 210.8–9 (trans. my own). Similar satires appear in *Sermones* 205.2; 207.2; 208.1.

66. *Sermo* 207.3 (Muldowney, 92). See also *Sermones* 208.2; 209.1; 210.10.

67. *Sermo* 206.2 (Muldowney, 87).

68. *Enarrationes in psalmos* 147.12 (trans. my own). For a survey of Augustine's and other patristic views on social justice, see Peter Phan, *Social Thought*; also, William J. Walsh and John P. Langan, "Patristic Social Consciousness—The Church and the Poor," in *The Faith That Does Justice*, ed. John C. Haughey (New York: Paulist Press, 1977) 113–51.

who has refused to hear the petition of the poor seek a generous response from God? For in the person of the poor, [God]—who experiences no hunger—wishes to be fed."[69]

Thus, as Augustine saw it, one sought Christ where he said he would be: among the poor.

Such an instruction on Lent would be the first of many for the *competentes*. From scattered references, it seems that the *competentes* joined the larger assembly for daily liturgies and sermons.[70] Several of these public catecheses have survived: *Sermons* 5, 352, and 392. The last offers a glimpse of the way Augustine might have catechized such a mixed audience. On this occasion, he divided the assembly into four groups and asked each to overhear admonitions addressed to others:

"Faithful, listen to what I am going to say to the *competentes*, and *competentes*, listen to what I am going to say to the faithful; penitents, listen to what I am going to say to the *competentes* and to the faithful; and catechumens, listen to what I am going to say to the faithful, *competentes*, and penitents; listen everyone . . ."[71]

He then exhorted each, by turns, on the perils of adultery and concubinage and on the scandals each group caused the others.

In *Sermon* 5, Augustine exhorted those who "rush to receive the grace of baptism" not to imitate the ungrateful servant in Jesus' parable; they were to remember the debts that would be forgiven them, and to extend the same magnanimity to others.[72] Later, Augustine referred, in passing, to a previous private instruction he had given them on the crucifixion. Suzanne Poque has suggested that this meant that the *competentes* were led through a whole sequence of special readings and instructions.[73] If so, then only the tiniest fraction of Augustine's Lenten curriculum has been preserved.

69. *Sermo* 206.2 (Muldowney, 87—altered).
70. Poque, "Introduction," 25.
71. *Sermo* 392.1 (trans. my own). The Maurists listed this sermon among the "dubii," but affirmed that it joined two authentic fragments from Augustine. Their assessment has been confirmed by Lambot and Verbraken; Verbraken, *Études critiques*, 156.
72. *Sermo* 5.2 (trans. my own).
73. Poque, "Introduction," 25.

In *Sermon* 352, Augustine addressed the *competentes* at length and with great warmth. He encouraged them "to hear the word with eagerness" as they "draw nearer to the moment of pardon" and begged them never to doubt God's lavish mercy: that no matter what they had done in the past they were to trust that "all absolutely, however great or small," would be forgiven them. He played on their curiosity, reminding them that they stood on the brink of witnessing great secrets; that just as at the death of Christ the veil in the Temple was ripped in two and opened up the holy of holies, so too with the celebration of Christ's dying and rising, all would be opened to them. He thus encouraged them: "Be joyful going to baptism; enter without fear on the road of the Red Sea." He tried to allay fears about certain future "enemies," those minor sins one committed daily. These would be destroyed the same way Israel destroyed the Amalekites: by standing, as Moses had stood, with arms raised in prayer.[74]

Besides daily public sermons of this sort, the *competentes* also received private instructions. These touched on matters cloaked under the *disciplina arcani*; thus neither pagans nor ordinary catechumens would be allowed in to hear them. We know of at least four occasions when these would be given (though, as *Sermon* 5 indicates, there may well have been others): (1) after the scrutiny; (2) on the handing over of the Creed; (3) on the giving back of the Creed; and (4) on the handing over of the Lord's Prayer. In the remainder of the chapter, these will be the focus.

EMANCIPATION PROCLAMATION: THE SCRUTINY

Both pagans and Christians worked, to some extent, from a common religious topography.[75] As they saw it, the stars and planets moved according to a sublime harmony and order; earth, on the other hand, remained a precarious realm tottering on the edge of chaos. Here below, invisible demonic forces wandered about wrecking havoc. These were responsible, in one way or another, for the vagaries that plagued human well-being: diseases, natural calamities, social ills. Christians tended to interpret these

74. *Sermo* 352.2 and 6–7 (trans. my own).

75. For what follows, see Dodds, *Pagan and Christian in an Age of Anxiety;* Van der Meer, *Augustine the Bishop,* 46–75; Macmullen, *Paganism in the Roman Empire,* 49–62, 73–94; Brown, *The Making of Late Antiquity,* 1–26.

threats as evidence of the power of Satan. His influence seemed everywhere: it masqueraded under the guise of paganism and its accompanying apparatus (idols, sacrifices, amulets, astrology); his pomps were displayed in cultural institutions (the bloody public games, the theaters, the annual festivals); and his dark powers had seeped into every crevice of ordinary social life (whether it be the widespread patterns of usury, drunkenness, or infanticide; whether the land-grabbing habits of the wealthy or the graft of imperial officials).

This world view shaped ancient Christians' vision of conversion. Sometimes, they would speak of *conversio,* of "turning," in terms familiar to us: as a sudden, inner-psychic experience; as a shift in one's institutional affiliation; as an integral process of intellectual, moral, and affective growth. But more often, they envisioned conversion in cosmological terms: it was marked by a metaphysical shift, a transfer of power from the reign of Satan to the reign of God. With this transfer of power came a change in status: the convert ceased to suffer Satan's tyranny and came to enjoy God's magnanimous rule. This awesome transition was necessarily tumultuous. As Brown notes:

"The Christian found himself committed to a wrestling match, an *agon.* This ring was clearly defined: it was the 'world,' the *mundus.* The enemy was specific and external to him, the devil, his angels and their human agents. The 'training' provided by his Church had equipped the Christian for the due reward of victory in any competition—a 'crown' in the new world. Simple men in the time of Augustine would . . . dream of fighting a wrestling match of horrible violence; they would long to escape from this 'double prison, the flesh and the world.' "[76]

The high drama of this turning was played out in one of major Lenten rites: the scrutiny (*scrutinium*).[77] In Hippo, this rite took place probably soon after enrollment (or, alternatively, just before

76. Brown, *Augustine of Hippo,* 244. On the "agon" image in Augustine, see also Poque, *La langage symbolique,* 1:69-97.

77. For a general study of the rite, see A. Dondeyne, "La discipline des scrutins dans l'église latine avant Charlemagne," *Revue d'histoire ecclésiastique* 26 (1932) 5-33 and 751-87. For the rite as held in Augustine's church, see Poque, "Introduction," 26-33; De Latte, "Saint Augustin et le baptême," 196-99.

the first handing back of the Creed).[78] Augustine alludes to its various elements in *Sermon* 216, delivered to the *competentes* immediately after the rite. However, a clearer picture of it emerges in a series of sermons attributed to Quodvultdeus, a Carthaginian who was a younger contemporary and friend of Augustine.[79] According to Quodvultdeus, the *competentes* would spend the night "not lulled with the delight of sleep nor with minds deceived by dreams . . . but by watching, by praying, by psalm-singing, by brandishing weapons against our adversary, the devil."[80] Then "from hidden places they were brought forward one by one in sight of the whole Church."[81] They would enter with head bowed low and possibly would kneel or prostrate themselves; these gestures symbolized that "pride was destroyed, [and] humility, brought in."[82]

78. The whole tone and tenor of *Sermo* 216 suggests that it occurred soon after the beginning of Lent. This is the view of T-A. Audet, "Note sur les catéchèses baptismales de S. Augustin," *Augustinus Magister* 1:158; Busch," De modo quo S. Augustinus descripserit initiationem christianam," 431; and DeLatte, "Saint Augustin et le baptême," 192–93. However, in Carthage, as is evident from the Lenten sermons of Quodvultdeus, it took place just before the *redditio symboli* (presumably one week before baptism). Poque, "Introduction," 26–27, favors this date; however, she ignores the tone evident in *Sermo* 216. All are agreed that the scrutiny/exorcism referred to several places in Augustine's sermon is clearly the same as that attested in Quodvultdeus. Either Augustine's church worked from a somewhat different calendar from that of Carthage; or there was more than one scrutiny (but Quodvultdeus implies that there was only one); or the tone of Augustine's sermon is simply misleading.

79. Most contemporary scholars accept Quodvultdeus as the author of the series which includes *De symbolo 1–3* and *Contra Iudaeos, Paganos, et Arrianos*. According to Vittorino Grossi "Adversaries and Friends of Augustine," *Patrology* 4:501–2, scholars are agreed that these are "homogenous collection of catechetical material of African origin which reflects fifth-century African baptismal catechesis"; while there is a homogeneity of content, some feel there is not homogeneity in style. For a thorough discussion of this, see R. Braun, "Introduction," *Livre des promesses et des prédictions de Dieu*, SC 101:88–113.

80. Quodvultdeus, *Contra Iudaeos, Paganos, et Arrianos* (trans. my own). Cf. Quodvultdeus, *De symbolo* 2.1. Augustine mentions an all-night vigil in *Sermo* Guelf. 1.11.

81. Quodvultdeus, *De symbolo* 1.1 (trans. E. C. Whitaker, *Documents of the Baptismal Liturgy*, rev. ed. [London: SPCK, 1970] 107).

82. Quodvultdeus, *De symbolo* 1.1 and *Contra Iudaeos, Paganos, et Arrianos* 1 (Whitaker, 107). The theme of embracing humility and renunciation of pride

Then the *competentes* would strip off their outer cloaks and stand barefoot "upon the stretched-out goatskin."[83] This goatskin sackcloth *(cilicium)*—not mentioned in the initiation rites of Constantinople, Rome, Milan, or Gaul—appears in association with exorcisms held in Antioch, Edessa, North Africa, and later in Spain.[84] (In chapter 2, we saw it mentioned by Theodore of Mopsuestia.) It was a multilayered symbol. In itself it was a sign of penitence.[85] But the gesture of standing (or perhaps stamping one's foot) upon it was equally important. In this way the *competentes* signaled their renunciation of their sinful inheritance—alluding to the widespread belief that Adam and Eve had worn tunics of goatskin.[86] Moreover, as Augustine notes in *City of God*, this gesture also expressed an eschatological hope: that at the Last Judgment one would be numbered not among the goats, but among the sheep.[87] While standing on the goatskin, the *competentes'* bodies were examined (Ambrose had mentioned a similar procedure).[88] What this entailed is not clear. Scholars have suggested possible motives for this: to see if they suffered from leprosy or some other contagious disease; to probe for signs of possession inscribed in their flesh; or simply to set them free from Satan's physical powers.[89]

At some point, an exorcist would come forward, and, according to Augustine, "invoke the name of your redeemer" and "heap

---

runs through Augustine's talk: see *Sermo* 216. Augustine refers to a prostration on the *cilicium* in *De civitate Dei* 15.20. Bettenson's translation is somewhat inexact here: not "prostrate ourselves *in* cloth of goat's hair," but rather "prostrate ourselves *on* the cloth of goat's hair." Poque "Introduction," 28, also sees a reference to prostration in *Sermo* 216.10.

83. Quodvultdeus, *De symbolo* 1.1 (trans. my own). Cf. Augustine, *Sermo* 216.10–11; Theodore, *Catechetical Homily* 12, synopsis.

84. Poque, "Introduction," 28.

85. *De civitate Dei* 15.20. Cf. *De consensu evangelistarum* 2.4.13.

86. Quasten, "Theodore of Mopsuestia on the Exorcism of the Cilicium," 218; Yarnold, *The Awe-Inspiring Rites of Initiation*, 10.

87. *De civitate Dei* 15.20. Cf. *Sermo* 216.10.

88. Ambrose, *Explanatio symboli* 1. See also Augustine, *Sermo* 216.11; Quodvultdeus, *De symbolo* 1.1; 2.1.

89. These three interpretations are given, respectively, by Busch, "De modo quo S. Augustinus descripserit initiationem christianam," 435 note 195; A. Dondeyne, "La discipline des scrutins dans l'église latine avant Charlemagne," 16; B. Capelle, "L'introduction du catéchuménat à Rome," *Recherches de théologie ancienne et médiévale* 5 (1933) 148.

well-deserved curses on [the devil]."[90] The invocations included calling down "the lowly, most high Christ"[91] and "the earth-shaking all-powerful Trinity."[92] According to another North African, Optatus of Milevis, the formula of imprecation against Satan was: "Cursed one, get out!"[93] Besides these verbal pleas, the exorcist would also breathe upon, or more precisely, "hiss at" the candidate. This gesture, the *exsufflatio*, was a conventional sign of contempt and had become, in Christian circles, a standard exorcistic act. For instance, Athanasius says that St. Anthony, when confronted by a demon, had hissed at it and called on the name of Christ.[94] Ordinary Christians used this same gesture to exorcise demonic spirits that they believed inhabited pagan statues. In fact, it was such a common Christian habit that at one time hissing at a statue of the emperor was declared a criminal act.[95] The use of breath was not accidental. For the ancients, one's breath was one's life, one's *spiritus*, the power that animated the flesh. Thus this *exsufflatio* meant spitting out the demonic breath that had invaded the candidates' God-given life-force.[96] Once, in a sermon to the *competentes*, Augustine explained its significance:

"Just as you saw today, even little children are hissed at and exorcised, so that the hostile power of the devil—who deceived one man to lay hold of everyone—might be knocked out of them. So it is not these children—God's creation—whom we hiss at and exorcise, but the one whose sway all those born with sin come under: that is, the prince of sinners."[97]

90. *Sermo* 216.6 (Muldowney, 156—altered).

91. Quodvultdeus, *De symbolo* 1.1 (Whitaker, 107). Cf. Augustine, *Sermo* 216.6.

92. *Sermo* 216.10 (trans. my own).

93. Optatus, *Libri VII [de schismate Donistarum]* 4.6 (trans. my own): "Maledicte, exi foras." Augustine frequently uses the expression "mittere foras" when speaking of exorcism: *De agone christiano* 1.1; *Sermo* 145.5; *Opus imperfectum contra Iulianum* 1.50 and 2.181.

94. Athanasius, *Vita S. Antonii* 40.

95. *Opus imperfectum contra Iulianum* 3.199.

96. John the Deacon, *Epistola ad Senarium* 3 (trans. Whitaker, *Documents*, 145): "[One] receives exsufflation and exorcism, in order that the devil may be put to flight and an entrance prepared for Christ our God, . . . so that a man who till recently had been a vessel of Satan becomes now a dwelling of the Savior."

97. *De symbolo ad catechumenos* 1.2 (trans. my own). The *exsufflatio* of children figures prominently in Augustine's debate with the Pelagians; *Epistola*

Finally, either at the scrutiny itself or soon after, the *competentes* would give voice to their new-found freedom by formally renouncing Satan.[98]

In *Sermon 216*, given just after this dramatic rite, Augustine spoke of conversion in the terms set by 1 Peter 2:9: that the *competentes* were being "rescued from the power of darkness and transferred into the kingdom of [God's] dazzling light."[99] Throughout, he used a mystagogical approach: weaving together cultural and biblical images with ritual actions, and drawing out their import for theology, spirituality, and moral action. While he did seek to hone the *competentes'* vision of conversion, he focused more often on making his own words a force to provoke it. Thus his dominant, but by no means exclusive, style seems to have been the grand, the style he reserved for moving hearts to conversion.

Apparently this address was one of his earliest, given soon after his ordination as a presbyter. He played on this fact in his opening words:

"The clumsy beginnings both of my ministry and of your conception—for you are beginning, by divine grace, to be quickened in the womb of faith—ought to be sustained by prayer; that way, my talk may invigorate and encourage you along, and your conception may console and help me along."[100]

Just as he was beginning his ministry, so the *competentes* were beginning theirs: he and they were "fellow new recruits" (*contirones*).[101] He saw a mutuality and interplay between their respective tasks:

Nos instruimus sermonibus,	I instruct by words;
vos proficite moribus!	you—advance by deeds!

194.46; *De gratia Christi et de peccato originali* 2.45; *De nuptiis et concupiscentia* 2.50.

98. Quodvultdeus, *De symbolo* 1.1 (Whitaker, 107). See also *De symbolo* 2.1; *Contra Iudaeos, Paganos, et Arrianos* 1. The formula is cited in Augustine, *Sermo* 215.1; and the renunciation is given in *Sermo* 216.6.

99. *Sermo* 216.6 (trans. my own).

100. *Sermo* 216.1 (trans. my own).

101. *Sermo* 216.2 (trans. my own).

265

Spargimus sermonem verbi,   I sow the teaching of the word;
fructum reddite fidei!   you—hand back the fruit of faith![102]

Note how even the rhetorical cast of his Latin echoes his message. The jingling rhymes link the phrases mirroring the idea that the catechist's ministry of words was linked to the *competentes'* ministry of deeds. This recalls the catechetical principle that Augustine outlined for Deogratias:

"So great is the power of sympathy, that when people are affected by us as we speak and we by them as they learn, we dwell in the other and thus both they, as it were, speak in us what they hear, while we, in some way, learn in them what we teach."[103]

For Augustine, the converting individual was as much a teacher as the catechist even though their media of eloquence were distinct. Moreover, while this back-and-forth dynamic—from word to deed to word—was inherent in all catechesis, it assumed particular urgency as baptism approached.

After this prelude, Augustine spun out further variations on the theme of mutuality, modulating from his relationship with them to their relationship with one another:

"Certainly, your very name—since you are called *competentes*—shows that you crave this, that you are striving for this with all the energy of your being. What else are *'competentes'* but people suing for something together? For just as *'condocentes,' 'concurrentes,'* and *'considentes'* mean nothing other than [teachers] teaching together, [athletes] running together, and [soldiers] pitching camp together, so the term *'competentes'* was welded together for no other reason than to describe people who were suing for one and the same thing at the same time."[104]

Augustine here combines etymology with spirituality to explain the hidden meaning of the title *competentes:* his hearers were not simply "petitioners," but "co-petitioners," for as the Latin itself implied, they were people "suing" *(-petere)* for something

---

102. *Sermo* 216.1 (BAC 24:186; trans. my own). Muldowney (FC 38:150 note 4) thinks that *sermonem* should be replaced by *semen;* in that case, the phrase would read: "I sow the seed of the word."

103. *De catechizandis rudibus* 12.17 (Christopher, 41—altered).

104. *Sermo* 216.1 (trans. my own).

"together" (com-). In other words, they had bound themselves together in a sort of class-action suit. The other compound words Augustine listed were equally evocative: the *competentes* were to be fellow teachers, fellow runners, fellow soldiers. Such wordplay was, of course, part of Augustine's rhetorical stock-in-trade and played to his hearers' native sense of *hilaritas*, that delight that sprang from "a mixture of intellectual excitement and sheer aesthetic pleasure at a notable display of wit."[105] Here, Augustine used rhetorical whimsy to draw in his audience, to render them, according to Cicero's dictum, "benevolent, attentive, docile." But with it, he got across an important point: conversion was not some individualistic pursuit, but a common enterprise which formed the *competentes* into a band of fellow seekers bound by a common task and shared ministry. As *concurrentes*, they were to run together towards a common goal. As *condocentes*, they were to teach one another the path. As *considentes*, they were to assemble as soldiers who would remain fearless of the "terrors of the world," even though rival "armies pitch camp" nearby and a "battle" threatens.[106]

Augustine then began exploring the deeper implications of conversion: its shape, its theological meaning, and its ethical consequences. He made no effort to be systematic. Instead, he flowed steadily from one theme to another, weaving aphorism with image, proclamation with exhortation. The remainder of the address leaves the impression of an order more musical than logical. To describe the metaphysical implications of conversion, Augustine focused on two underlying themes: God's action and the *competentes'* response. To highlight God's action, he appealed to a number of traditional biblical metaphors that accented in sharp, dichotomous terms the transfer of power and allegiance: the *competentes* were passing from darkness to light, from debt to solvency, from slavery to freedom, from the pangs of labor to the joy of new birth, from the desolation of exile to the consolation of coming home. These images would have had great poignancy for Augustine's hearers: ancients did not have the benefit of electric lights and so experienced darkness as a powerful, ominous reality; they lived in a world where slavery was commonplace and knew

105. Brown, *Augustine of Hippo*, 254.
106. *Sermo* 216.1 (trans. my own).

firsthand the dreadful cruelty slaves endured; they had no hospitals and few painkillers and knew childbirth to be a dangerous, painful process; they depended heavily on support from extended family, clan, and city, and knew of few punishments more fearful than exile.

Let us look at his handling of two of these. First, the slavery/emancipation motif: Augustine described conversion as a manumission wrought by God:

"Now your captivity, during which [the devil] held you in his tyrannical grip, will be wiped out. The slave-yoke with which he savagely used to weigh you down will be lifted off you and dropped on his own neck. To bring about your emancipation, you need only give your redeemer the word. . . . Refuse to cart around the yoke; instead, break open the fetters and toss the yoke away, so that you may never again be held fast by slavery."[107]

Here Augustine echoes the biblical theme of Christ the liberator, the one who shattered the shackles binding Satan's slaves. This biblical accent on emancipation moved against the grain of ancient thought. Ancients tended to be fatalists. They often saw their lives as one long, tedious subjugation to powers beyond their control: whether the tyranny of government or the whimsy of wealthy patrons; whether the sublime indifference of the gods or a fixity of fate dictated by the stars. Augustine insisted that conversion meant freedom from all that, a liberation won not by the *competentes'* own efforts, but by Christ. They had only to give their consent and the slave-yoke would be snapped off.

Second, the labor/new birth motif: As we have seen, this classic New Testament image of conversion was one Augustine played on regularly. Here he added several new twists:

"Behold the womb of your mother, the Church; behold how she labors in pain to bear you and to bring you forth into the light of faith. Do not, by your impatience, disturb your mother's body and make narrow the passage of your delivery. . . . God is your Father, the Church, your mother. . . . No labor, no misery, no weeping, no death will accompany this child-bearing, but only ease, blessing, joy, and life."[108]

107. *Sermo* 216.7 and 10 (trans. my own). See *De agone christiano* 7.7.
108. *Sermo* 216.7-8 (Muldowney, 156-58—altered).

As Augustine saw it, the *competentes* were the unborn whose confinement allowed them to be knit together in the Church's womb. He thus called them to passivity: to avoid disturbing the quickening by their impatience, to submit themselves to God's life-giving powers. What prompted their growth was "the word" by which "you are being nursed," by which "you are being fed"; this nourishment would allow them to advance in wisdom and age. Conversion also meant entering a new extended family. In this household, they would have God as "father" and the Church as "mother." This implied establishing new social bonds, new behaviors, new affections. The *competentes* thus stood on the threshold of a new status: they would become "children of God, children by adoption."[109]

The dichotomous imagery found in some sections of the sermon might give the impression that Augustine advocated a Christianity of discontinuity, a born-again view of things. However, he balanced such dichotomous images with other more gradualist ones. In one lengthy passage, he played on Jesus' parable of the sower and described conversion as a slow laboring to clear land which had been overgrown with thorns, but in time would produce high yields.[110] Later, he described how acquiring virtue would remain a lifelong task:

"Innocence will be your infancy; reverence, your childhood; patience, your adolescence; courage, your youth; merit, your adulthood; and nothing other than venerable and wise discernment, your old age. Through these age-divisions or stages, you are not developed [literally: 'unrolled'], but, though remaining the same, you are renewed. . . . Although all these stages do not come at the same time, within the devout and justified soul [their resonance] rolls on together in unending harmony."[111]

Here Augustine takes up a traditional scheme—dividing human life into "six ages"—and applies it to the life of faith. Like modern faith-development theorists, Augustine believed that conversion was a lifelong process, that one only slowly acquired the virtue of a given stage. Also like them, he argued that one did not outgrow

109. *Sermo* 216.7-8 (trans. my own).
110. *Sermo* 216.3.
111. *Sermo* 216.8 (Muldowney, 158—altered). On this traditional scheme and Augustine's use of it, see Markus, *Saeculum*, 17-29.

269

earlier virtues, but rather brought them along to the next stage. He denied that this constituted development in the sense that one ceased to be (ontologically) the person one was and became, as it were, someone else; instead, a new harmony, a new aesthetics of being, took shape as one subjected oneself more and more to God's power and thus became more fully and more perfectly the person one was created to be.

To accent the *competentes'* response, Augustine tapped on other images. At one point, he imitated the cadence and slogans of street vendors hawking their merchandise:

"Here, along with the auctioning and bartering of faith: behold, the kingdom of heaven is set up on the block and up for sale! Look inside your consciences' bank-account! And pile it all up! Put together your hearts' treasures, act together! And yet, you will pick it up for free—if you spot the great grace offered you. You spend nothing; and yet, what you get is great."[112]

Here, Augustine used his skills as a showman to drive home a simple point: that God's action was utterly gratuitous, that the *competentes* could buy the kingdom at bargain-basement prices. Yet elsewhere he suggested just the opposite—that conversion was a struggle, a hard-fought contest:

"Behold where your stadium is! Behold where the wrestling mats are! Behold where the race-track is! Behold where the boxing ring is! If you want to knock down a deadly sparring partner with a strong-armed faith, then overthrow your evil ways and entangle yourselves in good ones. If you want to run in such a way as to grab the prize, then run from the unjust and chase after the just. If you want to box in such a way that you do not punch thin air, but [instead] boldly pummel your opponent, then discipline your body and bring it back under control so that—controlling all your appetites and fighting according to the rules—you may triumph and share a heavenly prize and a laurel-crown that will never wilt."[113]

Here again Augustine compares conversion to an *agon*: a race, a wrestling bout, a boxing match. As we have seen, for Augustine

112. *Sermo* 216.3 (trans. my own).
113. *Sermo* 216.6 (trans. my own). See *De agone christiano* 1.1; 6.6. On the theme of victory, see Poque, *La langage symbolique*, 1:99–111.

and his contemporaries, conversion meant wrestling with Satan, and to prepare for such combat one had to undergo a variety of training exercises. Here he repeats ones cited earlier—overthrowing bad habits, embracing good ones, disciplining the body—but he also adds a new one: chasing after the just. Augustine was convinced that faith was much more than theological know-how; it was rather a *habitus*, a whole web of attitudes, feelings, and behaviors that imbued and shaped the lives of the faithful. He thus called on the *competentes* to apprentice themselves to seasoned veterans, to those who displayed a hands-on mastery of faith in the arena of the everyday.

Augustine warned the *competentes* that their past allegiance with Satan had left them vulnerable. But he assured them that if they put their bodies under God's protection they need not fear:

"As you once brandished your bodies as weapons of iniquity for sin, so now may you brandish your limbs as weapons of justice for God (cf. Rom 6:19). In a deadly ploy against you, your attacker has armed himself with your own javelins. In a saving counter-attack against him, let your protector, in turn, be armed with your limbs. Your attacker will not harm you if he does not grab hold of your limbs while you beat a retreat."[114]

Here again, Augustine speaks of the body as the locus of the war. As he saw it, Satan might use the *competentes'* own bodies against them as if they were an armory still under his control. Thus by their asceticism the *competentes* would try and wrest their bodies from the possession of Satan and return them to the armory of God. For this, they needed to muster formidable powers to counteract those of Satan.

This train of thought would lead Augustine to refer back to the earlier rite, in particular, the moment of exorcism:

"What I do for you—that is, by invoking your redeemer's name—you finish up by scrutinizing your heart and by contrition. On my part: I thwart ploys by pleading with God and by denouncing your old enemy. On your part: keep plying [God] with vows, and keep up your contrition of heart. That way, you may be rescued from the power of darkness and transferred into the kingdom of [God's] dazzling light. This now is your work; this, your task. On

114. *Sermo* 216.2 (trans. my own). See *De agone christiano* 2.2; 7.7–8.

271

my part: I heap well-deserved curses on [the devil] for his wickedness. On your part: declare war—a glorious one—by turning your
back on him and by devoutly renouncing [allegiance to] him."[115]

Here Augustine reassured them: he had joined his forces with
theirs in a common cause, and just as he and they were fellow
recruits and fellow teachers, so they were now fellow combatants.
Each had their respective tasks. During the rite, Augustine as
exorcist had battled with words: on the one hand, by imprecations
against Satan, and on the other, by invocations to God. Yet, he
insisted, they too had work to do: by turning public scrutiny into
interior scrutiny.

This turn appears again in his comments on another moment
within the rite: the bodily examination. He called on the *competentes* to probe the health of their hearts just as the ritualized
physical had tested the health of their bodies: "In joy I remind
you to preserve in your hearts the health which is evident in your
bodies."[116] This interior turn was Augustine's trademark. As
Brown notes:

"Augustine never questioned the broad outlines of . . . [ancient]
'religious topography.' . . . Augustine merely turned the Christian struggle inwards: its amphitheater was the heart; it was an
inner struggle against forces in the soul."[117]

Augustine certainly thought that demons wandered the earth, but
worried most about those that haunted the human heart. As he
once put it: "The devil is not to be blamed for everything: there
are times when a man may be his own devil."[118]

Augustine also commented on three other moments within the
rite: (1) the stripping off of the tunic, (2) the standing (or stamping) on the *cilicium*, and (3) the invocation of the Trinity. Echoing
Colossians 3:9, he encouraged the *competentes* to strip off their old
Adamic self just as they had stripped off their tunic: "Do you see,
my fellow recruits, what delights of the Lord you will come upon
when you toss away the delights of the world? . . . Strip off the
'old man' [i.e. Adam] that you may be clothed with the new [i.e.,

---

115. *Sermo* 216.6 (trans. my own).
116. *Sermo* 216.11 (Muldowney, 161—altered).
117. Brown, *Augustine of Hippo*, 244–45; also 311.
118. *Sermo* 163B.5 (=Frang. 5) (trans. Brown, *Augustine*, 245).

272

Christ]."[119] In the same way, he encouraged them to conquer and trample the world just as they had conquered and trampled the goatskin. Towards the end of the sermon, he alluded to both the goatskin and the invocation and drew out the moral import:

"When you were scrutinized and when that one who persuaded you to run away and desert [God] was rightly rebuked in [the name of] the earth-shaking all-powerful Trinity, you were not clothed in goatskin-sackcloth; however, your feet mystically stood on it. The vices and hides of goats must be trampled on; the rags from young goats [that will one day stand] on the left hand must be torn to shreds."[120]

For Augustine, ceremony and symbol was just the beginning: the *competentes* still had to make headway against bad habits, those vices that had led to their desertion.

Throughout, Augustine was alert to the *competentes'* subjectivity. He recognized that this whole process—the ascetical discipline, the scrutiny and exorcism, the dichotomous imagery—caused a kind of deconstruction: it disfigured their old sense of self; it tore down old patterns and old relationships. Thus he would again and again beg them to look beyond the present, to imagine a new transfigured self: "Do not despise yourselves, because it has not yet appeared what you will be"; "love what you are going to be, for you will be children of God, children by adoption."[121] He encouraged them to see themselves the way God saw them: "Do not feel you are worthless when your Creator and the Creator of everything has appraised your value at such a high price that daily he pours out the incredibly precious blood of his only-begotten Son."[122] He also claimed that they would enjoy a new self, one made no longer simply in "the image of him who is from earth" (Adam), but also in "the image of him who is from heaven" (Christ).[123] In other words, for Augustine, baptism marked the forging of a new interiority. No longer would the *competentes* be so racked by this *agon* with Satan, by the chaos and disorder of earthly life. Rather, they would have the divine life

119. *Sermo* 216.2 (Muldowney, 151).
120. *Sermo* 216.10–11 (trans. my own).
121. *Sermo* 216.2 and 8 (trans. my own).
122. *Sermo* 216.3 (trans. my own).
123. *Sermo* 216.2 (trans. my own).

implanted within their hearts; they would enjoy its power pulsing through their bodies; their hearts would no longer mirror only the tumult and transience of earthly life, but would begin to reflect the harmony and constancy of the upperworldly, that orderly procession of the stars and spheres of heaven.

A PACT AMONG PEARL-MERCHANTS: THE CREED

On Saturday, two weeks before Easter, the *competentes* would gather for a solemn ceremony: the handing-over of the Creed (*traditio symboli*).[124] During this rite, Augustine would recite the Creed and then give a phrase-by-phrase explanation of it. It would be an important milestone. It would mark the first time the *competentes* had heard the Creed and would be the first of the mysteries—previously cloaked under the *disciplina arcani*—now open for their perusal. Four of Augustine's sermons from this occasion have come down to us: *Sermons 212, 213, 214,* and *On the Symbol.*[125] Over the next week, the *competentes* were expected, with

124. The *traditio symboli* occurred a week before the *redditio symboli* and *traditio orationis; the traditio orationis* occurred one week before the vigil with a solemn *redditio symboli* sometime that day: see *Sermones 213.8* (=Guelferbytanus 1.9); Guelferbytanus 1.1; 58.1 and 13; 59.1. See the discussion of this in Poque, "Introduction," 26, 59, and 65. Verbraken, "Les sermons CCXV et LVI de saint Augustin: *De symbolo* et *de oratione dominica,*" *Revue Bénédictine* 68 (1958) 5–6, proposes a different chronology: three weeks before Easter, the *traditio symboli;* two weeks before Easter, the first *redditio symboli* and the *traditio orationis;* a week before Easter, a second *redditio symboli* and a *redditio orationis;* Easter Vigil, a third *redditio symboli.* He offers no justification for his views. Poque, 26 note 2, finds this chronology not borne out by the texts themselves; see also the excursus "La entrega del simbolo y del padrenuestro," BAC 24:792–93.

125. *Sermo 212* does not seem to be a complete sermon, but rather an *exordium* delivered immediately prior to the *traditio* itself. *Sermo 213* and *Sermo* Guelf. 1 are the same, except that 213 is slightly abbreviated: it lacks both the *exordium* given prior to the *traditio* itself and the *peroratio.* The Latin title of *On the Symbol*—*De symbolo ad catechumenos*—was assigned by later editors, not by Augustine; it is somewhat inaccurate in that Augustine carefully reserved the term *catechumenus* for simple catechumens and spoke of candidates in the Lenten discipline as *competentes* or *baptizandi. Sermo 214* is unusual in several respects: its opening words seem to indicate that Augustine is a newly ordained presbyter. Yet at the end of no. 1, someone has inserted these words: "Post hanc praelocutionem pronuntiandum est totum symbolum, sine aliqua interposita disputatione: Credo in deum patrem omnipotentem, et cetera quae sequuntur in eo. Quod symbolum nostis quia scribi non solet. Quo dicto, adiungenda est haec disputatio." Who inserted these? Augustine, or a *notarius,* or some later copyist? Some have presumed that these are the words of a

the help of their godparents, to memorize the Creed word for word.[126]

Then the next Saturday, eight days before Easter, they would gather again for a handing-back of the Creed (redditio symboli). Here Augustine would test them individually to see if each could recite it exactly as it had been given.[127] This served as a sort of dress rehearsal for the solemn redditio held on Holy Saturday at which they would stand before the assembled faithful—as Victorinus once had—and publicly proclaim the Creed.[128] After this dress rehearsal, Augustine would then give the competentes a second sermon on it. Only one of his sermons from this occasion has survived: Sermon 215. In these sermons, Augustine sometimes handed on the Creed he had learned in Milan and other times handed on the one used in North Africa.[129] (See chart 14.)

Both the traditio and redditio symboli apparently took place within a liturgical context. It is unclear, however, whether these rites were inserted into the regular Saturday liturgy (that is, sometime between the dismissal of the catechumens and the Eucharist) or whether they were free-standing liturgies. As we saw, Ambrose and the competentes had retired to the baptistery for the handing-over of the Creed; if the same tradition existed in Hippo, then Augustine and the competentes would have gathered in a wing separate from but connected to the main basilica, a wing which had both the font and a large adjoining vestibule.[130]

---

copyist. However, Verbraken, "Le sermon CCXIV de saint Augustine pour la tradition du symbole," Revue Bénédictine 72 (1962) 7–21, thinks that Augustine inserted them, and presumes that this means that this sermon was not actually delivered by Augustine, but was a model composed for presbyters charged with this work (i.e., similar to the sample addresses in De catechizandis rudibus). He disregards the Maurists' suggestion—too quickly, I believe—that Augustine may have retouched an earlier sermon for the benefit of fellow presbyters involved in the same work as he.

126. Sermo Guelf. 1.11.

127. Sermo 215.1.

128. Sermo 58.1.

129. For a discussion of this, see Kelly, Early Christian Creeds, 172–81; Poque, "Introduction," 62–63. Sermo 212 is hard to judge since it is not a commentary on each phrase of the Creed as the others are, but simply a prelude to the traditio; Kelly lists it with those commenting on the Milanese Creed while Poque claims that some of its phrasing reflects the African Creed.

130. There are certain passing remarks that seem to indicate that Augustine also held the traditio symboli in the baptistery complex. In Sermo 213.8, Augus-

In the *exordium* of these sermons, Augustine would stress the importance of memorizing the Creed. Typically he would suggest mnemonic techniques: "Say it on your beds; ponder it in the streets; do not forget it during meals; and even when your body sleeps, keep watch over it in your heart."[131] This memorization was meant, in part, to preserve its secrecy: "No one writes the creed so that it can be read; . . . let your memory be your codex."[132] But Augustine insisted that this had a deeper pedagogical significance: "You will believe what you hear yourself saying, and your lips will repeat what you believe."[133] Moreover, he felt that by repeating it, they were not simply inscribing words in their memory; they were also internalizing truth, learning it "by heart" in the truest sense of the term. This had theological implications. Augustine would cite Jeremiah 31:33—God would write a new covenant on people's hearts—and claim:

"The creed is learned by listening; it is written, not on tablets nor on any material, but on the heart. He who has called you to his Kingdom and glory will grant that, when you have been reborn by his grace and by the Holy Spirit, it will be written in your hearts, so that you may love what you believe and that, through love, faith may work in you and that you—no longer fearing punishment like slaves, but loving justice like the freeborn—may become pleasing to the Lord God, the giver of all good things."[134]

Augustine's concern was not knowledge per se, but knowledge that stirred up love, and not simply love that moved the heart, but love that ignited wise, justice-filled living. Thus he distinguished belief from understanding, and argued that while belief should lead to practice, it was practice that made authentic under-

---

tine seems to point in the direction of the font ("Ecce venturi estis ad fontem sanctum") In 213.11, he tells the *competentes* that they will return to this spot for an all-night prayer vigil: ". . . et quomodo vigiletis ad gallicantum, ad orationes quas *hic* celebratis." On the location of the outer vestibule (*catechumeneum*) and baptistery, see Marec, *Monuments chrétiens d'Hippone*, 100–112; Marrou, "La Basilique chrétienne d'Hippone," 149–50.

131. *Sermo* 215.1 (trans. my own). Cf. *De symbolo ad catechumenos* 1.1.

132. *De symbolo ad catechumenos* 1.1 (trans. Marie Liguori, FC 27:289). See also *Sermo* 212.2; *De fide et symbolo* 1.1.

133. *De symbolo ad catechumenos* 1.1 (Liguori, 289).

134. *Sermo* 212.2 (Muldowney, 120–21—altered). See also *De symbolo ad catechumenos* 1.1.

standing possible: "May this belief imbue your hearts and guide you in professing it. On hearing this, believe so that you may understand, so that by putting into practice what you believe you may be able to understand it."[135] Augustine would reassure the *competentes* not to be nervous about the handing back of the Creed: that catechists were not like schoolteachers of the day who used "canes and rods" on those who failed to memorize properly; that "though one may err in the words," one should "not err in the faith" they expressed.[136]

Augustine admitted that even though the precise wording of the Creed had been withheld until that day, the *competentes* were already familiar with its contents:

"These truths, that you are about to receive, that you will commit to memory and profess in words, are neither new nor unfamiliar to you. For you are used to hearing them laid out in a variety of ways in holy Scripture and in sermons given in church. But now they are to be handed over to you gathered together, compressed down, and arranged in a fixed order: so that your faith may be well grounded, your public profession prepared for, and your memory not overburdened."[137]

Augustine, like Cyril and Ambrose, saw the Creed as a compendium of the core elements of biblical faith. Thus one finds Augustine making few points in these catecheses that do not appear elsewhere in his public sermons. In other words, the Creed's wording may have been secret, but both its tenets and his explanation of them were very much part of the public domain. Yet both the Creed itself and the catecheses on it served an urgent pedagogical need. As Augustine makes clear in this passage and as we saw in the last chapter, the *competentes* had, as catechumens, learned Scripture in a wide variety of ways. They had, of course, heard the texts proclaimed and had chanted the psalms. But they had also listened to Augustine's long and frequent sermons, witnessing the way he had unfolded Scripture's twists and

135. *Sermo* 214.10 (Muldowney, 141). See also *De symbolo ad catechumenos* 2.4; *Sermo* 212.1.

136. *Sermo* Guelf. 1.11 (trans. my own). See the discussion of school discipline in Marrou, *History of Education in Antiquity*, 272–73; also *Confessiones* 1.14.

137. *Sermo* 214.1 (trans. my own). See also *De symbolo ad catechumenos* 1.1; *Sermo* 212.2; *De fide et symbolo* 1.1.

turns, the way he had elided disparate episodes through a cross-weave of verbal echoes, the way he had compressed complex themes into musical one-liners. But in the routine of the catechumenate, the emphasis had been depth over breadth; the journey had focused more on Scripture's nooks and crannies than its broad outlines. Thus what the *competentes* needed at this juncture was to step back and scan the horizon Scripture provided, to drink in its terrain in a single glimpse.

The Creed offered them a map by which to read this biblical terrain. Its brevity meant that it marked out complex depths with a few highly evocative signposts. For this reason, Augustine, like Ambrose and Theodore, would stress the Creed's compression: that from "a few words, much instruction may be drawn; . . . see how quickly it is said and how much it means."[138] Yet its truths were much more than propositions one assented to; they were to shape practice and link one to a community of searchers. To dramatize this, Augustine drew on and expanded an analogy Ambrose had used:

"We call it *symbolum*—shipping in a [business] term by a kind of metaphor: after all, merchants draw up among themselves a *symbolum*, a pact of fidelity by which they hold together their alliance. Your alliance too is a spirited partnership, for you are like brokers [bound together] by a quest for a valuable pearl: that is, the charity that the Holy Spirit will pour down into your hearts."[139]

Whereas Ambrose had used this financial analogy to warn of the perils of credal fraud, Augustine used it to instill a positive sense of solidarity: by reciting this symbol, one vowed to one's fellow pilgrims to share in their common search for that pearl of great price, charity.

After introductory comments of this sort, Augustine would pause. The *notarii* who recorded these addresses would stop writing, either marking the spot or breaking off altogether.[140] It was a solemn moment. Augustine would then formally hand over the

138. *Sermo* 213.1 (Muldowney, 121—altered). Cf. *Enchiridion* 2.7.
139. *Sermo* 212.1 (trans. my own).
140. In *Sermo* Guelf. 1.2, the *notarius* breaks off at the words, "Hoc est symbolum," and then picks up again noting "Et post symbolum." In *Sermo* 212.2, the *notarius* breaks off completely after the sentence beginning "Hoc est symbolum . . ." See also Augustine's or the *notarius's* insertion in *Sermo* 214.1.

Creed, reciting it slowly and in its entirety. The words, while not unheard of, were still part of the hidden lore: the Creed was a *symbolum*, a secret "password" that marked one off as an orthodox Christian.[141] Just to hear these words meant the *competentes* were passing an important threshold.

After this solemn recitation, Augustine would begin a phrase-by-phrase exposition, treating the wording of the Creed with the same minute attention he gave to Scripture. And, as might be expected, he would dip into his standard repertoire of rhetorical devices to tease out the Creed's meaning. Let me trace some of the most common of these. First, he would frame many matters paradoxically. For instance, he would speak of the incarnation as a "lofty lowly birth."[142] Sometimes he placed paradoxes in parallel sequence:

"By taking on the shape of a slave, the invisible [Word] became visible because he was born of the Holy Spirit and the Virgin Mary.
By taking on the shape of a slave, the all-powerful one became weak because he suffered under Pontius Pilate.
By taking on the shape of a slave, the immortal one died because he was crucified and was buried. . . .
In the shape of a slave, he will come to judge the living and the dead, for
in this shape he wanted to be a companion of the dead just as he is the life of the living."[143]

This sequence served a dual purpose: pedagogically, it aided memorizing by juxtaposing opposites; theologically, it joined event with meaning, setting in high relief the scope and scale of the divine condescension. Often Augustine used paradoxes to hold together different aspects of his theology: for instance, he noted that just as Mary gave birth to Christ and remained a virgin, so the Church would give birth to the *competentes* and yet remain a virgin, and that by both births the body of Christ was born, first as head, then as members.[144] By this simple paradox, he linked

141. *Sermo* 214.12. This idea figures prominently in Rufinus, *Expositio symboli* 2. See Kelly, *Early Christian Creeds*, 52–61.
142. *De symbolo ad catechumenos* 3.6 (trans. my own).
143. *Sermo* 212.1 (trans. my own). See also *Sermo* 215.5.
144. *Sermo* 213.7. See also *Sermo* 72A.7 (= Denis 25); *De sancta virginitate* 2.2.

Christology with ecclesiology, Mariology with sacramental theology.

Second, Augustine resorted, as usual, to rhyming antitheses. For instance, in *Sermon 214*, he juxtaposed Christ's two births—from the Father and from Mary—and stressed the marvel of each:

Illa est de patre	This one is from the Father
sine matre,	without a mother;
ista de matre	that one is from a mother
sine patre:	without a father;
illa est sine aliquo tempore,	this one is outside time,
ista in acceptabili tempore:	that one, in an acceptable time;
illa aeterna,	this one is eternal,
ista opportuna:	that one, timely;
illa sine corpore	this one, in heart of the Father
in sinu patris,	without a body;
ista cum corpore	that one, with a body
quo non uiolata	without violating
est uirginitas matris:	the virginity of the mother;
illa sine ullo sexu,	this one [happens] without sex;
ista sine ullo	that one [happened] without
uirili complexu.	a man's embrace.[145]

Similarly, he used rhyming antitheses to teach how Christ's divinity gave his humanity a unique configuration:

Nemo nostrum	No one of us
quia uult nascitur,	is born because we will it;
et nemo nostrum	and no one of us
quando uult moritur. . . .	dies when we will it. . . .
quomodo uoluit	[But] just as [Christ] willed it
natus est de uirgine,	he was born of a virgin;
quomodo uoluit	just as he willed it,
mortuus est in cruce.	he died on the cross.
Quidquid uoluit	Whatever he willed,
fecit:	that he did:
quia sic erat homo,	because he was human
ut lateret deus,	in such a way that God lay hidden,
susceptor deus,	God [becoming] the assumer,
susceptus homo,	humankind the assumed,

145. *Sermo* 214.6 (BAC 24:169; trans. my own).

unus Christus deus	[and thus] the one Christ, God
et homo.	and human.[146]

Third, Augustine would use analogies to explain difficult ideas. Sometimes he used them to accent the discontinuity between human experience and the divine nature. Thus to explain the equality of Father and Son, he noted: "Are we going to be in [God's] family in a position similar to a large household where there is a patriarch who has a son, so that we too shall call [one] 'the greater Master' and [the other] 'the lesser Master'? Shun the thought."[147] Other times, he used analogies to stress continuities between human experience and the divine nature. For instance, to explain the Nicene idea that the Son was "one in being" with the Father, he resorted to earthy, rather humorous examples:

"Consider earth-bound, mortal creatures: whatever something is, that is what it gives birth to. A human being does not give birth to an ox; a sheep does not give birth to a dog, nor a dog to a sheep. . . . A mortal being gives birth to what it is; an immortal one, to what it is . . ."[148]

Still other times, he would use a mixed analogy, one that revealed both continuities and discontinuities. For instance, while explaining the eternal birth of the Son, Augustine appealed to the classic phrase "light from light" and asked his audience to tell him which "gave birth" to which: fire generating the firelight, or firelight generating the fire. The *competentes* then shouted out: "fire, then firelight; not firelight, then fire." He acknowledged their shouted answers and noted that "an inborn wisdom makes you all cry out"—alluding to his idea that Christ as inner teacher had prompted their response. He then noted that the analogy showed that the "very instant fire begins, immediately it brings forth firelight." Thus the Father as fire instantly begets the Son as firelight. Yet this natural analogy only took one so far: while fires and firelight occur simultaneously, they have a beginning, while the Father and Son do not.[149] All three of these examples give a

---

146. *De symbolo ad catechumenos* 3.8 (CCSL 46:191; trans. my own).

147. Ibid., 2.4 (Liguori, 292—altered).

148. Ibid., 2.3 (trans. my own). Cf. *De fide et symbolo* 5.8.

149. *De symbolo ad catechumenos* 3.8 (Liguori, 296—altered). This appeal to the audience to elicit answers to his questions was a technique he used from time to time: see *Sermo* 265C.2 (=Guelf. 20).

glimpse into Augustine's gifts as a teacher. The question underlying each—the relationship of the Father to the Son—had formed the heart of the Arian crisis and had embroiled theologians of the previous century in some of the most complex wrangling the Church has ever witnessed. However, Augustine, with a deft use of analogies, was able to cut through the complexity while at the same time maintaining the necessary precision.

Fourth, he sometimes employed allegory. It was natural for him to invoke biblical allegories in an exposition on the Creed, for as noted earlier, he viewed the Creed as a dense summary of biblical teaching. For example, while discussing the meaning of "one baptism for the forgiveness of sins," he wove a complex allegory linking the Exodus, the Cross, and baptism:

"Your sins will be like the Egyptians following the Israelites, pursuing you only up to the Red Sea. What does up to the Red Sea mean? Up to the font, consecrated by the cross and blood of Christ. For, because that font is red, it reddens [the water]. . . . Baptism is signified by the sign of the cross, that is, by the water in which you are immersed and through which you pass, as it were, in the Red Sea. Your sins are your enemies. They follow you, but only up to the Red Sea. When you have entered, you will escape; they will be destroyed, just as the Egyptians were engulfed by the waters while the Israelites escaped on dry land."[150]

This explanation of baptism was one Augustine alluded to frequently, even in public sermons. Here he develops it at length. The turns he makes are easier to intuit than analyze. The core he relied on were various themes already paired within the New Testament itself: (1) the Exodus and the Cross; (2) the Cross and baptism; (3) Exodus and baptism; (4) the Cross and forgiveness; (5) baptism and forgiveness. In this passage, Augustine does not treat these five paired themes separately—as others often did—but instead weaves them into a complex, interlocking network of ideas, events, and images which nonetheless form a suggestive, memorable whole. Thus the "red water" of the font—red presumably because it was lined with red mosaic tiles—suggested both the Red

150. *Sermo* 213.8 (Muldowney, 128). This same theme appears in somewhat less developed form in *Sermo* 352.3 and 6; *Tractatus in evangelium Ioannis* 11.4; 28.9; *Enarrationes in psalmos* 80.38. See the excursus, "Exodo y vida cristiana," in BAC 7:745-46.

Sea and the blood of the Cross. The immersion in the water both reenacted the passage through the Red Sea, a passage from slavery to freedom, and bathed one in the blood of Christ, marking a participation in his death. By this immersion and passage, sins would drown in the baptismal pool as the Egyptians drowned in the Red Sea, thus linking the action of baptism with the idea of forgiveness.

Augustine had reason for explaining the tenets of the Creed with such care. First, he wanted to shape the self-understanding of the *competentes*, to firm up their identity as orthodox Christians. Thus he referred to the Creed as "a password [by which] the faithful Christian is recognized"[151] or as a "mirror [in] which you call your faith to mind and in which you see yourselves."[152] In addition, he knew that whenever his *competentes* strolled through the streets or marketplace, they would rub shoulders with pagans, Arians, Donatists, and Manichees, and these encounters could lead, often enough, to an exchange of jibes or a heated religious debate. So, in these sermons, he sought to arm his hearers, to help them combat competing religious views.

While Augustine did not often name opponents, still he would offer rebuttals to contested points. Against the pagans, he insisted on the resurrection of the body—both Jesus' and ours—since "the resurrection of the dead distills our faith-life out from the faithless 'dead.'"[153] Moreover, he reminded the *competentes* that, as catechumens, they had "received the sign of the cross on the forehead, as though on a house of shame" and so need not "fear the tongue of others" nor "fear the shame of the cross."[154] Against the Manichees, he insisted that the creator did not create evil: God "did not make [human beings] evil even though he created humankind, because he created their nature, not the sins which are contrary to nature."[155] Against the Arians, he insisted that the Word was not a creature nor had any beginning. In fact, Augus-

151. *Sermo* 214.12 (Muldowney, 142). Cf. Rufinus, *Expositio symboli* 2.

152. *Sermo* 58.13 (trans. my own).

153. *Sermo* 215.6 (trans. my own). See Marrou, *The Resurrection and Saint Augustine's Theology of Human Values*, St. Augustine Lecture Series, trans. Maria Consolata (Villanova: Villanova University Press, 1966).

154. *Sermo* 215.5 (Muldowney, 147).

155. *Sermo* 214.3 (Muldowney, 133). The whole section on God's omnipotence seems designed to combat Manichean views.

tine took the old Arian slogan—"there was a 'when' when the Word was not"—and turned it upside down: "Do not imagine any span of eternity when the Father was and the Son was not. From when the Father, from then the Son."[156] Against the Apollinarian view that the divine Word had replaced the human mind in Christ, Augustine insisted:

"The Word assumed a complete human being: that is, a reason-imbued soul and body so that the one Christ, the one Son of God, might not only be Word, but Word and human—a whole being [that] is the Son of God the Father according to the Word and Son of Man according to his humanity."[157]

Against the Donatists, Augustine would insist that rebaptism was horribly wrong, that baptism left an indelible "character" in the same way that Roman soldiers received a "brand" or "tattoo" marking them as soldiers.[158] Against Donatist claims that only Africa had the one true Church, he would insist that the Church included "however many faithful" there might be "in this city, this region, this province, across the sea, in the whole world."[159] Finally, against Donatist views on the pristine holiness of the Church, he insisted that while the Church was indeed holy, it nonetheless "tolerates the wicked . . . for the sake of the grain now growing amid the chaff."[160]

156. *De symbolo ad catechumenos* 3.8 (trans. my own).
157. *Sermo* 214.6 (trans. my own). Cf. *De fide et symbolo* 5.8; *Confessiones* 7.19. As Brian Daley notes ("A Humble Mediator," 103-4): "Drawing on the Neoplatonic philosophical tradition—the tradition that was for him the key to making intellectual sense of the Christian Gospel—Augustine understood the human soul to be a complete spiritual substance, independent of the body it vivifies, in control of the body, yet existing sufficient to itself. The soul, he assumed, is incorporeal, always engaged in knowledge and desire, immune to death and dissolution; more important, perhaps, it is the soul that is the real 'self' of a person, a person's subjective and unifying center. Throughout his career, then, Augustine seems to have seen it as metaphysically necessary . . . that the human soul of Christ should be the connecting link, the point of contact, between the divine Logos, the creative 'mind' of God, and Jesus the man." On Apollinarius, see Grillmeier, *Christ in Christian Tradition*, 220-37 and 322-28; G. L. Prestige, *Fathers and Heretics: Six Studies in Dogmatic Faith* (London: SPCK, 1940) 94-119.
158. *De symbolo ad catechumenos* 8.16. On the idea of baptism as a military tattoo, see *De baptismo contra Donatistas* 1.4.5; *Epistola* 185.43.
159. *Sermo* 213.7 (Muldowney, 126).
160. *Sermo* 214.11 (Muldowney, 141).

North Africa was racked by vociferous religious debates; and neither Augustine, his congregation, nor their opponents were ecumenists. He thus saw the Creed as "your tunic against shame, your armor against adversity."[161] In other words, the Creed was to serve the *competentes* both as a weapon for warding off opponents and as a tool for discernment—to help them sort through competing claims about God, about the world, about the Church, about sacraments. It thus marked off what was essential and set out a core which distinguished orthodox Christians from their competitors.

As usual, Augustine attended to the feelings of his hearers. For instance, he knew that discussing the meaning of Christ as the "judge of the living and the dead" would rouse the *competentes'* deepest fears. North Africans tended to think of God as a fearsome judge. It was a view Augustine both shared and modified. Here he offered the *competentes* a quite different and moving counterimage:

"If you were to have a case tried before a certain judge and were to prepare by hiring a lawyer, . . . and if, before he finished [preparing your case], you should hear that he has been made the judge, how you would rejoice! For the one who was your lawyer just a little while ago will now be your judge! Now the Lord himself pleads for us; he himself intervenes for us. We have him as our lawyer. Why should we fear him as our judge? Instead, let us hope he will be our judge—for we have already sent him ahead as our lawyer."[162]

Here analogy becomes parable. Augustine joins two biblical images, Christ as judge and Christ as advocate, but in joining them gives them an unexpected slant. He draws on an image from the Letter to the Hebrews—Christ as high-priest pleads for us—and converts it into a juridical image (cf. John 14:16): Christ pleads for us as a lawyer. He then adds a twist: Christ our lawyer does double duty by serving simultaneously as judge. Thus the *competentes* would not get an impartial trial, but a biased one, one rigged in their favor. With this imagistic sleight of hand, Augustine sought to counterbalance the old fearsome image of Christ's judgment and

161. *Sermo* 58.13 (trans. my own). See also *De fide et symbolo* 1.1.
162. *Sermo* 213.5 (trans. my own).

make it an icon of the radical mercy of God. By it, he hoped to quell the *competentes'* fears and at the same time adjust their unconscious image of God.

THE TWO WINGS OF PRAYER: THE OUR FATHER

One week before the Easter Vigil, Augustine would test the *competentes'* ability to recite the Creed. On one occasion, some did not fare well. Augustine told them not to panic; they still had a week to master it.[163] Sometime that same day, though probably not at the same service, they were handed on a second treasure: the Lord's Prayer.[164] This so-called *traditio orationis*, like the ceremonies surrounding the Creed, took place within a liturgical setting. Once again, we do not know whether this rite was inserted into the regular liturgy or whether it was free-standing. We do know that some of the faithful attended, for on one occasion Augustine turned to them and gave them a brief exhortation.[165] We also know that during this rite a Gospel text, Matthew 6:7-15, was read and, in fact, served as the medium for the formal handing-over of the prayer.[166] After the reading, Augustine would give a brief sermon on it, explaining it line by line, much as he did with the Creed. Four of these have come down to us: *Sermons* 56–59. The *competentes* were to memorize the Lord's Prayer as they had the Creed. They would also be expected to hand it back sometime on Holy Saturday, though this handing-back of the prayer seems to have occurred separately from the solemn handing-back of the Creed.[167] Augustine reassured the *competentes* that memorizing the prayer would pose few problems: for, while the faithful might hear the Creed spoken aloud only three times a year, "the Lord's prayer is said daily in the church before the altar of God."[168]

163. *Sermo* 58.1.

164. The timing of this rite can be pieced together from comments in *Sermones* 58.1 and 13; 59.1; 213.8 (=Guelf. 1.9); see also Poque, "Introduction," 65.

165. *Sermo* 58.7.

166. *Sermo* 58.1.

167. *Sermo* 59.1 (MacMullen, 288); see also *Sermo* 227. In *Sermo* 58.13, Augustine distinguishes the two *redditiones*. Theodore, *Catechetical Homily* 11.1, had insisted that the Lord's Prayer "be learned and kept in memory by those who come near to the faith of baptism."

168. *Sermo* 58.12 (MacMullen, 288). The three times that the faithful might have heard the Creed were: (1) the *traditio symboli* two weeks before Easter, (2) the preliminary *redditio symboli* one week before Easter, and (3) the solemn *redditio symboli* on Holy Saturday.

These sermons give the first clear example of this North African rite (though Tertullian's sermon *On Prayer* and Cyprian's treatise *On the Lord's Prayer* may have been prompted by it).[169] Because of this local tradition, Augustine's catechetical calendar differed from that of his mentor. As we saw earlier, Ambrose (and Cyril) explained the Our Father not during Lent, but during Easter Week, and did so because of its place within the Liturgy of the Eucharist. Augustine's timetable was more like that of his contemporary, Theodore of Mopsuestia, who explained the Lord's Prayer during Lent and linked it with the Creed as part of the necessary spiritual equipment for baptism.

Augustine typically began his catechesis by correlating the Creed with the Lord's Prayer. He did so because he believed that these two traditions, like all liturgical traditions, arose from and reflected some subtle inner logic. And as he saw it, these two—in both their content and order of delivery—flowed from a logic voiced by Paul: "How then shall they call upon [God] in whom they have not believed?" (Rom 10:14). According to Augustine, this meant:

"You have not first been taught the Lord's Prayer and then the creed. You have been taught the creed first, so that you may know what to believe, and afterwards the prayer, so that you may know whom to call upon. The creed contains what you are to believe; the prayer, what you are to ask for."[170]

For Augustine, the proximity of the two meant that *orthodoxia* ("right belief") was necessarily linked with *eusébeia* ("right worship"): the Creed gave the "what" of right belief, while the Our Father gave the "to whom" and "how" of right praise.[171]

Like his predecessors, Augustine insisted that the Our Father was *the* model of Christian prayer. Like them, he noted its compact form and argued that "our Lord pruned away long-windedness" and that one need not speak as though one were "teaching God by a flood of words"; rather what mattered was

---

169. De Puniet, "Catéchumenat," 2587. However, both Tertullian and Cyprian seem to refer to the Eucharist in such a way that presumes that the audience knew its shape—implying that their works were, in the main, intended for the faithful and not *competentes.*

170. *Sermo* 56.1 (trans. Denis J. Kavanaugh, FC 11:240). This appears in the *exordium* of each of the four: *Sermones* 57.1; 58.1; 59.1. Cf. *Enchiridion* 2.7.

171. *Enchiridion* 1.2–3.

"piety, not wordiness."[172] As Augustine saw it, the heart was the focus: "what you say, say it in your hearts," and the words themselves give "what our desires ought to be."[173] He would play on the dual meaning of "petition" (prex)—both a genre of prayer and a legal term—and would expand on his paradoxical image of Christ as lawyer and judge: "We have good hope of winning our case since such a [fine] jurist has composed the suit for us. . . . He who will be our judge is [now] our lawyer."[174]

After the exordium, he noted the prayer's opening words: Christians dared to call God "Father." On one occasion, he described this as a birthright extended to the unborn still in the Church's womb:

"You see, you have begun to have God for your Father, and you will have him so when you are born anew. But even now, before you are born, you have been conceived of his seed, for you are about to be born of the font, which is, as it were, the womb of the Church."[175]

Another time, he resorted to a sort of antithetical analogy and contrasted Roman anxieties over having large families with the Church's marital abandon:

"Parents sometimes, when they have one or two or three children, fear to give birth to any more, lest they reduce the rest to being beggars. But because the inheritance [God] promises us is such that many may possess it without anyone being put in a bind, [God] has called into his family the peoples of the nations; and the only Son has numberless brothers and sisters who say, 'Our Father . . .' "[176]

Augustine's hearers knew well why Romans practiced birth control and infanticide: they did not want family wealth divided up

172. Sermo 56.4 (trans. my own).
173. Sermo 56.4-5 (Kavanaugh, 242-43).
174. Sermo 58.1 (trans. my own).
175. Sermo 56.5 (Kavanaugh, 242-43); see also Sermo 59.3. Sometimes Augustine would claim that, strictly speaking, only the baptized could pray the Lord's Prayer: De symbolo ad catechumenos 8.16; Sermo 181.6.
176. Sermo 57.2 (MacMullen, 280-81—altered). A similar antithetical analogy discussing adoption habits occurs in Tractatus in evangelium Ioannis 2.13.

between too many beneficiaries.[177] As Augustine saw it, since the inheritance won by Christ knew no such human limits, the Church did not need to exercise such marital restraint. Moreover, calling God "Father" had implications for the social order:

"We all say in common, 'Our Father.' What an honor! This the emperor says, and this the beggar says; this the slave says, and this his master says. Therefore they have come to understand that they are brothers, seeing they have one Father. Now let not the master disdain to have his slave for a brother, seeing the Lord Christ has deigned to have him for a brother."[178]

Here Augustine followed the pattern of social critique found in Paul's Letter to Philemon: while he by no means denounced the institution of slavery, he did insist that the Christ-event required a countercultural understanding of human dignity.

After this, Augustine took up the petitions of the Lord's Prayer one by one. To aid the *competentes'* understanding, he suggested a mnemonic: "Of the seven petitions, three refer to life eternal, four to life here and now."[179] Augustine, like Cyprian, read the first three in a parallel manner. He claimed that prayer would not make God's name holy, nor would it bring on the coming kingdom, nor would it cause God's will to be done. These were simply present facts or future inevitabilities, and prayer did nothing to alter them; rather "it is for ourselves, not for God, that we pray."[180] Thus one asked not that God's name be holy, but that it "may be made holy in us"; not that the kingdom come, but that God "would make us worthy of the kingdom"; not that God's will be done, but that it "be done in us."[181]

As usual, Augustine indulged in allegorical excursus, for he saw in individual petitions a dense cluster of meanings. For instance, he claimed that in asking for "daily bread" one begged not only for bread, but for all the necessities of life: food and drink, cloth-

177. On Roman birth control practices and concerns about patrimony, see Veyne, *History of Private Life*, 9–14, 139–59.

178. *Sermo* 58.2 (MacMullen, 284—altered). See also *Sermo* 59.2.

179. *Sermo* 59.8 (trans. my own). See also *Sermones* 56.19; 57.6; 58.12; *Enchiridion* 30.115; *De sermone Domini in monte* 2.10.36.

180. *Sermo* 57.4 (MacMullen, 281). Cf. Cyprian, *De oratione dominica* 12–14.

181. *Sermo* 59.3-5 (MacMullen, 289—altered). See also *Sermones* 56.5-7; 57.3-6; 58.3-4.

ing and shelter.[182] At the same time and with the same phrase, one asked for the "bread of the Word"—whether as lections proclaimed, hymns sung, or sermons preached—as well as for "the eucharist, our daily food."[183] In mentioning Eucharist, he remained, because of the *disciplina arcani*, deliberately vague and said only that, after baptism, "you shall receive what the faithful receive."[184] He would then set these daily "breads" within an eschatological horizon: after this life, one would seek neither "that bread hunger seeks" nor "the sacrament of the altar," neither the bread of the Word "which we now speak" nor the "sacred codex which is read"; after this life, one would drink in not "roundabout words," but that one Word which the angels "feed on" and which causes them to "belch" contentedly in praise.[185] This reading differed markedly from Ambrose's: whereas Ambrose tended to leap immediately to the spiritual meaning and read the text only as referring to "the bread of eternal life," Augustine insisted that God fed the whole person and met our dual needs, both "the body's food" and "the spirit's nourishment."[186]

Usually Augustine devoted the most attention to the petition on forgiveness. In part, this was the emphasis he found in the Matthean text (Matt 6:14-15), and he wanted to stress what Christ had especially stressed.[187] In part, this was because he knew that lack of forgiveness was a local vice; thus this petition seemed "especially applicable to you."[188] People in North Africa could harbor fierce resentments and would thirst for revenge against those who had insulted them or those they envied. Augustine's congregation brought their ferocity to prayer: "Each day people come, bend their knees, touch the earth with their foreheads, sometimes moistening their faces with tears, and in all this great humility and distress say: 'Lord, avenge me. Kill my enemy.'"[189] It was

182. *Sermo* 57.7. See also *Sermones* 56.10; 59.6.

183. *Sermo* 57.7 (MacMullen, 282). See also *Sermones* 56.10; 58.5; 59.6; *De sermone Domini in monte* 2.7.25-27; *Enchiridion* 30.115.

184. *Sermo* 56.10 (MacMullen, 277).

185. *Sermo* 59.6 (MacMullen, 289).

186. *Sermo* 57.7 (trans. my own). Cf. Ambrose, *De sacramentis* 5.24-25.

187. *Sermo* 57.12.

188. *Sermo* 56.13 (Kavanaugh, 251).

189. *Sermo* 211.6 (Muldowney, 115—altered). Augustine describes the same mixing of vengeance and religiosity in the way his congregation sang the imprecatory psalms: see *Sermo* 22A.1 (=Mai 15).

against such attitudes that Augustine preached. He would beg the *competentes* not to let the sun go down on their anger, to see not the mote in their enemies' eye but the beam in their own. He would invoke analogies:

"If scorpions or asps were in your houses, how you would slave to clean them out—so you could live at home in safety! Yet you are angry—and it is a long-standing anger in your hearts: there is so much hatred, so many beams, so many scorpions, so many snakes. Are you not willing to clean out the house of God—your heart?"[190]

He would insist that their enemies, too, had a God-given dignity: "You have a soul; he does too. You are flesh; he is too. He is of the same stuff as you: from earth you both were made; from the Lord you both were in-souled. He is what you are. Look on him as your brother."[191] Thus when praying for their enemies, "Let your prayer be against the malice of your enemy; may his malice die, but may he live. . . . If his malice should die, then you would have lost an enemy and gained a friend."[192] Augustine stressed that this petition was "a promise, a covenant": that God would forgive them only if they forgave others. He also noted that many spoke words of forgiveness while continuing to nurse resentment in their heart. The *competentes*, by contrast, were to "forgive everything": if so, they would "come forth from the font, as from the presence of your Lord, with the assurance that all your debts are forgiven."[193]

Typically, Augustine would join exhortations on forgiveness with ones on almsgiving. This link might seem odd at first sight, but he habitually linked them because he found them linked in one of his favorite biblical texts: "Forgive and it will be forgiven you, give and it will be given to you" (Luke 6:37-38).[194] He found the quote apt because it joined prayer to practice. To explain the connection, he used an analogy his seafaring congregation could appreciate:

190. *Sermo* 58.8 (trans. my own).
191. *Sermo* 56.14 (trans. my own).
192. *Sermo* 56.14 (Kavanaugh, 253).
193. *Sermo* 56.13 (Kavanaugh, 251). Cf. *Sermo* 58.7.
194. See, for example, *Sermones* 58.10; 60.12; 83.2; 114.5; 205.3; 206.2. The monetary image is, of course, built into the Lord's Prayer itself.

"The baptized . . . pick up some debts due to human weakness. Although not shipwrecked, still the bilge-pumps must be used, for if the pumps are not used, water may slowly seep in so that the whole ship sinks. By praying this, we pump out the bilge-water. Yet we should not only pray, but also give alms. For, when we use the bilge-pumps that the ship not sink, we use both our voices and our hands. We use our voices when we say: 'Forgive us our debts, as we also forgive our debtors'; we use our hands when we act: 'Break your bread with the hungry, and bring the homeless into your house' and 'Stock up alms in the heart of the poor, and this itself will plead for you before the Lord.' "[195]

Augustine insisted that the work of prayer was coordinated with the work of our hands; otherwise, want of charity sinks us. The Lord's Prayer was not just said, but enacted. It was thus a prayer set within the larger ritual of rectifying the social order. He also noted that when people stood with arms raised in the traditional *orant* position, they were like birds with outstretched wings:

"[As for justice,] do as much as you can do, give from what you can muster, do it with joy, and send up your prayer fearlessly. It will have two wings, a double alms. What do I mean, a 'double alms'? 'Forgive and it will be forgiven you; give and it will be given you.' One 'almsgiving' is what you do from the heart when you forgive your neighbor his sin. The other 'almsgiving' is what you do with your resources—when you hand out bread to the poor. Do both: that your prayer not be grounded because it lacks one wing."[196]

Here Augustine uses a mystagogical style. He weaves together: liturgical gesture (the *orant* position), a scriptural theme (Luke 6), and an analogy from nature (a bird ready to take flight). In so doing, he links prayer with practice, and a two-pronged practice at that: both words of forgiveness and works of justice.

Sometimes when treating forgiveness, Augustine would stress that the Church was an abode of sinners, a *corpus permixtum*. Baptism marked the forgiveness of sin, not its end. The Lord's Prayer

195. *Sermo* 56.11 (trans. my own). The bilge-water image appears also in *Sermo* 58.10 and *Tractatus in evangelium Ioannis* 12.14.

196. *Sermo* 58.10 (trans. my own). See also *Sermo* 205.3; 206.2 and 3.

thus offered a "daily baptism," a "daily cleansing."[197] And in
Sermon 56, he insisted he too was a sinner needing its cleansing:
"You might ask, 'And you, too?' I [must] answer back: 'Yes, me,
too!' 'You, reverend bishop—you, a debtor?' 'Yes, I am debtor as
you are.' "[198] This may seem a paltry admission, but it would
have discomfited his original audience. Augustine regularly
debunked the veneration North Africans accorded bishops. And
he would scandalize some in the fifth-century religious world with
book 10 of *The Confessions*, a meditation on abiding weaknesses
that plagued him long after his baptism, long after his consecration as bishop.[199] Such talk seemed to undermine the old baptismal ideology of a radically new life, a life free from the least taint
of sin, a complete restoration of our primeval Adamic innocence.
This ideology was still very much in vogue, as the Pelagian movement makes amply clear. Yet Augustine kept his theology close to
his experience, even at the cost of undermining a venerable view
of baptism. He was acutely sensitive to his own woundedness and
sinfulness and saw the same wounds and sins in the Church he
pastored. And he was even willing to dampen some of the *competentes'* enthusiasm, if only to spare them the harsh disillusion-
ment that he and others faced on the far side of baptism.

LENT AND THE MIDWIFE'S ART

At this juncture, perhaps more acutely than at any other in
Augustine's catechumenal works, one senses the chasm between
the ancient and the modern experience of Christianity. One con-
fronts in these Lenten catecheses themes that would become some
of ancient Christianity's more troubling legacy to later ages: its de-
monology, its sometimes austere views on the human body, its
religious in-fighting and intolerance, its language of soldiery and
slavery. This thought-world was one Augustine both shared in
and altered—moderating some trends, radicalizing others—and his
views, both positive and negative, would figure prominently
within the trajectory taken by Latin Christianity. However, as we
have seen, it is critical to understand how Augustine actually used

197. *Sermones* 213.8; 56.12; 59.7. He sometimes uses a medicinal analogy: e.g.,
Sermo 17.5; *De fide et operibus* 26.48. See also *Enchiridion* 19.71; *Sermo* 352.6.

198. *Sermo* 56.11 (trans. my own).

199. Brown, "Pelagius and His Supporters: Aims and Environment," *Religion and Society in the Age of Saint Augustine*, 199–200.

these themes and what he meant by them. In any case, the task at this point is not to assess this legacy, but to try to see—as much as can be seen—Augustine as a teacher of early fifth-century *competentes.*

For the *competentes* in Hippo, Lent was time in the womb, and like any pregnancy, it would be both a delicate and a dangerous moment. It was, in anthropological parlance, a "liminal" or "threshold" phase during which they found themselves marked off—physically, socially, ritually—as people in transition.[200] According to Augustine and the tradition he inherited from the New Testament, the *competentes* were being "rescued from the power of darkness and transferred into the kingdom of God's dazzling light" (1 Pet 2:9). It was a drama with cosmological implications. Because of this, patristic Christianity erected around the *competentes* a complex ritual, disciplinary, and catechetical apparatus that would, by turns, ease and provoke their passage. It would be a transition at once awesome and eerie, a time of unmaking and remaking, of sloughing off the old and marking out the new. It also meant entering into terrible ambiguity: not knowing what one would be on the other side. Not surprisingly, the *competentes* experienced what Augustine himself had experienced: excitement and fear, sharp-eyed zeal and self-searching doubts.

In this transition, Augustine played midwife, mixing firmness and gentleness: on the one hand, calling them not to flee the labor pangs, and on the other, encouraging them to look forward and love the new self coming to birth. The core curriculum had, it seems, a twofold movement. On the one hand, the *competentes* themselves performed certain actions: (1) bodily exercises (fasting, abstaining from bathing and sex, vigils); (2) introspective exercises (prayer, assessing the past, forgiving wrongs endured); and (3) social exercises (almsgiving, begging pardon). On the other hand, the faithful—sometimes the laity, sometimes the ministers— performed certain acts: (1) bearing witness through their presence at liturgies and through their routine living-out of the gospel; (2) expressing solidarity by prayer and by taking on, as much as possible, the same ascetical discipline; (3) scrutinizing not only the *competentes'* way of life, but also their physical health; (4) exorcis-

200. The term is that of Victor Turner. For a summary of Turner's and other anthropological interpretations of rites of passage, see Ronald Grimes, *Beginnings in Ritual Studies* (Lanham, Md.: University Press of America), 117–59.

ing them with invocations, imprecations, and exsufflation. The program was thoroughgoing enough that Augustine and his contemporaries thought of it more along the lines of a boot camp or fitness program than schooling. They presupposed—rightly or wrongly—that the *competentes* were the spiritually flabby, that they suffered from any of a host of addictions, and that these ailments had penetrated every fiber of their lives and could be healed only with a radical reshaping of habit that touched the whole person: physical, psychological, intellectual, social.

Within this complex educative process, verbal catechesis played a part. We know more about the highlights—the catecheses on the scrutiny, Creed, and Lord's Prayer—than the daily routine. But we do know that in all his catecheses, whether public or private, Augustine fashioned a cross-weave of doctrine and moral admonition. On the one hand, he sought to interpret the meaning of conversion, particularly as it played itself out within the disciplines and the rites of scrutiny. As before, he taught with images: from warfare, slavery, business, seafaring, agriculture, jurisprudence, athletics. And as before, he exploited rhetorical devices—paradoxes, aphorisms, rhymes, antitheses—to make his message memorable. He would stress, by turns, the struggle of conversion and the gratuity of God's action. He would play on dichotomous images from the New Testament and insist that baptism meant new life, a passage from darkness to light, from slavery to freedom; yet he balanced these with developmental images, insisting that conversion was lifelong, that one only slowly acquired virtue. He also moved against inherited views and insisted that baptism marked the forgiveness of sin, not its end, that this coming to birth needed to be set within an eschatological horizon, and that on this side of eschaton the Church would remain a mix of wheat and chaff.

Lent also served, catechetically, as a time for integration, for sorting out the essential from the peripheral. Thus Augustine, following local tradition, would hand on two brief compendia: the Creed, the "what" of right belief; and the Lord's Prayer, the "how" of right praise. These he asked his hearers to memorize— all the while insisting that one was not just memorizing words, but taking their truth to heart. Yet they were more. The Creed was a covenant which bound the *competentes* together, joining them as fellow seekers in a common search for God and for the pearl of charity. It also aided self-understanding: it was a password to certify membership, a mirror for introspection, armor against outsiders. In his catecheses on the Creed, Augustine led the *competentes* through familiar terrain, the biblical landscape. He mapped it not as he had done when they first entered the catechumenate, that is, by sketching the broad lines of the biblical narrative; rather he highlighted its subliminal threads and fundamental presuppositions.

As before, Augustine focused on the heart: encouraging fervor, soothing certain anxieties, stirring up others. He also sought to forge bonds of solidarity—binding his ministry to theirs, and theirs with his and with one another's; together, they were fellow new recruits who shared a common quest and a common process of conversion. Yet Augustine's core concern was Christian living. He thus called the *competentes* to forge a *habitus* of faith: to imitate seasoned veterans. He worried much about social habits: sexual standards, civil rancor, indifference to the plight of the poor. And he insisted if their prayer was to take flight, they would have to help rectify this broken social order. Ultimately, his criterion was a simple one: that the *competentes* had begun to live lives that resonated in harmony with baptism, that they bore witness to a faith that labored in love.

Chart 12
Sermons to the *Competentes*

Sermon	Verbraken #	Text	Trans
1. Lenten Discipline: to whole assembly, beginning of Lent			
205	205	BAC 24	FC 38
206	206	BAC 24	FC 38
207	207	BAC 24	FC 38
208	208	BAC 24	FC 38
209	209	BAC 24	FC 38
210	210	BAC 24	FC 38
De utilitate ieiunii (?)	---	CCSL 46	PS 85, FC 16
2. Scrutiny: to the competentes, *probably early in Lent*			
216	216	BAC 24	FC 38
3. Traditio symboli: to the competentes, *two weeks before vigil*			
212	212	BAC 24	FC 38, Weller
213 = Guelf 1	213	BAC 24	FC 38
214	214	BAC 24	FC 38
De symbolo ad catechumenos	---	CCSL 46	FC 27
4. Redditio symboli: to the competentes, *one week before vigil*			
215	215	BAC 24	FC 38
5. Traditio orationis: to the competentes, *one week before vigil*			
56	56	BAC 10	FC 11, Weller
57	57	BAC 10	NPNF 6
58	58	BAC 10	NPNF 6
59	59	BAC 10	NPNF 6
6. Other sermons in which competentes *are addressed*			
5	5	BAC 7	---
352	352	BAC 26	---
392	392	BAC 26	---

Weller = Philip T. Weller, *Selected Easter Sermons of Saint Augustine* (St. Louis: Herder Book Co., 1959)

Chart 13
Passing References to the Training of *Competentes*

Sermon/Work	Verbraken #	Text	Trans	Topic
227	227	BAC 24	FC 38	Fasting, exorcism, *traditio orationis*
228	228	BAC 24	FC 38	Catechetical outline for Lent
229 =Denis 6	229	BAC 24	FC 38	Enrollment, fasting, exorcism
351	351	BAC 26	---	Penitence of *competentes*
Confessiones	---	CCSL 27	Pine-Coffin	Turn in names
Contra Faustum	---	CSEL 25	NPNF 4	Faithful join in Lenten discipline
De baptismo	---	CSEL 51	NPNF 4	*Exsufflatio*
De civitate Dei	---	CSEL 47	Bettenson	*Cilicium*
De consensu evangelist.	---	CSEL 43	NPNF 6	Forty days, *cilicium*
De cura pro mortuis	---	CSEL 41	FC 27	Story of Curma
De fide et operibus	---	CSEL 41	FC 27	Principles and criteria
De fide et symbolo	---	CSEL 41	LCC 6/FC 27	*Traditio symboli*
De quantitate animae	---	CSEL 39	ACW 9	Ambrose's Lenten teaching
Enchiridion	---	CCSL 46	ACW 2	Symbol, Lord's Prayer
Epistola 54	---	CSEL 34	FC 12	Forty days, bathing
Epistola 194	---	CSEL 44	FC 30	*Exsufflatio*
Epistola 227	---	CSEL 57	FC 32	*Redditio symboli*
Epistola 258	---	CSEL 57	FC 32	Turn in names
Guelf 7	229A	BAC 24	Weller	Fasting, exorcism
Opus imperf. contra Iul.	---	CSEL 85	---	*Exsufflatio*
Tract Jn 98	---	CCSL 36	NPNF 7	Symbol, Lord's Prayer

Chart 14
Creeds Found in Augustine's Sermons

1. *Creed of Milan;* reconstructed from *Sermones* 213–14 (also *Sermo* 212?) by J. N. D. Kelly, *Early Christian Creeds,* 3d ed., 173; cf. Suzanne Poque, SC 116:63-64.

Credo in deum patrem omnipotentem;
Et in Iesum Christum, filium eius unicum, dominum nostrum,
    qui natus de Spiritu sancto et Maria virgine,
    passus est sub Pontio Pilato, crucifixus et sepultus,
    tertia die resurrexit a mortuis,
    ascendit in caelum,
    sedet ad dexteram patris,
    inde venturus iudicare vivos et mortuos;
Et in Spiritum sanctum,
    sanctam ecclesiam,
    remissionem peccatorum,
    carnis resurrectionem.

2. *Creed of Hippo;* reconstructed from *Sermo* 215 (cf. *Sermo* 212) by Kelly, *Early Christian Creeds,* 176.

Credimus in deum patrem omnipotentem, universorum creatorem,
    regem saeculorum, immortalem et invisibilem;
Credimus et in filium eius Iesum Christum dominum nostrum,
    natum de Spiritu sancto ex virgine Maria,
    crucifixum sub Pontio Pilato, mortuum, et sepultum,
    [qui] tertia die resurrexit a mortuis,
    ascendit ad caelos,
    sedet ad dexteram dei patris
    inde venturus est iudicare vivos et mortuos
Credimus et in Spiritum sanctum
    remissionem peccatorum,
    resurrectionem carnis
    vitam aeternam
    per sanctam ecclesiam.

3. *Creed of Milan* (variant), reconstructed from *De symbolo ad catechumenos* by R. Vander Plaetse, "Praefatio," CCSL 46:181.

Credimus in deum patrem omnipotentem
et in Iesum Christum filium eius unicum dominum nostrum
    natus de Spiritu sancto et uirgine Maria
    passus sub Pontio Pilato crucifixus et sepultus
    ascendit in caelum
    sedet ad dexteram patris
    inde venturus iudicare vivos et mortuos
et in Spiritum sanctum
    sanctam ecclesiam
    remissionem peccatorum
    resurrectionem carnis in uitam aeternam.

Chapter 8

Mystagogy: Baking Bread, Fermenting Wine

Around the year 400, a man named Januarius wrote Augustine and asked about certain liturgical practices. One particularly bothered him: that the celebration of the Lord's Passion did not come around on the same day each year and that this shifting date was tied to the phases of the moon. This seemed reminiscent of a paganism which tied human fate to the stars or of a Manicheism which saw its myths played out in planetary movements.[1] Augustine answered Januarius with two long letters and, in the second, focused on the meaning and practice of Easter. He took pains to distance Christian practice from any foreign taint. He argued that watching the coursings of the moon or stars or planets might have legitimate ends: farmers watched the heavens to forecast the weather; pilots of ships used them to steer by; so did nomads who charted "their way through the sandy wastes of the south" where "no sure path" lay. According to Augustine, the Church saw the movements of the heavens as "parables." It believed that God had inscribed in creation a sort of eloquence which could woo people upwards and inwards, and that this had been adapted to the giving-out of sacraments. Thus the Church drew on this eloquence in creation. It did so sparingly in its rites, using things such as water, wheat, wine, oil. But it did so much more freely in its catechesis: drawing on "the whole of creation, the winds, the sea, the earth, birds, fish, flocks, trees, human-

---

1. *Epistola* 55.2. In the letter, Augustine grapples with the implications of this in terms of paganism and Manicheism, but he also touches on the Church's links to Judaism (which used a lunar calendar for determining certain of its festivals). Apparently, the shifting date of Easter raised the question of Christianity's Jewish roots and perhaps reminded Christians like Januarius of the objections of pagan critics, like Porphyry and Julian: that Christians were merely apostate Jews. See Wilken, *The Christians as the Romans Saw Them*, 126–205.

kind."[2] Augustine's baptismal candidates would taste this earthy, parabolic eloquence of rite and word with unusual intensity during Easter and the week that followed.

According to Augustine, the Easter *triduum*—or "Pasch" as he called it—was a "solemnity," that is, a religious celebration held annually.[3] Christmas was one as well, for it recalled a historical event, the birth of Christ, and was "marked by devout festivity." Similarly, at Easter, the Christian community as community called to mind what happened—that is, that Christ died and rose again. Yet Easter was not only a solemnity; it was also a "sacrament," in a way Christmas was not. This was because Easter not only celebrated that Christ died but that he "died *for our sins*"; not only that he rose again, but that "he rose again *for our justification*." Thus the community did not simply celebrate Pasch; rather, "we enact Pasch." Moreover, since the Pasch of Christ was a passing over, a passage from death to life, the Christian community likewise passed over:

"This passing-over is enacted in us only by faith—which works in us for the forgiveness of sins, with hope of life eternal for those who love God and neighbor. . . . According to this faith and hope and love, by which we begin to come under grace, we die together with Christ and are buried with him through baptism, as the Apostle says, 'because our old man has been crucified with him,' and we have risen again with him, and 'he has roused us up together and seated us together in the heavens.'"[4]

In this chapter, we will examine how Augustine led candidates for baptism through this Easter passage, this passing over in Christ from death to life. In the opening section, I draw together what is known of the celebration of the Easter Vigil in Hippo, how rite and catechesis intertwined. Then in the remaining sections, I will trace out the contours of Augustine's mystagogy: (1) his Easter morning sermons, delivered to the larger assembly but focused on the newly baptized; (2) his private catecheses on the Eucharist delivered to the newly baptized in the course of the

2. *Epistola* 55.13-15 (Parsons, 12:272-73—altered).
3. See *Sermones* 220; 223B.1 (=Guelf. 4); 223C (=Guelf. 6); 223D.1 (=Wilmart 4); 223E.1 (=Wilmart 5); 223I.1 (=Wilmart 15); etc. On Easter as a solemnity and sacrament, see Poque, "Introduction," 13-14.
4. *Epistola* 55.2-3 (trans. my own).

Easter morning liturgy; (3) the sermons of Easter Week which explored the meaning of resurrection; and (4) the celebration of the Octave during which Augustine offered the newly baptized a final solemn exhortation.

LAMPS AND HEARTS ABLAZE: THE EASTER VIGIL

From the beginning of Holy Week to the end of the Octave, the empire went on holiday. Official business came to a halt and all court cases went into recess.[5] People apparently made these weeks a time of leisure. But for those who were to be baptized, these days meant a busy round of church-going. On Thursday of Holy Week, the *competentes* broke their long fast and enjoyed a badly needed cleansing at the public baths. Many others would join them there for this brief relaxing of the Lenten routine.[6] On Friday, they celebrated "the passion of the one whose blood wiped out our sins."[7] In Augustine's church, the Passion according to Matthew was read. Augustine had once tried to implement a small liturgical innovation: "that the account of the Passion might be read, year by year, from each of the Evangelists in turn."[8] This caused such an uproar that he was forced to restore the traditional Matthean version.

On Holy Saturday, everyone fasted.[9] That evening, as it grew dark, Christians all over Hippo would light lamps for the great *lucernarium*: the vigil of the Lord's resurrection. The great basilica was lit by the flicker of flames in numerous oil lamps so that the whole interior shimmered in a golden light.[10] Throughout the long

5. *Codex Theodosianus* 2.8.19, delivered in 389 A.D.; 2.8.21 and 2.8.24, delivered in 405 A.D. For a translation, see Clyde Pharr, *The Theodosian Code* (Princeton: Princeton University Press, 1952) 44–45. See Augustine's comments on this in *Sermo* 259.6; cf. *Epistola* 34.2.

6. *Epistola* 54.10.

7. *Sermo* 218.1 (Muldowney, 164).

8. *Sermo* 232.1 (Muldowney, 210).

9. *Sermo* 210.1. For a careful gathering of the relevant material on the Vigil, see DeLatte, "Saint Augustin et le baptême," 204–23; Poque, "Introduction," 33–39, 75–83; see also Busch, "De modo quo sanctus Augustinus descripserit initiationem christianam," 446–65. For an imaginative reconstruction of the atmosphere of the vigil, see Van der Meer, *Augustine the Bishop*, 361–81; however, Van der Meer relies on sources beyond Augustine.

10. See *Sermones* 221.1; 223G.1 (=Wilmart 7); 223I (=Wilmart add. [15]); 223K (=Wilmart add. [17]).

night, all would "keep watch and pray," both those who had "already entered this great house" (the baptized) and those who were "arranging to enter it" (the *competentes*).[11] Throughout the night, the great events of salvation history were recounted in reading after reading, psalm after psalm: the separation of light from dark at the dawn of creation; the miracle of the burning bush and the revelation of God's hidden name; the crossing of the Red Sea and the victory hymn of Moses; the story of the three young men who preferred Nebuchadnezzar's furnace to apostasy; Isaiah's great prophecy of the last days when "the mountain of the Lord's house shall appear . . . and all the nations shall come together to it."[12] As Augustine saw it, the flow of readings and prayers resembled a great dialogue between God and his people: "May God speak to us in the readings; may we speak to God in our pleadings. If we listen compliantly to his eloquence, then the One we beg [shall] dwell within us."[13]

Augustine knew that the number and length of readings precluded commentary. Not only did his hearers lack the energy to listen to a studied exegesis; he lacked the wherewithal to give one.[14] So he kept his vigil sermons brief. Despite this, he would wield his few words with a baroque extravagance. For instance, he opened *Sermon* 220 with a long rhymed encomium: "Brothers and sisters, we know and we hold with firm faith that Christ died for us but once":

pro peccatoribus iustum,	the just for sinners,
pro servis Dominum,	the master for slaves,
pro captivis liberum,	the free for captives,
pro aegrotis medicum,	the physician for the sick,

11. *Sermo* 219 (Muldowney, 173).

12. *Tractatus in epistolam Ioannis* 1.13 (trans. Burnaby, LCC 8:269). There are scattered references to the lectionary readings: Genesis 1 (*Sermo* 223A.1 [=Denis 2]); Exodus 15 (*Sermo* 223E.2 [=Wilmart 5]; cf. *Sermo* 363); Exodus 3 (*Sermo* 223A.5 [=Denis 2]); Daniel 2 (*Contra litteras Petiliani* 2.92.211); Isaiah 2 (*Tractatus in epistolam Ioannis* 1.13). For an examination of possible psalms and Pauline readings, see Poque, "Introduction," 73–77.

13. *Sermo* 219 (trans. my own).

14. *Sermo* 223A.1 (=Denis 2). While the authenticity of this sermon is contested, the sentiment expressed here is not. Note the extreme brevity of Augustine's vigil sermons: *Sermones* 219–22; 223D–223K (=Wilmart 4–7 and Addimenta [14–17]).

pro miseris beatum,	the happy for the wretched,
pro egenis opulentem,	the rich for the needy,
pro perditis quaesitorem,	the seeker for the lost,
pro venditis redemptorem,	the redeemer for the sold,
pro grege pastorem,	the shepherd for the sheep,
et quod est omnibus mirabilius,	and—what is the most awe-inspiring of all—
pro creatura creatorem;	the creator for the creature;
servantem tamen quod semper est,	keeping to what he always is,
tradentem quod factus est;	handing over what he became;
Deum latentem,	hiding as God,
hominem apparentem;	appearing as human;
virtute vivificantem,	life-instilling by his power,
infirmitate morientem,	dying by his weakness;
divinitate immutabilem,	unchanging in divinity,
carne passibilem.	pained in the flesh.[15]

For Augustine and his hearers, the vigil celebrated the cosmic victory of Christ over death, over sin, over the demonic powers. The creation story from Genesis—particularly its description of God separating light from dark—would combine in his mind with the blaze of lamps that lit both basilica and town. He would proclaim: "the sun has gone down, but the day has not gone away, for a bright-lit earth has followed on a bright-lit sky."[16] For Augustine, this keeping night watch and lighting lamps united flesh to heart, physical act to interior affection:

"Keep the night watch humbly; pray humbly—with a devoted faith, a solid hope, a bright-burning charity—pondering what kind of day our [bright] splendor will result in if our humility can turn night into day. Therefore, may God—who ordered the light to blaze out of the dark—make our hearts blaze bright: that we may do on the inside something akin to what we have done with the lamps kindled within this house of prayer. Let us furnish the true dwelling place of God—our [inner] consciousness—with lamps of justice."[17]

15. *Sermo* 220 (BAC 24:226-27; trans. my own). Similar rhymed figures appear in *Sermones* 221 (=Guelf. 5); 222; etc.
16. *Sermo* 221.1 (=Guelf. 5) (trans. my own).
17. *Sermo* 223I (=Wilmart add. 15) (trans. my own).

As Augustine saw it, the vigil symbolized the preeminent gathering of time past and time future into time present so that it became, in Eliot's phrase, a "still point in the turning world." On the one hand, it was a "solemnity" that did "not permit the past to pass away."[18] So candidates and faithful would follow Christ's exhortation—to keep night watch and pray—in a way that the apostles had not.[19] On the other hand, this vigil offered a foretaste of endtime: a day uninterrupted by night, an open-eyed resting within God uninterrupted by the daily death of sleep.[20] Past and future met in the sacramental present of the baptismal candidates who would soon fulfill the great Pauline phrases: "once you were darkness, but now you are light in the Lord; walk as children of light"; "arise, you who sleep, and Christ will illuminate you"; "you are all children of light and children of the day."[21]

At some point—either during the all-night vigil itself or perhaps earlier in the day—two events took place which only the baptized and the candidates could have witnessed.[22] The first was the solemn handing-back of the Creed. The candidates would stand on a raised platform and recite before the assembled faithful the symbol they had memorized.[23] Adults were not the only ones who had to endure this moment in the spotlight. Anyone, age seven or older, would be required to do so, since by that time of life children were "able both to lie and to tell the truth, both to confess and to deny."[24]

18. *Sermo* 220 (Muldowney, 173). On Augustine's understanding of time vis-à-vis the vigil, see the valuable excursus: " 'Veritas' y 'sollemnitas' " and "Teologia de la vigilia pascual," BAC 24:795–97.

19. Augustine quotes Matthew 26:41 in *Sermones* 222; 223B.1 (=Guelf. 4); 223C (=Guelf. 6); 223E.1 (=Wilmart 5); 223K (=Wilmart add. [17]).

20. *Sermo* 221.3. See also *Sermones* 223B.2 (=Guelf. 4); 223D.2 (=Wilmart 4); 223G (=Wilmart 7); 223J (=Wilmart add. 16).

21. Ephesians 5:14 in *Sermo* 223J (=Wilmart add. 16); Ephesians 5:8 in *Sermones* 219 and 222; 1 Thessalonians 5:5 in *Sermo* 223K (=Wilmart add. 17).

22. Van der Meer, *Augustine the Bishop*, 363 and DeLatte, "Saint Augustin et le baptême," 205–6, presume that both occurred earlier in the day. Poque, "Introduction," 34 and 78–82, sees the solemn *redditio* and the catechesis on baptism as events held within the night-long vigil; this would imply that there was a dismissal of the catechumens. Poque also believes that prior to the dismissal, the resurrection narrative from Matthew was read, and a sermon was given on it.

23. *Sermo* 59.1; cf. *Confessiones* 8.2.

24. *De anima et eius origine* 1.10.12 (trans. Peter Holmes, NPNF 5:320). See also 3.9.12.

The second was a final solemn catechesis. Augustine would address the candidates and explain the meaning of the sacrament of the font.[25] Once, in a sermon directed to neophytes, he alluded to the content and time of delivery of this final baptismal catechesis:

"At your baptism, or rather before your baptism, on Saturday we spoke to you about the mystery of the font in which you were to be immersed. And we told you—I trust you have not forgotten—that baptism signifies a burial with Christ, as the Apostle says, 'For we are buried together with Christ by baptism into death, that as he was raised from the dead so we also may walk in newness of life.' "[26]

Scholars have examined Augustine's extant sermons and concluded that—unfortunately—none of these baptismal catecheses have been preserved.[27] However, his brief remarks here at least indicate something of his curricular timetable: that he, unlike Cyril and Ambrose, did not wait until Easter Week to explain the rite of baptism, but rather, like the Antiochenes Theodore and John Chrysostom, did so prior to its actual celebration.

25. *Sermo* 228.3.

26. *Sermo* 229A.1 (=Guelf. 7) (Weller, 100-101). This Pauline theme held pride of place in fourth-century baptismal catechesis; see Finn, "Baptismal Death and Resurrection. A Study in Fourth Century Eastern Baptismal Theology," *Worship* 43 (1969) 175-89.

27. Audet, "Notes sur les catéchèses baptismales de saint Augustin," *Augustinus Magister* 1:151-60, has carefully examined all the possible examples among Augustine's extant sermons and concluded that "les catéchèses augustiniennes sur le baptême sont irrémédiablement perdues." He does venture one slight possibility: *Sermo* Denis 8. However, Poque, "Introduction," 81-82, denies that this can be one. While it does give valuable indications of what such a catechesis would have been, it is clearly a sermon given to the neophytes on the Octave, and not to *competentes* during the vigil. For her part, she has suggested that *Sermo* 363 might be one. This sermon is on Exodus 15:1-21, one of the readings used during the vigil; it touches on several of Augustine's favorite baptismal themes; it quotes another of the vigil readings (Dan 2:6), and makes a brief allusion to Romans 6. But there are also indications against such a claim: the Maurists questioned whether this is indeed an authentic sermon of Augustine; there is no "turning" to the *competentes* such as one typically finds in his catecheses; nor is there any exegesis of Romans 6 nor any allusion to the rite. Thus it seem more likely that this sermon, if it is indeed the work of Augustine, was simply a sermon which Augustine gave in the course of the Easter Vigil. Thus DeLatte, "Saint Augustin et le baptême," 206, concludes: "Cependant, aucun de ses sermons n'a été conservé."

Sometime in the early morning dark, the candidates, together with Augustine and an entourage of ministers, would process out of the basilica to the strains of Psalm 41:

"As a deer longs for flowing streams,
so longs my soul for you, O God.
My soul thirsts for God, for the living God.
When shall I come and behold the face of God?
How I went with the throng,
in procession to the house of God,
with glad shouts and songs of thanksgiving,
a multitude keeping festival."

By this "truth-filled and long-sanctioned" hymn, the baptismal candidates were roused to "long for the fountain where sins are wiped out." But as Augustine knew well, "such a longing is not fully satisfied in baptism, even among the faithful." Only the vision of God, drunk in the deep draughts of endtime, could still such profound longing.[28]

The baptismal party would process to an annex just off the main basilica.[29] This annex included three rooms: the baptistery itself; an antechamber on its southwest side; and a small chapel with an apse on its northwest side. Erwan Marec, the director of archeological excavations in Hippo, has referred to the antechamber as a *catechumeneum*, presuming that either catecheses or prebaptismal rites took place there. Its floor was decorated with an intricate mosaic tableau: cruciform medallions inlaid with tesserae of chestnut, ebony, ruby red, and yellow, each medallion knit to others by a green-and-bronze garlanded latticework. Marec has called the small chapel with the apse a *consignatorium*, presuming that postbaptismal rites took place there. It, too, had a mosaic floor: eight-petalled violet- and rose-colored tulips alternating with oval-branched crosses on a blue-black backdrop, the whole held within a braided border. The baptistery itself was irregularly shaped: squared off on two sides and semicircular on the other. At its center was the font. It bore a close resemblance to the heated baths found in the houses of the wealthy. Some North African fonts were octagonal, like the one in Timgad; others, like

28. *Enarrationes in psalmos* 41.1 (trans. LF 25:178).
29. For what follows, see Marec, *Monuments chrétiens d'Hippone*, 110–12.

the well-preserved one in Cuicul and Augustine's in Hippo, were rectangular and had pillars at each of the four corners. A marble baldachin would have arched high over the font, while curtains perhaps hung between its pillars. The font itself was one meter deep, two-and-a-half meters long, and two meters wide, and may have had steps leading down into it. Possibly a jet of water streamed into the font, causing the water's surface to swirl and eddy. As Van der Meer points out:

"Living, that is to say, moving water was essential. Standing water, a natural seat of corruption, could never have been the symbol of new life which was not subject to corruption, nor could it ever have represented the soul's new potentiality for life."[30]

At some point—either soon after arriving at the baptistery or perhaps during the earlier *redditio*—the candidates once more renounced Satan and swore their allegiance to Christ. They may have turned west when renouncing and east when swearing allegiance, much as candidates did in Jerusalem. Once, in a sermon on Psalm 102, Augustine alluded to this bodily turning, speaking of it obliquely enough to respect the *disciplina arcani*:

" 'Look how wide the east is from the west, so far has [God] set our sins from us.' Those who know the sacraments know this. Nevertheless, I only say what all may hear. When sin is remitted, your sins fall, your grace rises. Your sins are, as it were, on the decline; your grace which frees you, on the rise. . . . You should look to the rising, and turn away from the setting."[31]

Also at some point—perhaps before the candidates' arrival or perhaps in their presence—the water was sanctified.[32] It was signed with the Sign of the Cross, and the name of Christ was invoked over it.[33] Apparently, this consecratory prayer was improvised, for Augustine reports that some clergy, "through lack of skill, utter

---

30. Van der Meer, *Augustine the Bishop*, 365.

31. *Enarrationes in psalmos* 102.19 (trans. LF 37:58–59—altered). Previous commentators do not seem aware of this passage. See also *Enarrationes in psalmos* 76.4; *Epistola* 97.9.

32. *De baptismo contra Donatistas* 5.20.27–38. Cf. Cyprian, *Epistola* 70.1.

33. *Tractatus in evangelium Ioannis* 118.5 and *Sermo* 352.3. See also *De baptismo contra Donatistas* 3.10.15.

words of error," and pray in ways "contrary to the Catholic faith."[34]

As the time for their cleansing neared, the candidates would strip off their clothes and make their way to the font. Such nakedness did not necessarily provoke embarrassment. As Brown notes, there was in the great public baths and public games an easy-going nudity; for them:

"nudity and sexual shame were questions of social status: the way people felt about being naked, or seeing others naked, depended to a large extent on their social situation. Thus, at the top of society, nudity in the public baths expressed the utter ease of the well-to-do, moving without a trace of sexual shame in front of their inferiors."[35]

However, in Augustine's church, we know that, during the baptismal rite, men were separated from women.[36]

People probably entered the font one by one. Like the pool of Bethsaida, the font "was so made that people had to step down . . . because the Lord's Passion searches for the humble": "Let the humble go down, let [them] not be proud, if [they] wish to be cured."[37] There they would stand waist-deep in the water. The celebrant would apparently break down the Creed into the three questions; after each, candidates would answer: "Credo" ("I believe").[38] Candidates also were immersed, or as Augustine would put it, "moistened" three times.[39] It is not clear how this was done: a minister (a deacon? Augustine?) perhaps held the person under the jet of water that rushed into the font or perhaps dunked the person's head and shoulders beneath the waters of

---

34. *De baptismo contra Donatistas* 6.25.47 (trans. J. R. King, NPNF 4:491—altered).

35. Brown, *The Body and Society*, 315.

36. *De civitate Dei* 22.8.

37. *Sermo* 125.6 (MacMullen, 478); cf. *Sermo* 258.2.

38. *Contra litteras Petiliani* 3.8.9. The interrogation formulas are alluded in references to the baptism of infants: *Epistola* 98.7; *Sermo* 294.12. See Poque, "Introduction," 35.

39. Augustine sometimes uses the word *tinguere* ("to wet" or "to moisten"—perhaps, playing on the word's other connotations, that is, "to dye" or "to imbue"): *Sermones* 213.8; 229A.1 (=Guelf. 7); *Tractatus in evangelium Ioannis* 15.3; 80.3. Other times he uses *conspergere* ("to moisten by sprinkling"): *Sermones* 227; 229.1 (=Denis 6); 272.

the waist-deep pool.[40] On several occasions, Augustine says that this baptism was "consecrated in the words of the gospel, . . . 'in the name of the Father, and of the Son, and of the Holy Spirit.' "[41] Despite such statements, liturgists believe that in Augustine's rite, as in Hippolytus's and Ambrose's, the triple interrogation may have substituted for the Matthean formula, and that the interrogations alternated with immersions.[42]

Those emerging from the font were thought to possess miraculous powers of healing and intercession. For instance, in *City of God*, Augustine tells the story of Innocentia, a woman of high standing in the community who had been diagnosed as having breast cancer: "When Easter was approaching, she was instructed in a dream to watch on the woman's side at the baptistery and ask the first newly-baptized woman who met her to sign the affected place with the sign of the cross."[43] She obeyed the instructions of the dream and found, to her great joy, that the cancerous lump in her breast had vanished. When she reported the cure to her doctor, he was nonplussed: "Why, I thought you were going to tell me something remarkable! . . . What is so extraordinary in Christ's healing a cancer, when he once raised to life a man four days dead?"[44]

Candidates were also anointed. Augustine, in one sermon, refers to an anointing in language reminiscent of that used to describe prebaptismal anointing: just as Christ had gone to the Mount of Olives before his death, so Christians went to the "mount of chrism"; by this "Christ has made us wrestlers against the devil."[45] We know that there was a postbaptismal anointing (or anointings). The chrism itself was consecrated by the Sign of the Cross.[46] According to conciliar decree, chrismation was the bishop's prerogative, and according to Augustine, oil was applied

40. Van der Meer, *Augustine the Bishop*, 367.

41. *De baptismo contra Donatistas* 3.14.19 and 15.20 (King, 442). Also *De baptismo* 6.25.46; *Epistola* 23.4; *Contra litteras Petiliani* 2.81.178.

42. DeLatte, "Saint Augustin et le baptême," 210–11; Poque, "Introduction," 35. See Hippolytus, *Apostolic Tradition*, 21; Ambrose, *De sacramentis* 2.20.

43. *De civitate Dei* 22.8 (Bettenson, 1037–38).

44. Ibid. (Bettenson, 1038).

45. *Tractatus in evangelium Ioannis* 33.3 (trans. John Gibb and James Innes, NPNF 7:197).

46. Ibid., 118.5.

to the candidate's head.[47] As he saw it, this "sacrament of chrism is . . . numbered among the class of visible signs, like baptism itself."[48] It meant that the newly baptized, like Christ the king, would have strength, "like kings, [to] rule over the flesh and overcome the world."[49] It also had sacerdotal implications: bishops and presbyters were not the only ones who enjoyed the title of priest; all the baptized enjoyed it, for "just as we call all Christians 'Christs' in virtue of their sacramental anointing, so we call them all 'priests' because they are members of the one Priest."[50] In addition, the "sevenfold Spirit" was invoked over the baptized, and hands were laid on them.[51] Augustine did not distinguish between baptism and confirmation as the medievals would do. Instead, he tended to describe each element—whether actions (exorcism, signing with the cross, bathing, anointing, hand-laying), objects (the font, oil), even time periods (Easter, the Octave)—as distinct "sacraments" in his sense of the term: "visible words," "sacred signs" of "the invisible."[52]

After these rites, the neophytes would don new robes made, in all probability, of white linen.[53] These linen robes were an ancient symbol of ritual purity and would have contrasted with the goat-skin sackcloth which the newly baptized had, as *competentes*, trodden underfoot. For the next eight days, they wore their baptismal robes to signal their commitment to a stainless life. They may also have kept their heads covered with a veil.[54] Finally, they would have donned special sandals lest their feet touch the earth.

47. *Contra litteras Petiliani* 2.104.237; Third Council of Carthage, *canon* 36.

48. *Contra litteras Petiliani* 2.105.239 (trans. J. R. King, NPNF 4:592).

49. *De civitate Dei* 17.4.9 (Bettenson, 723).

50. Ibid., 20.10 (Bettenson, 919). See also 17.4.9.

51. *Sermo* 229M.2 (=Guelf. 15). See also *Tractatus in epistolam Ioannis* 6.10; *Sermones* 248.5; 249.3.

52. *Tractatus in Ioannis evangelium* 80.3 (Gibb and Innes, 344); *De civitate Dei* 10.5 (Bettenson, 377). See also *Sermo* 324; *Epistolae* 54.1 and 138.7. These passages, of course, touch on only one strain in Augustine's multifaceted sacramental theory. For a careful elucidation of this, see M.-F. Berrouard, "Le *Tractatus 80, 3 in Iohannis Euangelium* de saint Augustin: La parole, le sacrement et la foi," *Revue des études augustiniennes* 33 (1987) 235-54; also helpful are Van der Meer, *Augustine the Bishop*, 277-316; Alexandre Ganoczy, *An Introduction to Catholic Sacramental Theology*, trans. William Thomas (New York: Paulist Press, 1984) 20-25; Kelly, *Early Christian Doctrines*, 422-24.

53. *Sermo* 120. See also *Sermones* 223; 260C.7 (=Mai 94).

54. *Sermo* 376A.1.

Augustine once remarked, caustically, that people were unusually superstitious about this tradition of not touching the earth during Easter Week but, at the same time, were quite lackadaisical about more serious matters, such as drinking themselves "dead-drunk."[55]

After these rites, the baptismal party would return to the main basilica and there be greeted by the faithful. The neophytes, or as Augustine called them, *infantes*, had crossed the Red Sea of baptism. Their first Eucharist followed immediately. As he once put it: "Where does [Christ] lead believers and the baptized? To manna."[56] During this first Eucharist, the neophytes simply listened and watched, apparently in baffled silence, for they had received no prior catechesis concerning it.[57] For the next week, they would witness the Eucharist at close range: standing within the *cancelli*, a sanctuary area which was sectioned off by a railing and within which the bishop, presbyters, and deacons normally stood.[58] This night, they would hear for the first time the dialogue that opened the Eucharistic Prayer:

"The Lord be with you.
And also with your spirit.
Lift up your heart.
We have [lifted them up] to the Lord.
Let us give thanks to the Lord our God.
It is right and just."[59]

The "sanctification"—as Augustine called the consecration of the bread and wine—would follow.[60] At its end, all would voice their approval with an "Amen."[61] They would then pray the Lord's

55. *Epistola* 55.35 (trans. my own).
56. *Tractatus in evangelium Ioannis* 11.4 (Rettig, 79:14).
57. *Sermo* 229.3 (=Denis 6). The lack of preparation is also mentioned explicitly in *Sermo* 272 and is clearly implied in *Sermones* 227 and 229A.1 (=Guelf. 7).
58. *Sermo* 260C.7 (=Mai 97) refers to the neophytes leaving the *cancelli* at the Octave. Cf. *Epistola* 34.2 in which Augustine refers to a Donatist neophyte standing within the *cancelli*.
59. *Sermo* 229A.3 (=Guelf. 7) and *Sermo* 227 (trans. my own). Also *Sermo* 229.3 (=Denis 6).
60. *Sermo* 227 (trans. my own). See also *Sermo* 229A. Cyprian used the same term: *Epistola* 63.13 *(in sanctificando calice)*; Ambrose, on the other hand, employed the word *consecratio*: *De sacramentis* 4.14 and 16; *De mysteriis* 54.
61. *Sermo* 229.3 (=Denis 6).

Prayer, and at the words "Forgive us our debts," all would strike their breasts.[62] After this, Augustine would proclaim, "Peace be with you," and all would offer one another the kiss of peace.[63] Finally, the neophytes would come up to Augustine. They would hear the words "Body of Christ" spoken to them and would receive the consecrated bread in their hands. A deacon would then offer them the cup.[64] The neophytes experienced all this—seeing, hearing, partaking in "what took place on the altar"—without comment or catechesis. Augustine's silence was deliberate. He would not take up the deeper implications of Eucharist—"what it is, what it means, and the great mystery it holds"—until the next morning.[65]

THE GREAT SWAP: EASTER MORNING

On Easter morning, the neophytes would return to the basilica for a second Eucharist. During the Liturgy of the Word, the opening of Acts and that of John's Gospel were read, and in between the two readings, all would sing Psalm 117 and the great Alleluia.[66] A sermon addressed to the whole assembly followed. Augustine kept his remarks brief, for it had been a long night, and both he and the neophytes felt weary after the previous night's labors.[67] Once, in fact, he had to beg off after only a few words, admitting that he was suffering acute exhaustion.[68]

In these public sermons, Augustine would direct the assembly's attention to the white-robed neophytes who stood in a special sec-

62. *Sermo* 227; see also *Sermo* 229.3 (=Denis 6). On beating of the breast at the Lord's Prayer, see *Sermo* 351.6.

63. *Sermo* 227.

64. *Sermo* 272. On the bishop giving the bread, see *Epistola* 151.9; *Contra litteras Petiliani* 2.23.53; on Communion in the hand, see *Contra litteras Petiliani* 2.23.53; on the deacon offering the cup, see *Sermo* 304.1. Van der Meer and DeLatte think that the neophytes were also offered a cup of milk and honey; Poque finds no real evidence of this in Augustine's works, nor have I.

65. *Sermo* 272 (trans. my own).

66. Augustine cites lectionary readings as follows: Acts 1 (*Sermo* 227); Psalm 117 (*Sermones* 120.3; 226; 229B [=Guelf. 8]; 230; 260D.1 [=Guelf. 18]); Alleluia (e.g., *Sermones* 228; 229B.2 [=Guelf. 8]; *Epistola* 55.32); John 1 (*Sermones* 119–21 and 225–26). On the lectionary of Easter, see Cyrille Lambot, "Les sermons de saint Augustin pour les fêtes de Pâques," *Revue bénédictine* 79 (1969) 163–64.

67. *Sermo* 228.1.

68. *Sermo* 320.

tion of the church. He would exclaim that if the assembly wanted to see the Scriptures enfleshed, it need only gaze at the neophytes: that on the night before, as at the dawn of creation, the Spirit had moved over the waters and God had said, "Let there be light," such that the neophytes themselves had become the first day of a new creation (Gen 1:2-5);[69] that they who "were once darkness" were now "light in the Lord" (Eph 5:8);[70] that "it is about [them] we sing, 'This is the day which the Lord has made: let us be glad and rejoice'" (Ps 117:24).[71]

Most importantly, Augustine regarded the neophytes as living reminders that "the Word became flesh and dwelt among us." As he saw it, Christ, like an import merchant from a foreign land, offered us a "great swap": he took on our flesh and we received his spirit.[72] He thus became a mediator, quite literally, a "middleman," one neither above nor below, yet neither departing from God nor departing from us.[73] In this swap, the Son of God became Son of Man that we might become children of God. And for Augustine, no one embodied this more concretely than the newly baptized who stood out so prominently in the assembly.

Augustine would, on occasion, publicly announce that the newly baptized enjoyed a new title and a new status:

"These people—who a little while ago were called *competentes*—are now called *infantes*. They were called *competentes* because they were thumping in their mother's womb, begging to be born; now they are called *infantes* because they—who had first been born to the world—are now born to Christ."[74]

He would lavish other titles on them: they were the "white-robed enlightened ones," the "new sprouts of mother Church," and

---

69. *Sermo* 226.

70. *Sermo* 225.4. See also *Sermo* 226.

71. *Sermo* 225. See also *Sermo* 226.

72. *Sermo* 121.5. Other aspects of the *Christus mercator* image appear in the Easter Week sermons: *Sermones* 229H.1 (= Guelf. 12); 233.3. On this theme, see the excursus, "Cristo mercader," BAC 24:800–801; Poque, "Introduction," 16–17.

73. *Sermo* 121.5. This figures in the Easter Week sermons as well: see *Sermones* 240.4; 245.4; cf. *Sermo* 47.12; *De civitate Dei* 11.2. On the larger outlines of this theme, see Daley, "A Humble Mediator," 105–8.

74. *Sermo* 228.1 (trans. my own).

most importantly, they were "faithful ones."[75] Augustine knew that new titles were not enough. He wanted people whose "lives move in harmony with their name": "I hear the name; let me see the real thing."[76] So he would beg the neophytes to focus on Christ "who called you, who loved you, who sought you when you were lost, who enlightened you when you were found."[77] He also knew celebrations would follow the liturgy and so warned the neophytes not to get drunk—on liquor at least. The only drunkenness permitted them was the intoxication that came from the Spirit and from psalm-singing.[78]

Once, in closing, Augustine pointed to what he saw as the catechetical high points in the neophytes' formation: (1) the "sacrament of the Creed," (2) the "sacrament of the Lord's Prayer," and (3) the "sacrament of the font." He reminded the neophytes that he had spoken on these great "traditions" (literally, "hand-ons") and that they had "seized hold" of them.[79] These were traditions in the ancient rabbinic sense: formulae memorized, revered, and passed on from one generation to another. Paul had used this very same terminology when speaking to the Corinthians—"I delivered to you as of first importance what I also received"—and had gone on to recite three ancient formulae: the story of the Lord's Supper; a credal fragment about the death and resurrection of Christ; and the list of the witnesses to the resurrection (1 Cor 11:23-26 and 15:3-7).[80] For Augustine's neophytes, one tradition remained: the "sacrament of the altar," something which they had witnessed but about which they had heard nothing.[81] So, after the dismissal of the catechumens, Augustine would hand on to the neophytes this one final mystery. It was, as he saw it, a debt he owed them.[82]

75. *Sermones* 120.3; 228.1 and 2 (trans. my own).
76. *Sermo* 228.2 (trans. my own).
77. *Sermo* 228.2 (Muldowney, 200).
78. *Sermones* 225.4 and 228. In *Sermones* 230 and 229B.2 (=Guelf. 8), he addresses this admonition to everyone.
79. *Sermo* 228.3 (trans. my own).
80. Keck, *Paul and His Letters*, 27. See also Jerome Murphy-O'Connor, "Eucharist and Community in First Corinthians," in *Living Bread, Saving Cup: Readings on the Eucharist*, ed. R. Kevin Seasoltz (Collegeville, Minn.: The Liturgical Press, 1982) 17; Stanley Marrow, *Paul: His Letters and His Theology* (New York: Paulist Press, 1986) 150–64.
81. *Sermo* 228 (Muldowney, 200); also *Sermo* 226.
82. *Sermo* 228.3.

BE WHAT YOU SEE, RECEIVE WHAT YOU ARE: THE EUCHARIST

The last of the catechumens would trickle out. The doors of the basilica would be closed, and the neophytes would find themselves once more permitted to stay on and enjoy their new privileges as full-fledged members of the body of Christ. "The prayer"—probably the prayers of the faithful—would follow.[83] Then, it seems, Augustine and his entourage would leave the apse and make their way to the sanctuary area, located within the central nave and surrounded by wooden railings (cancelli). At its center was a wooden table which served as the altar.[84] The neophytes would take their places quite close to it. It was here, apparently, that Augustine delivered a brief catechesis on the Eucharist. Four of these have been preserved: Sermons 227, 229, 229A, and 272.[85] (The authenticity of one other, Sermon 228B, has

83. *Sermo* 227. See the reconstruction by Van der Meer, *Augustine the Bishop,* 398-99; however, on North African terminology for prayer, see Edward J. Kilmartin, "Early African Legislation concerning Liturgical Prayer," *Ephemerides Liturgicae* 99 (1985) 105-27.

84. Marec, *Monuments chrétiens d'Hippone,* 28-29.

85. The authenticity of three of these has not been contested: *Sermones* 227, 272, and 229A (=Guelferbytanus 7). *Sermo* 229 appears to be a fragment of *Sermo* Denis 6. However, Karl Adam regarded Denis 6 as spurious, but viewed the fragment preserved by the Maurists, that is, *Sermo* 229, as unquestionably genuine; Adam's challenge centered on the description of the consecration. Busch personally questioned G. Morin on this, and Morin affirmed that Denis 6 was authentic, though he acknowledged that it may have been interpolated at this point. See Busch, "De modo quo s. Augustinus descripserit initiationem christianam," 397 note 46. As a result, some—Van der Meer, Audet, Albaric, Straw—continue to list this as "contested" without citing the reason it was contested. However, it was accepted as authentic by text critics such as Cyrille Lambot, "Les sermons de saint Augustin pour les fêtes de Paques," 148-72. It has also been listed as authentic by Poque, "Introduction," 38-39 and 83-84; and A. M. la Bonnardière, "Les commentaires simultanés de Matth. 6, 12 et de I Jo. 1, 8, dans l'oeuvre de saint Augustin," *Revue des études augustiniennes* 1 (1955) 129-47. Even the views on consecration have been treated as congruent with Augustine's by more recent commentators: see A. Sage, "L'Eucharistie dans la pensée de saint Augustin," *Revue des études augustiniennes* 15 (1969) 209-40; and most recently, Berrouard, "Le Tractatus 80, 3 in Iohannis Euangelium de saint Augustin" 235-54. I will focus for the most part on the section of the sermon whose authenticity is not in dispute, namely, *Sermo* 229.

been seriously challenged.)[86] Of these, two were given prior to the Eucharistic Prayer (229 and 229A), and two, just before communion (227 and 272).[87]

Augustine would first point to what lay on the altar, that is, bread and a cup of wine: "The food you see here on the Lord's table you are used to seeing on your own tables at home—as far as outer appearances go. It has the same look [visus], but not the same worth [virtus]."[88] He would then announce the mystery: once "the sanctification is added, this bread will be the Body of Christ, and this wine will be the Blood of Christ."[89] To explain the transformation of elements, he would point to the neophytes' own experience of transformation through baptism: "You are the same people you were before: nor do you bring new faces before us [here in the assembly]. Yet you are brand-new: your old selves on the outside; [but] new by the grace of sanctity, something—as it were—utterly new."[90] What sanctified the bread and wine, according to Augustine, was the Word of God, just as it had sanctified the baptismal waters the night before.[91] In asserting this, Augus-

86. *Sermo* 228B (=Denis 3) is rejected by Adam and others; listed as "doubtful" by Van der Meer, Mandouze, and Audet; affirmed by Wilmart, Morin, and Mohrmann; and accepted by Poque, Berrouard, and Lambot. See Verbraken, *Études critiques*, 160; Van der Meer, *Augustine the Bishop*, 378–79. While it may well be genuine, it is certainly markedly different in tone and theology. I will not treat it here.

87. See Poque, "Introduction," 83–84; Michel Albaric, "Une catéchèse eucharistique: le sermon 227," in *Saint Augustin et la Bible*, 88.

88. *Sermo* 229A.1 (=Guelf. 7) (trans. my own). Cf. *Sermones* 227, 229.1 (=Denis 6); 272.

89. *Sermo* 229A.1 (=Guelf. 7) (trans. my own); cf. *Sermo* 229.3. Since *Sermones* 227 and 272 took place after the Eucharistic Prayer, Augustine spoke of the bread and wine as already being the Body and Blood of Christ. For Augustine's views on the real presence, see Berrouard, "L'être sacramentel de l'eucharistie selon saint Augustin: Commentaire de Jean VI. 60–63 dans le *Tractatus* XXVII, 1–6 et 11–12 in *in Iohannis Evangelium*," *Nouvelle revue théologique* 99 (1977) 703–21; as well as the response by Kilmartin, "The Eucharistic Gift: Augustine of Hippo's Tractate 27 on John 6:60–72," in *Preaching in the Patristic Age: Studies in Honor of Walter J. Burghardt, SJ*, ed. David G. Hunter (New York: Paulist Press, 1989) 139–61; see also Kelly, *Early Christian Doctrines*, 440–49.

90. *Sermo* 229A.1 (=Guelf. 7) (trans. my own).

91. *Sermo* 227 (trans. my own). See also *Sermon* 229A.1 (=Guelf. 7); 229.3 (=Denis 6); also the excellent presentation by Berrouard, "Le *Tractatus* 80, 3 in *Iohannis Euangelium* de saint Augustin" 235–54.

tine touched on one strain of his multifaceted theology of sacrament. In his view, words—or more precisely, God's Word—made things sacraments. As he put it in his *Tractates on John:*

"What is the baptism of Christ? The bath of water in the Word. Take away the water; there is no baptism. Take away the Word; there is no baptism.[92]

"Take away the Word, and the water is neither more nor less than water. The word is added to the element, and there results the sacrament, as if itself also a kind of visible word."[93]

Augustine believed that God's Word imbued the material, whether the waters of baptism or the bread and wine, with a life-giving power. Thus the true dynamic of the sacraments was hidden from sight: "these are called sacraments because in them one thing is seen; something else, understood"; "what you see passes away, but the unseen—what the sign means—does not pass away, but endures."[94] Varied sources flowed together to shape Augustine's views: his neo-Platonic ontology and epistemology; his polemics against Donatists and Pelagians; and, of course, his long meditation on biblical texts, especially John and Paul. And these varied strains within his thought would later give rise to quite divergent trajectories first among the medieval Scholastics and later among the Reformers. Nearly all these strains appear, usually in nascent form, in these sermons.

The transformation of bread and wine into the Body and Blood of Christ did not preoccupy Augustine the way it would the medieval tradition. For Augustine, transformed bread and wine was but one-half of the mystery: the other half, transformed people, was what especially concerned him. He took his cue from St. Paul:

"The task now is to introduce you to what you have received or are about to receive—to commit it to your care—[and to do so] not from my own heart, nor by my own presumption, nor from human arguments, but on the authority of the Apostle. Now listen to what the Apostle says, or better what Christ says through

92. *Tractatus in Ioannis evangelium* 15.4 (Rettig, 79:80).
93. *Tractatus in Ioannis evangelium* 80.3 (Gibb and Innes, 344).
94. *Sermo* 272 and *Sermo* 227 (trans. my own).

the Apostle: 'We, being many, are one bread, one body' " (1 Cor 10:17).[95]

Augustine was fascinated by the dual meaning Paul gave the term "Body of Christ": on the one hand, the people of God and, on the other, the Eucharistic bread. Thus Augustine could assert bluntly: "The mystery that you are lies there on the table; it is your own mystery that you receive."[96] In other words, for Augustine, the Body of Christ appeared as a sort of diptych: at once as people and as "sanctified" bread. Moreover, this double image was at once a fact and an exhortation, an indicative and an imperative. He encapsulated this in one of his most memorable aphorisms:

| *Estote quod videtis,* | Be what you see, |
| *et accipite quod estis.* | and receive what you are.[97] |

Augustine did not conceive of real presence in strictly ritual terms. His thinking admitted no sharp fissure between the real presence of Christ in the bread and the real presence of Christ within the community.

Using this diptych of the Body of Christ as his starting point, Augustine would retrace the neophytes' long journey. He began by reminding his hearers how bread was made:

"Bear in mind what this creature [i.e., the wheat] was beforehand, when it still grew in the field; how the earth caused it to germinate, how the rains nurtured it, how it ripened in kernels; and later how laborers carried it to the threshing floor, treaded it, winnowed it, stored it in the granary, brought it out again to be milled, then added water to it and baked it, until at last it emerged as bread."[98]

He then would line up the steps in baking bread with those in the journey of initiation. (There are variants in his interpretation of these. See chart 17.) The first step was evangelization: "You were

95. *Sermo* 229A.1 (=Guelf. 7) (trans. my own). The same Pauline phrase is cited in *Sermones* 227 and 272 (the latter having the same cautious introduction).

96. *Sermo* 272 (trans. my own). Cf. *Sermo* 229.2 (=Denis 6).

97. *Sermo* 272 (BAC 24:768; trans. my own).

98. *Sermo* 229.1 (=Denis 6) (Weller, 108). Shorter descriptions of this "baking" process are found in *Sermones* 227 and 229A.2 (=Guelf. 7).

created [and] brought to the threshing floor of the Lord, threshed by hard-working oxen, that is, by the heralds of the Gospel."[99] The threshing floor was, of course, one of Augustine's favorite images of the Church; and he, at times, described his own role as preacher as that of an ox who threshed the wheat and chaff.[100] Here he seems to refer to any herald: whether the person who had first sponsored the neophyte, or perhaps the biblical writers themselves. (Interestingly he did not explore such images as seeds germinating, rain nurturing, kernels ripening, images which imply that prior to and within all human evangelizing is God's mysterious grace giving the growth.) After evangelization, "you were set aside as catechumens"; according to his bread-baking metaphor, this meant that "you were being stored up and watched over in the granary."[101] Then during Lent, after turning in their names, they were "milled" and "sifted" by fasts and exorcism.[102] At their baptism, they were "moistened" and kneaded into a single doughy mass.[103] Finally, they were baked: "Without fire, bread does not exist. What then does the fire signify? The chrism. For the sacrament of the Holy Spirit is [the oil of] our fire."[104] This linking of fire with chrism would be an obvious one for Augustine and his hearers, since they used olive oil in the lamps that lit their houses and churches.

This metaphor of baking bread served Augustine both pedagogically and theologically. Pedagogically, it enabled him to give the neophytes an insight into their long journey. Each stage had had its proper dynamic; each, its proper meaning. Yet the whole fit together. This extended metaphor integrated things much as the Creed did: that is, just as the Creed offered a way of surveying the horizon of Scripture in a single glimpse, so this bread-baking metaphor offered a way of surveying the journey of initiation in a single glimpse. It linked diverse threads—evangelization and catechesis, asceticism and liturgy—within a single overarching

99. *Sermo* 229.1 (=Denis 6) (Weller, 108—altered).
100. *Tractatus in evangelium Ioannis* 10.7; *Enarrationes in psalmos* 126.3.
101. *Sermo* 229.1 (=Denis 6) (trans. my own).
102. *Sermo* 227 (trans. my own). Also *Sermones* 229.1 (=Denis 6) and 272. A variant appears in *Sermo* 229A.2 (=Guelf. 7).
103. *Sermo* 227. Also *Sermones* 229 (=Denis 6); 229A.2 (=Guelf. 7); 272.
104. *Sermo* 227 (Muldowney, 196). Also *Sermones* 229 (=Denis 6) and 272. A variant appears in *Sermo* 229A.2 (=Guelf. 7) in which Augustine describes the "fire" as the fire of temptation (playing on Eccl 27:6).

framework. Theologically, it enabled Augustine to hold together Paul's dual image of the Body of Christ—at once the people of God and the "sanctified" bread—to show that the whole dynamic moved one towards both a liturgical end—Eucharist—and an ecclesiological one—unity. In all this, one can detect an echo of the ancient Eucharistic Prayer of the *Didache:* "As this broken bread was [once] scattered over the hills and, when brought together, became one, so let your Church be brought together from the ends of the earth into your kingdom."[105] Augustine's hope for the neophytes was similar, yet his frame was more explicitly Christological: they were to be the Body of Christ, that which they had become through baptism.

Augustine would then turn people's attention to the wine and show that it too served as an analogy for initiation, that what holds for bread-baking holds for wine-making.[106] He would first cite how wine was made: that grapes grew in clusters; that they were harvested and put through a wine press so that "what was once many individual berries now flows together as one liquid."[107] Only once would he point to its parallels in the initiation process: "And you, after these fasts, after hardships, after [this] humbling and grinding-down: you have come, in Christ's name, [and flowed] into the chalice of the Lord."[108] In the analogy of fermenting wine, Augustine's stress lay less on the individual steps and more on the end result: "In this way our Lord Jesus Christ has indicated his will: that we belong to him, for he has consecrated the mystery of our peace and our unity upon his table."[109] The neophytes would have known well what Augustine meant by "peace" and "unity." These were the traditional North African terms for that *communio* which defined being Church—and thus became for Augustine code-words which marked out what distinguished Catholics from Donatists. As he detailed in sermon after

105. *Didache* 9.4 (trans. R. C. D Jasper and G. J. Cuming, *Prayers of the Eucharist*, 2d ed, [New York: Oxford University Press, 1980] 15). On this echo, see Albaric, "Une catéchèse eucharistique," 94.

106. *Sermo* 272. See also *Sermones* 229.2 (=Denis 6) and 229a.2 (=Guelf. 7).

107. *Sermo* 272 (trans. Van der Meer, *Augustine the Bishop*, 363) and *Sermo* 229A.2 (=Guelf. 7) (trans. my own). Also, *Sermo* 229.2 (=Denis 6). This image seems to be based on Cyprian, *Epistola* 69.5.

108. *Sermo* 229.2 (=Denis 6) (trans. my own).

109. *Sermo* 272 (trans. Van der Meer, *Augustine the Bishop*, 373). Also *Sermones* 229.2 (Denis 6) and 229A.2 (=Guelf. 7).

sermon, treatise after treatise, the Donatists' great sin was their fracturing the peace and unity of the North African churches.[110] By so doing, they had betrayed the fundamental mystery of the Eucharist, just as their rebaptizing ways had betrayed the inviolability of baptism. Augustine begged his own neophytes not to imitate such contentiousness. They were to be what they saw, for the liturgy had its moorings in and was the privileged sign of genuine community: "In this sacrament you are united with us; together we are joined; together we drink, because together we live."[111] He would also repeat Paul's ominous warning: that to receive the bread and cup unworthily meant eating and drinking judgment upon oneself (1 Cor 11:27-29). For Augustine, that referred to anyone who "receives the mystery of unity and does not possess the bond of peace."[112]

Augustine would then offer guidance on the liturgy itself. He would touch on only a few ritual moments—or "sacraments," as he called them:[113] (1) the dialogue that opened the Eucharistic Prayer, (2) the great Amen, (3) the Lord's Prayer, (4) the kiss of peace, and (5) the words exchanged when receiving Communion. Because of this, liturgists have struggled to reconstruct the flow of the Eucharist in Hippo. We do not know, for instance, the contours of Augustine's Eucharistic Prayer, at least in the way we know that used by Cyril and Ambrose. It seems that Augustine's silence about the Eucharistic Prayer stemmed from his assessment of the pedagogical needs of his hearers: that is, he spoke not so much about what *he* said or did during the Eucharist, but about what the *neophytes themselves* would be expected to say or do. Explaining their role as faithful must have seemed more urgent, from a pedagogical standpoint, than explaining his role as presider. This meshes well with his abiding concern: that one speak ritual words not like "parrots, ravens, and magpies," but

110. See especially *Tractatus in epistolam Ioannis* 1–10 and *Epistola* 185; also Brown, "St. Augustine's Attitude to Religious Coercion," *Journal of Roman Studies* 54 (1964) 107–16; Bonner, *St. Augustine: Life and Controversies*, esp. 278–83.

111. *Sermo* 229.2 (=Denis 6) (trans. my own).

112. *Sermo* 272 (trans. my own). Cf. *Sermo* 227.

113. *Sermo* 227. Albaric, "Une catéchèse eucharistique," 89: "Chaque élément, chaque instant, du déroulement de la célébration est un 'sacramentum.' "

like a human being; that is, that one understand the meaning and import of what one is saying.[114]

Augustine focused especially on the dialogue that opened the Eucharistic Prayer. In his view, "these mystery-laden [words], are terse, but powerful; we say them quickly, but with great feeling."[115] The point-counterpoint of the dialogue was, according to Augustine, a testimony to grace: the presider greeted the assembly with a *Dominus vobiscum* since "without him we are nothing";[116] the call to lift up hearts befitted Christ's Body which yearned to follow its head's upward journey;[117] and the giving-thanks meant that uplifted hearts were a gift of God, and not something ascribable "to your own strength, your own merits, and your own labors."[118]

Augustine would sometimes touch on other words and gestures expected of the neophytes. At the end of the Eucharistic Prayer, they would "say 'Amen' . . . to subscribe to what has taken place."[119] He would quickly pass over the Lord's Prayer "which you received and gave back" since he had elucidated it during Lent.[120] In explaining the kiss of peace, he stressed the link between outward gesture and inner meaning: "This is a sign of peace; as the lips show, let peace be made in your [inner] consciousness, that is, when your lips draw close to the lips of your brother, let your heart not draw back from his heart."[121] Given the fractious resentments his hearers were prone to, such a sign always ran the risk of being an empty gesture. Augustine, who had fought so long and so fiercely to restore unity between Catholics and Donatists, wanted, at least within his own community, a sign of peace that was heartfelt. Finally, when the neophytes approached to receive the sanctified bread, they would hear the words "Body of Christ," and reply "Amen." This meant: "It is to what you yourselves are that you reply, 'Amen'; . . . Be therefore

114. *Enarrationes in psalmos* 18.2.1 (Hebgin and Corrigan, 29:182).
115. *Sermo* 229A.3 (=Guelf. 7) (trans. my own).
116. *Sermo* 229A.3 (=Guelf. 7) (Weller, 102).
117. *Sermo* 227.
118. *Sermo* 227 (Muldowney, 197). Also *Sermo* 229.3 (=Denis 6).
119. *Sermo* 229A.3 (=Denis 6) (Weller, 110).
120. *Sermo* 227 (trans. my own); cf. *Sermo* 229.3 (=Denis 6).
121. *Sermo* 227 (trans. my own).

truly a member of Christ's body, that your 'Amen' may be sincere."[122]

Augustine knew his brief catechesis on the Eucharist touched on only a few urgent matters: "You have heard a few things—but powerful ones. Measure worth not by number, but by weight. At the same time, these [words] should not weigh you down: that way, you might just hold onto what has been said."[123] He knew that over the previous twenty-four hours the neophytes had experienced much and that their memory had no doubt been taxed. They had passed through a long fast, an all-night vigil, a whole array of rites: the solemn *redditio*, the immersions and anointing, and the two Eucharists. And they had heard at least four sermons: two directed to the whole assembly (sermons during the vigil and Easter morning Liturgy of the Word) and two directed especially to them (the catecheses on baptism and on the Eucharist). It should not be surprising that Augustine kept his remarks on the Eucharist brief and passed over much in silence. In the days—and years—that lay ahead, there would be plenty of time for exploring deeper implications.

HUNTING DOWN DEATH: EASTER WEEK

In North Africa, the eight days from Easter until the following Sunday were known as "the octave days of the *infantes*."[124] Throughout the week, the newly baptized continued to wear their white robes and to stand together within the privileged confines of the *cancelli*—set off from the larger assembly both by dress and by location.[125] Eucharistic liturgies were held daily, and Augustine would preach at least twice a day, once in the morning and once in the evening. As Suzanne Poque has noted, "in Hippo, the Octave of Easter was a week especially set aside for catechesis, and the faithful were no less eager for instruction than the newly-baptized"; nonetheless, this catechesis was not reserved for neophytes and faithful, but was open to all.[126]

122. *Sermo* 272 (trans. Van der Meer, *Augustine the Bishop*, 373).
123. *Sermo* 229.3 (=Denis 6) (trans. my own).
124. *Sermo* 376A.1 (trans. my own); see also *Epistola* 55.32; *Sermo* 260; 260A.4 (=Denis 8).
125. *Sermo* 229P.4 (=Lambot 3).
126. Poque, "Introduction," 91. However, she may overstate things slightly when she claims that "les allocutions qui s'addressent spécialement aux nou-

During the morning Liturgy of the Word, the curriculum set by the lectionary followed a fixed rhythm: "During these days, we read of the Lord's resurrection according to all four evangelists. It is necessary that all be read because no single one has said it all."[127] From the sermons that have come down to us, it is clear that at some point during Augustine's career the order of these resurrection pericopes shifted (see chart 18).[128] Nonetheless, the theme remained the same: "These holy days we celebrate after the Lord's resurrection symbolize the life-to-come after our resurrection."[129] Augustine took special pains to spell out the meaning and implications of this, for, as he repeatedly noted, "the distinctive mark of the faith of Christians is the resurrection of the dead."[130] He knew that it was precisely this belief that pagans mocked. To deal with this, he once offered a special three-session series on pagan philosophers and their objections to bodily resurrection (Sermons 240–42). On this occasion, he wanted not so much to shore up people's faith as to train them as "physicians" for those who suffered the "wounds" of unbelief.[131]

After the morning liturgy, Augustine would take his familiar place in the apse of the main basilica and there would field questions from neophytes and faithful. On one occasion, the participants were interested in learning how to answer pagan objections to Christianity.[132] To help equip people for this apologetic work, a mock debate was set up. Augustine took the Christian side, while some of the assembly took the pagan side and challenged him to

---

veaux baptisés ne leur sont pas pour autant réservées." Augustine refers directly to the neophytes from time to time and often touches on topics of concern to them; but during Easter Week the neophytes were one group among several that Augustine took pains to address.

127. Sermo 234.1 (trans. my own). See also Tractatus in epistolam Ioannis, prologus; Sermones 231.1; 232.1; 235.1; 239.1; etc.

128. See Lambot, "Les sermons de saint Augustin pour les fêtes de Pâques," 148–72. Poque has claimed to find two additional ordines: see Poque, "Les lectures liturgiques de l'octave pascale à Hippone d'après les Traités de saint Augustin sur la Première Epître de S. Jean," Revue biblique 74 (1964) 217–41; summarized in "Introduction," 85–91.

129. Sermo 243.8 (trans. my own).

130. Sermo 241.1 (trans. my own). See also Sermones 229H.1 (=Guelf. 12); 234.3.

131. Sermo 240.1 (trans. my own).

132. De divinatione daemonum 1.1–2.6.

rebut subtle arguments on pagan oracles and divine providence. On another occasion, it seems, he took on a host of knotty problems within the Scriptures.[133]

In the evening, beginning on Easter Sunday, Augustine would offer a series on some special topic. One year, for instance, he spoke about the seven days of creation.[134] Another year—the same year he offered the intertwining series on the Psalms and John's Gospel—he spoke on the First Epistle of John.[135] He chose this text partly because it offered a way to continue listening to "blessed John whose gospel we have set aside for a while" and partly because its distinctive theme, charity, seemed especially well suited to the joy of Easter.[136]

In these sermons, Augustine would draw on a host of images—both from the Scriptures and from the local milieu—to tease out the meaning of Christ's resurrection. He would portray Christ as a teacher who made the cross his professorial chair;[137] as a merchant who imported into the land of birth and death an exotic novelty—eternal life;[138] as a physician whose blood became the medicine to cure his killers and whose scars became the medicine to heal the wounds of unbelief that festered in the apostles' hearts.[139] For Augustine and his hearers, time was the great ravager. And so he portrayed it as a swirling river which swept away everything in its fierce wake; thus Christ, whose roots lay in eternity, gave all a handhold against time's destructive coursings: "Time's river sweeps things down it; but there, like a tree born alongside the

133. *Sermo* 259.6. This sermon was given on the Octave; the implication seems to be that scriptural questions that Augustine had raised at a previous question-and-answer session had been left unanswered and he felt obliged not to leave them so. Apparently, it was unusual to hold such an open session on the Sunday of the Octave.

134. *Sermones* 229R–229V (BAC 24:376–88); only fragments of this have been preserved. See Lambot, "Une série pascale de sermons de saint Augustin sur les jours de la Création," *Revue bénédictine* 79 (1969) 206–14.

135. *Tractatus in epistolam Ioannis*, prologus; cf. *Tractatus in evangelium Ioannis* 13.1. See the discussion of this in Agaesse, "Introduction," 75:9–10; LeLandais, "Deux années de predication," 38; Rettig, "Introduction," 78:23–31.

136. *Tractatus in epistolam Ioannis*, prologus (trans. my own).

137. *Sermo* 234.2. Cf. *Sermo* 232.5–6.

138. *Sermo* 233.4; *Sermo* 229H.1 (=Guelf. 12).

139. *Sermo* 229E.2 (=Guelf. 9); *Sermo* 237.3. These images appear frequently: *Sermones* 229J.1 (=Guelf. App. 7); 229O.1 (=Guelf. 17); 242.2; *Tractatus in epistolam Ioannis* 2.1; 5.5; 6.8.

river, is our Lord Jesus Christ. . . . He planted himself—so to speak—alongside time's river. Are you rushing headlong down the rapids? Grab the tree!"[140]

Frequently Augustine paired Christological images with exhortations to the newly baptized. For instance, he would portray Christ as a wealthy man who paid off our debts and tore up the devil's promissory note. With this, he turned to the neophytes and reminded them that they had sworn to follow a new way of life and had been baptized and that the Lord had given them a prayer to free them from incurring further debt.[141] Similarly, he would portray Christ as a sojourner from a foreign land searching for hospitality. Thus his hearers, like the disciples from Emmaus, were to offer him shelter and recognize him in the breaking of the bread. Augustine knew that only insiders—which now included the neophytes—would have the eyes to spot this Eucharistic allusion.[142] But he was equally concerned that they see its implications for justice:

"Thus, let the hungry Christ be fed; let the thirsty Christ be given drink; let the naked Christ be clothed; let the foreign-born Christ be sheltered; let the ill Christ be visited. . . . On this pilgrimage, we must live where he is in need."[143]

Finally, he portrayed Christ as a great hunter who slew death, a fierce lion which had long terrorized humankind. The neophytes thus could enjoy the spoils—"you have captured it, held it fast, conquered it, sentenced it, struck it down and killed it"—and could join in Paul's taunt: "O death, where is your victory? O death, where is your sting?"[144]

Augustine insisted that faith in the resurrection set Christians apart. It meant that they did not share their culture's stock prejudices against the body, for (he insisted) "our faith praises the body."[145] Some of Christianity's most learned opponents, such as

---

140. *Tractatus in epistolam Ioannis* 2.10 (trans. my own).

141. *Sermo* 229E.2–3 (= Guelf. 9).

142. *Sermo* 234.2. See also *Sermo* 235.2 and 3; in *Sermo* 229E.4 (= Guelf. 9), this sort of allusion rouses applause.

143. *Sermo* 236.3 (Muldowney, 234—altered). See also *Sermo* 239.2.

144. *Sermo* 233.4–5 (trans. my own).

145. *Sermo* 241.7 (Muldowney, 261). For an excellent survey of Augustine's eschatological views, see the new study by Brian E. Daley, *Hope of the Early*

Porphyry, found such views absurd: "You [Christians] praise the body without good reason. No matter what kind of body it is, you must escape from it if you wish to be happy."[146] Some pagans would base their objections on ancient physics. To them, it seemed absurd that the human body—made of the stuff of earth, and thus heavy and slow-moving—could rise up to God the way the fleet and airy soul could. Augustine found their physics wanting: if a blacksmith could make iron bowls that floated on water, could not a body transformed by God have a remarkable lightness? Did bulk necessarily slow things down? Why then did the airy spider move ponderously while the bulky horse ran like the wind?[147] Other times, scoffers mocked the ugliness of the body—its internal organs such as intestines and lungs—and asked what use genitals or breasts or teeth would have after such a resurrection. Augustine would counter these jibes. As he saw it, every element within the body, whether internal organs or genitals or teeth, possessed a God-given beauty. The body's beauty came from harmony, like "tuned strings on a lute"; and "if all the strings were tuned the same, there would be no song; for from diverse-strung strings springs diverse sounds."[148] For Augustine, the body possessed its own harmony, its own musicality. Thus, he insisted, at the resurrection, the body would be restored, whole and untarnished; shame and lust would vanish; and even if parts of our bodies, like breasts or genitals, would no longer serve practical needs, they would still exist because of their beauty.[149] And most importantly, God would heal the ancient fissure between our bodies and our interiority. This, according to Augustine, was what Paul meant by a "spiritual body." At the resurrection, we would enjoy what Adam enjoyed: a body which would obey the spirit's direction.[150]

Church: A Handbook of Patristic Eschatology (Cambridge: Cambridge University Press, 1991) 131–50.

146. Porphyry, quoted in *Sermo* 241.7 (Muldowney, 262). See also *Epistola* 102.1; *De civitate Dei* 10.23–32; 22.25–27. On Porphyry's views on Christianity, see Wilken, *The Christians as the Romans Saw Them*, 126–63. For a survey of pagan objections against the resurrection that Augustine addressed, see Courcelle, "Propos antichrétiens rapportés par saint Augustin," 149–52 and 163–70.

147. *Sermo* 242.6–7.

148. *Sermo* 243.4 (trans. my own).

149. *Sermo* 243.6.

150. *Sermo* 242.11.

In these sermons, Augustine would exhort his hearers to cling to the Church and its faith. Orthodoxy meant sailing "between Scylla and Charybdis," between the "rocky jags" of Sabellianism and the "whirlpool" of Arianism.[151] His hearers were to believe as the Church believed: in the whole Christ, truly Word and truly human, and not just the divine mind in a human body, but a person with a fully human psychology, for the one "who created the whole person redeemed the whole person, assumed the whole person, liberated the whole person."[152] But right belief was not enough. Right practice—charity—was the acid test of true Christianity. He highlighted this especially in his series on the Epistle of John. In *Tractate 2*, he exhorted the neophytes:

"Our brothers and sisters [here] have now been born again of water and the Spirit. We too some years ago were born again of water and Spirit. . . . The bulwark of salvation is this: having the root of charity, having an [inner] force of holiness, not merely its [outer] form. The form is good, the form is holy, but what is the form worth if it does not hold to the root. The cut-off branch: is it not tossed on the fire? But how can you be rooted that you not be uprooted? By holding to charity—as the apostle Paul said: 'rooted and grounded in charity.' "[153]

Augustine insisted that outward pieties were not enough. For him, the Donatists were vivid proof that pieties mattered little if one had breached charity. As he sarcastically put it:

"Let them all sign themselves with the sign of the cross of Christ. Let them all respond Amen. Let them all sing Alleluia. Let them all be baptized, come to church, put up walls for [new] basilicas. You cannot discern the children of God from the children of the devil *except* by charity."[154]

Moveover, he would cite the neophytes as proof that possessing the Spirit lay in charity: at their anointing, they did not speak in

151. *Sermo* 229G.4 (=Guelf. 11) (trans. my own).
152. *Sermo* 237.4 (trans. my own). Through these sermons, Augustine uses a variety of heresies as foils for the Catholic position: Manicheism (*Sermones* 229J.1 [=Guelf. App. 7]; 237.1; 238.2); Priscillianism (*Sermo* 238.2); Photinianism (*Sermo* 246.4; 375C [=Mai 95]); Sabellianism (*Sermo* 229G.3-5 [=Guelf. 11]); Arianism (*Sermo* 229G.4-5 [=Guelf. 11]); Apollinarianism (*Sermo* 237.4; 253.4).
153. *Tractatus in epistolam Ioannis* 2.9 (trans. my own).
154. *Tractatus in epistolam Ioannis* 5.7 (trans. my own).

tongues as the first disciples in Acts had. This meant that the gift of the Spirit now manifested itself in love of neighbor.[155] And that charity expressed itself especially in one's care of the poor. Augustine, for his part, would have preferred a truly just social order: "You give bread to the hungry. But it would be better that no one should hunger, and you should not have to give. You clothe the naked. Would that all were so clothed that there be no need for it!"[156] Nonetheless, given an unjust world, the beginning of charity lay in the care of the poor.[157] Thus he encouraged the neophytes to make a beginning: their birth into God, unlike their birth into the world, had been something willed, and "where birth lies in the will, so does growth."[158]

CHIRPING TO FLEDGLINGS LEAVING THE NEST: THE OCTAVE

The days of leisure ended on the Sunday after Easter. The next day, the routine of work and the wrangling of the law-courts would begin afresh.[159] For the neophytes, this Sunday marked the end of their long journey, and they would be—for one last time—the center of attention. Augustine would tell them that this Sunday marked the "Octave of your birth," and that "today the seal of faith is completed in you."[160] The ceremonies that day were to be a distant echo, a figure, of the old Jewish rites of circumcision held on the eighth day after birth. But since, in the Christian dispensation, birth into the people of God was an event of the spirit, so too was its eighth day: this "sacrament of the Octave" would signal the neophytes' "circumcision of heart."[161]

The day was, according to Augustine, a busy one.[162] Unfortunately, we know only a little of what made it so busy. Early in the morning, it seems, people gathered at the *Memoria* of the Twenty Martyrs, a shrine built to honor those killed during the persecution of Diocletian. In the brief sermons given there, there is no

---

155. *Tractatus in epistolam Ioannis* 6.10. See also *Sermones* 229U; 229V; 249.3.
156. *Tractatus in epistolam Ioannis* 8.5 (trans. H. Browne, NPNF 7:508—altered).
157. *Tractatus in epistolam Ioannis* 6.1; cf. *Sermo* 229S.
158. *Tractatus in epistolam Ioannis* 3.1 (Browne, 476).
159. *Sermo* 259.6.
160. *Sermo* 260A.4 (=Denis 8) and *Sermo* 376A.2 (trans. my own). See also *Sermo* 260C.2 (=Mai 94).
161. *Sermo* 260 (trans. my own).
162. *Sermo* 260E.4 (=Guelf. 19); *Sermo* 260.

explicit mention of the neophytes, but scholars presume they were present. It is not clear whether this liturgy was held especially for their benefit, as Poque believes, or whether it addressed only a pious elite, as Perler supposes.[163] An instruction at a martyrs' shrine certainly formed part of the mystagogical routine in Antioch, and may have done so in Hippo as well.[164] Augustine would invite all present—presumably including the neophytes—to bear witness to their faith with the same fervor and courage their spiritual ancestors, the martyrs, had shown: "You too must say: 'We cannot *not* speak of what we have heard. We cannot *not* preach Christ the Lord.' . . . Thus preach Christ wherever you can, to whomever you can, in whatever way you can."[165]

Later that day, Augustine gave a final admonition to the neophytes (see chart 16).[166] During the previous week, the neophytes had stood as living icons: clustered together within the *cancelli*, dressed conspicuously in white robes.[167] They had stood before

163. Othmar Perler, "La 'Memoria des Vingt Martyrs' d'Hippone-la-Royale," *Revue des études augustiniennes* 2 (1956) 438–39; and Poque, "Introduction," 118 note 4.

164. Chrysostom, *Baptismal Instruction* 7.

165. *Sermo* 260E.2 (=Guelf. 19) (trans. my own).

166. The remaining Octave sermons fall into two groups: (1) a sermon on the readings of the day, probably given at the main liturgy, and (2) the final admonition to the neophytes. Augustine delivered at least one of the first type (*Sermon* 258) in the *Basilica Maior* (i.e, the *Basilica Pacis*), and at least one of the second type (*Sermon* 260) in the *Basilica Leontiana*. According to Perler, the *Leontiana* was perhaps the old cathedral, still used on certain occasions, and may well have been the smaller five-naved basilica that archaeologists have uncovered not far from the main church. This suggests two possibilities: (1) both the sermon on the readings and the exhortation to the neophytes were given during a single liturgy, and that this took place in the *Basilica Maior* on certain years and in the *Leontiana* on other years; or (2) the sermon on the readings was given in the *Maior*, while the exhortation to the neophytes was given in the *Leontiana*. If the second was the case, this would mean that each of the three Octave sermons took place in a different edifice and that the assembly would have had to process from site to site, hearing a sermon at each. Moving from site to site, from liturgy to liturgy, was certainly part of the routine in Jerusalem during this same period. See Poque, "Introduction," 112–15; O. Perler, "L'église principale et les autres sanctuaires chrétiens d'Hippone la Royale, d'après les textes de saint Augustin," *Revue des études augustiniennes* 1 (1955) 299–343; for an archeological description of the "basilica with five naves," see Marec, *Monuments chrétiens d'Hippone*, 183–212.

167. *Sermo* 260C.7 (=Mai 94). See also *Sermones* 229P.4 (=Lambot 3) and 260.

331

the assembly as a visual reminder of the high demands and great promise of baptism. On the Octave, the neophytes' infancy ended. They had come of age. They put off their white robes and mixed in once more with the larger assembly. This final rite of passage left Augustine feeling at once joyous and anxious:

"You see: today, the *infantes* mix with the faithful—as if flying out of the nest. It is necessary then that we birth-laborers address them. As you know, brothers and sisters, when young swallows . . . begin to fly out of the nest, their mothers flap around them noisily and, with dutiful chirpings, testify to dangers their children face."[168]

He would then begin chirping about the dangers his own fledglings faced. Like Chrysostom, he would focus on their baptismal robes. He reminded the neophytes that they, like the prodigal son, had once "tended pigs," but had given it up and journeyed a long road to be clad at last in new robes;[169] that they wore gleaming white on the outside because they had been cleansed bright on the inside;[170] and that even though they would soon take off "the outer signs of the sacraments," they were "always to wear [them] in the heart."[171]

But Augustine focused more often on the neophytes' leaving the nest of the *cancelli*. This liturgical action reminded him of his threshing-floor image of Church. As he saw it, this rite of passage meant that the neophytes would once more find themselves mixed in with the chaff. So he would exhort them: "Do not get mixed up by [taking on] a bad life-style. . . . Be grain!"[172] He did not fear their being influenced by pagans or heretics, but rather by the crowd of bad Catholics:[173] "We know that many who are called 'faithful' live badly and that their mores do not square with the grace they have received; that they praise God with the tongue

168. *Sermo* 376A.2 (trans. my own).
169. *Sermo* 260C.5 (=Mai 94) (trans. my own).
170. *Sermo* 223. See also *Sermo* 260C.7 (=Mai 94).
171. *Sermo* 260C.7 (=Mai 94) (trans. my own).
172. *Sermo* 260D.2 (trans. my own). The same theme, with different imagery—that of separating the catch of fish—figures prominently in his Easter Friday sermons: see *Sermones* 248.2–3; 249.2; 250.2; 251.3; etc.

173. *Sermo* 224. Certain interpolations have found their way into this sermon; see Lambot, "Le sermon CCXXIV et saint Augustin et ses recensions interpolées," reprinted in *Revue bénédictine* 79 (1969) 193–205.

and blaspheme him with their lives.''[174] Again and again, Augustine gave the same advice—that the neophytes should seek out and imitate exemplary Christians:

Bonos quaerite,	Seek out the good;
Bonis adhaerete,	Cling to the good;
Boni estote.	Be good.[175]

In these admonitions, he often mixed agricultural metaphors with rhymes and puns. He would remind the neophytes: they were still tender new shoots in the field of God; they had been *"irrigati fonte sapientiae, perfusi luce iustitiae"* ("irrigated by the fountain of wisdom, drenched with the light of justice"); most importantly, Christ "our farmer" had planted them to be "wheat-sprigs" *(spicas)*, not "thorns" *(spinas)*.[176]

Augustine often listed the "thorns" he feared most. The neophytes were to guard against business fraud and usury; against drunkenness and luxurious living; against lying and gossip; against consulting fortune-tellers and wearing amulets; against fornication and adultery.[177] Sometimes, in the course of such admonitions, he would shift his attention to the faithful and single out for rebuke men who used house-slaves as concubines. In Augustine's time, Christians abhorred adultery, but some of them would distinguish between going to a prostitute and visiting the servant quarters. They could claim that such-and-such a woman "is not a whore; she is my mistress."[178] Augustine was outraged by such behavior and did not mince words: "It is wrong, wrong, wrong"; such women made themselves "whores"—"There, go say that 'the bishop has insulted you'"; and men who carry on this way "will go to hell."[179] Moreover, he resorted to humor to chide wayward faithful who put off reform, who would say, "tomorrow, tomorrow" *(cras, cras)*: "when you say 'cras, cras,' you turn into a

---

174. *Sermo* 376A.2 (trans. my own). See also *Sermo* 260.

175. *Sermo* 223.1 (BAC 24:239; trans. my own). See also *Sermones* 224; 260D.2 (=Guelf. 18); 260C.7 (=Mai 94).

176. *Sermones* 260B.1 (=Mai 89); 223; and 376A.2 (trans. my own).

177. *Sermones* 224; 260; and 260D.2 (=Guelf. 18).

178. *Sermo* 224 (trans. my own). On concubinage in antiquity, see Veyne, *History of Private Life*, 1:75–85; on its practice in Christian communities, see the excursus, "El concubinato," BAC 24:797–98.

179. *Sermo* 224 (trans. my own).

crow."[180] Finally, he would exhort the veterans, those baptized one year or many years before. They were to take the neophytes under their wing without, of course, leading them down the road of perdition.[181]

Augustine offered the neophytes no illusions about life on the far side of baptism. Using Exodus imagery, he reminded them that while they had indeed crossed the Red Sea, they had yet to enter the Promised Land; that while they need not fear a rear-guard attack from enemies drowned in the Red Sea of the font, desert wanderings still lay ahead of them.[182] On this desert sojourn, they would face the same mix of joy and temptation that the Jewish people had faced. They too would eat "manna," both the bread of the altar and the bread of God's word. They too would drink from "a cup sweetened by wood," the wood of the cross. They too would face serpents' venom and be healed by gazing at the medicinal cross of Christ. They too would face enemies and defeat them with prayer, with arms uplifted and stretched out in the Sign of the Cross.[183]

Augustine also explored the symbolism of the Octave. As he saw it, its preeminent meaning was eschatological: "Today is a great sacrament, [a sign] for us of unending joy. Today itself will pass away, but the life it symbolizes will not pass away. . . . For this day, the Octave, symbolizes the new life at the world's end."[184] According to Augustine, the Octave offered a dim, fleeting foretaste of that day when the Church would appear no longer as an unsifted mass of wheat and chaff. On that final day, only fine-milled wheat would remain and—Augustine would add ominously—"we know where chaff ends up."[185] As he saw it, the vast scope of history converged—albeit via liturgical signs and passing feelings—within Easter Week. On the sixth day of creation, God had impressed his image on humankind; in the sixth

180. Ibid.

181. *Sermo* 260D.3 (=Guelf. 18) (trans. my own). See also *Sermo* 223.2.

182. *Sermo* 353.2. See also *Sermones* 260.1 and 259.3.

183. *Sermo* 353.2 (trans. my own). *Sermo* 260B.1 (=Mai 89) treats the same images but with variant interpretations: the manna is the bread of the altar; the drink comes from the "rock" which is Christ; the serpents are evil Christians.

184. *Sermo* 259.1-2 (trans. my own). See also *Sermo* 260C.1 (=Mai 94).

185. *Sermo* 259.2 (trans. my own).

age of history, Christ had restored that image; and so at the vigil, "as if on the sixth day of the whole era, we are renovated in baptism so that we may receive our maker's image." On the seventh day of creation, God rested; in the seventh age of history, the future rest of the saints on this earth will take place; and so the Church had celebrated a seven-day sabbath. Finally, on the eighth day, Christ rose with body renewed, separating light from dark as on the first day of creation; and in the eighth and final age, "we shall return to that immortality, that blessedness, from which humankind tumbled." It was for this reason that "the Octave brings to fulfillment the sacraments of the *infantes*."[186] The Octave thus set world history against an eschatological horizon. And for Augustine and for his congregation, the neophytes stood as the fragile bearers of that accumulated symbolic weight. Thus he would exhort the neophytes to "keep your concentration fixed on the eighth day."[187]

It was within this eschatological perspective that Augustine once ventured a long and eloquent plea on behalf of the poor. He stressed "the medicinal power in good works of mercy." He noted that those who had suffered shipwreck sympathized with other victims of shipwreck; that ex-slaves sympathized with the plight of others enslaved; that farm laborers felt compassion for those deprived of rightful pay; that a father who had lost a child—as Augustine himself once had—shared in the lament of parents grieving over children who had died; that "therefore no matter how hard the human heart, shared suffering softens it." He wished that the "common bond of human nature" would be enough to bend people to mercy, but he recognized that more often people remained wounded healers. Thus he begged the neophytes and others to recognize their own wounds—"to fear what you have not been, to remember what you have been, and to consider what you may be"—and thus to show mercy to others as God had shown and would yet show mercy to them. And, he insisted, these works of mercy always had to be done with great sensitivity, with graciousness and humility. Moreover, almsgiving held a profound lesson: when the giver's hand is placed in the needy person's hand, the giver learns compassion and glimpses

186. Ibid. See also *Sermo* 260C.2–6 (=Mai 94).
187. *Sermo* 260C.6 (=Mai 94) (trans. my own). See also *Sermo* 259.1.

into the depths of our "common humanity and common infirmity."[188]

Augustine knew that many of the neophytes would leave that day and travel home to small towns or farms and that many would not return except, perhaps, for some major celebration.[189] He thus pleaded that they faithfully attend church:

"Come back often and visit this 'mother' who gave you birth. See what she has brought together: she has united creature to Creator, has made slaves into children of God. . . . You will not seem ungrateful of such great favors if you offer her the gift of your presence."[190]

He would beg them "not [to] abandon such a mother"—as he had once abandoned his own mother, Monica, and left her standing on the docks of Carthage while he sailed off to Rome. Rather, they should come daily for Spirit-filled food: "the bread of heaven" and "the chalice of salvation." Finally, he pleaded, "let her lead you free and injury-free to life everlasting."[191]

MYSTAGOGY TUNED TO THE KEY OF ENDTIME

Augustine's mystagogy, like that of his contemporaries, drew together various threads: (1) liturgical actions and words, (2) scriptural images and themes, (3) analogies drawn from nature or culture. And these threads came together into a distinct weave due to (1) Augustine's personal temperament, (2) his theological stance, (3) local liturgical traditions, and (4) local culture and physical surroundings. Like his contemporaries, Augustine catechized on the rites of the vigil, and like them, he maintained a silence about the Eucharist itself until after the neophytes had experienced it. While he did offer catecheses on baptism and Eucharist, the individual moments within these liturgies did not shape his mystagogical curriculum the way they did for Ambrose, Cyril, and Theodore. Augustine stood closer to Chrysostom both in timetable and in emphasis: both men catechized on baptism prior to the rite itself; and both brought a paraenetic slant to their catechesis.[192]

188. *Sermo* 259.3–5 (trans. my own); cf. *Tractatus in epistolam Ioannis* 8.5.
189. *Sermo* 259.4; also *De cura pro mortuis gerenda* 12.15.
190. *Sermo* 255A (=Mai 92 and Wilmart 18) (trans. my own).
191. Ibid.
192. The similarity may stem partly from the fact both were trained as rhetoricians, an art in which exhortation figured prominently. Also, at least late in

Using analogies, Augustine would draw out the mystery and paradox of Christ so that here, as before, Christ appeared in varied guises: as a deep-rooted tree in time's rushing stream; as a hunter whose quarry was death itself; as a physician whose scars healed the wounds of unbelief. Sometimes, Augustine used image clusters as maps for tracing out the neophytes' journey. With his baking-bread metaphor, he helped them to grasp the dynamic underlying each stage of initiation and to see that initiation moved towards both a liturgical telos (Eucharist) and an ecclesiological one (unity with God's people). With his Exodus typology, he showed the neophytes that, by entering the Church, they had not entered some Promised Land; that they had, instead, embarked on a desert sojourn; and that for its duration, life would remain a mixed blessing.

Augustine, like St. Paul, reminded people to guard the traditions, those terse formulae that he had handed over and that they had received. He cited four: two given during Lent (the "sacraments" of the Creed and the Lord's Prayer) and two given during the Triduum (the sacraments of the font and the altar). The first two were verbal emblems, catechetical heirlooms to be treasured and passed from one generation to the next; they were to be held as laconic, venerable reminders of a long, meandering journey through God's mysteries. The latter two were enacted symbols whose meaning Augustine found best expressed by St. Paul: in baptism, the neophytes had been buried together with Christ; in Eucharist, they had become one with the one Body of Christ.

While Augustine made little use of the sequence of the liturgy for his curricular outline, nonetheless his mystagogical reflections often revolved around liturgy: its words, its movements, its objects, even its calendar dates. Most often, he used these as starting points for excursions into salvation history, Christology, ecclesiology, eschatology. In his catecheses, the sweep and swirl of time came to the fore. He saw in the liturgical present a convergence of past and future, of history and eternity. Various moments

***

his life, Augustine testifies to a familiarity with at least one of Chrysostom's sermons to neophytes and uses it in his debate with Julian: see Jean-Paul Bouhot, "Version inédite du sermon 'Ad Neophytos' de S. Jean Chrysostome, utilisée par S. Augustin," *Revue des études augustiniennes* 17 (1971) 27–41; Paul W. Harkins, "Chrysostom's *Sermo ad Neophytos*," *Studia Patristica* 10, ed. F. L. Cross (Berlin: Akademie-Verlag, 1970) 112–17.

or movements within the liturgies echoed moments or movements spanning from the dawn of creation to the final trumpet blast of endtime. Thus the white-robed neophytes stood before the larger assembly as living sacraments: they were the first day of a new creation; embodied proof that the Word had become flesh and dwelt among us; the tangible sign of history's Octave when humanity would stand again sealed with the impress of God's image.

One point should not be overlooked or underestimated: all these symbolic reverberations within the liturgies of Easter came to the fore only because Augustine spelled them out verbally. In other words, Augustine the liturgist and sacramental theologian was at one and the same time Augustine the catechist; and it was precisely as catechist that he did his liturgical and sacramental ruminating. He "liturgized" catechetically; that is, publicly, orally. And he chose this public, oral medium because he considered these matters vital to the faith-education both of the newly baptized and of the larger assembly. Sometimes a pragmatic pedagogical assessment shaped liturgical catechesis: for example, his focusing on the neophytes' role within the Eucharist, a rite that was new to them. More often, he was concerned that people see through sacramental emblems to their inner meaning. Yet for Augustine as catechist and mystagogue, expounding the mysteries did not mean explaining them away. Rather, it meant both piling up and uncovering the dense cluster of meanings and letting them set off vibrations among themselves. Moreover, for Augustine, mysteries had consequences: they shaped how one saw Christ and the Church, how one felt and probed one's heart, and how one treated everyone else. The neophytes were to be what they see and receive what they are—the Body of Christ—and that meant being people rooted and grounded in charity.

Still, Augustine's mystagogy was not so much liturgical as eschatological. For him *the* mystery was endtime, and teaching on mystery meant situating things—life and liturgy, salvation history and the history of one's heart—against that final horizon. This perspective was conditioned, in part, by the lectionary tradition in his church; in part, by pagan antagonists who thought the resurrection of the flesh a crude thing; and in part, by Augustine's own theological and philosophical outlook. His debate with the Donatists, his long meditation on his abiding weaknesses, and his painful awareness of the half-sifted mix of good and bad within his own congregation had left him acutely aware that baptism was only a beginning, admittedly dramatic, but a beginning nonetheless. He had no wish that the *infantes* simply be socialized into his Church, for on this side of the eschaton, that Church would remain very much a mix of wheat and chaff. He considered mere socializing a threat. Thus he begged the neophytes to imitate the good and begged the good to take the neophytes under their wing. Repeatedly, he presented the neophytes as the fragile icons of creation's eighth day—that mystery which the eye could not see nor ear hear, a timeless time when humanity would stand restored in body and spirit, in heart and society, and peer into the mystery that God is. He wanted the neophytes, the assembly, and himself to keep eyes fixed on that eighth day and order their pilgrimage accordingly. And that meant imagining a new world where justice was the norm and poverty had been overcome. But for these times in between, set within endtime's horizon, works of mercy were an imperative. The poor were to be fed, clothed, sheltered, welcomed, for in them, the Body of Christ still suffered, and they stood before all as an indictment against an unjust social order and as poignant bearers of the mystery too often fled from or ignored: that all human beings shared a common humanity and infirmity.

Chart 15
Sermons for the Easter Vigil

Sermon	Verbraken #	Text	Trans
1. Liturgy of the Word: to the whole assembly			
219	219	BAC 24	FC 38, Weller
220	220	BAC 24	FC 38
221 = Guelf 5	221	BAC 24	FC 38, Weller
222	222	BAC 24	FC 38
363	363	BAC 26	---
Denis 2+	223 A	BAC 24	Weller
Guelf 4	223 B	BAC 24	Weller
Guelf 6	223 C	BAC 24	---
De resurrectione Domine (fragment)	228 A	BAC 24	---
Wilmart 4	223 D	BAC 24	---
Wilmart 5	223 E	BAC 24	---
Wilmart 6	223 F	BAC 24	---
Wilmart 7	223 G	BAC 24	---
Wilmart add. [14]	223 H	BAC 24	Weller
Wilmart add. [15]	223 I	BAC 24	---
Wilmart add. [16]	223 J	BAC 24	---
Wilmart add. [17]	223 K	BAC 24	---

2. Baptismal Catechesis: to the competentes

[None of these have been preserved: it is referred to in *Sermons* 228 and 229A
(=Guelf 7). Given sometime on Saturday, either in the course of the vigil or perhaps
earlier during the day.]

+ Authenticity of *Sermo* 223A (=Denis 2) is contested. Poque lists others which Verbraken
and others assign to Easter morning: *Sermons* 229D (=Guelf 8), 229C (=Wilmart 8), and 229D
(=Wilmart 9); also 375A (=Denis 4) and 375B (=Denis 5) whose authenticity has been contested.

Chart 16
Sermons Explicitly Mentioning the Neophytes

Sermon	Verbraken #	Text	Trans	Day of Week
1. Liturgy of Word*: to the whole assembly				
119	119	BAC 23	NPNF 6	Easter morning
120	120	BAC 23	NPNF 6	Easter morning
121	121	BAC 23	NPNF 6	Easter morning
225	225	BAC 24	FC 38	Easter morning
226	226	BAC 24	FC 38	Easter morning
228	228	BAC 24	FC 38	Easter morning
2. Eucharistic Catecheses: to the neophytes (and faithful)				
227	227	BAC 24	FC 38, MF 7 Weller, MF 6	Easter morning
229+	229	BAC 24	FC 38	Easter morning
272	272	BAC 24	MF 7	Easter morning
Denis 3	228B	BAC 24	MF 7, Weller	Easter morning
Denis 6+	229	BAC 24	MF 7, Weller	Easter morning
Guelf 7	229A	BAC 24	MF 7, Weller	Easter morning
3. Easter Week Sermons*: to the whole assembly				
146	146	BAC 23	Weller, NPNF 6	Saturday
233	233	BAC 24	FC 38	Monday
245	245	BAC 24	FC 38	Wednesday
249	249	BAC 24	FC 38	Friday
Guelf 9	229E	BAC 24	Weller	Monday
Guelf 15	229M	BAC 24	Weller	Friday
Lambot 3	229P	BAC 24	---	Saturday
Tract epist Jn 1	---	SC 75	LCC 8, NPNF 7	Easter Sunday evening
Tract epist Jn 2	---	SC 75	LCC 8, NPNF 7	Monday
Tract epist Jn 3	---	SC 75	LCC 8, NPNF 7	Tuesday
Tract epist Jn 6	---	SC 75	LCC 8, NPNF 7	Saturday
4. Final Exhortation: to the neophytes (and faithful)				
223	223	BAC 24	FC 38	Octave Sunday
224	224	BAC 24	FC 38	Octave Sunday
260	260	BAC 24	FC 38	Octave Sunday
353	353	BAC 26	Weller	Octave Sunday
376A+	376	BAC 26	---	Octave Sunday
Denis 8	260A	BAC 24	Weller, FC 11	Octave Sunday
Guelf 18	260D	BAC 24	---	Octave Sunday
Mai 89	260B	BAC 24	Weller	Octave Sunday
Mai 92	255A	BAC 24	---	Octave Sunday
Mai 94	260C	BAC 24	---	Octave Sunday

Chart 16 *(cont.)*
Sermons Explicitly Mentioning the Neophytes

Sermon	Verbraken #	Text	Trans	Day of Week
5. Liturgy of the Word: to the whole assembly				
258	258	BAC 24	FC 38	Octave Sunday
259	259	BAC 24	FC 38	Octave Sunday

*For a complete list of Augustine's Easter Sermons: see Suzanne Poque, *Sermons pour la Paques,* SC 116:356–65; A. Wilmart, "Les sermons de saint Augustin pour les fetes de Paques," *Revue bénédictine* 79 (1969) 148–72.

+ *Sermo* 229 is a fragment of Denis 6; see note 85. The authenticity of *Sermons* 228B has been contested; see note 86. *Sermon* 376 of the Maurists is now seen as a composite of a least two sermons (now listed as 376 and 376A in BAC).

Weller = Philip T. Weller, *Selected Easter Sermons of Saint Augustine* (St. Louis: Herder Book Co., 1959).

Chart 17
Augustine's "Baking Bread" Image of Initiation

Steps in baking bread (as cited in Denis 6)	Sermon 227	Sermon 229 = Denis 6	Sermon 229A = Guelf 7	Sermon 272
1. Germinated in field, nurtured by rain, ripened	---	---	---	---
2. Threshed by oxen and brought to granary	---	threshed by heralds of gospel (evangelization)	---	---
3. Set aside under observation in granary	---	catechumenate	---	---
4. Threshed	---	---	fasts observances vigils exorcisms	---
5. Milled	fasts, sacrament of exorcism	fasts exorcisms	exorcism	exorcism
6. Wetted into dough	baptism	baptism	baptism	baptism
7. Baked by fire	chrism of Holy Spirit	Holy Spirit	temptations	Holy Spirit

Chart 18
Lectionary Readings for Easter Week

Day	Homiliary of Pseudo-Fulgentius	Homiliary of Fleury; Alleluia Collection
Easter Vigil	Matt 28	[Matt 28]
Easter Morning	[John 1]	John 1
Monday	Luke 24	Mark 16
Tuesday	Mark 16	Luke 24:1-32
Wednesday	John 20:1-18	Luke 24:33-53
Thursday	John 20:19-23	John 20:1-18
Friday	John 21:1-14	John 21:1-14
Saturday	[John 21:15-25]	John 21:15-25
Octave Sunday	[John 20:24-31]	John 20:24-35

*From C. Lambot, "Les sermons de saint Augustin pour les fetes de Pâques," *Revue bénédictine* 79 (1969) 148–72. Poque claims that two other "ordines" can also be detected: see "Les lectures liturgiques de l'octave pascale à Hippone d'après les Traités de saint Augustine sur la Première Épitre de saint Jean," *Revue bénédictine* 74 (1964) 217–41.

Chart 19
Special Easter Week Catecheses

Sermon	Verbraken #	Text	Trans
1. Seven Days of Creation (fragments)	229R–229V	BAC 24	---
2. *Tractatus epistolam Ioannis, 1–6 (7–8?)*	---	SC 75	LCC 8, NPNF 7
3. *De resurrectione corporum, contra Gentiles*	240–242	BAC 24	FC 38
4. Special question-and-answer sessions:			
De divinatione daemonum	---	CSEL 41	FC 27
[cf. *Sermon* 259, 7]	259	BAC 24	FC 38

Chapter 9

Peroration

A final question: what, if anything, of Augustine's practice and reflections might be gleaned and adapted for use by contemporary catechists who struggle to create curricula and ways of teaching appropriate to the RCIA? Obviously this question needs to be approached with care, given the profound distance and difference between Augustine's world and ours. As a point of entry, I would like to draw on some reflections from Jaroslav Pelikan, one of the foremost contemporary historians of the Christian tradition. First, as Pelikan notes, investigations into the Christian tradition offer no pre-packaged solutions. Instead, they give us—or at least one hopes they give us—a glimpse into "the living faith of the dead."[1] Admittedly, the burning concern of contemporary catechists must lie, above all, in the living faith of the living. Still, scholarly excavations of this "living faith of the dead" flow from a simple presumption: that to nurture the living faith of the living, we need to "include the dead within the circle of [our] discourse."[2] In other words, such efforts presume that the dead have something to say to us; that there is a continuity between their living faith and ours; and that they possess a wisdom, admittedly a wisdom with quite definite limits, but a wisdom nonetheless. Thus, scholars hope that by including the dead within the circle of our conversation, we might not forget a hard-won wisdom and, at the same time, might gain from their guidance the ability to ask new questions and to explore new courses that may indeed serve the task of living faith.

What has hopefully emerged from the preceding chapters is an image—or more precisely, a set of vignettes or tableaux—of Augustine's catechumenate. Like any historical portrait, it can be looked at in and of itself. But, as Pelikan suggests, images from the

1. Pelikan, *The Emergence of the Christian Tradition*, 9.
2. Pelikan, *The Vindication of Tradition* (New Haven: Yale University Press, 1984), 82.

Christian tradition can also serve as icons.[3] What might this mean? Icons are images that one does not simply look at. Rather, they are images that one looks through, as one looks through a window. They help fix our gaze at mysteries that lie beyond any particular historical image: that is, the mystery that God is, the mystery that the Church is, the mystery that we ourselves are. In this sense, Augustine's catechumenate as icon—in its very particularity, its very concreteness—can help fix our gaze "beyond it to the living reality of which it is an embodiment."[4] But an icon is not simply a window. It is, in another sense, an image that helps us look back at ourselves, as one might look into a mirror. Its very otherness, its strangeness, casts a reflection back. In this sense, Augustine's catechumenate as icon might help us see ourselves more clearly. In its reflection, the contours and limits of our own teaching on the mysteries—that God is, that the Church is, that we ourselves are—might come into better focus. In this chapter, I will take Augustine's catechumenate as an icon—as both a window and a mirror—and suggest some ways that his example may prove helpful or suggestive.

Before beginning, however, I must note several limits. First, rustling beneath these reflections on Augustine and the modern catechumenate, one will detect a whole web of educational, epistemological, and theological issues at play. To name but a few: What constitutes knowledge—particularly of faith and about faith? What forms of knowing—cognitive, affective, verbal, practical— most need to be promoted and in what ways? What does teaching mean—especially when it involves teaching mysteries? What roles do Scripture, dogma, liturgy, and theology play within the catechetical enterprise? What is the relationship between intentional formation and grace? What is the relationship between tradition and transformation? These questions have been treated in detail by those who have reflected on the larger enterprise of religious education, and their work has aided my own.[5] Still these

3. Pelikan, *The Vindication of Tradition*, 54–57. I have somewhat extended Pelikan's line of thought here. See also Pelikan, *The Spirit of Eastern Christendom (600–1700)*, vol. 2 of *The Christian Tradition* (Chicago: The University of Chicago Press, 1974) 91–145.

4. Pelikan, *The Vindication of Tradition*, 55.

5. See, for instance, Groome, *Christian Religious Education*; Boys, *Educating in Faith*; Warren, *A Sourcebook for Modern Catechetics*.

questions need to be explored more systematically as they apply specifically to the catechumenate, particularly in light of the contributions of Augustine and other ancient catechists. In these few pages, I can do no more than touch upon these questions.

In addition, these meditations on Augustine and the catechumenate are attempts to look, as it were, through a glass darkly—to speak more of possibilities than actualities. That alone makes these reflections tentative. After all, the catechumenate is, in large measure, an enterprise "unbegun"—to use Kavanagh's term. Thus to try to speak systematically about what Augustine might contribute to this larger enterprise would at this juncture be risky. Moreover, Augustine is not the only ancient voice that needs to be included in this larger conversation on the catechumenate and catechesis. Others who made passing appearances in the preceding pages— Tertullian, Origen, the Cappadocians, Cyril of Jerusalem, John Chrysostom, Theodore of Mopsuestia, Quodvultdeus—deserve to come center stage and to receive equal hearing. Their works invite investigations of equal length and detail.

THE SPOKEN WORD: RHETORIC

In large measure, rhetoric shaped the "how" of Augustine's catechesis. He knew its perils quite well: that it was in itself a neutral art, that it could be pressed into service either for urging evil or for urging justice. Still he regretted that catechists of his day were ignorant of the art, and he pleaded that they take it up as an instrument for the service of the gospel. Augustine's complaint rings even truer today. Rhetoric has become a lost art. It appears today, if it appears at all, under the guise of written composition and has been shorn almost entirely of its original oral character. While one certainly finds some accomplished rhetoricians today, both in the Church and in the political sphere, their artistry has been, in large measure, self-taught and won through an intuitive grasp of basic rhetorical strategies. No longer is rhetoric a self-conscious discipline. No longer is it routinely the object of systematic study. No longer, certainly, is it a pre-requisite in the formation of catechists. This study has illustrated, I believe, the power of catechesis in the hands of an accomplished rhetorician. Admittedly, some of Augustine's rhetoric—orchestrated according to a fifth-century aesthetic and tuned to turns possible only in Latin—is out-of-date. But Augustine does offer us some strategies, some principles, and some perspectives for a catechesis honed by rhetoric. These touch, for the most part, on a limited but vital area of catechesis: the catechist's own words.

A. Catechesis as a Performing Art. Catechesis is an art, or more precisely, a performing art. It was no accident that Augustine compared his efforts to the theaters he so often denounced. His catechesis was a theater of the Word: its drama was salvation history, its script was the Scriptures, and its actors included everyone. He recognized some risks: that he might execute his artistry as though it were a one-man play rather than an epic drama in which he served as soloist singing amid a larger chorus; that his people might well prefer cheering to changing, nodding assent to moral living. And thus he insisted that the measure of artistry depended on God's good grace and expressed itself in people who enfleshed the faith, embodied its charity, and enacted its justice.

Still, Augustine tended to underestimate how vital his own rhetorical training had been. We cannot. Catechists, like other performing artists—musicians, dancers, actors, athletes—need to undergo an exacting discipline. That means, in part, practice, practice, practice. One need only reflect how many times a gymnast might rehearse a dismount from the high bar, how many times a pianist might go over a Mozart cadenza, how many times an actor might recite a Shakespearean soliloquy. With practice, the difficult can become effortless. Despite this, the art of catechesis—like the art of jazz or of stand-up comedy—includes improvisation. And, ironically, such improvisational skills themselves come from practice, from having within one's repertoire a host of standard turns and ornaments.

Moreover, catechesis, like other performing arts, has a fragile beauty whose artistry is tied to one-time performances. Performing artists necessarily wield their craft at specific times, in specific locales, before specific audiences. Thus, the beauty of catechesis, as with other performing arts, flowers in the fleeting heat of live performance. Because of this, history—at least before the advent of records, films, and videotapes—has tended to remember its dramatists, not its actors; its composers, not its musicians; its theologians, not its catechists. By its very nature, catechesis is an art etched in the ephemeral. It is precisely this fragile beauty that Possidius alluded to when he regretted that his readers had missed the better part if they had not seen or heard Augustine preach. It is precisely this fragile beauty that Augustine himself acknowledged when he alerted Deogratias to the difference between writing with a future reader in view and speaking to a flesh-and-blood inquirer. The written word can only dimly capture the living voice. Utterly lost is the cadence of speech and intonation of voice, the pauses and gestures, the choreography of body and word. For this reason, one learns catechesis as one learns other performing arts: from living masters. It is no accident that Augustine offered Deogratias an apprenticeship. It is also no accident that Augustine belittled the ancient obsession with rule books, that he insisted, as Cicero had, that orators needed raw talent, much practice, and good models, and that great orators fulfilled rules because they were eloquent, rather than applying them that they might be so.

Augustine's example suggests that the oral character of catechesis has a complexity and rigor all its own—and that this be respected in the formation of catechists. It also suggests that while catechists obviously need a thorough grounding in scholarship—lest their artful performances rely on ill-founded or ill-digested ideas—their use of that scholarship necessarily orients itself according to demands of an oral medium. Consider musicians: the studied phrasing of a musicologist writing in a scholarly journal differs from the studied phrasing of a classical guitarist performing before a live audience. Both demand scholarly expertise, but their respective expressions of that expertise differ. For the catechist, as for classical musicians, erudition is less visible; its expression, more spontaneous; its effect, more immediate. Yet for the performing catechist, as for the full-time scholar, the search for truth remains an abiding, passionate concern.

B. *The Well-Tempered Word.* In recent years, religious educators have begun to recover storytelling as a catechetical medium. Not surprisingly, some have made it a stock item in the repertoire of RCIA catechesis. Augustine used other tools: metaphors, epigrams, antitheses, puns, paradoxes, parallelisms, jingling rhymes, to name only a few. Such rhetorical figures were, of course, part of the orator's stock-in-trade. Certainly such figures sometimes find their way into the words we use when teaching, but rarely in the concentration and with the artistic self-consciousness that

Augustine and his contemporaries brought to their own performances. Moreover, such figures are but the flickering surface of a deeper sensibility and sensitivity: a care for the well-tempered word. Catechists today are more liable to worry about *what* they are going to say than *how* they are going to say it. The focus tends to lie more on clarity of thought than crispness of expression. Augustine too sought clarity, not cultivation. But for him clarity meant making his message memorable. Clarity meant forging images that would flash in the mind long after the fire of live performance had passed. Clarity meant crafting ear-catching phrases that would echo in the memory long after the actual sounds had left his lips and lapsed into silence.

Augustine offers, I believe, some helpful devices. Certainly, some of his favorites can be executed in English only with difficulty. For instance, his long rhyming passages presume Latin's flexible word order and consistent ways of conjugating verbs and declining nouns. But other Augustinian devices might be more easily imitated. Let me retrace three: the epigram, the antithesis, and the metaphor, and suggest not only their pedagogical import, but also their theological significance. I mean only to be suggestive, not exhaustive. Other Augustinian devices—the knotty problem, the parallelism, the soliloquy—could prove equally valuable and deserve exploration.

(1) *The Epigram.* Augustine's sermons on the Eucharist offer a number of examples. For instance, he gave his hearers an easy-to-remember definition of sacraments: "In them, one thing is seen, something else, understood" (*"in eis, aliud videtur, aliud intelligitur"*). He used an epigram to stress the link between liturgy and life: "Together we drink because together we live" (*"simul bibimus, quia simul vivimus"*). Finally, he used an epigram to turn his two-edged theology of Eucharist into an exhortation: "Be what you see, and receive what you are" (*"Estote quod videtis, et accipite quod estis"*).

These examples suggest that epigrams help both to summarize and to exhort. As an intellectual tool, the epigram can concentrate a chain of reasoning, making its subtleties manageable and its insights memorable. As an exhortative device, it can make moral consequences clear and the moral task urgent. Obviously, teaching with epigrams has risks. It can substitute for the hard-nosed task of theological thinking a soft-minded merchandising of theological slogans. But the epigram remains one tool—among others—for lessening the intellectual fissure between ordinary believers and the educated elite, a problem that plagues the contemporary Church as least as much as it did Augustine's. And it remains one tool—among others—for highlighting that theology has consequences and that mysteries have imperatives.

(2) *The Antithesis.* Dual figures dot the Augustinian landscape: the Church as wheat and chaff; Christ as Head and Body; the gospel as the love of God and the love of neighbor; history as the tale of two cities. Such dual figuration shaped even the minute turns of his thought: he thought of himself as the "servant, not the master of the house"; he called the *competentes* to "fast from hatred and feast on love"; he denounced Christians who "praise God with the tongue and blaspheme him with their lives." Augustine's oratory is, in large measure, the art of the antithesis. It is an art full of promise and full of peril. Its promise lies in the way it can catch the clash of light and dark in the human heart and in human history. Its peril lies in its overbold contrasts which can sever Church from world, spirit from flesh, divine life from human life. Augustine's work is reminiscent of those master photographers who prefer shooting in black-and-white. If they underexpose a photo, things appear too dark. If they overexpose it, things appear too bright. But when they balance light and dark with a discerning eye, they capture the world's subtle shades of gray.

Antithesis is, to a large degree, the native language of baptism and of baptismal catechesis. After all, candidates are called to strip off the old and to put on the new; to prefer the folly of the Cross to the wisdom of the world; to die to sin and to be reborn to grace. More importantly, antithesis is the native language of Christian faith itself. As the Council of Chalcedon formulated it, we are to confess faith in "our Lord Jesus Christ, the same, perfect in divinity and perfect in humanity, the same, truly God and truly human, . . . the same, one in being with the Father as to the divinity and one in being with us as to the humanity." If orthodoxy itself balances antitheses, then how much more do catechists today need to make such balancing part of their own language. In the end, this art of antithesis is like the art of tightrope-walking: one, in a sense, falls off in both directions at the same time and so keeps one's balance. The effect can be breathtaking.

(3) *The Metaphor.* Augustine's catecheses teemed with images from the life around him: from sea-faring, agriculture, jurisprudence,

352

commerce, athletics, warfare. He rarely used these images in simple ways. Sometimes they served to highlight often-unexpected continuities between the ways of culture and nature and the ways of God and Church: for example, the Lord's Prayer as a bilge pump; the Creed as a pact between pearl merchants; the Spirit as a hot southern wind. Sometimes they served to stress discontinuities so that the ways of culture and nature appeared as a photographic negative of the ways of God and Church: for example, in ordinary households, the father is greater than the son, whereas in God's household, Father and Son are equal; in ordinary law courts, judge and lawyer are different so that the trial is impartial, whereas in God's law court judge and lawyer are the same so that the judgment is rigged in our favor. Sometimes Augustine crafted extended metaphors (or if biblically based, typologies and allegories) so that an image cluster became a map: for example, initiation as baking bread; the Church as the inn of the Samaritan; Christian life as an Exodus out of Egypt and into the desert. Sometimes he turned images inside out so that a well-worn theme became once more astonishing: for example, Christ the physician whose scars healed wounds; Christ the import merchant who swapped our death-bound flesh for his death-defying spirit.

This style of teaching keeps one's message close to the audience's experience. Moreover, it can give one's message a poignant and, on occasion, threatening proximity to everyday life. With images, one can, in a single stroke, elide a cluster of meanings, sentiments, and attitudes into an imaginative whole. If used frequently and over time, images mount up so that a cumulative religious vision begins to form. The images thus undergird and support the cross-weave of the everyday and the religious so that the religious becomes incarnated into the everyday and the everyday becomes imbued with religious overtones. At the same time, they mark off and hold the rightful tension between faith and culture, Church and world, divine logic and human logic. This style of teaching—both as a pedagogical method and in its pedagogical outcomes—meshes quite naturally with a faith that dares to make the paradox of incarnation its doctrinal centerpiece.

While teaching by image has much potential, it also has hazards. Images rarely mean one thing or elicit a single association, something poets both recognize and exploit. Certainly images have great power, but they also have a life of their own. They often mean more than we want them to mean, precisely because they are drawn from the thicket of everyday life. Images can twist and turn in one's hands, and, if mishandled, have a bite that can poison one's best intentions. Thus one must know when to pick them up and when to drop them.

C. *The Art of Persuasion.* Augustine felt that what Cicero had said of any orator applied equally to the Christian: that the one who is eloquent teaches, delights, and motivates, and that the greatest of these is motivating. In other words, the art of rhetoric is the art of persuasion. And persuasion means convincing people's minds, stirring their hearts, and leading them to action. Augustine recognized that these aims, when transposed into a Christian setting, assumed definite contours. Certainly teaching—bringing people to understand the Christian message—remained a vital concern. He took great pains to introduce people to the best theology he knew and to do so using the best methods at his disposal. Moreover, he took special care for those who walked a little slower and would not move on until he had heard their shouts of understanding. Delighting, too, had its place. At one level, he knew that he had to entertain, if only that his hearers might be retained as hearers. But at a deeper level, he recognized that delighting meant forming hearts. Thus he made his first concern to read his hearers' hearts and to let them read his. He also sought to sweep them up so that they would taste the full spectrum of religious emotions: awe, fear, joy, sorrow, zeal, yearning. Still, motivating remained his ultimate measure. It meant, of course, setting out the Christian wisdom and way of life. It also meant moving people that they would do what they knew should be done. Thus, for Augustine, the measure of catechesis was persuasion. And persuasion meant informing minds, forming hearts, and transforming lives. It meant, in a word, conversion.

These three aims—teaching, delighting, motivating—are not the usual way catechists today would frame their task. Certainly there are some who not only teach, but delight, who not only instruct, but persuade. But the more common category of self-reflection remains "teaching," and often enough, "teaching" in the narrow sense of instructing. This seems to come, in part, from force of habit: as Americans, we spend many years in schools, and schools often define educational success in terms of cognitive knowledge and cognitive skills; and as Catholics, we are heirs to a religious education which has too often equated faith with assent to propositions. Moreover, since Vatican II, instructing has seemed especially urgent since new theological insights and skills have displaced many older ones. However, rustling beneath this emphasis on instructing and on cognition may also be certain Enlightenment presuppositions: for instance, that true knowing comes only from the exercise of critical and dispassionate reasoning.

This modern preoccupation with cognition, with topics to be covered and knowledge to be gained, can miss the tasks Augustine thought equally important: delighting and motivating. Certainly, it is essential to give contemporary candidates the best that theology has to offer. But it is not enough. Certainly it is essential to use the methods that best promote cognitive understanding. But it is not enough. What a content-and-method mindset tends to miss is the profoundly human dynamic of catechesis. Catechesis is not just something said about some topic at hand. It is something said between people: catechist to candidates, candidates to catechist. And in this exchange, as Augustine observed, a natural sympathy tends to spring up so that supposedly clear lines between teacher and learner blur. Catechesis is thus more than subject matter, more than learning techniques. It is an activity rooted in a human relationship. Augustine sensed this. He thought it natural to compare the experience of evangelical catechesis to the experience of one friend giving another a tour through the countryside, an expanse well known to the one, novel to the other, and enriching to both.

It is from the deeply human dynamic of catechesis that care for delight and for persuasion has, or should have, its moorings. (I say "should have" because any talk of delighting, motivating, and persuading inevitably raises an ominous specter: turning catechesis into ploys, play-acting, and the hard sell. I shall touch on this later.) Augustine's example suggests that we need to give delighting and persuading the same care now lavished on instructing. This would mean recognizing that the affective dynamic of catechesis has a complexity all its own. It was a complexity that Augustine and his contemporaries gave studied attention to. They had a knack for sizing up, in a glance, the unique chemistry of a group and learned to attune their words to the ebb and flow of their hearers' moods. And they incorporated this sense into their catechesis precisely because they were concerned with forming hearts and transforming lives. Such a fine-tuned sensitivity cannot easily be analyzed, dissected, or categorized. But it can be learned and it can be given its due.

Equally critical is the mood of the catechist. Augustine's exchange with Deogratias makes this clear. When Deogratias had asked advice on method, Augustine obliged, but insisted that the heart of the matter lay less in method and more in the affections of the catechist. He insisted that the catechist needs—and that the gospel deserves—*hilaritas:* delight, enthusiasm, passion. The dour catechist is a poor spokesperson for the awe-inspiring mercy and love of God. What Augustine recognized—and what we may, at times, overlook—is that no hard-and-fast line can be drawn between the Christian message and the Christian who bears that message. Inevitably, the bearing of the messenger affects the bearing of the message. A listless messenger tends to make the message listless, while an inspired messenger tends to make the message inspiring. This is scarcely to reduce catechesis to emotional outbursts. Augustine could hardly be invoked as an example of mere emotionalism. He brought to the art of catechesis the full resources of a critical reason nurtured according to the philosophic tools of his age. But he also brought along the full spectrum of his own emotions. At the end of a long study of Augustine, Van der Meer remarked that he found himself "impressed not so much by [Augustine's] powers of reasoning as by the personal passion that lies behind the arguments."[6] Catechists today may well choose to offer arguments very different from those of Augustine, but the need for passion, a passion for Christ and for the gospel, remains no less a part of the task.

Nonetheless, neither eloquent words nor passionate speech persuade the way lives persuade. Thus Augustine insisted—and it remains no less true today—that the life of the speaker has greater weight in persuading than the most eloquent speech. This truth testifies in a different way to the principle cited earlier: that no hard-and-fast line can be drawn between the Christian message and the Christian who bears the message. Christianity in our time, as in Augustine's, celebrates its martyrs. And the word *martyr,* as Augustine would remind his hearers, means "witness," for mar-

6. Van der Meer, *Augustine the Bishop,* 567.

tyrs give testimony not so much by eloquent words as by eloquent deeds.[7] The reverse is no less true. Christians who live badly are eloquent dissuaders, and lead people to protest now as they protested in Augustine's time: "Do you want me to be like so-and-so?"

Finally, catechists need to exercise caution and humility by admitting the limits of Christian persuasion. Consider Augustine the catechumen. He was deeply impressed by the eloquence of Ambrose's speech, and he was deeply impressed by the eloquence of Ambrose's life. Yet his conversion moved slowly, by fits and starts, and the formation he received as a catechumen was only one factor among many in his conversion. In the end, neither eloquent words nor eloquent lives have the final word. Grace does. As Augustine repeatedly insisted, the catechist, the outer teacher, matters far less than Christ, the inner teacher. Thus Augustine once pleaded with a procrastinating catechumen named Firmus and reminded him—and us—of whose eloquence matters:

"I [persuade] in one way; God, in another;
I, on the outside; God, on the inside; . . .
I, by speaking; God, in an ineffable way;
I, only through his gift; God, through his very self;
I, as a minister, who have this ministry from him; God, as a
    crafter of ministers, who, though needing no minister, uses
    faithful ministers for this that he may lavish the good of his
    workings even on them;
finally: I, as a human being who, most of the time, cannot persuade much; God, as the one—when he so wills it—to whom the power of persuasion submits."[8]

D. The Dark Side. Rhetoric grew up in a tough neighborhood: the ancient law courts. There it developed a mean streak, despite all its cultivated veneer. The ancient rhetorician knew how to use words as weapons. He learned not only how to take apart an opponent's argument, but also how to demean an opponent's character. In other words, the ancient rhetorician learned strategies for conducting a smear campaign. This habit of mind appears in Augustine. He was, by training and temperament, a debater, not

7. *Sermo* 260E.1 (=Guelf. 19), given on the Octave. See also *Sermones* 286.1; 299F.1 (=Lambot 9); 328.2; 335A.1 (=Frang. 6).
8. *Epistola* 2* (Divjak) (trans. my own).

an ecumenist. Dismantling an opponent's case or scoring debating points sometimes mattered more than seeing things from an opponent's standpoint. He had a knack for pitting "us" against "them," and, despite protests to the contrary, may have exacerbated civil tensions between Catholics and Donatists.[9] These tendencies, it must be acknowledged, were no less true of his opponents who could be equally vituperative and unbending. This strain within ancient rhetoric lived on and enjoyed a long career within Catholicism in the campaigns against the Reformers, against the Enlightenment, against the Modernists. Vatican II moved consciously and decidedly against such polemics. It insisted that Catholics approach other religious communities in the spirit of dialogue, a dialogue aimed at mutual understanding. Vatican II's stance obviously sets the tone for contemporary baptismal catechesis. This does not mean that catechists should cease marking out positions that distinguish the Catholic community from other communities. But it does mean acknowledging that other people and other faiths can possess a truth and a wisdom that only God's spirit can give.

The rhetorical tradition has a second dangerous drift within it. It can easily become self-absorbed—as it did in Augustine's time—and lapse into a frivolous aestheticism. Augustine had to worry about educated dilettantes more attuned to style than truth. The danger today lies elsewhere. A catechesis honed by rhetoric could easily follow the drift of some popular art forms and descend into mere entertainment. It could reduce teaching to mere showmanship, theology to glitz, and the gospel to what sells on prime time. In an era in which thinking, whether political or religious, threatens to be reduced to TV sound-bites, this drift should not be underestimated. Given the contemporary milieu, it becomes even more imperative that catechists, whatever their rhetorical gifts, be well informed, that they have at their fingertips the best that scholarship has to offer.

Finally, rhetoric must be seen for what it is: a technology of the word. Like any technology, it can be used for good or for ill. Augustine noted (as Cicero had before him) that the combination of rhetoric's power and its indifference made it a dangerous tool.

9. This view—admittedly disputable—is set out by Frend, *The Donatist Church,* chapters 14 and 15 and is repeated in his more recent work, *The Rise of Christianity,* 668–73.

More often than not, it was, is, and will be used for ill. In our century, politicians have used it for promoting wars and playing on ethnic hatred and racial prejudice; advertisers have used its stratagems for purveying useless consumer goods and for fueling a crass materialism. Our culture, like Augustine's, teems with rhetorically astute voices. And these voices, often enough, seek to persuade people to accept values that stand in stark contrast to the gospel. Nonetheless, rhetoric can also serve the good. One need only look at the example of Martin Luther King, whose eloquence gave the moral truth for which he gave his life a force and a power it would not have otherwise had. King's career is itself eloquent testimony to Augustine's insistence that eloquence, if rooted in wisdom, can in fact do much good.

THE VISIBLE WORD: LITURGY

Augustine thought of the liturgy as a sequence of "visible words." And it was within the visible words of liturgy that his spoken words, his catechesis, usually resided. The two intertwined. Each nurtured and shaped the other. On the one hand, Augustine's catechesis moved according to liturgical rhythms: his classroom was his basilica; his lectures were his sermons; his textbooks were the Scriptures proclaimed by readers and sung by cantor and congregation; and his lessons, often enough, drew on a repertoire of ritual gesture, movement, and word. On the other hand, he used catechesis to rescue ritual from unthinking ritualism. With catechesis, he would draw out how liturgy held hidden theological meanings and glaring moral imperatives. In his catecheses, he would probe the liturgy for echoes of salvation history or for reverberations from endtime. In his catecheses, he would trace out how the shape of a rite might shape the heart or how ritual mores might clash with cultural ones.

At no time was this play of rite and catechesis more obvious or more concentrated than during the Triduum. During one thirty-six-hour period—from Holy Saturday to Easter Sunday evening—candidates would move through rite after rite: the solemn *redditio;* the lighting of vigil lamps; the all-night round of readings and psalms; the baptismal immersions and anointings; the two Eucharists. And yet again and again this succession of rites was punctuated by catechesis of the highest order: by the public sermons during the vigil and the morning Liturgy of the Word; by the private sermons on baptism and on Eucharist; by a Sunday evening sermon that inaugurated the special Easter Week sequence. The Triduum was indeed the culmination of a long journey. And at that journey's end came initiation, marked not simply by a sacramental crescendo, but also by a catechetical one.

The ancient symbiosis between catechesis and liturgy no longer exists. The two have parted paths. Each has become a separate discipline; each has its expertise; each, its distinctive methods and concerns. This division of labor has admittedly yielded some gains, but it has also meant certain losses. One of these is what Kavanagh termed the "de-ritualization of catechesis." No longer does catechesis move first and foremost within a liturgical ambience. No longer is catechesis knit simply within the ritual rhythm of Scriptures proclaimed, psalms sung, prayers uttered. No longer do ministers see or use the sermon as the preeminent catechetical medium. The inverse, what I would term the "de-catechization of ritual," has also taken place. No longer is liturgical theology a genre of catechesis. No longer does it breathe the spontaneous orality that Augustine and his contemporaries brought to it. No longer does it address itself to audiences with little education and even less background. No longer does it use a language pruned of jargon and spiced with music and imagery.

In moving from the basilica to the classroom, catechesis has gained as well as lost. This move made it possible for the laity to once more serve in this vital ministry. It opened the way for catechumens to gather apart from the larger assembly, so that they might receive a catechesis better attuned to their unique needs. It also opened the way for using a variety of educational methods. For instance, a classroom ambience allows informal dialogue, something virtually impossible in a liturgical setting. Admittedly, moving from liturgy to classroom has sometimes meant little more than moving from a monological sermon to a monological lecture. Nonetheless, accomplished catechists now use a spectrum of dialogical methods. With these, candidates learn to give voice to the religious within their own experience, to tell their own history of salvation, and to grapple in their own words with biblical texts and doctrinal traditions.

Augustine himself did not always use a liturgically based catechesis. His evangelizing of inquirers often took place outside of liturgy, and his address to them would be profoundly shaped by an opening, and sometimes ongoing, dialogue. During Easter Week he held special open sessions with neophytes and faithful, and in these, too, dialogue played an important part. No doubt, other important, though informal, exchanges took place—but these are exactly the types of experiences rarely preserved in the historical record. We do know, thanks to the *Confessions*, that one such exchange figured prominently in Augustine's own conversion: his conversation with Simplicianus. Simplicianus recounted to him the story of Victorinus's conversion and, in so doing, fired Augustine's enthusiasm and offered him a model to be imitated. Even Augustine's liturgical catecheses moved according to a dialogical rhythm. Again and again, his hearers broke in and punctuated his words with outcries and applause—so much so that he used their noisy responses as a barometer of his pedagogical effectiveness.

It would be a mistake to treat Augustine's liturgically imbued catechesis—or that of his contemporaries—as though his or their efforts offered some norm for contemporary catechesis. Some of what he and they did may be desirable, but not feasible; and some of what he and they did may be feasible, but not desirable. Nevertheless, his and their examples, while by no means normative, may still prove suggestive. Let me cite several examples:

A. The Sermon as Catechesis. Augustine routinely preached for an hour. Perhaps more surprising, his hearers were liable to think themselves cheated if he shortened his remarks unduly. Obviously, most Catholic congregations today have very different expectations and would understandably revolt against such unabashed prolixity. Sermons may now be shorter. Nonetheless, they remain a form of catechesis. What may well be overlooked is a simple, obvious fact: catechumens still listen to sermons. So do the elect and so do neophytes. In fact, over the course of their formation, candidates may well hear more than a hundred Sunday sermons. Do preachers avert to this? Do they look out and see the catechumens or elect or neophytes mixed in with the larger assembly? Does the presence of such candidates in any way shape what preachers say or how they say it?

The example of Augustine may offer contemporary preachers several helpful strategies. First, preachers inevitably address mixed audiences—a fact that Augustine and his contemporaries both recognized and exploited. When Augustine came upon a biblical text with baptismal overtones, he routinely turned to the catechumens and offered them a brief instruction or exhortation. Such turns, in effect, make the catechumens the hearers and the larger assembly the over-hearers. In this way, as Augustine noted, the catechumens are instructed and the faithful roused from forgetfulness.

A second strategy moves in the opposite direction: the preacher singles out the candidates, but addresses his remarks to the larger assembly. Augustine's Easter Sunday and Octave sermons illustrate the basic dynamic. He would have the assembly turn its gaze to the white-robed neophytes clustered in the *cancelli*. He would then invest the gathered neophytes with symbolic force by linking them to classic scriptural phrases. In this way, the neophytes became living icons that pointed to the high cost of conversion and the high dignity of baptism. This approach is one way that preachers might make the RCIA a vehicle for renewing the whole local community. At the most obvious level, this helps instruct the community about a rite that is new and unfamiliar. But more importantly, it helps the community come face to face with a simple, but often overlooked principle: the way one becomes a Christian is the way one remains a Christian—that is, by conversion—and the journey of conversion is lifelong, communal, and required of all.

B. The Pedagogy of Silence. Augustine's neophytes emerged from the baptistery freshly washed, freshly anointed, and freshly clothed. They were then invited, for the first time, to join the assembled faithful for Eucharist. No one had explained the Eucharistic Prayer to them. No one had explained the kiss of peace to them. No one had even explained to them how to receive Communion, let alone what it meant. Only later, at a second Eucharist, did Augustine offer any instruction.

This suggests that the first movement in liturgical catechesis is—or, at least, might be—a pedagogy of silence. In other words, the catechist recognizes that silence can teach; that the rite itself teaches; and that the rite, not the catechist, should perhaps have the first word. Such silence presumes what cannot, unfortunately, be presumed: namely, that we use liturgical symbols and gestures that are generous enough and lavish enough to speak for themselves; that baptism be a real bath and not a few dribbles of water, that chrismation be a real anointing, applied thickly enough for its fragrance to be sensed, and that our Eucharistic bread look, feel, and taste like real bread.

The pedagogy of silence is related to, but distinct from, the larger and thornier question of the *disciplina arcani*. When the RCIA resurrected the rite of dismissing catechumens, it reinstituted, in effect, something of the old *disciplina*. This rite of dismissal—and the whole tradition of the *disciplina arcani*—has been ignored by many, defended by some, and attacked by others. Those who object argue that it is a liturgical anachronism. Even worse, it is bad manners and smacks of spiritual elitism. However, two of Augustine's contemporaries, Cyril and Ambrose, suggested that the *disciplina arcani* had a value beyond simply shielding the Christian mysteries from the uninitiated. They felt it had a pedagogical value all its own. Cyril, for instance, believed that in matters of mystery, experience should precede explanation; and Ambrose believed that the inner light of the mysteries infused itself better in the unsuspecting. Similar views may have governed Augustine's practice. In any case, he consciously chose not to explain the Eucharist until after the neophytes had first experienced it themselves.

One may choose to dismiss the *disciplina arcani*. Nonetheless, a pedagogy of silence may have a value all its own. It implies that catechists refrain from explaining the rites in advance, that they cease trying to pre-program candidates' experience. Because this moves against common practice, a simple analogy might prove helpful: we expect film critics to alert us whenever a worthy film comes along; we also expect them to pique our curiosity and to point out a few salient features from the film; but most of all, we expect them to have the common decency not to tell us the ending—as if their review were a substitute for the actual experience of seeing the film. If critics know how to be circumspect about films, then how much more should catechists be circumspect about the Church's rites. Certainly, catechists need to alert candidates to a rite's worthiness and the responsibilities that accompany its passage. Certainly, catechists need to pique their curiosity and alert them to a few of the rite's salient meanings: that becoming a catechumen means committing oneself to following Christ; that baptism marks the forgiveness of sin; that the Eucharist means real presence. But like film critics, catechists need to have the common decency not to tell everything—as if their preparatory catechesis were a substitute for sacramental experience. Good films have an immediate intelligibility to those who watch them; likewise, good rites have an immediate intelligibility to those who participate in them. And if good films have a richness and meaning that provoke discussion among appreciative viewers, how much more do the Christian mysteries have a richness and meaning that naturally provoke meditative reflections among appreciative participants.

In other words, a pedagogy of silence flows from a respect for the candidates and a respect for the mysteries. In practice, it means that one would not explain the rites in advance and certainly not hold rehearsals. All that is needed is to alert candidates to doctrinal essentials and to the high responsibilities and blessings that will come on the far side of the rite. Usually, one may need to quell anxieties. To do so, one simply has to reassure candidates that they will not be embarrassed, that a master of ceremonies will make sure that they are in the right place at the right time, and that they need only to listen for and answer the simple questions asked them. As for the rest, the mysteries can speak for themselves.

C. *The Shape of Mystagogy.* Mystagogy, the teaching of mystery, is itself a mystery to many. Patristic examples may provide guidance not only in restoring the term, but in restoring the art itself. As we have seen, fourth- and fifth-century mystagogy braided into a single weave with three distinct strands: (1) liturgical actions and words, (2) scriptural images and themes, and (3) analogies drawn from nature or culture. Also, it assumed different contours in the hands of different mystagogues. For instance, Cyril, Theodore, and Ambrose used their respective baptismal and Eucharistic liturgies as their outline, but differed from one another in emphasis: Cyril stressing how the liturgical present imaged the scriptural past; Theodore stressing how the liturgical present foreshadowed an eschatological future; and Ambrose stressing how visible rites pointed to invisible realities. Chrysostom and Augustine, on the other hand, used the liturgy less systematically. For them, liturgical symbols and gestures served as springboards for theological exploration or, more often, moral exhortation. The difference between these two lay less in intent and more in framework: Chrysostom drew especially on figures from the scriptural past that they might serve as moral exempla; Augustine, by contrast, drew on scriptural figurations of the future that his moral dicta might be tuned to the key of endtime.

The art of mystagogy, it seems, begins with two presuppositions. First, candidates need to understand. They need to know what the liturgies mean and how liturgical symbols form them for Christian life. As Augustine insisted, human beings must not act like parrots, ravens, or magpies who mimic things they cannot understand. People have minds, and with their minds, they are to pierce through sacramental emblems to glimpse their inner meanings. This has its dangers. Explaining rites can easily lapse into explaining them away. Moreover, inner meanings can be stressed so that outer symbols become mere husks. To put it in Augustinian terms: just as human beings have a spirit that enlivens their flesh, so sacraments have a meaning that enlivens their flesh; and just as one kills a human being by trying to extract the spirit from the flesh, so one can kill a sacrament by trying to extract its meaning from its flesh. In effect, a wrong-headed approach to teaching sacraments violates the second presupposition: namely, that sacramental mysteries are, in fact, mysteries and need to be treated as such. Mystagogical catechesis is thus less an explanation and more an exploration; it is less an explication and more an evocation. It works like sonar: it plumbs the depths not to deny the depths, but rather to point out how deep they actually are. It works like diving gear: it allows one to breathe in depths otherwise inaccessible and to swim down and surface buried treasures otherwise overlooked. In other words, the mysteries should appear, on the far side of catechesis, not less mysterious, but more mysterious.

In practice, the art of mystagogy is a good deal simpler than one might think. One way is to begin with a liturgical symbol: for instance, the baptismal water. One then free-associates to gather scriptural stories: the waters of creation, Noah's ark, the Red Sea, Christ walking on the water, the woman at the well, etc. One then repeats the same process, but focuses on how water appears in natural settings: spring rains, snow on mountains, salmon leaping upstream, dolphins swimming in the ocean, etc. One then repeats this a third time, focusing on water experiences in the local culture: turning on tap-water, taking a shower, nearly drowning in a lake, polluting a stream with chemicals, etc. In this way, one assembles a whole reservoir of biblical, natural, and cultural images. One then probes each in terms of baptism so that it appears either as a type or an antitype. For example: "Christ bathes us in baptism's pure waters, not in some polluted stream, for he desires from us not polluted lives, but pure ones"; "Just as salmon struggle up mountain streams to return to their birthplace, so too Christians struggle up a baptismal stream to their birthplace in Christ"; "Both dolphins and Christians swim in depths over their heads, dolphins in the depths of an ocean, Christians in the depths of God's love."

A more difficult approach is to weave a mystagogical strand around liturgical words. Take, for instance, the words "The Lord be with you / And also with you." First, one ponders its resonances: it is both a greeting and a blessing. Then one free-associates to give these ideas some concreteness: for example, one greets people at the door of one's house; one blesses food at one's table. Then one assembles biblical episodes and themes to set this within the light of faith. Thus, one might say:

"With the words 'The Lord be you / And also with you,' we greet one another. Yet we not only greet one another; we also bless one another. Why do we greet one another? Because God has greeted us first, just as Christ once greeted the frightened apostles in the upper room. Why do we greet one another? Because Christ the homeless one has welcomed us into his home. Why do we bless one another? Because God has blessed us first, just as Christ blessed all those he healed. Why do we bless one another? Because God has blessed us with this feast, this Eucharist."

One then explores whether this liturgical pattern might evoke a cultural one: for example, homeless people have no door to be greeted at nor regular meals to bless. One can thus turn this liturgical exploration into a moral admonition:

"We greet one another and bless one another at the liturgy, but the homeless sit in the streets ungreeted and unblessed. Should we only greet them and bless them with words? No. We need to greet them with emergency aid. We need to bless them by pressing their just cause. In that way, they too may have houses where they may greet friends. In that way, they too may have food which they may bless. We Christians are greeters and blessers in worship because, before all else, we are greeters and blessers in

366

our lives—particularly to those who might otherwise know neither greeting nor blessing.''

Mystagogical thinking is not difficult; it is simply different. It obviously can lapse into liturgical ''alchemy'' if not based on a knowledge of the structure, history, and theology of worship and sacrament. Yet mystagogy is an oral art and differs from a scholarly text on sacramental theology. Mystagogy moves by a logic more associative than discursive, more poetic than philosophical. This logic is not its only salient feature. There is another: a preference for surplus, whether a surplus of cultural images or scriptural echoes or both. The mystagogue tends to let these images and echoes pile up so that the meanings cluster and set off vibrations among themselves; the scholar, by contrast, tends to sort them out into discrete bits of meaning. Sorting out creates conceptual clarity; piling up evokes experience—an experience that presses the hearer beyond the words themselves. The mystagogue uses this method of surplus to achieve a conscious pedagogical aim: namely, that while each image and each echo point to the mystery at hand, no one image or echo can subsume it. This method is thus a way of telling the truth about mystery: that a mystery can be pointed to, hinted at, even glimpsed, but it cannot be defined or exhausted.

D. Catechesis as Liturgical Theology. Certain rites and symbols from the North African liturgy do not appear in the RCIA: catechumens no longer receive the sacrament of salt; the elect no longer go through a prebaptismal physical nor do they stamp their feet on a goatskin-sackcloth; neophytes no longer wear their baptismal robes during Easter Week nor do they walk about in special sandals. However, others rites and symbols from the North African liturgy do appear in the RCIA: catechumens are once more signed with the cross on the forehead; Lent once more begins with an enrollment of names; the Creed and the Lord's Prayer are once again handed over; the elect are once more expected, in a solemn ceremony, to recite the Creed from memory; the neophytes once again gather in a special ''nest'' set apart from the larger assembly. This second cluster of rites and symbols played prominent roles in Augustine's catecheses. The care and focus he gave them should alert us to features of the RCIA whose importance might be easily overlooked and whose symbolic potential might be left untapped.

Augustine took the details of liturgy seriously. He presumed that every gesture, every sign, every word mattered. Each held some import for how one believed, felt, and acted. It is for this reason that he did not reserve catechesis on liturgy for neophytes and for Easter Week. He recognized that inquirers were signed with the Cross, that catechumens joined in Liturgies of the Word, that *competentes* were exorcised and were handed over the traditions. All these rites and symbols needed—indeed, required— exploration. Thus, a mystagogical strand threaded its way through the catecheses he gave at every stage of initiation.

This attitude and approach is not out-of-date. Catechesis has an ongoing role to play vis-à-vis the RCIA's panoply of liturgies. Candidates now, as then, experience rites and symbols at every stage in their formation. And these need—indeed, require— exploration. Thus, for better or for worse, we catechists must serve as liturgical theologians. Like Augustine, we do our liturgical ruminating catechetically; that is, orally, publicly. And we use this public, oral medium because the symbolic reverberations within the many liturgies of the RCIA are vital to the faith of candidates and of baptized alike. In other words, catechesis and liturgy necessarily intertwine. As Augustine recognized, the two share a common language: the eloquence of the earth. They also share a common aim: a people transformed into the Body of Christ. It is this mystery—transformed people—that guides both rite and catechesis. Both hope to point to it. Both hope to evoke it. And both hope against hope that it may come about.

THE WRITTEN WORD: SCRIPTURE

What are we to teach? A generation ago, the answer—at least in many circles—seemed obvious: teach inquirers about the "cathedral" of Catholic doctrine. This cathedral, despite centuries of modification, retained the old Gothic outlines of the *summae: de trinitate, de incarnatione, de gratia, de sacramentis.* The task of catechists was, in a sense, to walk inquirers around this cathedral of doctrine, to explain each pillar and each niche, in hopes that they would understand and agree. Often enough, tours were conducted using a small handbook, the catechism. This cathedral-tour approach was, on occasion, sharply criticized—for instance, by

Josef Jungmann and the kerygmatic movement. Yet in the right hands and with the right person—say, a Thomas Merton or a Dorothy Day—it could aid a conversion of mind, heart, and life.

With Vatican II, the old doctrinal architecture was altered radically. Naturally, new guidebooks arose to replace the old, to reflect more accurately the radically refurbished interior and the radically reworked groundplan. Nonetheless, many retained the old doctrinal focus, even the old Gothic outline: so much on Trinity, so much on incarnation, so much on grace, so much on sacraments. (The *Dutch Catechism* and its imitators remain the most obvious exceptions to this.) Thus when the RCIA appeared, it seemed only natural to use these new catechisms, despite contrary indications within the RCIA itself and despite often impassioned protests from commentators on the rite. Even now, I continue to find parish after parish following, almost unconsciously, the old outline: so much on Trinity, so much on incarnation, so much on grace, so much on sacraments. Sometimes parishes no longer follow one catechism, but instead offer a survey of theological topics. In effect, the old unified doctrinal structure is replaced to better reflect the pluralism of disciplines within contemporary theology. More recently, however, the trend has begun to shift towards using the lectionary. Certain of its advocates (Hinman Powell, for instance) insist that the lectionary is *the* curriculum, ignoring the fact that the RCIA concilium prudently refrained from dictating a curriculum. And now, just as some parishes have begun to experiment with the lectionary, one hears rumbles, like distant thunder: a new universal catechism has come onto the horizon, and no one knows exactly what storms it may raise up. To this legacy and to this setting, the example of Augustine offers, I believe, not answers, but questions, not solutions, but challenges.

A. The Bread of the Word. Augustine taught candidates Scripture: Scripture in quantity and Scripture in depth. Like the advocates of the lectionary method, he presumed that people need a certain biblical literacy, that they need to have a great many scriptural stories and a great many scriptural sayings at their fingertips, and that these stories and sayings need to infuse their minds, stir their hearts, and shape their way of life. Moreover, he insisted on something that a catechism or theological-topics approach tends to lose sight of: that God's Word is bread, that it feeds the hungry.

Augustine's example suggests that the first priority is to give people the Scriptures themselves, in quantity and in depth; and that one not let second-level theological reflections—however brilliant and however necessary—be put forward as though they were substitutes for the Word itself. It is this perception that seems to have guided the RCIA's insistence that catechumens feast—before all else and for years if need be—at the table of the Word. Vatican II put the matter even more pointedly when it quoted Augustine's contemporary, Jerome: "Ignorance of the scriptures is ignorance of Christ."[10] Moreover, Augustine insisted that the duty of Christian teachers and preachers, above all else, is to break open this bread of the Word and to multiply its loaves. In other words, catechists should think of themselves not as servants of theology nor as servants of a catechism, but rather as servants of the Word. And as Augustine insisted, both they and those they guide live off the same scriptural diet.

B. *Breaking Open the Bread of the Word.* Breaking open the bread of the Word means interpreting. To do this, most of us are liable to turn first to the fine biblical commentaries and tools produced by highly trained and knowledgeable exegetes. The work of these exegetes has radically altered our understanding of Scripture. They have alerted us to the Jewishness of Jesus, to the eschatological strains in his preaching, to the subtle elusive nature of his parables, to competing groups like the Pharisees, Sadducees, and Zealots. Moreover, exegetes have sought to ferret out what lies behind the inherited text: earlier sources, oral traditions, editorial patterns, social settings. All this work, the fruit of the historical-critical method, orients itself according to a quite deliberate end: to understand what Scripture (and the traditions behind it) *meant* in its (and their) original settings.[11] Moreover, the exegete as exegete tries to set aside—as best as an interpreter can—two other questions: what a scriptural text *has meant* in the tradition and what a scriptural text *means* now.

It was precisely these two questions—what Scripture *has meant* in the tradition and what Scripture *means* here and now—that

10. Jerome, *Commmentariorum in Isaiam prophetam,* quoted in Vatican II, *Dei Verbum,* 25.

11. See Raymond E. Brown, *The Critical Meaning of the Bible* (New York: Paulist Press, 1981) 23–44. See also Edgar Krentz, *The Historical-Critical Method* (Philadelphia: Fortress Press, 1976).

preoccupied Augustine. His example suggests that we today cannot be content to repeat the findings of exegetes, to teach only what Scripture meant in its original setting. After all, catechumens are not being initiated into the first-century community of Luke or of Matthew. They are being initiated into a twentieth-century Catholic community. And that means, in part, finding ways to help initiates learn to read Scripture with Catholic eyes. We saw that during one four-month period, Augustine took catechumens (among others) through the opening chapters of John's Gospel. He explored at length what reading those chapters with Catholic eyes entailed. He knew that his Catholic reading differed sharply from the reading given these chapters by others (Arians, Donatists, pagan neo-Platonists). But his concern was not simply to mark out the Catholic view. He treated these chapters at length because they grappled with questions that the orthodox tradition had wrestled with for centuries: Who is our God? What does it mean to call Christ the Word made flesh? What meaning does baptism have? What responsibilities come with it? What is creation and salvation? And what difference does any of this make?

Augustine's example has something to say to any who use a lectionary approach. It suggests that exploring the Scriptures with catechumens is not the same as exploring the Scriptures with exegetes. Exploring the Scriptures with catechumens requires helping them read the Scriptures in the light of the Catholic tradition—for it is into that tradition that they are being initiated. Moreover, that tradition has expressed itself in many and varied ways: in art and music, in liturgy and popular piety, in the lives of saints and the spirituality of mystics, in the pronouncements of councils and the insights of great theologians. And these traditions inevitably take as their taproot one or another Scripture verse or theme. If catechumens are to be initiated into the Catholic tradition via Scripture, then they will need to grapple not only with the texts themselves, but also with the rich and varied streams within the tradition that those texts touch upon. That includes, of course, handing on doctrine, the self-conscious, communal, and canonical understanding of the Catholic community. However, as Augustine demonstrated, one must teach doctrine not as a free-floating set of abstractions, but as both a summary of beliefs and attitudes rooted in Scripture and a lens for reading Scripture.

There is another side to this: Augustine taught what it meant to read the Scriptures according to the rule of faith long before he actually taught the rule of faith. As we saw, the Creed in no sense subsumed his initiatory curriculum—a fact that should challenge those who use the catechism approach. The example of Augustine suggests that learning the Creed or a catechism cannot substitute for nor offer a shortcut around a long, meandering pilgrimage through the Scriptures. The Creed offers a map for reading the biblical terrain. It is not, strictly speaking, the terrain itself. Its brevity marks out complex depths with a few words. And if those depths are not explored, its few evocative signposts risk becoming overly abstract, if not altogether unintelligible. The Creed is a symbol—neither more nor less. It is a catechetical heirloom passed from one generation to the next as a sign that the tradition itself has been passed from one generation to the next. Yet passing on the Catholic tradition demands a good deal more than passing on the Creed. In and of itself, the Creed is a summary of what the Catholic Tradition understands about crucial matters. But the knowledge of summaries, while crucial, indeed imperative, is not the same as knowledge of the Tradition: for knowing the Tradition, in an Augustinian sense, means not only knowing in mind, but loving in heart and loving in deed. Thus, as Augustine suggested, the Creed is ultimately a covenant between merchants who have committed their energies and their resources to a single-hearted quest for the pearl of great price, that is, charity.

But teaching what Scripture *has meant* through the Tradition is not enough. Augustine's example suggests that catechists also need to teach what Scripture *means*: in a particular locale, at a particular moment, before a particular assembly. It is this point that no catechism, universal or otherwise, can effectively anticipate. Consider how Augustine taught. He sat in the apse of the basilica with an eye focused as much on his audience as on the text in his hand. And what he taught depended a great deal on who he taught and where he taught it. He was not, after all, teaching Scripture to candidates of all the Catholic communities in the empire; he was teaching Scripture to candidates of the Catholic community in Hippo. Thus he often used the local milieu as a lens for reading the Scriptures. As a result, Scripture would appear outfitted in North African colors: the Spirit blowing like a wind out of the Sahara; the Church appearing like a granary for sifting wheat and chaff; Christ sailing into town with precious goods like an import merchant. Other times, Augustine used the

Scriptures as a lens for reading the local milieu. Thus he would pit gospel teaching on the forgiveness of enemies against the local revenge ethic, or he would denounce the scandalous gap between rich landlords and the beggars in the streets. His example thus suggests that the catechist is a mediator: one who brings Scripture to culture and culture to Scripture. It also suggests that we may need to shift the burden of reflection away from universal catechisms and toward local catechists, away from pre-packaged curricula and towards on-site discernment. It suggests that proclaiming the Christian message means more than proclaiming timeless truths; it means proclaiming timely truths. And it is perhaps for that reason that class preparation in an RCIA setting needs to root itself as much in prayer as in any straightforward lesson planning and that the local catechist must take care to come before God as a petitioner and listener before he or she comes before catechumens as a teacher.

C. *The Musicality of the Word.* If one approaches Augustine with a programmatic eye, one leaves disappointed. He offers no neat lesson plans, no orderly scope-and-sequence chart, no clear and distinct curricular architecture. Yet if one comes to Augustine not with an eye for architecture, but with an ear for music, patterns begin to emerge. One detects a different order: that his catecheses moved melodically, not structurally; that their flow was more fugal than linear. It is this musicality that makes his work so hard to outline or to summarize.

Within a single sermon, often the only unifying thread might be the Scripture text at hand. Yet focusing unduly on this thread misses what Augustine was doing: producing intricate variations on the Word of God. In a single variation—what might be printed in a modern text as a single paragraph—Augustine might quote the same verse three or four times, first setting it alongside verses from elsewhere in Scripture (e.g., from Paul or the psalms); then setting it against an image from the local milieu; then teasing out its implications for Christology or ecclesiology or sacraments; then sounding out its emotional resonances or turning it into a quick series of exhortations. The excitement his hearers felt came not so much from an intellectual clarity assembled piece by piece, but from the surprise of links suddenly forged or turns unexpectedly taken. And they were liable to leave not with a mental outline, but with a string of insights, feelings, and imperatives knotted in tight-wrapped clusters.

This musicality touched not only Augustine's individual catecheses. It also shaped his approach to each of the four periods, or movements, of Christian initiation. For him, each had its distinctive repertoire of melodies and moods. Evangelization meant a brief, energetic *ouverture*—setting out within a single kerygmatic address the vast sweep of salvation history. In the catechumenate, Scripture remained the focus, but the emphasis shifted from breadth to depth. And as we saw, during one four-month period, Augustine alternated between John's Gospel and the psalms of ascent—in effect, moving in a musical counterpoint between an education of mind and an education of heart. Lent brought to a crescendo the New Testament theme of conversion, of turning from darkness to light, from slavery to freedom. During this phase, Augustine made his catechesis harmonious with a complex ritual and ascetical round that touched mind, heart, even body. And in passing on the Scripture-imbued Creed and the scriptural Lord's Prayer, he would draw together earlier strains into a easy-to-remember melodic core. During Easter, the mysteries of baptism and Eucharist set the tone. Yet Augustine transposed these into an eschatological key—lest initiation be mistaken for mere socializing into a wheat-and-chaff Church instead of a prelude to the resurrection of the flesh and the coming kingdom.

Augustine's musical ordering moves against the grain of contemporary catechesis. Catechists are more accustomed to parceling up theology into discrete topics. Augustine's approach suggests an alternative: individual sessions need not have a single intellectual thread nor a single coherent argument; faith can be also passed on via small tight-wrapped clusters of insights, feelings, and imperatives. Moreover, Augustine's example suggests that it may be less important to cover, for example, ecclesiology as a unified body of theological reflection and more important to probe each ecclesiological insight for its links with Trinity or spirituality or ethical action. In part, this approach springs from a respect for the structure of the oral memory. But more importantly, such an approach presumes that Christianity is not an intellectual system, but a way of life. And one does not acquire a way of life by beginning with some long, systematic intellectual reflection on it and then making some long, systematic effort at doing it. Rather, one acquires a way of life in a more piecemeal fashion: by a flash of insight here or there, by picking up a feel for this part or that part, by imitating this expert or that old hand.

In addition, the example of Augustine suggests that catechists attune themselves and their message to the unique moods and aims of each of the four movements; that an evangelical *ouverture* is not the same as a catechumenal *andante* or a Lenten *grave* or a mystagogical *vivace*. Clearly, he challenges any who would turn a period of the RCIA into a unit in which candidates cover material so as to graduate on to the next unit. Rather, he suggests that RCIA catechesis should move more by circling around a common source—Scripture—but in varied ways, with varied moods, and for varied ends.

Obviously, this does not imply that one needs to abandon a fine-crafted curricular architecture for Augustinian musicality. On the contrary: a catechetical cathedral—like a cathedral of stone and stained glass—can be a splendid setting for music. Moreover, Augustine's example in no way suggests that catechisms need be snatched from the hands of catechumens or catechists. Rather the question is how and why one uses a guidebook to the cathedral of Catholic doctrine. Augustine himself once authored such an *enchiridion*, or "handbook." Yet in sending it on, he advised: "It will not suffice to place a small manual in one's hands; rather it will be necessary to enkindle a great zeal in one's heart."[12]

THE WORD MADE FLESH: CHRIST

A. The Melody of Christ. Classical composers have traditionally used a set form to hold together a lengthy composition. Typically, they open the work by introducing a melodic core, or theme. As the work unfolds, this theme appears again and again, but rarely in its original form. Rather it is transposed into a different key or moved from the treble line to the bass; or it might quicken to match a quickened tempo or be set in counterpoint to some contrasting theme. It can even disappear for a time through certain bridge passages. However, in the closing bars, it returns, this time in its full-voiced sonority, set within and against a recapitulation of contrasting themes, so that the composition as a whole ends with a crescendo before the final cadence.

12. *Enchiridion* 1.6 (Arand, 14).

Augustine's baptismal catechesis followed a similar pattern. He too composed around a melodic core or theme: Christ. Augustine introduced the melody of Christ at the climax of his evangelical *ouverture*—proclaiming Christ as the breakthrough that marked the sixth age of world history, as the sign that human interiority had once more been made in the image and likeness of God. And Augustine would frame this melody in a long series of paradoxes: Christ the hungering one who sated all hunger, Christ the thirsting one who quenched all thirst. This melodic core would appear again and again throughout his catecheses, transposed in true musical fashion, according to the demands of the moment: Christ was thus a plague doctor who made himself the medicine; a king who made himself the royal road; a jurist who will rig the case in our favor by serving as both lawyer and judge.

Augustine lifted this paradoxical melody from the prologue of John's Gospel. There, he believed, one finds the true two-edged identity of Christ; on the one hand, Christ the divine Word, and on the other, Christ the Word made flesh. So fond was Augustine of John's prologue that he quoted it more frequently than any other passage of Scripture—some one thousand times in his surviving works.[13] Not surprisingly, in his four-month catechumenal sequence, he devoted no less than three full sermons to the Johannine prologue. Similar, though briefer, expositions appeared in other catecheses, especially those given on the Creed and on Easter morning. What is striking—from a pedagogical point of view—is not so much the centrality Augustine gave this, nor the detail in which he investigated it, nor even the number of times in which it appeared; rather it is the musical inventiveness he brought to it. He always seems to have had the ability to give this paradoxical melody some new turn or unexpected variation.

Augustine's method parallels the method of classical composers in other ways as well. Just as a composer might set contrasting themes in counterpoint with the main theme, so Augustine typically set other themes into play with Christology. For instance, he linked Christology to spirituality (Christ the inner teacher); to Trinity (Christ the eternal Word); to soteriology (Christ the ransomer of slaves, Christ the physician); to ecclesiology (Christ as Head, Church as Body); to ethical exhortation (welcoming Christ

13. Marrou, *Saint Augustine and His Influence through the Ages*, 83.

the foreigner; "tattooing" the Cross of Christ on catechumens' foreheads). Moreover, just as classical composers, in drawing their work to a close, recapitulate earlier themes, so Augustine, between Easter and the Octave, recapitulated earlier themes: the Church as wheat and chaff; baptism as passing through the Red Sea; care for the poor. Finally, just as composers draw out the full-voiced sonority of their principal theme just before the cadence, so Augustine drew out the depth and intensity of his Christological melody by setting his farewell words to the neophytes against the backdrop of Christ's resurrection and the resurrection at endtime.

Augustine's method was probably simpler than it may seem from this overview. I do not think that he consciously set about to create this rather complex musical rhythm. Instead, I suspect that he did no more than ask himself, at each juncture, one basic question: "How does such-and-such a point I am making relate to the mystery of Christ?" Because he was attentive to the text at hand as well as to the liturgical season, this musical rhythm flowed rather naturally.

Augustine's Christological method may prove helpful in avoiding certain pitfalls. For example, a lectionary approach runs the risk of becoming so many biblical readings that—while perhaps moving or engaging in and of themselves—have no inner cohesiveness or guiding thread. A theological-topics or catechism approach faces a different pitfall: it can tend to relegate Christology to the status of one discipline among many others. Augustine's approach suggests that amid the diversity of theological concerns, there is in fact a guiding thread, a linchpin: and that is the person of Christ. It is Christ who stands as the point of entry into the mystery of creation and salvation, of human history and the human heart, of Church and sacrament, and, of course, of God— or, as Augustine would put it, of "the Trinity which God is."[14]

Also instructive is Augustine's Christological faith itself, its content, its vitality. As Brian Daley has noted, Augustine tended to avoid technical language; instead, he "preferred to speak of the mystery of Christ in concrete, rhetorically challenging phrases that let the believer savor the inherent paradox of preaching an incarnate God" and, in so doing, underlined "the complexity and

14. *De trinitate* 15.4 (trans. my own).

inner tensions of the Christian message."[15] Augustine's example suggests that one obviously take care to hand on and explore in depth the faith of the orthodox Churches, what Augustine found expressed in Nicaea and Constantinople and what we find in Chalcedon; but that, in doing so, one not be content with abstract propositions, but rather take care to bring alive the bristling paradox of Christ, the Word made flesh.

B. Christ and Conversion. Theology is multidisciplinary. It includes Trinity, ecclesiology, sacraments, eschatology, ethics, etc. For Augustine, the melodic core which held together his catechesis on all these matters was Christ. In an analogous sense, conversion too is multidisciplinary. It touches one's interior, both mind and heart. It touches moral action, both personal charity and social justice. It touches one's relationship with Church, both the local community and the larger communion of Churches. It even touches one's body: sacramental acts in which one's body is signed, immersed, anointed, and fed, as well as the hard-to-define, yet quite real, links and fissures that exist between our inner desires and bodily habits. For Augustine, the cadence toward which conversion in all these areas moved was Christ. As he said to his catechumens and congregation: "Where do we go? To Christ. How do we go? Through Christ."[16] In other words, the journey of conversion is a journey in which Christ serves as both means and end, as both mediator and measure. In *City of God*, Augustine set out this theme more fully:

"The way to humanity's God is, for the human being, the human God: namely, 'the mediator between God and humanity, the man Christ Jesus' [1 Tim 2:5]. For it is as a human being that he is a mediator, and through this too, that he is the way. If there be a way between the one walking and the point towards which one is walking, [then] one has a hope of reaching one's goal; but if there is none, or if one is unaware of how to get there, of what use is it to know where one wants to go? There is only one way that is assured against all error: [and that is] that the very same person should be God and a human being—God, as the goal to which we are going, and a human being, as the way by which we go."[17]

15. Daley, "A Humble Mediator," 101.
16. *Enarrationes in psalmos* 123.2 (trans. my own).
17. *De civitate Dei* 11.2 (trans. Daley, "A Humble Mediator," 107-8—altered).

Augustine, of course, did not collapse the many layers of conversion into a conversion to Christ of a narrow sort, such as the me-and-Jesus conversion found among certain fundamentalists. Instead, he recognized that a conversion to Christ had profound interior, ecclesial, sacramental, interpersonal, and social implications. If one surveys Augustine's catecheses in terms of the ways he sought to evoke conversion, one can see that he addressed, at one time or another, every layer. In fact, he would often touch several at once: for instance, he touched on three—interior, interpersonal, and social—when he insisted that one pray the Lord's Prayer with two "wings": on the one hand, begging forgiveness from those one has hurt, and on the other, handing out alms to those in need.

Moreover, just as baptismal formation neared its final cadence, that is, between Easter and the Octave, the profound links between Christology and conversion came to the fore. He begged his neophytes to focus on Christ who called them, who loved them, who sought them when they were lost, who enlightened them when they were found. At the same time, he would set forth to his congregation how Christ, the Word made flesh, could be glimpsed in the flesh-and-blood neophytes who had, after the hard discipline of Lent, tasted grace's definitive favor. Yet he never let this moment be treated as an end in itself. Rather it was a sign, a flickering glimpse, of the final grandeur of history's Octave when human beings would no longer have to endure the quirky fissures that divided their minds from their hearts from their flesh; when they would no longer pine under oppressive social structures; when they would taste and feel and hear—in bodies utterly transfigured—what it means to be a human being fully alive; when human beings, at long last, would see and hear the mystery that neither eye has seen nor ear heard: the mystery that God is. Thus Augustine made it quite clear that baptism—however dramatic—is only a foretaste, nothing more and certainly nothing less.

By using this eschatological frame, Augustine downplayed, in a sense, the momentousness of adult baptism. We may not wish to. Today, for many congregations, the connection between baptism and conversion, between the high dignity of the one and the high cost of the other, has been obscured, in part by the practice of infant baptism. Nonetheless, Augustine's example suggests vigilance, lest we tame the RCIA and turn it into a fine-calibrated instrument for socializing people into a wheat-and-chaff Church. He reminds us that it is God, not baptism, that is the end of the journey; that it is the coming kingdom, not baptism, that will ultimately transfigure the world and humankind.

Augustine's vision of conversion had its darker strains. For instance, he seems to have worked from the traditional North African view that there could be no salvation outside the Church—a view consciously overturned by Vatican II. He could darken this North African perspective further in the way he portrayed human history as a somewhat desolate story of the saved few and the lost many. Another weak point—from a contemporary perspective— was the way he dealt with the larger social order. While he certainly exhorted candidates to help repair the unjust social order through almsgiving, he only rarely pushed this in the sharp, prophetic manner of a Chrysostom, not to mention a contemporary liberation theologian. Moreover, he tended to despair at the intractability of sinful social structures and to turn people's gaze away from life here and now to the life hereafter. Partly, he was too much of an enthusiast for the city of God. Creation's grandeur seemed too pale, and life on earth seemed too often like an unduly protracted and painful pilgrimage, a walk more to be survived than celebrated.[18]

On the other hand, Augustine grappled with an area of conversion utterly ignored in contemporary catechetical circles: the need to catechize the body. He had insisted, against Porphyry and the neo-Platonists, that our faith praises the body, precisely because of the resurrection of Christ. In practice, he praised the body little. Instead, he stressed the problems bodiliness brings on. Yet he insisted that the real culprit behind the body's self-destructive habits is the unruly human heart. Thus, during Lent, he (and his contemporaries) insisted that the body too needs catechesis. And so he (and they) imaged Lent as a boot camp or Olympic training. Lent was a time to purge the poisons out of one's system, to root out slovenly habits, and to sober up with others who sought recovery from an addiction to the world. This way of thinking, however alien to contemporary catechesis, is routine in secular

18. Despite this, one finds passages of great lyric beauty which celebrate the magnificence of the earth: e.g., *De civitate Dei* 22.24.

circles. The media routinely charts the widespread devastation that comes from addiction to alcohol, to drugs, to sex. And addiction, for all its many layers and forms, has a bodily dimension. Moreover, asceticism need not be anti-body. We recognize that people routinely subject their bodies to a stringent discipline of diet and exercise in order to maintain fitness and health. It is this perspective that Augustine and his contemporaries worked from. They insisted that our bodiliness had profound spiritual consequences. It is an insight that we catechists need to reintegrate into our catechesis and our vision of conversion, precisely because Christian faith is a faith in the fleshy incarnation and the fleshy resurrection of Christ. We may choose to recommend very different disciplines than those Augustine used to help people come to grips with addictive or disordered habits; and we may choose to celebrate more loudly than he the gift of the earth and the flesh. But Augustine does at least challenge us to let our catechesis reflect our faith, for our faith praises the body.

Conversion is, of necessity, many-layered, for human beings are themselves many-layered. The seismic turnings of conversion vibrate through the whole person because—as Augustine reminded his neophytes—Christ created the whole person, redeemed the whole person, liberated the whole person. Still, any individual catechist tends to focus effort more on one layer than on others. Augustine too had his preference. For all his intellectualism, he focused most often on the human heart, for he believed that there is no voice to reach the ears of God save the voice of the heart. Moreover, he believed that we are, in the end, lovers—lovers who may perhaps spend most of the time loving the wrong things or loving the right ones in the wrong ways. Nonetheless we are lovers, for we are made in the image and likeness of God, and God is love. Thus for Augustine, to guide people through the new birth of conversion meant evoking rightly ordered loves and quelling wrongly ordered ones. For him, this was the standard—indeed, the essence—of Scripture: love of God and love of neighbor. And as he pointed out to Deogratias, this twofold love itself flowed from Christ:

". . . Christ came chiefly for this reason: that we might learn how much God loves us, and might learn this to the end that we might begin to glow with love of him by whom we were first loved, and so might love our neighbor at the bidding and after the example of him who made himself our neighbor by loving us.''[19]

For those of us baffled by the intricacy of the RCIA, by its many rites and its subtle catechesis, Augustine calls us back to a simplicity on the far side of complexity. He reminds us that Christian initiation is ultimately an apprenticeship in the love of God and the love of neighbor. It is, in the end, that simple.

19. *De catechizandis rudibus* 4.8 (Christopher, 23—altered).

Select Bibliography

I. WORKS OF AUGUSTINE: TEXTS AND TRANSLATIONS

Nearly all of Augustine's works can be found in J. P. Migne, Patrologia Latina, vols. 32–47. Migne reproduced the late seventeenth-century edition of the Benedictines of St. Maur. This text is slowly being replaced by modern critical editions in the Corpus Scriptorum Ecclesiasticorum Latinorum (CSEL) and the Corpus Christianorum, Series Latina (CCSL).

Translations of many of Augustine's works are found in The Fathers of the Church (FC), Ancient Christian Writers (ACW), and The Library of Christian Classics (LCC). In some cases, the only translation is that found in the Select Library of the Nicene and Post-Nicene Fathers (NPNF), done in the late nineteenth century. A new series has just begun to be published: John E. Rotelle, ed., *The Works of Saint Augustine: A Translation for the 21st Century* (Brooklyn: New City Press, 1990–). The initial volumes have just begun to make available Augustine's many *Sermones ad populum* (the majority of these have never previously been translated into English). This new series appeared too late for me to use. Listed below are the texts and translations that I used or consulted.

Confessiones. CCSL 27. Ed. Lucas Verheijen. Turnholt: Brepols, 1981.
   Confessions. Trans. R. S. Pine-Coffin, New York: Penguin Books, 1961.
   Confessions. Trans. Henry Chadwick. Oxford: Oxford University Press, 1991.

De baptismo contra Donatistas. CSEL 51:107–244. Ed. M Petschenig. Vienna: 1908.
   On Baptism, Against the Donatists. NPNF 4:411–514. Trans. J. R. King. Reprint. Grand Rapids, Mich.: Wm. B. Eerdmans Publishing Co., 1983.

De catechizandis rudibus. CCSL 46:115–78. Ed. I. B. Bauer. Turnholt: Brepols, 1969.
   The First Catechetical Instruction. ACW. 2. Trans. Joseph P. Christopher. New York: Newman Press, 1946.

De civitate Dei. CCSL 47–48. Eds. B. Dombart and A. Kalb. Turnholt: Brepols, 1955.
   City of God. Trans. Henry Bettenson. New York: Penguin Books, 1972.

De doctrina christiana. CSEL 80. Ed. Wm. Green, 1963.

> *On Christian Doctrine.* Trans. D. W. Robertson, Jr. Indianapolis: Bobbs-Merrill Educational Publishing, 1958.

De fide et operibus. CSEL 41:35–97. Ed. Joseph Zycha. Vienna: 1900.

> *Of Faith and Works.* In *Treatises on Marriage and Other Subjects,* FC 27:213–82. Trans. Marie Liguori. Washington: The Catholic University of America, 1955.

De fide et symbolo. CSEL 41:3–32. Ed. J. Zycha. Vienna: 1900.

> *Faith and the Creed.* In *Augustine: Earlier Writings,* LCC 6:351–69. Ed. John H. S. Burleigh. Philadelphia: Westminster Press, 1953.

De symbolo ad catechumenos. CCSL 46:179–99. Ed. R. Vander Plaetse. Turnholt: Brepols, 1969.

> *The Creed.* In *Treatises on Marriage and Other Subjects,* FC 27:283–307. Trans. Marie Liguori. Washington: The Catholic University of America Press, 1955.

Enarrationes in psalmos. CCSL 38–40. Eds. D. Eligius Dekkers and Johannes Fraipont. Turnholt: Brepols, 1956.

> *On the Psalms.* 2 vols: Ps 1–37. ACW 29–30. Trans. Scholastica Hebgin and Felicitas Corrigan. New York: Newman Press, 1960–61.

Enchiridion ad Laurentium [De fide, spe, et caritate]. CCSL 46:49–114. Ed. E. Evans. Turnholt: Brepols, 1969.

> *Faith, Hope, and Charity.* ACW 3. Trans. Louis A. Arand. New York: Newman Press, 1947.

Epistolae. CSEL 34.1–2, 44, 57–58. Ed. A. Goldbacher. Vienna: 1895–1923.

> *Letters,* 5 vols. FC 12, 18, 20, 30, 32. Trans. Wilfrid Parsons. Washington: The Catholic University of America Press, 1951–56.

Epistolae ex duobus codicibus nuper in lucem prolatae. CSEL 88. Ed. Johannes Divjak. Vienna: 1981.

> *Letters VI (1*–29*).* FC 81. Trans. Robert B. Eno. Washington: The Catholic University of America Press, 1989.

Sermones. Obras Completas de San Agustin 7, 10, 23, 24, 25, 26. Ed. Miguel Fuertes Lanero; trans. Pio de Luis and others. Madrid: Biblioteca de Autores Cristianos, 1981–85.

> *Selected Easter Sermons of Saint Augustine.* Trans. Philip T. Weller. St. Louis: B. Herder Book Co., 1959.

> *Sermons on Selected Lessons of the Gospels.* NPNF 6:245–545. Trans. R. G. MacMullen. Reprint. Grand Rapids, Mich.: Wm. B. Eerdmans Publishing Co., 1980.

Sermons on the Liturgical Seasons. FC 38. Trans. Mary Sarah Muldowney. Washington: The Catholic University of America Press, 1959.
Sermons pour la Pâque. SC 116. Trans. Suzanne Poque. Paris: Éditions
du Cerf, 1966.

Tractatus in epistolam Ioannis. SC 76. Text, with French trans. P. Agaesse.
Paris: Édition du Cerf, 1961.

Homilies on the First Epistle General of St. John. In *Augustine: Later
Works,* LCC 8:251–348. Trans. John Burnaby. Philadelphia: Westminster
Press, 1955.

Tractatus in evangelium Ioannis. CCSL 36. Ed. R. Willems. Turnholt:
Brepols, 1954.

Homilies on the Gospel of John. NPNF 7. Trans. John Gibb and James
Innes. Reprint. Grand Rapids, Mich.: Wm. B. Eerdmans Publishing
Co., 1956.

Homélies sur l'evangile de Saint Jean, I–XVI. BAug 71. Text, with French.
Trans. M. F. Berrouard. Paris: Desclée de Brouwer, 1969.

Tractates on the Gospel of John. FC 78 and 79. Trans. John W. Rettig.
Washington: The Catholic University of America, 1988.

II. OTHER ANCIENT AUTHORS:
TEXTS AND TRANSLATIONS
The most up-to-date and comprehensive anthology of documents from the
ancient catechumenate is that of Thomas M. Finn, *Early Christian Baptism
and the Catechumenate,* MF 5: *West and East Syria* and MF 6: *Italy, North
Africa, and Egypt* (Collegeville: Minn.: Michael Glazier / The Liturgical
Press, 1992). Two other useful anthologies are: E. C. Whitaker, *Documents
of the Baptismal Liturgy,* rev. ed. (London: SPCK, 1970) and Edward J.
Yarnold, *The Awe-Inspiring Rites of Initiation: Baptismal Homilies of the 4th
Century* (Middlegreen: St. Paul Publications, 1972). Listed below are com-
plete texts and translations of some key figures:

Ambrose. *De Helia et ieiunio.* Text, with trans. M. J. Buck. PS 19. Washington: The Catholic University of America, 1929.

—————. *De mysteriis.* SC 25. Text, with French trans. Bernard Botte.
Paris: Éditions du Cerf, 1961.

The Mysteries. In *Theological and Dogmatic Works,* FC 44. Trans. Roy J.
Deferrari. Washington: The Catholic University of America Press, 1963.

—————. *De sacramentis.* SC 25. Text, with French trans. Bernard Botte.
Paris: Éditions du Cerf, 1961.

The Sacraments. In *Theological and Dogmatic Works,* FC 44. Trans. Roy J.
Deferrari. Washington: The Catholic University of America Press, 1963.

_____. *Explanatio symboli ad initiandos.* Texts and Studies 10. Text, with trans. R. H. Connolly. Cambridge: Cambridge University Press, 1952.

Cyril of Jerusalem. *Catecheses 1–18.* PG 33:369–1060. Paris: n.d.

Lenten Catecheses. FC 61, 64. Trans. Leo McCauley. Washington: The Catholic University of America Press, 1969–70.

_____. *Catecheses 19–23.* In *St. Cyril of Jerusalem's Lectures on the Christian Sacraments.* Ed. F. L. Cross. Crestwood, N.Y.: St. Vladimir's Press, 1986.

Mystagogical Catecheses. FC 64. Trans. Anthony A. Stephenson. Washington: The Catholic University of America Press, 1970.

_____. *Procatechesis.* In *St. Cyril of Jerusalem's Lectures on the Christian Sacraments.* Ed. F. L. Cross. Crestwood, N.Y.: St. Vladimir's Press, 1986.

Procatechesis. FC 61. Trans. Anthony A. Stephenson. Washington: The Catholic University of America Press, 1969.

Egeria. *Peregrinatio.* SC 296. Text, with French trans. Pierre Maraval. Paris: Éditions du Cerf, 1982.

Diary of a Pilgrimage, ACW 38. Trans. George E. Gingras. New York: Newman Press, 1970.

Gregory of Nazianzus. *Oratio 40: In sanctum baptisma.* PG 36:360–77. Paris: 1885.

Oration 40: On Holy Baptism. NPNF, second series, 7:352–77. Trans. Charles G. Browne and James F. Swallow. Reprint, Grand Rapids, Mich.: Wm. B. Eerdmans Publishing Co., 1955.

Gregory of Nyssa. *Oratio catechetica magna.* PG 45:11–106. Paris: 1863.

Address on Religious Instruction. In *Christology of the Later Fathers,* LCC 3:268–325. Ed. Edward Hardy. Philadelphia: Westminster Press, 1954.

Hippolytus. *La tradition apostolique* SC 11. 2d ed. Text, with French trans. Bernard Botte. Paris: Éditions du Cerf, 1968.

Hippolytus: A Text for Students. Ed. and trans. Geoffrey J. Cuming. Bramcote: Grove Books Limited, 1987.

John Chrysostom. *Catechesis prima et altera.* PG 49:223–40. Ed. B. Montfaucon. Paris: 1862.

Baptismal Instructions. ACW 31. Trans. Paul W. Harkins. New York: Newman Press, 1963.

_____. *Huit catéchèses baptismales inédites.* SC 50 bis. Text, with French trans. A. Wenger. Paris: Éditions du Cerf, 1957.

Baptismal Instructions. ACW 31. Trans. Paul W. Harkins. New York: Newman Press, 1963.

Minucius Felix. *Octavius* CSEL 2. Ed. C. Halm. Vienna: 1867.

Octavius. ACW 39. Trans. G. W. Clarke. New York: Newman Press, 1974.

Possidius. *Sancti Augustini Vita.* In *Vita di S. Agostino, Verba Seniorum,* new series, 1. Ed. Michele Pellegrino. Edizoni Paoline, n.d.

Life of St. Augustine. Trans. Audrey Fellowes. Introduction, Michele Pellegrino. Villanova: Augustinian Press, 1988.

Tertullian. *De baptismo.* SC 35. Text, with French trans. R. F. Refoulé. Paris: Éditions du Cerf, 1952.

Tertullian's Homily on Baptism. Text, with trans. Ernest Evans. London: SPCK, 1964.

_____. *De idolotria: Critical Text. Translation, and Commentary.* Eds. J. H. Waszink, J. C. M. Van Winden. Leiden: E. J. Brill, 1987.

_____. *De paenitentia.* CCSL 1:319-40. Ed. J. G. Ph. Borleffs. Turnholt: Brepols, 1954.

On Penitence. ACW 28. Trans. William LeSaint. New York: Newman Press, 1959.

_____. *De spectaculis.* CCSL 1:225-53. Ed. E. Dekkers. Turnholt: Brepols, 1954.

Spectacles. In *Disciplinary, Moral and Ascetical Works,* FC 40:33-107. Trans. Rudolph Arbesmann. Washington: The Catholic University of America Press, 1959.

Theodore of Mopsuestia. *Les homélies catéchétiques de Théodore de Mopsueste.* Studi e Testi 145. Text, with French trans. G. Finaert. Vatican: Biblioteca Apostolica Vaticano, 1949.

Commentary on the Nicene Creed [Homilies 1-10]. Woodbrooke Studies 5. Ed. A. Mingana. Cambridge: 1932.

Commentary on the Lord's Prayer and on the Sacraments of Baptism and the Eucharist [Homilies 11-16]. Woodbrooke Studies 6. Ed. A. Mingana. Cambridge: 1933.

III. WORKS ON AUGUSTINE

Bonner, Gerald. *Augustine and Modern Research on Pelagianism.* St. Augustine Lecture Series. Villanova: Villanova University Press, 1972.

_____. *St. Augustine of Hippo: Life and Controversies.* 2d ed. Norwich: Canterbury Press, 1986.

Brown, Peter. *Augustine of Hippo: A Biography*. Berkeley: University of California Press, 1967.

_____. *Religion and Society in the Age of Saint Augustine*. New York: Harper & Row, 1972.

_____. "Augustine and Sexuality." *Center for Hermeneutical Studies*, Colloquy 46:1–13. Berkeley: Graduate Theological Union, 1983.

Busch, Dom Benedict. "De initiatione christiana secundum sanctum Augustinum" and "De modo quo sanctus Augustinus descripserit initiationem christianam." *Ephemerides Liturgicae* 52 (1938) 159–78 and 385–483.

Chadwick, Henry. *Augustine*. Past Masters. Oxford: Oxford University Press, 1986.

Courcelle, Pierre. *Recherches sur les Confessions de saint Augustin*. Paris: E. de Boccard, 1950.

_____. "Propos antichrétiennes rapportés par S. Augustin." *Recherches augustiniennes* 1 (1958) 149–86.

Daley, Brian E. "A Humble Mediator: The Distinctive Elements in Saint Augustine's Christology." *Word and Spirit* 9 (1987) 100–117.

DeLatte, R. "St. Augustin et le baptême. Étude liturgico-historique du rituel baptismal des adultes chez saint Augustin." *Questions liturgiques* 56 (1975) 177–223.

Evans, G. R. *Augustine on Evil*. Cambridge: Cambridge University Press, 1982.

Frend, W. H. C. *The Donatist Church*. 2d ed. Oxford: Clarendon Press, 1985.

Hagendahl, Harald. *Augustine and the Latin Classics*. Studia Graeca et Latina 20. Guteborg: Acta Universitatis Cothoburgensis, 1967.

LeLandais, Maurice. "Deux années de predication de saint Augustin: Introduction a la lecture de l'*In Joannem*." *Études augustiniennes* 28:1–95. Paris: Aubier, 1953.

Marec, Erwan. *Monuments chrétiens d'Hippone: Ville épiscopale de saint Augustin*. Paris: Arts et Métiers Graphiques, 1958.

Markus, R. A. *Saeculum: History and Society in the Theology of St. Augustine*. Cambridge: Cambridge University Press, 1970.

Marrou, Henri-Iréné. *Saint Augustin et la fin de la culture antique*. Paris: Bibliothéque des Écoles Francaises d'Athénes et de Rome, 1938.

_____. *Saint Augustine and His Influence through the Ages.* Trans. Patrick Hepburne-Scott. New York: Harper Torchbooks, 1957.

_____. *The Resurrection and Saint Augustine's Theology of Human Values.* St. Augustine Lecture Series. Trans. Maria Consolata. Villanova: Villanova University Press, 1966.

Mohrmann, Christine, "Saint Augustin prédicateur." *Études sur le latin des Chrétiens*, 2d ed, 1:391-402. Rome: Edizioni di Storia e Letteratura, 1961.

O'Connell, Robert J. *St. Augustine's Confessions: The Odyssey of Soul.* Cambridge, Mass.: Harvard University Press, 1969.

O'Meara, John J. *The Young Augustine: The Growth of St. Augustine's Mind up to His Conversion.* London: Longmans, Green, and Co., 1954.

Pelikan, Jaroslav. *The Mystery of Continuity: Time and History. Memory and Eternity in the Thought of Saint Augustine.* Charlottesville: University Press of Virginia, 1986.

Pontet, Maurice. *L'exégèse de s. Augustin prédicateur.* Paris: Aubier, 1946.

Poque, Suzanne. *Le langage symbolique dans la prédication d'Augustin d'Hippone.* 2 vols. Paris: Études augustiniennes, 1984.

TeSelle, Eugene. *Augustine the Theologian.* New York: Herder & Herder, 1970.

Trapè, Agostino. "Saint Augustine." *Patrology.* Vol. 4, *The Golden Age of Latin Patristic Literature from the Council of Nicea to the Council of Chalcedon: 342-462.* Ed. Angelo di Berardino. Westminster, Md.: Christian Classics, Inc., 1986.

Van der Meer, Frederic. *Augustine the Bishop.* Trans. Brian Battershaw and G. R. Lamb. London: Sheed & Ward, 1961.

Verbraken, Pierre-Patrick. *Études critiques sur les sermons authentiques de saint Augustin.* Instrumenta Patristica 12. Steenbrugis: 1976.

IV. WORKS ON THE PATRISTIC ERA

Barnes, Timothy D. *Tertullian: A Historical and Literary Study.* New York: Oxford University Press, 1971.

_____. *Constantine and Eusebius.* Cambridge, Mass.: Harvard University Press, 1981.

Brown, Peter. *The World of Late Antiquity.* New York: W. W. Norton, 1971.

_____. *The Making of Late Antiquity.* Cambridge, Mass.: Harvard University Press, 1978.

_____. *The Cult of the Saints: Its Rise and Function in Latin Christianity.* Chicago: The University of Chicago Press, 1981.

_____. *Society and the Holy in Late Antiquity.* Berkeley: University of California Press, 1982.

_____. *The Body and Society: Men, Women, and Sexual Renunciation in Early Christianity.* New York: Columbia University Press, 1988.

Campenhausen, Hans von. *The Fathers of the Latin Church.* Trans. Manfred Hoffman. Stanford: Stanford University Press, 1964.

Carroll, Thomas K. *Preaching the Word.* MF 11. Wilmington, Del.: Michael Glazier, 1984.

Chadwick, Henry. *Early Christian Thought and the Classical Tradition.* Oxford: Clarendon Press, 1966.

_____. *The Early Church.* Pelican History of the Church 1. New York: Penguin Books, 1967.

Chitty, Derwas J. *The Desert a City: An Introduction to the Study of Egyptian and Palestinian Monasticism under the Christian Empire.* Crestwood, N.Y.: St. Vladimir's Seminary Press, 1966.

Crouzel, Henri. *Origen.* Trans. A. S. Worrall. San Francisco: Harper & Row, 1989.

Daley, Brian E. *The Hope of the Early Church: A Handbook of Patristic Eschatology.* Cambridge: Cambridge University Press, 1991.

Davis, Leo Donald. *The First Seven Ecumenical Councils, 325–787: Their History and Theology.* Theology and Life Series 21. Wilmington, Del.: Michael Glazier, 1987.

Dodds, E. R. *Pagan & Christian in an Age of Anxiety.* New York: W. W. Norton & Co., 1965.

Fox, Robin Lane. *Pagans and Christians.* New York: Alfred A. Knopf, 1987.

Frend, W. H. C. *Martyrdom and Persecution in the Early Church: A Study of a Conflict from the Maccabees to Donatus.* Garden City, N.Y.: Doubleday & Co., 1967.

_____. *The Rise of Christianity.* Philadelphia: Fortress Press, 1984.

_____. *Saints and Sinners in the Early Church: Differing and Conflicting Traditions in the First Six Centuries.* Theology and Life Series 11. Wilmington, Del.: Michael Glazier, 1985.

Froelich, Karlfried. *Biblical Interpretation in the Early Church,* Sources of Early Christian Thought. Philadelphia: Fortress Press, 1984.

Grabar, André. *Early Christian Art: From the Rise of Christianity to the Death of Theodosius.* Trans. Stuart Gilbert, James Emmons. New York: Odyssey Press, 1968.

Grant, Robert M. *Augustus to Constantine: The Rise and Triumph of Christianity in the Roman World.* San Francisco: Harper & Row, 1970.

_____. *Greek Apologists of the Second Century.* Philadelphia: Westminster Press, 1988.

Grillmeier, Aloys. *Christ in Christian Tradition: From the Apostolic Age to Chalcedon.* Trans. J. S. Bowden. New York: Sheed and Ward, 1965.

Hinson, E. Glenn. *Understandings of the Church.* Sources of Early Christian Thought. Philadelphia: Fortress Press, 1986.

Homes Dudden, F. *The Life and Times of St. Ambrose.* 2 vols. Oxford: Clarendon Press, 1935.

Hunter, David G., ed. *Preaching in the Patristic Age: Studies in Honor of Walter J. Burghardt, S.J.* New York: Paulist Press, 1989.

Jones, A. H. M. *The Later Roman Empire 284–602: A Social, Economic, and Administrative Survey.* 2 vols. Baltimore: Johns Hopkins Press, 1986.

Kelly, J. N. D. *Early Christian Creeds.* 3d ed. New York: Longman Inc., 1971.

_____. *Jerome: His Life, Writings, and Controversies.* New York: Harper & Row, 1975.

_____. *Early Christian Doctrines.* Rev. ed. New York: Harper & Row, 1978.

Kennedy, George A. *Classical Rhetoric and Its Christian and Secular Tradition from Ancient to Modern Times.* Chapel Hill: University of North Carolina Press, 1980.

MacMullen, Ramsay. *Paganism in the Roman Empire.* New Haven: Yale University Press, 1981.

_____. *Christianizing the Roman Empire, A.D. 100–400.* New Haven: Yale University Press, 1984.

Markus, R. A. *The End of Ancient Christianity.* Cambridge: Cambridge University Press, 1990.

Marrou, Henri-Iréné. *A History of Education in Antiquity*. Trans. George Lamb. Madison, Wis.: University of Wisconsin Press, 1982.

Momigliano, Arnaldo, ed. *The Conflict between Paganism and Christianity in the Fourth Century*. Oxford: Clarendon Press, 1963. See especially the essays by Momigliano, Pierre Courcelle, and A. H. M. Jones.

Pelikan, Jaroslav. *The Christian Tradition: A History of the Development of Doctrine*. Vol. 1: *The Emergence of the Catholic Tradition (100–600)*. Chicago: University of Chicago Press, 1971.

Prestige, G. L. *Fathers and Heretics: Six Studies in Dogmatic Faith*. London: SPCK, 1940.

Quasten, Johannes. *Patrology*. 3 vols. Westminster, Md.: Newman Press, 1965.

Rousseau, Philip. *Ascetics, Authority and the Church in the Age of Jerome and Cassian*. Oxford: Oxford University Press, 1978.

Sider, Robert D. *The Gospel & Its Proclamation*. MF 10. Wilmington, Del.: Michael Glazier, 1983.

Stevenson, J. *A New Eusebius: Documents Illustrating the History of the Church to A.D. 337*. Rev. ed. W. H. C. Frend. London: SPCK, 1987.

_____. *Creeds, Councils, and Controversies: Documents Illustrating the History of the church A.D. 337–461*. Rev. ed. W. H. C. Frend. London: SPCK, 1989.

Trigg, Joseph W. *Origen: The Bible and Philosophy in the Third-Century Church*. Atlanta: John Knox Press, 1983.

_____. *Biblical Interpretation*. MF 9. Wilmington, Del.: Michael Glazier, 1988.

Tugwell, Simon. *The Apostolic Fathers*. Outstanding Christian Thinkers Series. Harrisburg, Penn.: Morehouse Publishing, 1989.

Van der Meer, Frederic, and Christine Mohrmann. *Atlas of the Early Christian World*. Trans. Mary F. Hedlund and H. H. Rowley. London: Thomas Nelson and Sons, Ltd., 1959.

Veyne, Paul, ed. *A History of Private Life*. Vol. 1: *From Pagan Rome to Byzantium*. Trans. Arthur Goldhammer. Cambridge, Mass.: Harvard University Press, 1987.

Wilken, Robert L. *The Christians as the Romans Saw Them*. New Haven: Yale University Press, 1984.

Young, Frances M. *From Nicaea to Chalcedon: A Guide to the Literature and its Background.* Philadelphia: Fortress Press, 1983.

V. WORKS ON THE ANCIENT CATECHUMENATE AND THE RCIA

Austin, Gerard. *The Rite of Confirmation: Anointing with the Spirit.* New York: Pueblo, 1985.

Duggan, Robert. "Conversion in the *Ordo Initiationis Christianae Adultorum.*" *Ephemerides Liturgicae* 96 (1982) 57–83, 209–52; and 97 (1983) 141–223.

Dujarier, Michel. *The Rites of Christian Initiation: Historical and Pastoral Reflections.* New York: Sadlier, 1979.

Finn, Thomas M. *The Liturgy of Baptism in the Baptismal Instructions of St. John Chrysostom.* Studies in Christian Antiquity 15. Washington: The Catholic University of America Press, 1967.

Jungmann, Josef A. *The Early Liturgy to the Time of Gregory the Great.* Trans. Francis A. Brunner. Notre Dame: University of Notre Dame Press, 1959.

Kavanagh, Aidan. *The Shape of Baptism: The Rite of Christian Initiation.* New York: Pueblo, 1978.

_____. "Unfinished and Unbegun Revisited: The Rite of Christian Initiation of Adults." *Worship* 53 (July 1979) 327–40.

_____. *Confirmation: Origins and Reform.* New York: Pueblo, 1988.

_____. "Critical Issues in the Growth of the RCIA in North America." *Catechumenate: A Journal of Christian Initiation* 10 (Mar 1988) 10–21.

Kavanagh, Aidan, et al. *Made, Not Born: New Perspectives on Christian Initiation and the Catechumenate.* Notre Dame: University of Notre Dame Press, 1976.

Mazza, Enrico. *Mystagogy: A Theology of Liturgy in the Patristic Age.* New York: Pueblo, 1989.

McDonnell, Kilian, and George T. Montague. *Christian Initiation and Baptism in the Holy Spirit: Evidence from the First Eight Centuries.* Collegeville, Minn.: The Liturgical Press (A Michael Glazier Book), 1991.

Mitchell, Leonel. "Ambrosian Baptismal Rites." *Studia Liturgica* (1962) 241–53.

Mohrmann, Christine. "Le style oral du *De sacramentis* de saint Ambroise." *Vigiliae Christianae* 6 (1952) 168–77.

Puniet, P. de. "Catechuménat." *Dictionnaire d'archéologie chrétienne et de liturgie* 2:2579–2621.

_____. "Baptême." *Dictionnaire d'archéologie chrétienne et de liturgie* 2:251–346.

Quasten, Johannes. "Theodore of Mopsuestia on the Exorcism of the Cilicium." *Harvard Theological Review* 35 (1942) 209–19.

Riley, Hugh M. *Christian Initiation: A Comparative Study of the Interpretation of the Baptismal Liturgy in the Mystagogical Writings of Cyril of Jerusalem, John Chrysostom, Theodore of Mopsuestia, and Ambrose of Milan.* Washington: Consortium Press, 1974.

Rordorf, Willy, and others. *The Eucharist of the Early Christians.* Trans. Matthew J. O'Connell. New York: Pueblo, 1976.

Searle, Mark. *Christening: The Making of Christians.* Collegeville, Minn.: The Liturgical Press, 1980.

Sheerin, Daniel J. *The Eucharist.* MF 7. Wilmington, Del.: Michael Glazier, 1986.

Trigg, Joseph W. "Origen's Understanding of Baptism." *Studia Patristica* 17.2:959–65. Ed. E. A. Livingston. Oxford: Pergamon Press, 1982.

Wagner, Johannes, ed. *Adult Baptism and the Catechumenate.* Concilium 22. New York: Paulist Press, 1967.

Index

104; ordination forced on, 105, 265; as preacher, 158–159, 164–174, 186–188, 194–195, 198–203, 223–227, 235–237, 293–296, 336–339, 349–358, 360–362, 368–375; prayer of, 165, 188, 189, 196–198, 220; relationship with Ambrose; 82–91, 116–118; simplicity of lifestyle, 256; son of, 81, 93, 105, 335; teacher of rhetoric, 81–82, 123–126

WORKS: *Confessiones*, 31, 80–92, 98–99, 113, 116, 118, 361; *Contra Faustum*, 124; *De beata vita*, 88; *De catechizandis rudibus*, 29, 31, 35, 107–154, 168, 266, 382; *De civitate Dei*, 111, 144, 151, 263, 310, 378; *De cura pro mortuis gerenda*, 244; *De doctrina christiana*, 29, 35–36, 170, 172–188; *De fide et operibus*, 29, 35, 93–94, 156, 245–250; *De fide et symbolo*, 202; *De magistro*, 210; *De peccatorum meritis et remissione*, 150; *De quantitate animae*, 93; *De symbolo ad catechumenos*, 274–285, 297; *De trinitate*, 200, 377; *De vera religione*, 105, 144; *Enarrationes in psalmos*, 158–160, 171, 191–193, 194–198, 203–227, 234–243, 307, 308; *Enchiridion*, 375; *Epistolae*, 29, 180, 183, 184, 196, 220, 300–301, 357; *Sermones*, 29–30, 116–117, 120–121, 133, 151, 161–172, 186–188, 191–193, 228, 248, 252–260, 264–293, 297–298, 303–306, 313–330, 332–336, 340–343; *Soliloquia*, 217; *Tractatus in evangelium Ioannis*, 29, 158–160, 171, 191–193, 194–195, 198–203, 207–243, 318; *Tractatus in epistolam Ioannis*, 326–330, 341–342, 345

Baptism; in Acts, 245–246, 256; biblical types of, 57, 102–103, 106, 170–171, 246, 257; character, 215, 240, 284; credal interrogations, 44, 309–310; and cross, 282, 308; deathbed, 60–61, 75; delay of, 47–48, 50, 59–61, 162, 229–230, 237, 244n; disappointment with ceremony, 48, 101; Donatist views on, 214–215; dying with Christ, 16, 301, 306, 337; at Easter, 7, 10, 38, 98, 307; in Hippo, 307–311; in Hippolytus, 44; Holy Spirit, 13, 220–221; infant, 13–14, 50, 80, 379; of Jesus, 49, 61, 195, 215–216, 229, 253–254; and lifestyle, 46–47, 57, 63, 74, 94, 250; in Milan, 93, 100, 196; new creation, 233, 273, 335; norm of, 13–14; not separated from Confirmation, 8, 12; rebirth, 91, 233, 234, 257, 317; Red Sea, 143, 171, 232, 236, 246, 260, 282–283, 334; remission of sins, 65, 230, 282, 292; secrecy, 158, 170, 232–233, 237; unrepeatability, 215, 234, 236, 284, 322; visible sign, 70, 101; as water and Word, 318 (*see* Font, Immersion, Mystagogy, Rite of Christian Initiation of Adults, Renunciation, Stripping off of clothes, Water, White robes)
Baptistery, 39, 71, 96, 275, 307–308, 310, 362
Bathing, abstaining from, 44, 64, 251–252, 294, 298, 302
Basil of Caesarea, 55n, 59, 61n, 85, 88, 90, 97, 348
Basilica, 39, 52, 99, 329; in Hippo Regius, 139, 161–163, 205, 235, 275, 275n, 302, 304, 307–308, 312, 313, 316, 325
Bible, 4, 6, 9, 22–23, 50, 55, 57, 65–66, 78, 91, 118, 163–164, 168–169, 368–375; Ambrose on, 86–87, 94–95, 102, 106; bread of the Word, 11–12, 160–161, 223, 290, 369–370; Augustine's exegesis of, 127–130, 143, 160–161, 180–188, 202, 206–207, 219, 224–226, 235–237, 246–247, 277–278, 336–337; quoted in ser-

315, 322–323, 337, 353, 367, 374, 379; as daily baptism, 292–293 (*see Traditio orationis*)

Love, of God, 3, 16, 70, 129–130, 143–144, 148, 149, 153–154, 185–186, 203, 210, 212–213, 221, 249, 273, 301, 315, 352, 366, 379, 381; of neighbor, 5, 129–130, 144, 148–149, 153–154, 185–186, 203, 213, 249, 258, 301, 330, 352, 381; Spirit-filled, 144, 213, 219, 247, 276, 296, 330 (*see* Charity)

Lucernarium, 56n, 302

Madaura, 112, 117

Manichees, Manicheism, 79, 81–82, 88–89, 105, 139, 162, 164, 195, 201–202, 239, 283, 300

Manlius Theodorus, 88, 105n

Martyrs, 50–51, 55, 76, 115, 116, 192, 239, 240, 250, 331, 356–357; feasts of, 161, 163, 181, 187, 203–205, 330–331

Maximus Confessor, 136n

Melito of Sardis, 147

Metaphor, 160–161, 178, 209, 212–214, 223, 224–225, 235–236, 253, 256, 265, 268–270, 285–286, 295, 326–327, 334, 337, 352–354

Milan, 82, 93, 94, 95, 102, 104, 263, 275, 299

Minucius Felix, 109, 110n, 125n, 150n

Miracles, 48, 115–117, 143, 219–220, 240, 244, 310

Missa (*see* Dismissal)

Monica, 80, 89, 115, 336

Mosaics, 39, 162, 181–182, 282, 307

Moses, 49, 72, 102, 257, 260, 303

Mystagogy, 3, 9, 17, 22, 38, 45, 336, 364–367, 375; of Ambrose, 69, 94, 99–104, 106, 336, 364; of Augustine, 29, 32, 265, 292, 301–302, 306, 316–330, 336–339, 341–343, 365, 368; of Cyril, 69, 71–72, 78, 103, 336, 364; Egeria on, 70–71; eschatological, 72–73, 325, 334–335, 338–340; of Chrysostom, 70–71, 73, 75–76, 103, 331, 336, 337n, 364–365; liturgical, 71–72, 102, 316–324, 337–338, 364; morality-centered, 73, 103, 336, 364; of Theodore, 70, 72–73, 77, 336, 364; timing of, 66–67, 69–70, 306, 324, 336, 360

Narratio, 107, 124–130, 140, 142–147, 152–153, 155

Neophytes, 9, 29, 32, 38, 45, 48, 69–73, 55, 75–76, 94, 98–104, 115, 151, 156, 238, 248, 310–342, 361–363, 367–368, 377, 379, 381

Neoplatonism, 79, 83n, 84n, 88, 90, 104–105n, 135, 136, 151, 199, 202n, 210, 254, 284n, 318, 371, 380

Nicea, Council of, 54, 202, 281–282, 378

Nicodemus, 57, 195, 231–233

Noah, 49, 102, 143, 146, 213, 236, 241, 250

North Africa, 34, 36, 50, 54, 80–81, 197, 201, 222, 224, 290, 372–373; Christianity in, 45–46, 54, 111–115, 132–133, 162, 285, 293, 307, 321; rites of initiation in, 107, 150, 263–264, 287, 302–313, 367; paganism in, 111–113, 162

Notarius, notarii, 97, 99, 111n, 137n, 165–166, 189, 274n, 278

Octave of Easter, 70, 302, 311, 324, 330–336, 338, 341–342, 362, 377, 379

Optatus of Milevis, 264

Oration: aesthetic, 129–130; six parts of classical, 124–125, 152–153, 155, 181

Origen, 39n, 42n, 51, 85–86, 88, 195, 211, 348

Pagans, paganism, 34, 41, 46–48, 53–54, 59, 82n, 83, 104n, 111–119, 129, 131–133, 149, 155, 162, 164, 183, 211, 223–224, 228, 240, 260–261, 264, 283, 300, 325–326, 327–328, 332, 338, 371; objections to Christianity, 131–133, 151–152

Parallelism, 93, 169, 178, 210–211, 279, 350

Paul, the apostle, 73, 76, 90, 92, 119, 134, 184, 188, 209, 210, 213, 214, 218, 241, 247, 250, 255, 305, 315, 318–322, 327, 328, 337, 373

Paulinus of Milan, 94

Pelagians, Pelagianism, 55, 250, 264n, 293, 318

Pentecost, 9, 38

Peroratio, 124–125, 148, 153, 155, 181, 206

Perpetua, 51, 115

Petitioners (*see Competentes*)

Philo of Alexandria, 86

Photizomenoi, 62, 65, 75

Plato, 121

Plotinus, 83n, 88, 188, 203

Ponticianus, 92

Pontius, 115n

Poor, 43, 52, 118, 138, 162, 183, 187, 218; Augustine as, 256; care of, 64, 85, 95, 222, 225, 229, 251, 258–259, 291–292, 330, 335–336, 339, 377

Porphyry, 83n, 88, 300n, 327–328, 380

Possidius, 105, 113n, 166, 187n, 226n, 255n, 256, 349

Prayer, 50, 100, 251, 257–259, 262, 265, 290–292, 294, 303–305, 327, 334, 373; of Augustine, 165, 188, 189; blessing of baptismal water, 308–309; eucharistic, 312, 317, 321, 322–323, 362; of the Faithful, 44, 190, 196, 316; at Liturgy of the Word, 4, 41, 57–58, 83, 189, 196, 360; teach catechumens, 5, 17, 32, 220–221

Preaching (*see* Rhetoric, Sermon)

Presbyter, 40, 45, 63, 105, 139, 162–163, 265, 311, 312

Presentation: of the Creed, 7, 37, 367; of the Lord's Prayer, 7, 37 (*see Traditio orationis, Traditio symboli*)

Priest, 8, 11, 16, 60, 311, 361–362, 370; Christ as, 285, 311; neophytes as, 11, 311

Prophecy, 87, 111, 128–129, 143, 144, 145, 153, 155, 185, 204, 205, 229, 240, 257, 303

Protrepticus, 130

Prudentius, 112

Psalms, 65, 83, 94, 99, 158–160, 164, 171, 182, 191–193, 194–198, 203–227, 234–243, 303, 307, 308, 315, 326, 360, 373, 374

Pseudo-Dionysius the Areopagite, 136n

Punic, 225–226, 239

Purification/Illumination, period of, 6–7, 37 (*see* Lent)

Quodvultdeus, 262–265, 348

Reader, 163–164, 189, 359

Recitation of the Creed, 7, 38, 367 (*see Redditio symboli*)

Red Sea, 49, 102, 143, 171, 232–233, 236, 246, 260, 282–283, 303, 312, 334, 365, 377

Redditio symboli, 65, 78, 91–92, 274–285, 297, 305 (*see* Creed)

Renunciation, 38, 46, 71–72, 75, 77, 78, 261–262, 265, 308

Resurrection, 6, 16, 71, 78, 98, 127, 131–132, 148–149, 151, 153, 155, 211, 283, 302, 315, 325, 327–328, 335, 338, 339, 374, 377, 379, 380–381

Rhetoric, 123–128, 136, 173–180, 235–236, 348–358; affective dynamic, 135–136, 154–155, 168, 249–250, 296; art of persuasion, 81, 174–177, 354–357; audience response, 126–127, 137–139, 153, 169–170, 178–179, 265–266, 355–356; Augustine as professional, 81–82, 124–126, 164–165; dangers of, 180, 358–359; delivery, 140; education in, 55, 81, 121–122; figures of speech, 173–174, 178, 223, 235, 295, 333, 350; oral performance, 139, 153, 165–166, 174, 349–350; three aims, 174–177, 354–355 (*see* Antithesis, Applause, Metaphor, Parallelism, Oration, Rhyme, Style, Wordplay)

Rhyme, 101, 173, 210–211, 233–234, 235, 265–266, 280–281, 295, 303–304, 333, 350, 351

Rite of Christian Initiation of Adults (RCIA), 1–18, 20–21, 35–38, 363, 368, 370, 380; catechesis in, 17, 21–24, 26, 346, 368, 375; conversion dynamic, 4, 14–17, 22, 34; ministries of, 6, 8, 10–11; patristic roots, 3–4, 24, 26–27, 367; rites, 3–9, 12–13; silences, 18–20, 24, 369; stages, 3–9, 14–15, 18, 22, 29

Rome, 1, 40–45, 52, 63, 81, 82, 91–92, 112, 151, 203, 263, 336

Rufinus, 91n, 97n, 98n, 147n, 279n, 283n

Sabellians, Sabellianism, 246n, 329

Sacrament(s), 38, 57, 94, 102–103, 120, 171, 249, 253; of the altar, 290, 315, 337; Ambrose on, 99–103, 106; catechumens' ignorance of, 170–171, 191, 232, 237, 308; character, 215; Christ's power in, 217–218, 311; Church and, 279–280, 322; Creed as, 315, 337; cross on forehead as, 150–151, 227–228; Donatists' view of, 214–215; Easter as, 301, 305; exorcism as, 248; of the font, 94, 306; Holy Spirit, 311, 320; and lifestyle, 73, 250; Lord's Prayer as, 315, 337; material element, 300, 315; Octave of Easter as, 311, 330, 334–335; salt as, 150–151, 189; visible and invisible, 310, 311, 318; unity of initiation, 7–8, 12–14

Salt, 80, 150–151, 189, 193, 367

Satan, 46, 67, 75, 102, 142, 201–202; defeated by Christ, 208, 223, 253, 268, 304, 327; exorcism of, 6n, 67–69, 80, 227, 262–264, 271–272; renunciation of, 46, 71–72, 261–262, 265, 308; catechumens wrestling, 64, 73, 98, 115, 218, 233, 271, 310

Scripture (*see* Bible)

Scrutiny, 6–7, 32, 37, 68–69, 96, 245, 249, 260–274, 295, 297, 367

Secrecy (*see Disciplina arcani*)

Sermon(s), 2, 4, 47, 61, 139; of Ambrose, 83–91, 94–95, 99–100, 106; audience, 162, 195, 235, 259; as catechesis for catechumens, 31–32, 56–57, 83–39, 157–160, 164–172, 194–195, 235, 361–362; catechumens addressed during, 57, 158, 195, 201, 227–234; collections of Augustine's, 29–31; on the Creed, 274–275, 297; on the Eucharist, 316–317, 341; frequency, 161, 241; length, 167–168; on the Lord's Prayer, 286, 297; oral performance, 165–166, 349–350; prayer at close of, 189; scripture quoted in, 182–183; sequences of, 158–159, 194–198, 238, 325, 345; setting for, 161–164, 167–168; themes in Augustine's, 206–223, 236–237, 239–241

Seven ages, 146–148, 240, 334–335

Sex, abstinence during Lent, 95, 251, 255, 294

Sign of the Cross, 4, 16, 37, 80, 97, 143, 150, 191, 193, 227–229, 232, 239, 282, 283, 308, 310, 329, 334, 367, 368, 378

Simplicianus, 91–92, 361

Sin, 3, 5, 7, 16, 34, 48, 141, 203, 222, 224, 228, 230, 258, 271, 333–334, 380; remission of, 50, 57, 60, 65, 98, 132, 143, 282, 292, 307–308; Christ takes away, 60, 65, 208, 301–302, 304; prayer and forgiveness of, 64, 260, 290–293

Slaves, slavery, 41, 52, 58, 61, 68, 194, 267–268, 289, 293, 295, 333, 335; catechumens as household servants, 228, 232; sin as, 69, 268, 276, 283, 374

Social justice, 64, 85, 95, 187, 225, 258, 296, 330, 339, 379–380

Soliloquy, 172, 216, 223, 229, 235, 351

Sponsor, 6, 10–11, 16, 37, 41, 63, 65, 75, 113–114, 152

Stripping off of clothes, 44, 309

Styles, three oratorical, 177–179, 199, 205, 265

Sunday, 4, 6, 83, 86, 94, 96, 161, 171, 203, 224, 227, 231, 251, 313–315, 330, 361

Symmachus, 82

Tertullian, 25, 40, 45–50, 59, 67, 101, 103, 115, 287, 348

Thagaste, 104

Theater, 46, 59, 80, 133, 148, 164–165, 187, 223–224, 227–228, 234–235, 261, 349
Theodore of Mopsuestia, 62, 66–73, 77, 94, 263, 278, 286n, 287, 306, 336, 348, 364
Traditio orationis, 285–293, 295–296, 297–298, 315, 337, 368 (*see* Lord's Prayer)
Traditio symboli, 65–66, 93, 96–98, 106, 274–286, 295–296, 297–298, 315, 337, 368 (*see* Creed)
Trinity, 8n, 54–55, 61, 75, 97–98, 99, 148, 198–201, 211, 264, 272, 280–282, 310, 374, 376, 377
Two cities, 144, 147–148, 153
Tyconius, 144, 185

Valerius, bp. of Hippo, 105
Vatican Council II, 1, 4, 11, 12n, 358, 369, 370, 380
Vergil, 121, 181
Victorinus, Marius, 91–92, 108n, 114, 120, 124, 275, 361
Virgin Mary, 216, 240, 279–281
Volusianus, 151, 183

Washing of feet, 102, 106
Water, 6, 8, 13, 44–45, 46, 48–49, 101–103, 106, 217, 231, 234, 282–283, 292, 300, 308–309, 314, 317–318, 319, 329, 362–363, 365–366
White robe, 38, 67, 71, 73, 99, 106, 311–312, 313–314, 324, 331–332, 338, 362
Word of God (*see* Christ)
Wordplay, 211, 266–267, 333–334